The Saffron Condition

The Saffron Condition

Politics of Repression and Exclusion in Neoliberal India

Subhash Gatade

Three Essays
COLLECTIVE

First Edition September 2011

ISBN 978-81-88789-75-7

Three Essays
COLLECTIVE

B-957 Palam Vihar, GURGAON (Haryana) 122 017 India
Phone: 91-124 2369023, +91 98681 26587, +91 98683 44843
info@threeessays.com Website: www.threeessays.com
Printed and bound by Glorious Printers, New Delhi

To the Juneds

Contents

SECTION 2

Logic of Caste in New India

Section 3

State and Human Rights

Preface

Earth sticks to earth
And makes a wall
Poor people stick to poor people
And overthrow a kingdom

A Chinese Poem

There are times in the life of a people when the challenges confronting them and their resolution have a decisive bearing on humankind's onward journey. People's history of the world records many such moments, when humanity appeared to take a turn.

Who would have imagined that the second decade of 21st century would witness massive people's movements in the countries of the Arab world, culminating in successful uprisings in some countries, around issues of unemployment, corruption, the opulent life styles of the rich, and for democracy, shaking the much despised autocratic/monarchical pro-US regimes to the core. Undoubtedly these tumultuous developments have demonstrated that new players have come to the fore in yet another 'backyard' of the US, for whom neither an appeal around faith nor paying obeisance before the great ruler are factors of much concern.

Gone are the days when we were given sermons on the elixir of life which capitalism had supposedly discovered; gone are the days when we were told that a revolutionary anti-capital politics is non-feasible and non-viable; gone also are the days when questions on the neo liberal model of development were met with endless gibberish around the TINA factor. Everyone can now see how the global financial crisis, which seems to have abated somewhat, had suddenly changed the situation. Die hard votaries of free play for market forces had suddenly discovered the virtues of the dirigiste model. The idea of socialism has suddenly acquired new force.

Interestingly this critical look at capitalism and the revival of the idea of socialism has also been the period during which many unsavoury aspects integral to capitalism came to light. The criminal dimensions of the economic system as a whole were clearly evident during the period. It was revealed that drugs money, worth billions of dollars, had kept the financial system afloat at the height of the global crisis. How the regime of corporate frauds contributed to the smooth functioning of tax havens to facilitate tax evasion by the super rich had also made headlines.

India, which yearns to become a superpower in the 21st century, presents one of the worst pictures on both counts.

According to a recent survey by the global accountancy firm KPMG, titled 'India Fraud Survey Report', India stands at No. 1 when it comes to fraud both at the employee and the management levels. Transparency International, another international watchdog, included India in its list of most corrupt nations (2009). When it comes to slashing away black money in Swiss Banks or other similar banks, there too India holds the No. 1 position among the comity of nations. In fact in a communiqué sent sometime ago the Swiss Banking Association had put five countries on top. India: 1,456 billion dollars; Russia: 470 billion dollars; Britain: 390 billion dollars; Ukraine: 100 billion dollars; China: 96 billion dollars.

Considering that 37 per cent of the Indian population lives below the poverty line (if one were to consider the Suresh Tendulkar Committee's readjusted poverty statistics, which also appear to be a gross underestimate of the overall situation) and 77 per cent of the population subsists on mere Rs 20 per day, one can quite imagine the plunder of resources engaged in by the high and mighty and the conspiracy of silence maintained by the elite.

In this part of the world, which boasts of an interesting mix/amalgam of different cultures, with its multilingual/ multiethnic/multireligious strands clearly visible, we are in fact witness to a dual process. On the one hand we are in the midst of a greater deepening and widening of liberal democracy from the parliament to the panchayat level, with hitherto marginalised sections asserting themselves through it, and as a response to it we have the coercive machinery of the State perfecting its repressive apparatus against popular movements in various parts of the country. Rampant application of draconian laws against voices of dissent, and unleashing of brutal violence against people who dare challenge its supremacy, seems to have become the norm.

The growing disjunction between the life worlds of the elite and the majority of the people is evident in the manner in which their very right to protest and resist is being severely restricted. Anti systemic movements aiming for a life of dignity, justice for a broad cross-section of people – the most exploited and the most marginalised – are being branded as the "biggest internal threat" to the country.

On the other hand, we are beset with problems that have their origins in the historical makeup of our society. Nothing illustrates this better than the covert/overt societal violence against sections of people on account of gender/caste/community/ethnicity. Keezhavenmani, Thanjavur district where 44 dalits – mainly women and children – were massacred by the local landlords supposedly for demanding better wages in a struggle led by the Communist Party epitomizes this type of violence (1969). The perpetrators of this massacre (like several other massacres in post-independence India) were allowed to go scott free by the judiciary under the specious argument that '... [I]t was difficult to believe that the landlords would have gone walking to the dalit hamlet.' Women find themselves vulnerable to violence not only in the public sphere but also in the private spaces.

1. Dead Hence Guilty!

What could be said to be the most brutal manner in which the might of the State gets unleashed on its people?

The atrocious practice of 'encounter killings' or custodial killings, when protectors of citizens and enforcers of law themselves violate law, represents the height of brutality of the State against its own citizens. Police and law enforcement agencies in various states resort to such encounters supposedly to fight crime or terrorism. The practice is akin to institutionalization of death squads by the system, which suits more a ruthless dictatorship than a nation flaunting its democratic ideals.

Statistics reveal that it is an old practice and is quite widespread. The National Human Rights Commission (NHRC), the prime human rights body in the country, received about 1,560 complaints between 1993 and March 2010 alleging fake encounters. On further investigations, the NHRC found 856 to be genuine. According to human rights activists these figures are a gross underestimate. A most disturbing aspect of this 'method' of countering crime and/or terrorism is that it has become acceptable in public consciousness.

Commenting on a fake encounter the Supreme Court (SC) remarked (Nov 2010) that policemen involved in fake encounters must face stern action, including dismissal and even murder charges. Of course, this was not the first time that the courts/commissions expressed their disagreement over this 'method'. Justice MN Venkatachallaiah, Chairperson of the NHRC, had in 1997 explicitly asked governments to book cases of culpable homicide against policemen who participated in such encounters. But it is a fact that there has been no change in the ground situation.

The routine practice adopted by policemen to avoid prosecution is to register a case against the dead. To make their blatant illegal act look stronger, the police even manages to pull out a variety of old cases against the dead. The idea is to prove that the policeman found himself in a life threatening situation and he fired in self defense in an encounter against a hardened criminal. As the victim (who is projected as a perpetrator) is already dead, the case is not investigated any further. File closed.

Case study of an encounter killing some time ago and its coverage by the media reveals many such gory details of this 'method'.

The National Capital Region (NCR) witnessed a police encounter on the eve of Republic Day, 2009. Two young men--supposedly carrying a big cache of arms and ammunition--were killed on the spot. We were told this duo was part of a larger LeT (Lashkar-e-Toiba) module which planned to wreak havoc in the capital city.

The killing of the two young men did not cause much uproar.

The police officers appeared jubilant over having 'foiled these attempts'. To blunt any possible criticism of the incident an enquiry was duly ordered by the powers that be, with a promise that it would be completed within a stipulated time.

A nation, yet to come to terms with the terrorist attack in Bombay (26/11), which saw deaths of more than 200 innocents, largely remained silent on this encounter. One could say this silence reflected a fatigue among people due to the frequency of such incidents. Or, what is more likely, one could interpret this silence as expressing the emerging consensus among articulate sections of our society that human rights are for humans not 'terrorists'. A senior judge of the Supreme Court had given vent to similar feelings in a public meeting where he went on to say "... [a] terrorist is not fit to be called a human. He is an animal, so what are required are animal rights." (*Indian Express*, 28 January 2009).

The only consolation in this otherwise bloody episode was that a few conscientious journalists, including some civil rights activists, tried to look beyond the official truth. They were perplexed how the 'terrorists' happened to be killed in the same lonely and uninhabited area which had already witnessed two encounters in a span of one month and how, despite the 'heavy exchange of fire between the ATS (Anti Terrorist Squad) team and the terrorists' as claimed, only one cop suffered a minor injury on his hand, while the terrorists received four bullets each.

The Times of India (26 January 2009) plainly posed all these 'curious questions'. Questioning the ATS version, which stated that the terrorists were chased on a 25 km stretch and then shot, it asked why the ATS had not alerted the three police posts on the wayside during this 'chase' and why there were no bullet marks on the car carrying the terrorists despite the 'heavy exchange of fire'. The reporter also expressed incredulity over the fact that despite being on 'an undercover operation', the 'terrorists' were carrying a Pakistani passport.

Another daily also deemed it necessary to express disagreements over the official truth. In its first editorial 'Encounter begs answers of UP Police' *Mail Today* (27 January 2009) wrote:

> To begin with, we would have been a wee bit surprised had the police not produced some "terrorists" – slain or alive – in the run-up to the

> Republic Day. For the past many years, encounters and arrests have been as regular as the official ceremony on these occasions.

Questioning a few other oddities which 'don't fit so well' it ended on a somber note:

> What surprises in no less measure is their 'confession'. If the police story is to be believed, the terrorists confessed – after they had received four bullets each – how they had come to India and what they intended to do, before they succumbed to their injuries. Who tells stories while at death's door, and in such detail?

One can see for oneself that there was a sense of deja vu with the official version. It is worth noting that the spot, which witnessed this 'encounter', appears to have become a regular site for encounters. There were seven 'encounters' at this same spot during a period of ten months between December 2008 and October 2009.

In fact the Delhi 'encounter' on the eve of Republic Day was accompanied by newspaper reports questioning the 'Singhavaram encounter' in Chhattisgarh, which had witnessed a merciless killing of 15 tribals by a joint team of security personnel and Special Police Officers (SPOs). It would be opportune to state here that these Special Police Officers are nothing but ordinary civilians who have been asked or coerced into joining the counter insurgency operations. In addition to arming them the State also pays these individuals some money at regular intervals.

Whatever the outcome of this particular case it will not erase the fact that in each and every state, each and every city, in fact each and every police station in the country, there are countless stories of barbarity and brutality by the very forces supposed to guarantee life and liberty of the people.

Imagine, for a moment, a team of dedicated sociologists and social activists engaged in collecting data on encounter killings, custodial deaths or sentences of capital punishment administered by various courts, what would they find? In addition to the fact that jails are crowded by people from the poor economic strata, most belonging to oppressed communities/castes, they would discover that the majority of those dying an unnatural death at the hands of the police also belong to similar socio-economic categories.

Apart from killing innocent people in fake encounters, another sinister phenomenon quite widespread is the fabrication of false charges by the police against innocents, consequent to which these people have had to spend many years in jail on trumped up charges. In one instance which is an exception, an additional sessions judge, Virendra Bhat, in Delhi absolved and acquitted seven men accused of terrorism in a case dating to 2005, while declaring four officers of the Delhi Police guilty of manufacturing a fake story about an 'encounter'. In this particular case the police claimed to have recovered AK-47 assault rifles, fake currency and ammunition from the men they claimed were ISI agents--which was a false claim. (February 2011).

Jamia Teachers' Solidarity Association (JTSA), a group of human rights activists from Delhi, held a press conference demanding the arrest of the guilty police officials:

> ...What is incredible is that the Special Cell officers work with the same script each time. In 2008, Tyagi was indicted by the CBI for planting evidence such as RDX, J & K bus tickets and pistols on two men, Irshad Ali and Md. Qamar, whom they charged with being Al Badar operatives. In both instances, it was noticed that the police rested content having once 'recovered' the explosives and arms, making no effort to trace their source. It's obvious why the source was not traced. It would lead perhaps to the Special Cell Lodhi Road office.

In any civilised country, such simple facts would have caused unease, but since the victims often belong to the minority religion or lower castes and poor strata of society, while a large majority of the opinion makers are at peace with the graded hierarchy based on purity and pollution, all such differentiations appear to them coincidental statistical data. An India that presumes itself 'meritorious' and seems in a hurry to become a Super Power in the 21 st century has no interest in knowing such details about the subalterns.

2. Mythology of Merit!

The manner in which the reservation discourse has developed in our society reflects a very static understanding of merit.

Interestingly all those who have become upholders of the 'merit mantra' would be shocked to find how badly their own forefathers and foremothers fared when they took their first hesitant steps in the education system initiated by the British. The very genesis of III rd division in education in the Madras Presidency College way back in the first half of the nineteenth century was necessitated by the large numbers of failures among the students, most of them upper castes (Tamil Brahmins), who were unable to pass their examinations in first and second divisions.

An analysis of the reports Selections from Educational Records (1781-1938, 1840-1859, and 1860-1887) and Progress of Education in India reveals a similar picture. According to the authors 'the native-Indians were highly disinterested in Science and Education; two, they fared very poorly in science subjects; and three, failure rates in science was very high'.

Certainly much water has flown down the Ganges (as well as the Kaveri) since those times. There is no denying that despite these initial failures, these sections of society, never having to face any social handicaps due to the Varna ordained structure of our society, have been able to carve out a niche for themselves in different fields.

An interesting find is that while the top echelons of the hierarchical Varna society performed badly when they first encountered British education, the experience of the 'lowest castes' among them was exemplary under the circumstances. P.S.Krishnan, in an article 'Logical Step' (Frontline, May 8, 2006) tells us how Monstuart Elphinstone, the legendary British administrator, recognised in the mid-19th century that "the missionaries find in the lowest caste the best pupils." It goes on: "the Board of Education of Bombay Presidency in its report for 1850-51 was confident that if the doors of education were opened to 'the despised castes' they would turn into 'men of superior intelligence to any in the community'."

It needs be underlined here that this was for the first time, after thousands of years of varna-caste servitude, that the doors of education were gradually being opened for the 'shudras-atishudras'. And in their first steps in modern education they had not only proved themselves 'best pupils' but had also shown that 'with such qualifications, as they would then possess', there would be nothing to prevent them from rising 'to the highest offices open to native talent'.

Imagine for a moment if, considering the 'poor performance' of the upper castes and the promise shown by the 'despised castes', the British had decided to chart an alternate path in educating Indians, what would have been the picture today? Would it have been the same, as it exists today?

In the context of the 'strong opposition' by upper castes to enabling measures such as reservations for the oppressed classes in institutions of higher education, supposedly on grounds of 'loss of merit', one needs to ask why no such protests took place when payment-seats were introduced in different institutions a decade ago, under the impact of the neo liberal agenda in education? Do they believe that 'payment' substitutes well for merit? Interestingly, in the historic Inamdar case, which precipitated a demand from many quarters to extend reservation to private as well as other institutions through a constitutional amendment, the highest courts of the country denied any fixed seats for the 'socially deprived' sections of our society, but had no hesitation in reserving a fixed percentage for the NRIs (Non resident Indians) who could pay for it.

Even as India is debating the pros and cons of its reservation policy in a highly charged atmosphere, it may be opportune to recall how the US handled and defended its affirmative action programmes introduced in the 60s.

Two white students of Michigan University had approached the Supreme Court of USA alleging they had been denied admission because of the 'discriminatory' affirmative action programme. In a historic decision on 23 June 2003 the Supreme Court of USA, which had seen the entire society vertically divided on this contentious issue, upheld the prerogative of colleges and universities to give preference to members of minority groups in admissions.

It is a tragedy of our times that in India, more than sixty years after independence, the age old exclusivist mindset which stunted the growth of our society, remains unchanged. It is a mindset based on notions of purity and pollution, which has helped strengthen the structured hierarchy in our society, and claims religious sanction as well.

These hierarchies and inequities in our society have in turn provided the material basis for internecine conflicts based on religion, community and other identities.

3. Fighters for a Sectarian Cause

It was in the late eighties that one witnessed the growing surge of the 'biggest movement in independent India' led by the Sangh Parivar, which ultimately resulted in the demolition of the Babri mosque. One still remembers one's naivete: it was sincerely felt that whatever may be the claims of the Hindutva brigade, they would not dare touch the five hundred year old mosque.

All that is now passé.

It is almost two decades since the mosque was demolished and the people of India experienced some of the worst riots in the history of independent India. One recognizes that this was a consequence of the dangerous mix of the hard Hindutva practiced by the Sangh Parivar and the soft Hindutva of the Congress. Many senior leaders of the Parivar stand accused in the case, yet till date criminal proceedings against them have not moved a bit.

The Lieberhans Commission appointed to look into the conspiracy of the demolition of the mosque finally submitted its report after sixteen and a half years and forty eight extensions, and the same was finally placed before the Parliament. The report shows that the demolition was indeed a conspiracy and provides details of the planning at the highest levels of the Hindutva brigade and the dubious role played by the leaders of the movement.

A judicial verdict given by the three member Lucknow bench of the Allahabad High Court has effectively turned the suit of the ownership of land into a dispute between three parties and emphasised people's beliefs and sentiments as opposed to actual facts in deciding the case. This celebration of faith as opposed to law, and theology as opposed to hard scientific evidence, could be considered a new low in the judicial history of independent India.

Much on the lines of the Supreme Court judgement in the late nineties which called Hinduism 'a way of life' in India and provided new legitimacy to the exclusivist project of the Sangh Parivar, this judgement which upholds majoritarian claims and disregards justice would be discussed for a long time to come.

Ayodhya, which has been a symbol of our composite heritage for centuries, is gradually experiencing the erasure of the signs of its shared history from the minds of people.

I was a resident of Varanasi in the days when one of the 'lunatic fringes' of the Sangh Parivar had given a call for lighting mashaals (torchlight) at a particular time in the evening as a mark of support for their agenda. People were asked to raise mashaals from their rooftops to protest 'government inaction' and to underline their support for the Ram temple movement. It was a frightening experience for us that ours was the only house in the sprawling neighbourhood which had not lit a mashaal.

This particular image of ordinary people raising provocative slogans in unison and lighting their mashaals in support of the sectarian call still remains with me. Some of my neighbours had even gone as kar sevaks on the trip to Ayodhya, supposedly to demolish the 'age old symbol of slavery'.

No one, not even those only slightly concerned with peace, justice, progress and a more inclusive world, could today say that there has been an improvement in the situation. On the contrary, it would not be incorrect to say that the 'Right' has now become the new 'Centre'. It was inconceivable then that an exclusivist formation like the Sangh Parivar would install one of its Swayamsevaks on the top post of the Republic and a section of the secular fraternity would have no qualms in singing paeans to the idea of 'one nation, one people, one culture'.

The percentage of votes garnered by the BJP during the last few decades has been on the rise with minor hiccups now and then. From 11.5 per cent in 1989 it gained 20 per cent vote in 1991 and 1996, which rose to 25.5 per cent in 1998. It dropped to 23.7 in 1999 and 22.1 in 2004. Elections in the year 2009 showed a decline in the number of votes garnered by the Hindutva combine. Yet there is no ground for complacency as one can see.

In social terms many decades of communal propaganda, accompanied by systematic and planned violence against the 'others', has helped create a certain set of attitudes about how things should be run and what constitutes a 'nation'. These have gained wide currency and acceptability in the minds of the people. The Congress which deftly unseated the BJP in two consecutive elections by stitching together a 'secular coalition' has not taken any serious steps to combat these attitudes, nor has it attempted to take the 'anti-communal struggle' beyond the facile Sarva Dharma Sambhav (Equal Treatment to All Religions). In fact, instead of adopting an uncompromising position on the issue of secularism to defang the hard Hindutva of the Sangh Parivar, it has rather been rediscovering the virtues of soft Hindutva. Anyone can see that issues not finding favour with the communal and majoritarian forces could not be brought on the agenda by the Congress in this interregnum.

The competitive electoral politics in India gives rise to a complex scenario wherein any consolidated vote bank may gain political bargaining power quite disproportionate to its actual electoral strength. More than any other political formation this possibility has been exploited by the right wing formations. In fact with a minority share of votes in their kitty, these formations are able to unleash processes, institutionalise mechanisms and create situations which force powers that be to acquiesce to their demands. Here we find a strange commonality between South Asia's two anti-human forces, those promoting the political project of Hindutva and that of fundamentalist-political Islam. Mapping the trajectory of such forces would throw some light on the yet unexplored dimensions of their growth and provide answers to a few unanswered questions.

4. Rose Petals for Terrorists

Pakistan, a country of 170 millions, had made headlines recently for altogether wrong reasons. The manner in which a murderer, Malik Qadri, member of the elite police force, who had killed Salman Taseer, Governor of Punjab, was declared a 'Gazi of Islam' (warrior for Islam) by some fundoos, and the jubilation which awaited him when he was presented in the Islambad court, with someone from the crowd even showering rose petals on him, was seen on television throughout the world.

It is known that Salman Taseer was killed for his defense of Aasiabi, a Christian working woman, falsely implicated under the infamous blasphemy law. Perturbed over her conviction, and despite his party's -Pakistan People's Party -refusal to take a firm stand on the issue, Taseer stood his ground and even demanded a repeal of the infamous blasphemy law. There is no denying that with the growing belligerence of the fundamentalist forces in Pakistan, with a few Mullahs even declaring Salman Taseer *Wajib ul Qatl* (worth to be killed), few from the ruling dispensation summoned the courage to support him.

Under this law, introduced under the Zia ul Haque regime in the mid eighties, anyone can be charged on the simple claim of having shown disrespect towards the founder of Islam or the Quranic scriptures. Although nobody has faced judicial execution under this law till date, many have been killed by reactionary forces after their acquittal by the court.

It is to the credit of the vibrant civil society in Pakistan that it not only opposed the judicial verdict in Aasiabi's case but also demanded that the infamous law be repealed or amended. Sherry Rehman, a former minister in the cabinet, had even moved a bill in the senate to that effect. It was clear that these efforts to save Aasiabi's life and seek repeal/revisions in the controversial law have received a tremendous setback with Salman Taseer's assassination. As expected the fundamentalist forces are jubilant.

A letter sent by Pakistan's foremost progressive intellectual and physicist, Dr Pervez Hoodbhoy, which had appeared on the website 'New Age Islam' makes chilling reading. In this letter the leading public intellectual shares his 'deep depression' over the state of affairs in Pakistan and the unfolding situation after Mr Taseer's assassination. It mentions the interior minister – a political colleague of Mr Taseer – as having said that 'he too would kill a blasphemer with his own hands.' According to the letter:

> Whatever one might think of Governor Salman Taseer's politics, he was killed this Wednesday for what was certainly the best act of his life: trying to save the life of an illiterate, poor, peasant Christian woman. ...Pakistan once had a violent, rabidly religious lunatic fringe. This fringe has morphed into a majority. The liberals are now the fringe. We are now a nation of butchers and primitive savages. Europe's Dark Ages have descended upon us. Sane people are being terrified into silence. Islamo-fascism is a reality.

Noting that the 'culture of religious extremism was resulting in a bloodbath in which the majority of victims are Muslims' Dr Hoodbhoy adds:

> This country is destined to drown in blood from civil war. I wish people would stop writing rubbish about Pakistan having an image problem. It's the truth that's really the problem.

These are no ramblings of an ordinary man; they voice the anguish of the people in Pakistan who still cherish the liberal dream. The letter concludes with a frank appraisal of the situation (...battle for sanity has been lost) and a resolve to fight. (Many friends have written to me to leave Pakistan. How can I? One must keep fighting as long as possible. It is what we owe to future generations).

It is notable that barring the 'lunatic fringe' in Indian polity, most people have felt discomfort over the developments in Pakistan.

On the other hand, the developments in Pakistan have been witnessed with glee by Talibans of a different kind, namely the Hindutva Supremacists in India, who have been pursuing their very own agenda of majoritarianism. As the saying goes, reactionaries/ bigots grow together. Any turn towards Talibanisation of Pakistan would further augment the strength of these fanatics here. We should not forget that the ascendancy of these forces in India towards the end of 20th and the beginning of the 21 st century has also been the period when for the first time in Pakistan's history fundamentalist forces have gained dominant position in the electoral arena in two of its states.

It is no sheer coincidence that much on the lines of Malik Qadri's visit to the Islamabad courts and the crowd gathered there to greet him, the terrorists of the Malegaon bomb blast (2008), namely Lt. Col. Purohit, Pragya Thakur, Dayanand Pandey etc were also greeted similarly by a crowd owing allegiance to the Hindutva formations when they were presented in the courts in Pune and Nashik, and showered with rose petals.

5. Manu's Orphans!

Despite thoroughgoing and many in-depth analyses of the rise and spread of communal fascism in the country, few points, which appear inconsequential on the surface, have remained largely ignored by activists and scholars. One is referring to the many pioneers or stalwarts – ranging from the Savarkars, Hedgewars and Golwalkars to the likes of Deorass and Thakres in recent times – of the movement for Hindu Rashtra. Is it a mere coincidence that all of them belong to the western geographical terrain of the country, namely Maharashtra? Does it have something to do with the social make up of the area and the long history of social movements which have posed tremendous challenges to Brahminism and Patriarchy? Does it have anything to do with a very instrumental understanding of Modernity?

Why should a region that witnessed one of the first successful challenges to the Mughal imperial rule and where the population of Muslims has never crossed the ten percent mark, become a 'lighthouse' for the anti-minority project? Perhaps one needs to look into the cultural revolt led by Mahatma Phule in the nineteenth century which was taken forward by Shahu Maharaj, Ambedkar and many others. These glorious movements of the hitherto oppressed subaltern classes proved to be the biggest challenge to the stranglehold of Brahminical forces in the region. Hedgewar, the founder-member of the RSS (as stated in his 'official' biography *Sanghvriksha ke beej* – C.P. Bhishikar), gave two clear reasons for the founding of the RSS: one, 'menace of minorities' and two, the non-brahmin movement which had created dissensions in society. It may be noted that after the death of Mahatma Phule and Savitribai Phule, the movement for social upliftment metamorphosed into a non-Brahmin movement.

Time and again, leaders of the Hindutva project have exhibited their love and preference for the Brahminical mode of governance as laid down in the *Manusmriti*. In fact, when the Constituent Assembly was engaged in framing a constitution for independent India based on one wo/man one vote and was keen to do away with the graded hierarchy inherent in Manu's code, these leaders stated bluntly that independent India should be run on the principles enshrined in the *Manusmriti*.

It is a tragedy of our times that the anti-communal struggle in our country has not taken into account this important aspect of the Brahminical counter revolution couched in the language of Hindutva. It would not be an exaggeration to say that till date the strategy to combat communalism has suffered from this lacuna.

As Braj Ranjan Mani rightly puts it:

> The Hindutva of the RSS-BJP is predominantly hegemonistic, it is more social than political, and the so-called Hindu backlash against the past humiliations supposedly heaped on it by Islam and Christianity is a shrewd tactic to arrest the democratic upsurge of the hitherto excluded and marginalised majority. Earlier, the Hindu brahminic forces treated the toiling majority as the mlecchas. Now, dalit-subalterns are being co-opted into Hindu politics as tools against religious minorities. (*Debrahminising History*, p.26, Manohar 2008).

The timing and forms in which the Ram temple movement unfolded makes it abundantly clear how the affirmative action programme for the other backward classes was cleverly utilized for bringing the politics of religious symbolism to the national centre stage. It aimed at creating polarizations between Hindus on one side and the Muslims and Christians on the other and proved successful in keeping people disunited along class lines. It logically followed that during the course of the upsurge of the Ram temple movement the ruling classes could not be effectively confronted on the issues of mass poverty, illiteracy, malnutrition and unemployment and the central issue of making producers also collective appropriators.

6.

The articles included in this collection have appeared earlier in different publications: newspapers, magazines as well as blogs and websites. Many people – comrades, friends, acquaintances and family members – have contributed in various ways in helping me systematise my ideas and in putting them together in a more readable and communicable format. It is impossible to name each and everyone here. I thank them all for the support they have rendered me through many years.

Of course, as always happens in such compilations, there is a danger that the concerns expressed remain immersed in the pool of contemporaniety. Nevertheless, one sincerely hopes that the reader will find the collection useful and of relevance to our struggles. Also, as inevitable in such collections, some ideas and a bit of information overlap. In the interest of continuity of argument and the specific context in which this occurs, I have allowed it in a few instances.

Before I end I would like to share with you the story of one Juned Salim Sheikh, aged seven, resident of Anjanwa village, Panchmahals district, Gujarat, published in one of the reports ('The Next Generation: In the Wake of the Genocide') brought out in the aftermath of the Gujarat genocide 2002.

The team met the kid with his grandparents in a relief camp at Iqbal High School. "He sat with us with a vacant wide-eyed look, neck bent at an angle, head falling into chest, like he had lost all interest in holding it up." Juned had witnessed 13 members of his family being killed, houses looted, women brutalised and all of them thrown into a nearby well. Three days later only Maqsooda, Juned's aunt could be recovered from the well, still alive. After reaching the camp, for full days Juned stayed hungry, kept fleeing from one place to another...

Would it be asking for the moon if one were to demand that the perpetrators of this misery on Juned and the real masterminds behind it are punished and also no Juned – belonging to any faith or outside it – encounters a similarly brutalised childhood in any part of the world?

Section I

Saffronization and the Neoliberal State

The 'Civil Warriors' for Hindu Rashtra

What is common between George Bush, King Gyanendra (now the titular head of secular Nepal), and controversial minister in the UP cabinet, Haji Quereshi, or BJP stalwarts like Vinay Katiyar and Sahib Singh Verma? Prima facie one may not discern any commonality in their demeanour or language. In fact Gyanendra in his ceremonial medieval attire would appear a museum relic in the company of George Bush, and 'the character builders' of the nation have their own distinct appearances.

What connects them is their *weltanschauung* (world view), and the absence of any qualms in putting bounties on heads of people with whom they do not agree. It is a different matter that the Bushes and the Gyanendras have already learnt the hard way that this strategy does not always pay. The controversial minister has also realised that there is not much to gain from temporary publicity, while the acolytes of the Sangh Parivar are a bit late in deriving their own 'pearls of wisdom'.

It all began when Sahib Singh Verma, Vinay Katiyar and many leaders of the BJP-RSS Parivar were in Jammu in connection with the party's 'save Doda, save nation satyagraha' aimed supposedly at saving Jammu from "de-Hinduisation". As part of this Satyagraha these people have been holding public meetings and courting symbolic arrest. The "bounty speeches" by the Vermas and Katiyars were made before these symbolic arrests. According to the police Rs one lakh was offered by them to any civilian who kills a militant, and if a civilian dies fighting a militant, his family would be paid Rs 2 lakhs.

As of now both these BJP leaders --Vinay Katiyar and Sahib Singh Verma – find themselves booked by the Jammu and Kashmir police for 'inciting communal passion' and engaging in 'seditious activities' by announcing monetary rewards to civilians killing militants. According to a newspaper report 'An FIR has been registered against them for "making provocative statements" and "inciting communal passions" under section 123-A (inciting people against the state or government) and 153-A (spreading disaffection among people) Ranbir Penal Code (RPC) in Nowabad Police Station here, deputy inspector general of police Niaz Mehmood, told PTI.' According to legal experts, under 123-A and 153-A, the guilty could be punished with life imprisonment besides a severe fine.

Even a layperson understands that vigilante justice of this kind would further help militarise the civil society. The ensuing culture of death and destruction would further enhance the culture of communalism and religious sectarianism in the country. Such offers of bounty for killing militants is clearly aimed at creating a civil war like situation in the country where a section of the citizenry belonging to a particular religion is given the liberty to kill anyone from the other community under the garb of curbing militancy.

This recipe for civil war rather authorises every man on the street, especially a Hindu in this case, to kill anyone for settling personal scores or just for money under the specious argument of liquidating a terrorist. It would be height of innocence to assume that these two leaders were talking of their own sweet will and had no authorisation from the top echelons of the party. In fact this was the party's way of gauging public reaction. Obviously they did not expect an adverse action. As it happens the party has now been compelled to formally dissociate itself from these views and to claim allegiance to the law of the land, and to also direct Vinay Katiyar and Sahib Singh Verma to tender an apology.

It was a positive sign that the provocative statements by the Katiyars and the Vermas received condemnation from all quarters of Kashmir's civil and political society. Leaders of the National Conference, who shared power with the BJP for six years, also joined in the chorus of voices asserting that nobody had a right to take the law into their own hands. The duplicity of the BJP however became evident when it came to light that during its own regime in the Centre, the graph of killings in Doda had been on the higher side but the party had never tried to rake up the issue.

As has been rightly noted in an editorial in *Kashmir Times* (10 June 2006) 'Setting Chenab on Fire' these speeches smack of the fascist and communal policies of the party. According to it they

> ...[b]etray the sinister designs of not just provoking communal violence and fear psychosis but also creating anarchy. In fact, the bid to create lawlessness by rewarding those who kill militants is nothing but a step towards creation of a civil war. In exhorting civilians to kill militants in lieu of a reward, in the name of protection of Hindus, the BJP has not only revived the archaic glory of 'eye for an eye' concept but has also revealed its fancy for the Hindutva's hate soaked agenda of branding all non-Hindus as militants and anti-nationals.

It is an open secret that such attempts at spreading fear, provoking violence, creating a communal holocaust can help trigger displacement of Doda's minorities from the region, which suits the BJP in very many ways. It can be used as a card elsewhere in the country to exploit religious sentiments and promote its fascist and hate soaked Hindutva ideology.

Interestingly, the duo of Katiyar and Sahib Singh Verma, who looked rather adamant after making these statements were directed by the party to seek 'apologies' when it dawned upon it that the two are liable for prosecution, and if the powers that be show enough political will both would have to cool their heels behind bars.

The fact is that provisions of law are clearly unambiguous in all such cases involving 'sedition' or 'promoting dissonance between two communities'.

Under Indian Law promoting enmity between different groups on grounds of religion is a recognized criminal offence. According to a news release issued by the Secretariat of Amnesty International (dated 16th October 2002) "... the Indian Penal Code (IPC) prescribes criminal prosecution for "wantonly giving provocation with intent to cause riot" (section 153); "promoting enmity between different groups on grounds of religion" (section 153A); "imputations, assertions prejudicial to national integration" (section 153B); "uttering words with deliberate intent to wound the religious feelings of any person" (section 298); "statements conducive to public mischief" (section 505 (1), b and c); and "statements creating or promoting enmity, hatred or ill-will between classes (section505(2). Section 108 of the Code of Criminal Procedure, in addition, allows an Executive Magistrate to initiate action against a person violating section 153A or 153B of the IPC." The "Guidelines to promote communal harmony" issued by the Ministry of Home Affairs in October 1997 also point towards precise responsibility of the state machinery to deal with potentially inflammatory statements in the context of communal tension. Guideline 15 states that "effective will needs to be displayed by the district authorities in the management of such situations so that ugly incidents do not occur. Provisions in section 153A, 153B, 295 to 298 and 505 of IPC and any other Law should be freely used to deal with individuals promoting communal enmity". Article 20 of the International Covenant on Civil and Political Rights, which India ratified in 1979, affirms that "Any advocacy of national, racial or religious hatred that constitutes incitement to discrimination, hostility or violence shall be prohibited by law".

While the provocative speeches in Jammu seem to have backfired on BJP, similar attempts by members of the *Parivar* in the past have gone unattended despite knowledge that they contributed to inter communal disharmony at various levels. There have been innumerable instances when the top bosses of the BJP-RSS-VHP looked the other way when one among them was threatening minorities in no uncertain terms. "Moderates" like Vajpayee are also known to deliver the not so well received "Goa Musings" and tell the "minorities to behave" lest they become exposed to some revised edition of the Gujarat experiment.

Delivering hate speeches is in fact normal practice for these people. It was as part of this 'routine exercise' that, in its very first meeting after the debacle of NDA at the hustings in 2004, the VHP had glorified the Gujarat pogrom of 2002. As reported in a section of the press, Mr Ashok Singhal, working president of VHP said that "the events in Gujarat post-Godhra killings had Lord Ram's blessings". (*Jansatta*, Delhi, 'Gujarat riots had Ram's blessings', July 4, 2004).

Of course the six year tenure of the BJP at the centre could be said to be the 'golden period' for these hate mongers. It was a marker when the

VHP top brass had called for "direct action" after the Supreme Court rejected the central government's petition to allow any religious activity on the "undisputed land" in Ayodhya then. One of the top leaders of this outfit, Mr Praveen Togadia, did not even hesitate to claim responsibility for the demolition of Babri Mosque and was also candid enough to say that it was his organisation which took lead in the post-Godhra reaction.

The unhindered flow of such speeches went on unabated during those times despite the fact the highest court of the country did not take a kind view of such utterances. The last week of February 2003 had witnessed the Supreme Court issuing a notice to the Centre on a petition to prosecute Narendra Modi and Ashok Singhal for making "inflammatory speeches" to the effect that the "Gujarat Hindutva experiment" would be repeated throughout the country. A bench comprising Justice Lahoti and Justice Brijesh Kumar had also issued a notice to the State governments of Maharashtra and Gujarat. The said petition was filed by well known journalists and civil liberty activists, including Alyque Padamsee, BGVerghese, Kuldip Nayar, Valjibhai Patel and Teesta Setalwad.

Remember the attack by terrorists belonging to Lashkar-e-Toiba in Ayodhya last year which was foiled successfully by the security people? Interestingly, while ordinary people had heaved a sigh of relief, the triumvirate of the VHP-BJP-RSS became more uneasy. Fearing that loss of interest would prove a death knell to their brand of politics they tried all sorts of ways to foment a fresh bout of tension. Ranging from the likes of Lal Krishna Advani to the local level leaders of the VHP, they tried in vain to create a fresh wedge between the communities.

In a public meeting held in Ayodhya they tried to demonise the whole Muslim community and asked for the eviction of Muslims from the periphery of the acquired land in Ayodhya. Ramvilas Vedanti, a VHP leader from Ayodhya who received enough bytes the day the terrorist attack occurred, had spewed venom on the occasion. "Muslims should be shifted from the adjoining areas and the localities acquired in Ayodhya. There will be no guarantee of security of Ram Lalla till they are not shifted." Acharya Giriraj Kishore, the vice president of the VHP, categorically made the same demand in his New Delhi press conference.

None of them were even sent a summons to explain their conduct.

Last but not least, the speeches by Katiyar and Verma, which have generated a nationwide controversy, also remind one of the infamous "Rivers of Blood" speech in England by Enoch Powell in 1968. It is now history how he was stigmatised and became a parliamentary leper.

Is it not high time that a hatemonger of any shade should meet a similar fate in the Indian context? Is it asking for too much at a time when we are preparing to celebrate the150th anniversary of India's First War for Independence – the historic struggle in which Hindus and Muslims fought shoulder to shoulder against foreign rule?

July 2006

Hindutva is the Real Threat

> Hyderabad: BJP leader LK Advani has said that after naxalism and terrorism, infiltration of Bangladeshi nationals from across the border was the third biggest threat to country's security. *The Hindu,* April 19, 2006.

> (They) were doomed to the flames and burnt, to serve as a nightly illumination when daylight had expired. Nero offered his gardens for the spectacle. Tacitus (Roman historian and official, c.58 to 115 C.E.), *The Annals, Book XV*, C.E. 62-65.

Lal Krishna Advani, ex President of BJP would not have imagined that the Sangh Parivar's own people would get caught making illegal bombs just as he was busy sermonising to all and sundry about the threats before the nation. The coincidence was, in fact, striking. According to a write up in *Mid Day* (9th April 2006) "...[o]n the eve of Lal Krishna Advani's Bharat Suraksha Yatra in Maharashtra, police officials in Nanded said Bajrang Dal activists were actually making a bomb before a bomb exploded in an activist's house." Two people died on the spot in the blast and three others were badly injured. The investigating officer was categorical that the duo, Naresh and Himanshu, who died on the spot were 'office bearers of Bajrang Dal from time to time and used to attend their meetings'.

As expected the state Bajrang Dal leader flatly denied that these people had anything to do with his organisation and also ascribed the powerful explosion to 'crackers'. The most interesting comment came from the state BJP spokesperson. "In any case, what does the Bajrang Dal's involvement in this, if at all, have to do with us? We are an independent political party with an independent political agenda."(*The Telegraph*, 10 April 2006).

One does not know Advani's reaction to the Nanded episode. Possibly he had vouched for their innocence or as usual saw in it a larger conspiracy at the behest of some foreign hand.

One still remembers how he had delivered a 'certificate of good conduct' to the Bajrangis in Orissa after the Graham Steins case. 'I know them. They would not engage in this type of work' was his crisp reply about Bajrang Dal then. Along with George Fernandes he had rushed to Orissa to give a 'clean chit' to them although all evidence pointed at their involvement in the burning alive of the Australian missionary, who was engaged in serving lepers, along with his two kids.

These same bajrangis were part of a mob carrying tridents and lathis that had stormed the Orissa Assembly four years ago. As reported in many newspapers, around 500 activists of the Vishwa Hindu Parishad, the Bajrang Dal and the Durga Vahini had stormed the Orissa Assembly building and indulged in massive vandalism causing extensive damage. These activists were on a dharna outside the Assembly to demand the handing over of the disputed land in Ayodhya to the Ramjanmabhoomi Nyas for the construction of a Ram temple. And they forcibly entered the premises through the main entrance at 2.10 p.m. in the presence of a posse of policemen. "The activists, many of whom were armed with tridents and lathis, broke glass doors, windowpanes of the Assembly library and rooms allotted to the Ministers and smashed the flowerpots in the corridors of the building." (*The Hindu*, Mar 17, 2002). People may be reminded that this attack had come just a few months after the infamous attack on Indian parliament, which had been rightly condemned and dealt with as a 'terrorist act'. But as far as this attack on the Orissa Assembly was concerned, it did not attract a 'terrorist' tag and ironically Naveen Patnaik categorised it as an 'unpleasant act'. And for all practical purposes there the matter ended.

Of course it remains to be seen whether the act by the Nanded trio would be brought under the ambit of a law meant for 'terrorist' acts.

We know that the draconian law POTA (which was allowed to lapse) enacted during Advani-Vajpayee's 'reign' had made it explicit that such acts could be bracketed as ' terrorist act'. It said:

> CHAPTER II, 3. (1): Whoever (a) with intent to...strike terror in the people or any section of the people does any act or thing by using... inflammable substances or firearms or other lethal weapons...or by any other means whatsoever, in such a manner as to cause, or likely to cause, death of, or injuries to any person or persons or loss of, or damage to, or destruction of, property...commits a terrorist act.'

This is not the first time that the Bajrang Dal cadres have been found engaged in acts which go against the established civilian norms of our society. Only two years ago Bajrang Dal, along with its parent organisation Vishwa Hindu Parishad (VHP), was keen on demolishing the Afzal Khan memorial at Pratapgarh Fort in Satara district, Maharashtra. "We had given an ultimatum to the state Government that if it did not demolish the objectionable construction then the job would be done by VHP and Bajrang Dal activists", VHP International general secretary Praveen Togadia had then told reporters at Pune. (*PTI*, September 5, 2004). It is a different matter that the whole experiment to repeat 'Babri' at Afzal's Tomb proved to be a damp squib.

Two years ago many newspapers also reported on how the 'Bajrang Dal activists made a village in Rajasthan Muslim free'. *The Indian Express* (29 September 2003) report had given a vivid description of the whole episode :

> Aklera (Rajasthan): It couldn't be less subtle. A bright saffron board welcomes you to the "Ideal Hindu Village", Mishroli. Nestled in picturesque green surroundings, the village has acquired this tag just this month. The past 10 days have seen armed Bajrang Dal activists on the rampage, driving out about 25 Muslim families from their homes, ransacking their houses and setting them on fire.

For more than five years now organisations like the Bajrang Dal, and others of the same ilk, have been engaged in training their cadres in the use of arms. One gets to read stories from different parts of India on this. As the annual summary brought out by *Communalism Combat* (2001-2002) puts it:

> Over the past three years, different wings of the Hindu right wing have proclaimed publicly that they are training their cadres in the use of arms. While at one level the statements proclaim that the training is in the use of air guns only, the threat of violence, and the rhetoric that accompanies these pronouncements portend ill for internal peace in India. Since August 01 even the pretence of using 'harmless air guns' has been given the go-by.

One is also witness to other sinister ways in which the militarisation of civil society is being achieved at the behest of the affiliated organisations of the Parivar. The Bajrang Dal, through its programme of distribution of *trishuls*, has actually been systematically arming young men with sharp edged weapons. As a report brought out by the People's Union for Civil Liberties, April 2003, rightly put it:

> And there was a definite correlation between Trishul distribution ceremony in an area and violent communal conflict therein."

As the report makes clear, although the distribution of Trishuls is called a symbolic religious exercise, supposedly to awaken the Hindus, the

> ...[d]istributed Trishuls were not at all the iconic harmless Trishuls, which are not sharp at all, associated traditionally with Shiva temples and Shaivite orders. The VHP Trishuls were in fact sharp three bladed daggers meant to cause grave injury and even kill. These Trishul distribution ceremonies were invariably accompanied by VHP leaders, led by Pravin Togadia, delivering inflammatory hate speeches against religious minorities, which immediately exacerbated communal temperature in the area concerned.

As per the Indian Constitution, private militias arming themselves represent a threat to law and order and the peace and tranquility that the State is bound to preserve. The Indian Arms Act, 1959 also expressly prohibits the possession of arms by private parties without license. But despite all these rulings there is no stopping this forcible militarisation of Indian society by the Hindutva cadres.

There are several ways and instances which go to show how the social fabric is being communalized, rather militarized, by the Bajrang Dal and other affiliated organisations of the Parivar who have become key players in this process.

The question naturally arises as to what purpose these 'violent acts' serve. There is no doubt that the acts of violence reinforce the cleverly constructed idea of restrictive and discriminatory nationhood, which is a hallmark of the RSS. This nationhood posits (upper caste) Hindu as the true legatee of the Indian nation, and Indian culture is equated with a particular religion.

One can imagine the ramifications of giving primacy to a particular religion or a particular people in a multireligious, multicultural, multilingual nation at the dawn of the 21st century. One can imagine the havoc this can create where such blatant 'majoritarianism' is peddled as 'democracy' in a composite culture like ours. For L.K. Advani Naxalism, terrorism or infiltration of migrants from across the borders is the biggest threat to India's security. But any impartial, objective student of Indian society and state would agree that the idea of Hindutva and its paraphernilia of numerous organisations posit the biggest threat to the cause of justice and peace in the Indian subcontinent.

May 2006

Soft Hindutva of the Congress

Dr Surendra Parikh, practising allergist and President of the Federation of Indian Associations in USA. Does the name sound familiar? All those closely following the Gujarat genocide and the dubious role played by Narendra Modi and others from his Parivar would know this man for other reasons. He is associated with the Hindutva brigade there and was one of the main organizers of a 'Gujarat Gaurav Yatra' on the streets of New York City in the aftermath of the genocidal killings in the state. It was a futile attempt to whitewash Mr Narendra Modi who has been facing a lot of flak there for his 'successful Gujarat experiment'.

Back home a professedly secular dispensation at the Centre selected Dr Parikh to be one of the recipients of the prestigious Pravasi Bharatiya Samman, given to him during a three day meet held at Hyderabad. A small group of Indians residing in the USA, present at the meet, deemed it necessary to lodge a protest when he was presented the award by the President of India. This group was part of a larger coalition of secular organisations and individuals based in north America called 'Coalition against Genocide' which had spearheaded a successful campaign last year to prevent Modi from coming to USA.

Is it for the first time that a secular government at the Centre has been found wanting when it comes to upholding secular principles? The meeting of the National Integration Council, held last year after a gap of 13 years, showed that the UPA government has not really broken with the mindset of the previous NDA government. The agenda papers circulated at this gathering tried to peddle a convenient lie, which is very dear to the Sangh establishment. It said that forcible and fraudulent conversions (to Christianity) are the main cause of civil unrest in tribal and other rural areas. We know well that within the Hindutva *weltanschauung* 'conversion' is a very convenient ploy to put the religious minorities on hook. On this pretext the Hindutva front organisations have played havoc with the lives of the tribals and have been successful in re-converting thousands of them to their 'original' religion. The ground reality however is that the unrest in such backward areas is primarily because of the material-cultural deprivation felt by the local population vis-à-vis policies of the establishment.

A leading Christian rights activist and leader of the All India Christian Council conveyed his clear disapproval over the understanding of the government on this issue. His letter stated that it "[i]s a malicious myth propagated by obscurantist and fundamentalist – and often violent – political groups and their frontal organisations of a well known exclusivist ideology which believed in the thesis of 'One nation, One people, One Culture' totally negating the Indian reality of Unity and Diversity." (*Milli Gazette*, Wednesday 31, August 2005).

One also remembers how the UPA government retreated on its promise of repeal of POTA with retrospective effect. When out of power the Congress had called the law "draconian". In power it has conveniently forgotten the plight of hundreds of innocents still languishing in jails without any trial. The number of arrests made in Gujarat under this law in the aftermath of the carnage is in hundreds. It is also well known that the goons of the Hindutva brigade responsible for the genocide with due connivance of the state machinery roam free while those apprehended belong to the religious minorities.

Mukul Dube, a leading writer, in an introductory essay to *The Parivar Raj and After* (Vikas Adhyayan Kendra, Mumbai, August 2005) has rightly asked:

> Can the Congress not see what POTA has left behind of itself? … POTA will continue to apply to those who were arrested under its provisions. People who have suffered on account of a bad law will be tried under the provisions of that very bad law – although that bad law has been thrown out precisely because it was a bad law. It is difficult to conceive of a more putrid example of brahminical double-speak.

Many eyebrows were raised when the Congress Party, the leading constituent of the UPA government, welcomed in its ranks the rebels of the Shiv Sena, a Fascist formation based mainly in Maharashtra. One has seen how its Supremo, Bal Thackray, has openly praised Hitler, spewn venom against the minorities and dalits, and was instrumental in the demolition of the historic Babri Mosque. Justice Sri Krishna Commission, which enquired into the Bombay riots of 1992-1993, has on several accounts held the Shiv Sena responsible for the tragic happenings in the city. Questions naturally arise as to why these very people, who till the other day were henchmen of the fascist formation and some of whom had criminal cases slapped against them, could overnight be absorbed in a party that swears by secularism.

Close observers of the Congress recall with horror how the party had embraced the path of soft Hinduism in the eighties, thereby facilitating the rise of the 'hard Hindutva' forces. Whether it was the issue of the Meenakshipurm conversions in the early 80s, or the genocide of the Sikhs in 1984, or the opening of the gates of the Babri Mosque supposedly to 'free Ramlalla', one could see the growing commonalities of views between the 'secular' Congress and the Hindutva brigade. The then Prime Minister of India, Rajiv Gandhi, had even kick started his election campaign for the Parliamentary polls in 1989 from Ayodhya. And in his opening speech he had given a call for the formation of 'Ram Rajya'. The majoritarian forces of the Hindutva kind had certainly gained an upper hand due to the Congress slide back on secularism. In hindsight it could be said that the eighties were the turning point in the fortunes of the Hindutva brigade, helped by the Congress, which helped bring it from the margins to the centre stage of Indian polity.

The dubious role played by the Congress in facilitating the ascendance of the Hindutva forces may be a thing of the past but it cannot be said that this will not be repeated for short term political gains. Professor Aijaz Ahmad rightly says that the Sangh-BJP are "programmatic communalists" but insofar as Congress is concerned it should be noted that it is a party of "pragmatic communalists".

It would not be surprising that given the disarray in the Hindutva camp and the slackening of secular vigil in the country the Congress Party may well reinvent itself in a soft Hindutva garb. An inkling of this churning within the Congress can be had from the grassroot political rivalries which find local cadres of both formations fighting on the same turf and speaking the same language of 'politics of appeasement'.

The 'soft Hindutva detour' of the Grand Old Party of Indian democracy is definitely a wake up call. It remains to be seen how the motley coalition of organisations and individuals who have helped turn the tide against the resurgent communal BJP reinvigorate themselves to stem the tide of communalism.

A Metaphor Called Hashimpura

After 13 years, Bombay courts in September finally began to return verdicts on the 1993 bomb blasts in that city that had left 257 dead and 713 injured. The findings included the convictions of five Bombay policemen. Over the years, nearly 700 witnesses had been called and 35,000 pages of evidence racked up. But the number that continues to be discussed with the most awe – and anger – is '13', as in 13 long years. Other cases in India suffer for being less sensational, and are forced to wait even longer for justice – if it comes at all.

A study by the Bureau of Police Research and Development, a Union Home Ministry body, shows that "Between 1954 and 1996, almost 16,000 people lost their lives in 21,000 incidents of rioting, while over one lakh were injured. Only a handful have been held accountable." ('Communal Riots', *India Today*, July 21, 2003).

One such 'incident' was the 1987 massacre of 42 Muslims by a group of PAC (Provincial Armed Constabulary) personnel at Hashimpura in Uttar Pradesh. It has taken 19 years to even file a charge sheet for the case, which finally took place mid-July of this year. The following month, the Supreme Court succeeded in having the case transferred to Delhi – four years after it had first ordered the action. But for the perseverance exhibited by a few committed activists, the tragedy at Hashimpura would have joined the growing pile of largely forgotten massacres in the history of post-Independence India.

I

Ujma, who lives in Hashimpura, Meerut, never celebrates her birthday. She was born 19 years ago, and little time goes by without either her grandmother or mother recalling that terrible day. On the day of her birth, 22 May 1987, a communal conflagration suddenly ignited in their city. The Congress party was in power then, both in the state and at the Centre. The riots were fallout from the decision by Rajiv Gandhi's government to open the gates of the Babri Masjid in Ayodhya to allow Hindus to worship at a shrine there. After both police and PAC personnel were posted at the mosque, a curfew was imposed to contain the escalating unrest in Meerut.

On that late May evening, some hours before Ujma was born, her father, a daily-wage labourer, was at home when a PAC team stormed in and demanded he come with them. Days later, his body would return, riddled with bullets. Under circumstances similar to that of Ujma's father, 41 other Hashimpura residents, from ages 14 to 70, lost their lives that night. All of them were shot at point-blank range, and their bodies subsequently dumped in a nearby canal. No PAC member allegedly implicated in the incident has yet been forced to leave his job.

Sluggish investigations

A 1994 report by the Central Bureau of Investigation shed more light on what happened in Meerut on that summer night. At around eight in the evening, 40 to 42 alleged rioters were loaded into a PAC truck, ostensibly to be taken to the police station. Instead, the platoon's commander reportedly drove them to a canal of the Ganga in Ghaziabad, where they were "unceremoniously" shot down.

Commenting on the massacre, Vibhuti Narain Rai, then-superintendent of police in Ghaziabad, wrote in a later study critical of the police actions: "Most of the police personnel posted in Meerut saw the riots as a result of Muslim 'mischief', while ignoring the role of Hindutva groups in fanning them. They claimed that Meerut had become a 'mini-Pakistan' because of 'Muslim intransigence', and that it was necessary to teach the community a lesson."

Reports by senior journalists such as Nikhil Chakravarty and Kuldip Nayar, and organisations including the People's Union for Civil Liberties and the People's Union for Democratic Rights, revealed that the incident was largely a case of cold-blooded murder on the part of the PAC personnel. Chakravarty compared the event with "Nazi pogroms against the Jews, to strike terror and nothing but terror in a whole minority community". A report filed by Amnesty International in the immediate aftermath of the massacre stated that, "There is evidence to suggest that members of the PAC have been responsible for dozens of extra-judicial killings and disappearances".

The state government of Uttar Pradesh also asked the Criminal Investigations Department (CID) to look into the incident. This investigation was only completed in 1993, and its report did not come out until the following year. Even after this delay, there was massive procrastination in implementing the report's recommendations, with orders issued only in 1995 and 1997. Even then, the state government recommended action against only 19 policemen, even though the CID report had recommended action against 66. Due to the fact that most of the accused were public servants, the state government's sanction was needed in order to prosecute them. Even the 19 individuals named in the report did not comply with the court's summons – despite six bailable and 17 non-bailable warrants issued between January 1997 and April 2000. Although all of the accused were in active service when the court issued the summons, the government declared them 'absconders'.

According to Iqbal A Ansari, an Aligarh lawyer and founding member of the Minority Council, an organisation that has long worked for justice for the Hashimpura victims: "The UP government says that the INR 40,000 it paid for each of those killed is enough. It needs to be kept in mind that Hashimpura's is a case of custodial killings by PAC, not that of killings during riots because of failure of governance, as was the case in 1984 in Delhi, for which the Delhi High Court awarded compensation of INR two lakhs [for each person killed]."

A close look at the trajectory of the case exposes connivance between the state and police machinery in denying justice to the victims. This delay in justice, it should be noted, cannot be pinned on any one political group – the case has dragged on for nearly two decades due to the apathetic attitudes of several mainstream political formations.

If the Supreme Court had not intervened in the Hashimpura case, the legal process would have been postponed still further. But in 2002, following complaints that the accused were "exerting pressure and influence" to stall the proceedings in Ghaziabad, an appeal to the Supreme Court succeeded in getting the case transferred to New Delhi. The state government subsequently delayed appointing a special public prosecutor, and the framing of charges eventually took four years, until this last July. A three-judge bench headed by then-Chief Justice AS Anand lamented, while hearing a petition on the Meerut case: "We are at a loss to understand why the state has been taking this matter so casually, and why we were not informed over all these years of the correct position," referring to the inordinate delay in appointing a prosecutor and framing the charges.

2.

'84, '87, '89, '92-'93, '02... Hashimpura is not an aberration in post-Independence India. Indeed, it is one in a line of furious riots that have taken place in the Subcontinent during the past half-century, as well as their unjust aftermaths. The pattern playing out in Hashimpura has been repeated time and again: people lose their family members and friends to terrible violence, and spend much of their remaining years battling for justice. The guilty, meanwhile, remain free years and even decades after the atrocities.

The events of 1984 can be seen as a watershed in the history of communal violence in India, and the whole of South Asia in the post-Independence era. While the region had previously experienced riots, the assassination of Indira Gandhi by her Sikh bodyguards on 31 October of that year, followed by the organised massacre of Sikhs with the collusion of the Congress party, ushered the region into an era dotted all too frequently with pogroms and genocidal assaults – many of which enjoyed the active connivance of the state.

Of what took place in 1984, Supreme Court lawyer HS Phoolka wrote in 2004: "4000 innocent citizens belonging to the Sikh community were massacred in Delhi, and another 3000 were massacred in other parts of India. The government recorded a figure of 2733 deaths for Delhi alone ... Even after the horrendous task of pursuing the cases for 20 long years, only nine murder cases have resulted in conviction, which is not even one percent of the official figure of killings." None among the senior politicians or senior police officers of the time were included in the list of accused.

The scale of the 1989 riots in Bhagalpur District in Bihar dwarfed any previous riot in that state. Indeed, a 1990 report prepared by the People's Union for Democratic Rights called the violence "the largest Hindu-Muslim riot since 1947". The first round of rioting went on intermittently from the third week of October until early December. More than three months later, in March 1990, rioting again erupted in the town. During the course of the riots, over 2000 people lost their lives, a majority of whom were Muslim; 11,500 houses were also torched and nearly 50,000 people displaced. In Chanderi village, women and children under the protection of the local police were slaughtered by a mob. Despite the ferocity of the Bhagalpur riots, the subsequent delivery of justice was no different from that in many other cases. Of the 864 cases filed by the police in Bhagalpur, 535 were closed, and most of the accused were acquitted for lack of evidence.

The run-up to the Babri Masjid demolition in 1992 witnessed rioting throughout India, which only increased in the demolition's aftermath. Although thousands of people died in the tumult, there have been almost no significant convictions to date. Even though the Liberhans Commission, appointed by the then-Congress government of PV Narasimha Rao to look into the causes of the demolition and riots, has yet to submit a report, there is reason to believe that little will change after it does so. Its fate will undoubtedly be similar to the report of the Srikrishna Commission, which investigated the 1992-93 Bombay riots, and whose recommendations are by now largely forgotten.

Reports by various human-rights groups, and the various recommendations and strictures passed by the Supreme Court and the National Human Rights Commission, have castigated Hindutva organisations for their roles in the Gujarat genocide of 2002. The names of scores of activists of the Vishwa Hindu Parishad and the Bajrang Dal, including members of the ruling BJP, found mention in the numerous First Information Reports (FIRs) filed by victims. But subversion of investigations and justice for the surviving victims is continuing with impunity. Chief Minister Narendra Modi, who allegedly spearheaded this organised attack on minorities, is still holding the reins of power (See 'Gujarat as another country', *Himal* Oct 2006).

Teesta Setalvad and Javed Anand, leading anti-communal activists and editors of the Bombay-based *Communalism Combat*, wrote in an editorial in late 2004:

> For the perpetrators of a pogrom or genocidal killing, impunity from prosecution and punishment appears to be guaranteed in advance. Armed with this impunity, the mass murderers have mastered techniques of subversion of investigation. And the destruction of evidence is now 'in-built' into the very modes of killing adopted. This was clearly visible in Gujarat, where a chemical powder was extensively used while burning people so that no trace of the victims remained and which made it all the more difficult to count the dead.

In a newspaper article entitled '1984 in the Life of a Nation', also printed in late 2004, Supreme Court lawyer Indira Jaisingh noted:

> Our legal system has failed to answer the question: What is the constitutional and personal responsibility of the head of state for mass killings ... Apart from holding all those who committed the acts of killing liable, we also have to hold liable people in positions of power, who not only failed to prevent the killings, but encouraged by hate speech, justified it as an understandable response.

Revisiting communal carnage always brings a dilemma. Some advocate moving ahead and forgetting the terrible past, questioning the good that would come from disturbing the delicate inter-communal peace by dredging up past murders, pogroms or genocides. It is crucial to realise, however, that lasting peace can never be achieved without justice. We have no alternative but to keep talking about these issues, and to keep searching for ways of achieving that goal.

> On the contrary, I said to myself, and to a former district magistrate in Aligarh, that there existed in these towns what I called "institutionalised riot systems." The ex-DM, who knew very well how riots were organised, nevertheless reacted with an uncomprehending look. I was somewhat discouraged by his reaction, but ultimately found in my data from interviews, official and non-official reports – but not from the media – that the existence of such systems was to my mind incontro-

> vertible. Moreover, it was much more highly developed and elaborately organised within the network of militant Hindu organisations radiating out from the RSS than from any comparable network of Muslim organisations, at least in northern India. (Paul R. Brass, *The Hindu*, 23 rd August 2006)

> Moreover, it was also now clear enough to me that what have been called Hindu-Muslim riots in India of the past several decades are misnamed, that they could not have been carried out with such force in so many places, in many cases for extended periods of time, and repeatedly, without the complicity of the police and the failure of the political parties in control of government and the administrative and police officers in the districts to prevent riots or at least to contain them once they had begun. In short, what are called Hindu-Muslim riots in India are, in fact, more like pogroms, and have recently, in Gujarat and elsewhere, taken the form of genocidal massacres and local ethnic cleansing as well. (Paul R Brass, *The Hindu*, 23 rd August 2006)

November 2006

Auschwitz of Our Times

For if I shall not burn
And you shall not burn
If we shall not burn
Then who will dispel the dark

Nazim Hikmet

I

A place called Auschwitz, approximately 270 kms. from Warsaw, the capital of Poland, is today a museum for the cruelty and barbarism of the Nazi regime. It is now more than sixty years since the brick kiln structures there, which housed the detainees, witnessed the silent sufferings of lakhs of people put to death in myriad ways by the henchmen of Hitler.

A majority of the victims were simply hurled into a gas chamber to immediate deaths caused by inhaling a poisonous gas like cynaide. Many of them were literally choked to death and many starved to death. Quite a number died due to the intense hard labour and malnutrition.

In hindsight, thanks to meticulous research by some scholars, we know that the killings were no spontaneous actions on the part of the Nazis. Hitler in his autobiography *Mein Kampf* had specifically talked of '*submitting twelve to fifteen thousand of these Jews who were corrupting the nation' to be '... to poison-gas'.*

The recent revelations in the *Tehelka* expose of the Gujarat carnage of the year 2002 vividly brought back to 'life' the deaths of 11 lakh people in Aushwitz. One could easily draw a parallel between the likes of Rudolf Hoess, Dr Joseph Mengele, Dr Clark Clauberg, Arthur Libenatial, Richard Baer and the likes of Dr Praveen Togadia, Dr Maya Kodnani, Dhimant Patel, Jaideep Patel, Babu Bajrangi, Haresh Bhatt, Anil Patel, and heading them all, Herr Modi.

History bears witness to the weird 'scientific' experiments conducted by the likes of Dr Joseph Mengele on the detainees during which caustic chemicals were injected into the bodies of women to test a new series of contraceptives.Perhaps the perpetrators of Gujarat carnage were no less 'innovative'. If the Germans had devised special gas chambers for the hapless Jews and many dissidents of the Nazi regime, the likes of Babu Bajrangi turned a sewer line into a gas chamber by placing a big boulder on the opening of a sewer line in which a group of Muslims were hiding from the marauders of the Hindutva brigade. Only their dead bodies were recovered from the pit a few days later. If the Nazis had adopted the practice of confining detainees into a small pit with very little source of oxygen so that they may die for want of oxygen, the followers of Modi-Togadia contrived to pour hot oil on their hapless victims hiding in a pit and burnt them alive. Babu Bajrangi, the main perpetrator of the Naroda Patiya massacre, a leading Bajrang Dal/VHP figure, proudly boasting about his 'heroism' in the said killings, narrated how '*they were clinging to each other in the pit. Then we threw in oil and burning tyres and killed them*'. One could go on drawing attention to the parallels between the Aushwitz experiment and the Gujarat Genocide which many of us witnessed before our own eyes – thanks to the 24 hour news channels beaming out 'war' and 'riots' live into our homes.

It is now history how humanity has tried to exorcise itself of Auschwitz and the ghosts of Nazism and Fascism. The historic Nuremberg trials gave its final verdict on the Nazi criminals. Leading perpetrators of Auschwitz were sent to gallows in front of Aushwitz itself. Rudolf Hoess, who headed the Auschwitz camp for full three years and gave graphic descriptions of the working of Auschwitz in his memoirs and also before the court, was the first to be hanged.

Perhaps it is a sign of changed times or the slackening of the resolve of humanity to prevent such atrocities that today, sixty years after Auschwitz, the 'Neros' of Gujarat have been allowed to go scot free. Forget punishment, these perpetrators of ghastly killings – the strategists, the planners and the actual footsoldiers – are today regarded a respectable lot. All those who have conceded their crimes before cameras, including details on the planning that went into making the genocide happen and their own specific roles in burning down houses, killing innocent people or raping innocent girls/women have been allowed to go scot free. If the electoral victories of their political masters over the dead bodies of thousands of people in a 'democratic' process could be hailed by them as 'vindication of their succesful experiment', an encore in a similar exercise in coming days could further legitimise their crimes against humanity in the eyes of a very wide section of people.

A question naturally arises: are sensitive, humane, justice loving persons/formations in this part of the world ready to tolerate this further humiliation with folded hands, or are they willing to break asunder the carefullly maintained conspiracy of silence? Would it be correct on our part to look on the carnage as acts of some 'psychotic killers', as 'products of a few crooked minds', leaving the Rashtriya Swayamsevak Sangh and its affiliated organisations – who planned and executed it – absolved of the crimes? Would it be correct on our part to accept the fictitious division between 'Hindutva' and 'Moditva' and reserve our scorn for Narendra 'Milosevic' Modi alone? Is there not a need to focus on the imminent dangers of majoritarianism in a multireligious/multicultural country like ours?

II

> At the beginning of the Great War, or even during the War, if twelve or fifteen thousand of these Jews who were corrupting the nation had been forced to submit to poison gas...then the millions of sacrifices made at the front would not have been in vain.
>
> Adolf Hitler, *Mein Kampf*

The year 1933 saw an interesting presentation by a Polish-Jewish scholar Raphael Lemkin at a legal conference held under the auspices of the

League of Nations (a precursor to the United Nations) at Madrid. This gentleman who had closely studied the massacre of Armenians in Turkey during the First World War and the genocide of Assyrians in Iraq the same year, and how many such crimes against humanity went unpunished, made a novel suggestion in his paper 'Crime of Barbarity'. According to him all such crimes against humanity which take the form of killing of innocent people merely because they belong to a particular community, region, or ethnicity etc should be considered crimes under international law.

As expected the imperialist countries, cosying up to the Nazi and Fascist regimes in Germany and Italy, did not find any merit in Lemkin's argument. And his own government, which had established a good rapport with the Nazis by then, also disapproved of his suggestions. In fact, a few of his comments at the Madrid Conference so infuriated the Polish government that he was asked by the Polish Foreign Minister to resign from his job as Public Prosecutor and as teacher in a college.

Of course, very few people realised then that it was an idea whose time had come. Only the experience of the genocidal Second World War, the establishment of concentration camps like Auschwitz and the persecution of particular communities under the Nazi dispensation pushed humanity to seriously consider measures to avoid such genocides in future.

The year 1944 saw publication of Lemkin's magnum opus *Axis Rule In Occupied Europe* in the United States. The book comprised detailed legal analysis of the Nazi rule in the occupied countries during World War II. Lemkin further concretised his ideas on Genocide as an offence against international law in later writings.

The international community did not find much difficulty in accepting Lemkin's ideas now and it formed the legal basis of the historic Nuremberg Trials which were held against the Nazi leaders who 'conducted deliberate and systematic genocide – namely, the extermination of racial and national groups.' The year 1948 saw the adoption of a Convention by the international community in the form of *Convention on the Prevention and Punishment of the Crime of Genocide* by the UN General Assembly (9th December 1948) which came into effect on 12 January 1951. This contained an internationally-recognized definition of genocide which was incorporated into the national criminal legislation of many countries, and was also adopted by the Rome Statute of the International Criminal Court, the treaty that established the International Criminal Court (ICC). The Convention (in article 2) defines genocide as:

> ...any of the following acts committed with intent to destroy, in whole or in part, a national, ethnical, racial or religious group, as such:
>
> (a) Killing members of the group;
>
> (b) Causing serious bodily or mental harm to members of the group;
>
> (c) Deliberately inflicting on the group conditions of life calculated to bring about its physical destruction in whole or in part;
>
> (d) Imposing measures intended to prevent births within the group;
>
> (e) Forcibly transferring children of the group to another group.

III

> *After killing them, I felt Like Maharana Pratap ...* Babu Bajrangi, Bajrang Dal leader
>
> *As the CM, Narendra Modi couldn't say 'Kill the Muslims'... I could say it because I was from the VHP.* Rajendra Vyas, VHP leader, Ahmedabad
>
> *Put lathis aside and pick up AK-56s, if you are to develop Hinduism. It is clear who the enemies are, Muslims and Christians.* Dhimant Bhatt, Chief Auditor of M.S. University, Vadodara
>
> DCP Gadvi promised VHP's Kalupur Zila Mantri Ramesh Dave that he would kill "at least four-five Muslims" if Dave pointed them out to him. Dave took him to a house from where a group of Muslims could be seen. "Before we knew it, he'd killed five people." Dave said. Quoted in *Tehelka*

Any sensible person who has browsed through the sting operation done by *Tehelka* or who has seen its telecast on some TV channels would confirm that there was nothing spontaneous about the carnage which occurred in Gujarat which officially saw deaths of more than 1,000 people.

The sting operation done by a young journalist Ashish Khetan, over a period of six months, during which he managed to make many ringleaders of the RSS-BJP-VHP who spearheaded the carnage talk about their role in the events, is definitely 'the most important story of our time'. Ashish Khetan and the Team *Tehelka* need to be given kudos for the marvellous job done to persuade the 'killers' to themselves speak of what they had done.

Any sane person would also agree with Tarun Tejpal about the three particularly disturbing things about Gujarat 2002. "The first that the genocidal killings took place in the heart of urban India in an era of saturation of media coverage"; "the second that the men who presided over the carnage were soon after elected to power not despite their crimes but because of them"; and, "the fact that there continues to be no trace of remorse, no sign of penitence for the blood-on-the hands".

The 'sting operation' makes it clear that right from the giving of the green signal to the Sangh workers to start an attack on the Muslims to the planning that went into making it happen the top bosses of the Sangh Parivar were involved at every level. In fact they met and strategised about every aspect of the attack very carefully. To shield the attackers from the law, they even consulted prominent lawyers as well as senior police officers. All sorts of weapons – from bombs to guns to trishuls – were either manufactured by the Sangh workers or were smuggled through Sangh channels from all over India. One BJP MLA from Gujarat even managed to manufacture rocket launchers in his factory. Its other contacts in the quarrying area managed to manufacture other explosives also. Since 'cremation is considered un-Islamic' fire was the 'most favoured weapon in the rioters hand'.

But it is a sign of our changed times that neither the Congress nor other secular parties nor the highest court of the country deemed it necessary to go in for either 'prosecuting Narendra Modi' or 'go in for arresting the bloodthirsty criminals who had the audacity of sharing their exploits during the genocide without any sign of remorse'.

A question that naturally arises is: why did the people in power not act despite clear-cut evidence before them of the culpability of the

Hindutva goons in the carnage? The foremost reason appears to be the calculations of electoral politics, where the 'secular parties' feared and wanted to forestall any attempt on the part of Modi to further polarise voters on communal lines. Apart from their own game plan, the muted reaction of the articulate sections of our society could have guided their consideration.

A few of the doubting Thomases even raised the issue of the 'timing' of the exposure and its likely impact on the electoral (mis) fortunes of the parties involved.

It may also be argued that despite signing the UN Convention on Genocide way back in 1959 India has failed to comply with international legal norms, by formulating a suitable domestic legislation. In fact the absence of domestic legislation to not only prevent and punish genocide, but also designate a tribunal for the trial of those charged, has helped create a strange situation where the ability of the Indian criminal justice system to dispense justice – when it comes to mass crimes – seems to be in grave doubt.

IV

How many ears must one man have
Before he can hear people cry?
How many deaths will it take till he knows
That too many people have died?
The answer, my friend, is blowing in the wind,
The answer is blowing in the wind

Bob Dylan, *Blowing in the Wind*

There are very many ways in which India is presented and projected to the outside world. For some it happens to be the biggest democracy in the world, while for others it is one of the fastest growing economies of the world, which has now 'arrived'. Many talk about its becoming the new superpower with the demise of the US from the world scene.

But rarely does anyone talk about its being a 'land of mass crimes' where the perpetrators of such crimes have always gone unpunished. None of the opinion makers talk about the unholy alliance between politicos, mafiosi and the law and order machinery which has emerged down the years, of the site where the art of 'invisibilising mass crimes' is being perfected. And the targets of such mass crimes are mainly the religious minorities or people on the lowest rung of the social matrix or the toiling masses of the country.

Would anyone believe that the 'first' massacre of around forty Dalits – mainly women and children – in independent India at Keezhavenmani (Tamilnadu, 1969) by the local upper caste landlords went unpunished with the specious argument on the part of the judiciary that 'these are upper caste people and it is impossible to believe that they would have gone walking to the dalit hamlet'. It is a well known fact that the dalits and other toiling masses of the area had begun a strike for better wages under the leadership of the Communist Party.

Would anyone believe that Delhi, the capital city of the great democracy called India, was witness to the killings of around 3,000 innocent people (the Sikhs in 1984) merely 23 years ago and today, ten enquiry commissions and three special courts later, merely three people have been found guilty of killing the hapless 3,000 Sikhs.

It is a sad commentary on the 60 year old history of post-Independence India that neither the killing of around 40 dalit women and children in Keezhavenmani (Tamilnadu, 1969) nor the massacre of around thousand plus Muslims in Nelli (Assam 1983), nor the genocide of 3,000 Sikhs in Delhi (1984), nor the cold blooded murder of 42 Muslims in Hashimpura (UP, 1986), nor the killing of around 1,800 people (majority of them Muslims, Bombay 1992), nor the massacre of scores of Dalits in Kumher (1993, Rajasthan) have been punished till date.

It is also enlightening how such mass crimes are rationalised or legitimised by the powers that be. The Prime Minister of the country had no qualms in commenting after the massive carnage of the Sikh community led by his own party people, that "When a big tree falls, the earth shakes". A chief minister of a state shamelessly discovers the Newtonian 'action-reaction' thesis to cover up the crimes of his own Parivar.

Intellectuals enamoured with the idea that tolerance is inherent in 'our great culture' must be rather shell-shocked to find how the ordinary, peace loving people imbued with this great culture can 'metamorphose overnight' into murderers and rapists of neighbours they have lived together with. All the orgy of violence and their 'joyous participation' in it is followed by a conspiracy of silence where nobody is then ready to tell the truth. Bhagalpur in Bihar which had become a site of violence where officially over a thousand people had been slain, most of them Muslims, is still remembered for a particular incident. In Logain village, 116 Muslims were massacred, buried in a field and cauliflowers grown over their bodies.

This scenario of the guilty going unpunished needs to be changed if India is to emerge as a humane society. It is a challenge before every one of us. If people of the subcontinent resolve that 'the biggest democracy in the world' should not henceforth tolerate these mass crimes, then it can actually be so.

However, times are such that this simple proposal appears utopian to most people. But there is no alternative than to persist in one's attempts at the individual as well as collective level, to unleash processes and strengthen institutions so that positive change can be expedited.

As mentioned above, it was in the year 1933 that the Polish-Jewish scholar Raphael Lemkin first gave voice to this idea on a public platform. We are also told that in his personal life Lemkin faced tremendous tragedy. He lost 49 relatives in the holocaust, among the 3 million Polish Jews killed during the Nazi occupation. But all such personal tragedies did not deter him from continuing his work to convince humanity of the necessity to create deterrents that such barbarities are not committed again.

Where are our Raphael Lemkins who can yell: *It's Enough*!

November 2007

Modi's Gujarat

The Fascists don't view the Jews as a minority but as an opposing race, the embodiment of the negative principle. They must be exterminated to secure the happiness of the world. Adorno and Horkhheimer

'Memory for Forgetfulness'

More than two and half years ago, at a gathering of activists in Gujarat comprising of many 'outsiders' like me, a young film maker from the state made this passionate appeal: 'Keep returning to Gujarat'. Faced with a bewildered silence he immediately explained what he meant. "Even if it is not possible for you to physically come here, keep 'revisiting' Gujarat one way or the other."

Perhaps he had a premonition that the havoc wreaked on Gujarat by the Hindutva brigade would unfold itself so tortuously that to 'forget' Gujarat would become impossible.

There is no comparable example in the history of post independence India of a genocide of such a scale, and of executing it with such military precision and thereafter presenting it as 'spontaneous outburst' of people.

There is no comparable example of such continuous subversion of justice despite the extraordinary intervention of the Supreme Court to rein in the 'modern day Neroes'.

As things stand today the 'other' people may have gained some respite from direct violence, but ongoing low intensity violence still continues to be inflicted on them. The economic boycott of the minorities remains unabated, the intimidation of witnesses continues with impunity and steps are being taken to deprive the victims of any sense of hope for justice. The highest court of the country has rightfully observed in its historic judgment on the 'Best Bakery Case (April 12, 2004): "[T] he fanatics who spread violence in the name of religion are worse than terrorists and more dangerous than an alien enemy...." .

What does one do in such a situation?

It would be worthwhile to remember Mahmoud Darwish, the great Palestinian poet. "It was August 1982 when Darwish was living in Beirut when it was intensively bombed by the Israeli air force and navy. The bombardment was spread over two months, and almost every day about two to three hundred Lebanese and Palestinian civilians were killed. To come to terms with that experience, he wrote a diary which he called 'Memory for forgetfulness'." (Excerpted from a speech 'Political Culture of Fascism,' by Jairus Banaji).

One knows that 'memory' is not neutral. It is subversive. It helps people remember each and every insult, humiliation they have had to face at the hands of the powers that be. It helps people 'carry on such sedimented memory' from generation to generation. It keeps reminding people to avenge all the sufferings, all the trauma, all the grief they have had to endure from times immemorial

Here is an attempt to share a few such 'stray memories' which somehow remained buried on the editor's table. They may seem a bit old, but are still worth recounting. We should know and remember how these Indian versions of the Taliban celebrate violence, glorify people who have helped them 'design' it and how have they 'modi'fied terrorism, driving the minorities to a permanent secondary status in their 'model state'.

Felicitating a Hatemonger

It was a gathering not much reported outside the Hindutva laboratory. After their humiliating defeat at the hustings at the Centre it was the first gathering of its kind. Many stalwarts of the Sangh Parivar had assembled to felicitate one among them. One could see all the big names of the Parivar hierarchy – the ex deputy PM LK Advani, Narendra Modi and the likes of Togadias and Singhals, and quite a galaxy of saffron robed sadhus. The programme held in Ahmedabad to felicitate Prof Keka Shastry on his entering the centenary year seemed an ideal occasion for them to air their views in Gujarat.

For those not conversant with the VHP's who's who in Gujarat, Prof Keshavram Kashiram Shastry, a one time famous Gujarati literary figure, has been state president of the Vishwa Hindu Parishad and is part of its triumvirate, along with international general secretary Mr Praveen Togadia and Jaideep Patel, all key figures in the organisation.

Whatever may be the pluses and minuses of Prof Keka Shastry's literary works, the rest of India learnt of him only in the aftermath of Godhra.

It was through one of his interviews to the rediff.com people ('It had to be done, VHP leader says of riots', Sheela Bhatt, 12 March 2002) that people heard how things unfolded in an organized way after the Godhra incident. The interview was an admission for the first time by the Hindutva brigade of their direct role in the carnage which officially saw over 2,000 deaths, uprooting of lakhs of people from their homes and hearth and loss of hope and peace for millions of people.

Rarely had one come across an interview so direct and so chilling. He told the correspondent that "[t]he list of shops owned by Muslims in Ahmedabad was prepared on the morning of 28 February itself." In the tape recorded interview he said, "In the morning we sat down and prepared the list. We were not prepared in advance."

When the correspondent asked him why they did it, he responded "It had to be done, it had to be done. We don't like it, but we were terribly angry..."

When the correspondent asked him how he, a scholar and littérateur could condone the burning of innocents, he responded: "The youngsters have done some things which we don't like. We don't support it. But we can't condemn it because they are our boys." He added for good measure "We don't believe that the boys have done anything wrong, because this was the result of an outburst.... We needed to do something."

The interview had also explained the inactivity of the police in simple terms by underlining that "they feared death" and "some of them were Hindus who thought "Let the mob do whatever it wants." While talking to the interviewer his future prognosis was clear. He said the situation could get aggravated and bigger riots were possible.

There is no doubt that if the Parivar people would not have been in power this 'literary' figure would have been hauled up and put behind bars for "promoting enmity between different groups on grounds of religion, race, place of birth, residence, language" etc. and for "acts prejudicial to maintenance of harmony (Section 153-A, IPC)", or "deliberate and malicious acts intended to outrage religious feelings of any class, by insulting its religion or religious beliefs (Section 295-A,IPC) ", or "uttering words, etc with deliberate intent to wound religious feeling (Section 298, IPC)", or similar other provisions which have clearly laid down punishment for offences committed under such acts.

But he was not even called to the police station to explain his utterances. He seemed to be putting in black and white what others of his ilk were implementing through this 'successful experiment'.

What is disturbing is that his was not the first or only admission of the role of the VHP and the likes of Keka Shastry in the carnage. In the 'Letters to the Editor' column Prof JS Bandukwala, Vice President, PUCL Gujarat, whose house had also come under attack, pointed out that similar utterances had also appeared in the print media. Prof Bandukwala questioned the rationale behind the state government's felicitation ceremony. He said "[T]his is the same gentleman who on March 4, 2002, praised those who carried out the Naroda Patiya and Gulberg society massacres. In his words, widely reported by the media, including the *Times of India* 'these were our boys, from respected families, who were trained to do this thing'. He never retracted this statement. As expected the Gujarat Government did not even file a case against him, for incitement to murder and rape."

Even the 'Swayamsevak' Prime Minister, who had advised Mr Modi to remember his 'Raj dharma' while on a visit to the Shah Alam Camp, did not deem it necessary to exercise the central government's powers under Section 355 in order to make a decisive intervention. The self proclaimed 'iron man' also preferred to remain silent and rather concentrated on singing eulogies to Prof Shastry.

Indian mythology, which has been made a handmaiden of the saffrons, is filled with many stories of wise men who chose silence at opportune moments.

'Modi'fying 'Counter Terrorism'

It is surprising that the revelations of the 'counter terrorism' plans of the Gujarat police (*The Rediff Special*, Sheela Bhatt in Ahmedabad, 'How Gujarat plans to counter terrorists', July 15, 2004) which sent shivers down the spine of the religious minorities in the state, especially the Muslims, who were yet to recover from the trauma and tribulations of the post Godhra carnage, could not become a matter of debate at the national level.

The implicit understanding (as per the Gujarat government) behind this plan is that the 'state has become a haven for terrorists' (read Islamic terrorists)'. In an interview to the same e-magazine the additional CP of Ahmedabad, Mr Vanzara, hammered this point home in no uncertain terms: "After the Godhra carnage and the subsequent riots terrorists of a variety of types and shapes are aiming at Gujarat. Gujarat has become the destination for terrorists." ('The Rediff Interview' July 27, 2004).

As a precursor to these plans of 'counter terrorism' a detailed survey was done of the number of mosques and madrasas in the state, and a list prepared of the various Islamic organisations active in the state and their alleged 'linkages with other national-international organisations' also noted. As per these plans every police person above the rank of constable has been instructed to keep a close watch on the situation on the ground. S/He has been asked to keep tabs on meetings at masjids and the goings on in the madrasas. Activities of the Tablighi Jamaat are also to be keenly watched.

It is clear that the neatly designed 'counter terrorism plan' of the Gujarat government stigmatizes the whole minority community and, as expected makes no mention of the extremist elements within the Hindu community at whose behest the post Godhra pogrom against the Muslims was systematically carried out. The need to keep a close watch on the controversial activities of the Hindutva brigade and its leaders is firmly scuttled. It was only an year ago that the 'intelligence bureau people overseeing the national scene had warned the central government to rein in elements like Praveen Togadia and Ashok Singhal if it was keen to nip the fresh sources for terrorist activities in the bud.' *(Jansatta,* Hindi Daily, 5th Sep, 2003, Delhi, 'Intelligence bureau warns the government about Togadia and Singhal').

According to the top bosses of the Gujarat police the plan originated in the context of the murder of former state home minister and senior Bharatiya Janata Party leader Haren Pandya. It is being said that the murder opened the eyes of the state government to the phenomenon of the state having become a breeding ground for terrorists belonging to the Pakistan-based Lashkar-e-Tayiba and Jaish-e-Mohammad. It is, of course, another matter that till date Mr Vithalbhai Pandya, father of Mr Haren Pandya, has consistently maintained that his son's murder was politically motivated and has pointed fingers at the higher ups in the state BJP for their complicity in the same. As a mark of protest against the state government's reticence to investigate his charges, he even contested as an independent candidate against Mr LK Advani in the recent elections to the Parliament.

Given the track record of the state government in pursuing such matters and its role in the 2002 pogrom the 'counter terrorism plan' causes no surprise. Innumerable reports have brought out details of police and state administration complicity in the carnage. Many victims of the riot also later reported that the police, instead of protecting them, had handed them over to the rioters.

It is a fact that the trauma of the minorities has not ended with the pogrom. They have been subjected to all round harassment in matters of relief distribution and in apprehending the guilty. Till date a significant section of the Muslim population in the state is facing economic boycott. The misuse of the draconian POTA and the victimization of innocent persons in the post pogrom months is also a fact that has been well documented. A report filed by the AFP (New Delhi, Sep 03) has shown that of the 240 booked under POTA (which carries a death penalty) 239 were Muslims and one was a Sikh. While Muslims had been booked for three different attacks on Hindus, the burning of Sabarmati Express at Godhra last year, the attack on Ahmedabad's Akshardham temple and murder of former minister Haren Pandya, despite the participation of thousands of Hindus in mass killings not a single case has been filed under POTA.

A report compiled by the Indian People's Tribunal, comprising renowned legal luminaries, intellectuals and human rights activists, exposes the dreaded misuse of POTA and several other security legislations. What is even more shocking is that these laws are being selectively used against the weaker sections of society, the poor, the minorities, juveniles and other marginal groups. The tribunal noted that a "deliberate communal bias in the application of security legislations" was evident in the fact that Muslims form an overwhelming majority of POTA detainees.

The 'counter terrorism plan of the state police' has come as a sequel to the amended Gujarat Control of Organised Crime Bill (GUJCOC), which was passed by the Gujarat Assembly in the beginning of June 2004. The Bill incorporates almost all the provisions of POTA, including the authority to hold the accused in jail without trial and provisions giving jurisdiction only to Special Courts to try the cases under the Act. The Bill has armed the BJP government in the state with an alternative coercive law in the event of the Centre repealing the Prevention of Terrorism Act (POTA) with retrospective effect.

The action plan, so partisan in nature and communal in content, could hardly have seen the light of day without direction from the top bosses of the Sangh Parivar. The rationale for the plan is not difficult to decipher. With a changed political ambience in the country which brought about the exit of the Hindutva brigade from the citadels of power in Delhi, and possibilities of a filing of criminal complaint of culpable homicide against Narendra Modi and others on the increase, perhaps this is a bold attempt by the saffrons to once again polarise the populace on communal lines.

Modi's Ringtones ?

A few months ago, during the *Rakshbandhan* festivities, the media had reported on the one lakh women from different parts of Gujarat who had sent their *Rakhis* to 'brother' Mr Modi. The figures may be inflated but there is no denying that a person whose regime presided over one of the worst genocides which also involved brutal violence against women, is being accepted as 'protector' and a 'benefactor' by a significant section of women.

The popularity of 'Modi Ringtones' has also been widely reported recently. A Modi fan copied a portion of his speech and sent it to a friend, who in turn sent it to many of his friends, and then somehow it reached some people from a private company. A spokesperson from the Company told a newspaper reporter that there is a huge demand for that particular ring tone and that it is now competing with many popular numbers from Bollywood.

Another aspect of this 'popularity of Modi' is the absence of remorse among people of the state over the tragic incidents. Reports emanating from the state keep underlining this fact. The language of those days remains unchanged. 'They had invited it.' 'They had it coming', 'They needed to be taught a lesson', 'Hindus have shown that they cannot take it lying down' etc. At any discussion in any public place, the words may differ but the content remains the same.

Will this situation continue indefinitely or is a radical rupture with the recent past possible?

In Germany and Italy it has been seen that the people as whole have more or less been redeemed of their Nazi or Fascist past.

The famous left-wing American playwright David Campian has written a beautiful play '*Us*' *and* '*Them*' which depicts inter communal tensions arising out of false pride and the absence of tolerance towards other peoples and cultures. Only last year the leading poetess of Gujarat, Saroop Dhruv, took the initiative and staged this play in the Juhapura area of Ahmedabad, with children from both communities participating in it. The play evoked a good response where ever it was staged.

Perhaps it is time to make fresh beginnings in Gujarat, perhaps it is time to rededicate ourselves for a world devoid of hatred and full of harmony, perhaps it is time to break new ice.

2004

Gang Rape in Modirashtra

What should a Chief Minister do if a victim of gang rape and her batch mates – who have similarly faced assault at the hands of the rapists – and their parents come to seek audience with him to demand strict action against the perpetrators of a crime that has shocked the entire state?

Courtesy demands that the chief minister at the very least spares a few minutes for them and tries to assure them that 'no guilty would be spared'. But then if it happens to be Narendra Modi, to expect such courteous behaviour is perhaps to hope for too much.

The latest case of a gang rape of a student in the Primary Teachers Training College (PTC) in Patan, 130 kms from Ahmedabad, by her own teachers evoked no sympathy from the Chief Minister. It is being reported that the high profile CM of Gujarat did not deem it necessary to meet the victim because of his otherwise 'busy schedule'.

The reasons for his not meeting the victim are not far to seek.

In fact this case has exposed the stark reality in the much tom-tommed 'vibrant Gujarat'. Only recently the media was singing paeans to the 'dynamic leadership' of Modi who had 'vanquished his opponents' inside and outside the party. This coincided with the time when he was anointed No. 2 in the BJP hierarchy at the national level and the BJP president had asked the other CMs of his party to follow the 'Modi model'.

Therefore, the manner in which the whole case came to light was rather unexpected for Mr Modi.

In fact once the matter spilled beyond the confines of the college, the anger of the Patan residents against the whole episode knew no bounds. The whole town remained closed in protest for two consecutive days to demand prompt action against the guilty. Angry residents of Patan town took out a massive rally, which saw the participation of more than 25,000 people, to demand action against the six teachers. Anandiben Patel, who is the MLA from the area, and other ministers from the region became so terrified of the citizens' anger they did not have the courage to meet them.

Apart from Patan, most of the major towns and cities in Gujarat witnessed similar rallies in support of the dalit girl victim.

The media in general and the Gujarati media in particular felt the pressure to bring into focus some facts relating to the case. The media duly reported that the alleged rapists – the six teachers in the Primary Teachers Training College, namely Manish Parmar, Suresh Patel, Ashwin Parmar, Kiran Patel, Atul Patel and Narendra Patel – are close to Ms Anandiben Patel, who in turn is a close confidante of Mr Narendra Modi himself. A section of the media also reported that Atul Patel – the ringleader of these rapist teachers – was the election agent for Ms Anandiben Patel during the 2002 elections. The importance of Ms Anandiben Patel in the government can be gauged from the fact that she was awarded the much coveted Revenue Department after the recent Assembly elections.

It also came to light that the PTC in question, meant for girls, has only a single lady teacher. This sole lady teacher Bharatiben Patel was earlier shifted/ transferred out of the college as she had reported to higher authorities similar cases of misdemeanor by her colleagues in the college. It is significant that Ms Anandiben Patel handled the education department during that period. It was also discussed in the media, how the system of internal markings had become a weapon in the hands of such teachers to abuse and brutalise the girl students in other PTC colleges as well. (There are 134 such 'girls only' PTC colleges all over the state where 16,000 girl students were undergoing the two year residential course.) And how a insensitive administration slept over earlier demands raised by concerned citizens to not only remove the system of internal markings but also take serious action in earlier cases of sexual assault in colleges.

Perhaps the other no less shocking aspect of the case (at least as far as Mr Modi was concerned) is that it happened in Patan, the venue of the official celebrations for 15th August since the last few years. The shifting of the official venue to Patan was then seen as a shrewd move by Mr Modi to connect himself to the historical legacy of the Rajput kings who ruled Gujarat for a considerable period of time.

It is now well known that the sexual exploitation of the hapless Dalit girl continued for around six months during which period she was raped 14 times by these six teachers. The matter came to light only because she fainted during prayers on January 31st.

The plight of this hapless daughter of a dalit labourer, Babubhai Makwana, who hailed from Jetalvasana village of Mehsana district, touched a wide cross-section of people. It is not surprising that ordinary people, who had rarely joined any anti-Modi demonstration, felt compelled to register their protest on this account.

People learnt from the media reports that the victim was the most intelligent and smart amongst her brothers and sisters. When she scored distinction in the10th and 12th standards it became news not only in her village but in the adjoining villages as well. The only handicap faced by her with regard to her studies after the 12th standard was her father Babubhai Makwana's poverty. Babubhai, father of five children did not earn enough to finance the studies of all his children.

Aware that his daughter showed extra promise, he asked a son to discontinue his studies and help in the daily chores. Babubhai hoped that when his bright daughter took up a job on completing her Training Course their difficult days would end.

At the time of admission to the College Babubhai even met a few of the teachers and explained to them his pathetic economic condition. He was pleased when the teachers assured him full support. Little did Babubhai know what was in store for his daughter.

The indifference shown by the administration was not lost on the media. According to a signed write-up in the *DNA*, reporter Jumna Shah raised the question: Is the Modi government insensitive towards the Patan gang rape case? According to babus in the Sachivalaya, the government should have handled the case with a little more sensitivity, which is completely missing from the government's response to the issue.

For example, the education minister's aide dubbed the issue as "routine", while home minister Amit Shah said that the police had done their job and now it's up to the education department to act.

The CM, who launched 'beti bachao' movement with great fanfare, had no time to even meet the victim or her family members due to his 'busy' schedule. "This is not expected of any government in a democracy," remarked a senior official.

It was rather shocking to note that despite the involvement of colleagues, the state association of teachers in Gujarat – a body close to the Sangh Parivar – did not deem it necessary to issue a condemnatory statement.

A four member team of *National Commission for Women* which met the victim (as reported in newspapers on 8th Feb 2008) said that it was not 'only a one-off incident'. In fact the initial investigations indicated that 'more girls have been raped, but are scared or unwilling to register their complaints.'

The severe indictment of the Gujarat government and of its no. 2 minister in particular, by the National Commission for the Scheduled Castes, has exposed the chinks in the Parivar's armour. In fact, the very day when the BJP had organised a mass meeting of women in Delhi to set the agenda for the coming elections, the Chairperson referred to the incident and this appeared in the media.

Quoting Mr Buta Singh, the *Times of India* report (21st February 2008, 'Gujarat minister shielding Patan rape accused') stated that

> ...[t]he accused teachers were close supporters of Patel who was Education and Women's Welfare Minister when the sexual exploitation started'. Accusing the college administration of complicity in the nefarious activities, he added that the said girl's college had turned into a fief of the accused as the only lady teacher was transferred out after she reported on the conduct of the Principal to the Department of Education two years ago. The preliminary report also makes it clear that 'while the six have been arrested, the cases against them were weak and left sufficient room for them to get scott free.

The biggest problem for the Modi regime seems to be the exposure to a wider populace of the 'myth of women's security' in Gujarat. People came to know that there is tremendous 'gender disparity in the police' which 'hampers probe in crimes against women.' (*Indian Express* Feb 21, 2008).

The Gujarat police is facing a handicap as it battles an upswing in violent crimes against women. The police have to make do with the presence of a lone lady police constable in the controversial Patan gang rape case. Similar is the minor girl sex scam in Vadodara. The state has just five women IPS officers, three deputy SPs, four women police inspectors and seven police sub-inspectors (PSI), and except for one woman PSI, none of them are posted to handle the Patan gang rape case.

It has been more than ten years since the Supreme Court, in its 'Vishakha Judgment' case, issued guidelines for the formation of Gender committees in various institutions to redress and prevent Sexual Harassment at Workplace. According to independent surveys most of the workplaces in Gujarat (this includes the educational institutions) have not put in place appropriate mechanisms for redressal of such complaints. According to the Supreme Court guidelines, it is mandatory that the complaint committee formed in such cases be headed by women and not less than half of its members be women. Participation of representatives of a voluntary organisation in the complaints committee is also necessary.

Can the BJP government escape the blame that it flouted Supreme Court guidelines in this case?

As of now although magisterial probe has been announced in the case, no terms of reference have been set. The Patan district collector would conduct the enquiry as per the rules set up by the state government. And from what has preceded one can gauge what the fate of any such enquiry would be.

As noted in a detailed write-up on the issue by Dwarakanath Rath, a famous TU leader from Ahmedabad, the need of the hour is a firm administrative action against the accused. The accused teachers can be blacklisted and de recognised from their degrees by the Education Department as is the practice for Doctors and Lawyers in certain circumstances. He adds "This administrative action can encourage the victim and the concerned people to face the trial further. Always it seems that in the judicial trial one is going to face a very difficult task. 1832 applications related to crime against women were withdrawn in past one year." (*DNA*, 11.2.2008).

Of course the most notable aspect of the whole case is the courage shown by the victim and the support she received from her batch mates and the sole lady teacher Bharatiben Patel. In fact, had it not been for this support and their determination to follow things through, this case might just have remained confined within the walls of the PTC college.

97 students gave a signed memorandum to the Principal on 31 st January. The Principal went to Gandhinagar and placed the complaint before the higher authorities. Although he was assured of action in the matter, the students were doubtful of the outcome. Following the advice of Prof Bharatiben Patel, they informed their guardians about the issue. The guardians rushed to the college.

It is reported that on the morning of February 4 the guilty teachers were assaulted with sticks and bricks. Their bikes were also damaged. If the police had not intervened, the angry mob could have lynched the perpetrators.

The exposure to the case has brought back memories of the recent past in Gujarat. Everyone is aware of the victory of Bilkees Bano in the gang rape case (2002). The tough fight which Bilkees with due support from her husband Yakoob, waged against her perpetrators is a saga well known.

The gang rape of Bijal Joshi by her own friends on 31 st December 2003 had also made national headlines.

Bilkees, Bijal, and now the hapless Dalit girl from Mehsana – all faced a similar plight.

The biggest silver lining in all these dark cases is that the victims did not remain silent, and preferred to speak out. While some may consider these to be lone voices, it is clear that by their actions these brave women have challenged the patriarchal notion that rape is a crime which brings shame to women.

February 2008

Saffron Terror: Nanded

Nanded, in Maharashtra, is a town with a significant population of different faiths – Hindu, Muslim, Sikh and Buddhist. Nanded could well have become a new metaphor for secularism as practised in the subcontinent. But this was not to be. Instead, Nanded has come to represent the emergent danger of a violent new brand of Hindu militancy, with due support from a section of the state machinery. A place that was once witness to the final days of Guru Gobind Singh, Sikhism's Tenth Guru, has today metamorphosed into an epicentre of violent Hindutva. Indeed, Nanded represents the build-up of the violent fundamentalist Hinduism of the past half-century. The town has been witness to a new spate of acts that can be inarguably dubbed 'terrorism'.

The inner workings of this new form of Hindutva were on show recently in two, evidently accidental, explosions in Nanded within a span of nine months, in April 2006 and February 2007. These blasts, which killed four people, took place at the houses of activists from the Rashtriya Swayamsevak Sangh (RSS), Bajrang Dal and Shiv Sena. The arrival of Nanded on India's 'terror' map was followed by media investigations into similar previous incidents, which also showed the involvement of Hindu youth in terrorist actions.

The new element here is the increasing similarity between Hindu militancy and 'terrorism' of other hues. While various enquiry commissions have looked into riots in post-Independence India and corroborated the proactive role played by the RSS in instigating riots, the irony of the situation is that the organisation is still able to maintain its 'missionary' image. Partly this is because the group has long maintained a strict division of labour within its ranks, delegating much of the 'dirty work' to fringe workers. The Nanded blasts proved to be an exception to this pattern, as the RSS links were obvious. This is why, in the immediate aftermath of the explosions, the Sangh Parivar leadership went to great lengths to suppress the news. Indeed, activist friends of this writer in Maharashtra were also unaware that any such incident had taken place.

One set of blasts took place in a house belonging to Laxman Rajkondwar, an old RSS activist, and killed two youths belonging to the Bajrang Dal and RSS, while injuring three others. The explosives that were being manufactured were to be used during the entry into Maharashtra of Bharatiya Janata Party (BJP) leader L K Advani's Bharat Suraksha Yatra, the idea being to warn of the grave security situation existing in the country. Later investigations revealed that the plan had been to instigate communal riots in Nanded, which would have been made to spread to adjoining areas. Such a situation, it was hoped, would boost the sagging morale of both the BJP and its ageing stalwart, Advani.

The aim was clearly to instigate a communal conflict. A police raid on one of the deceased's houses found maps of nearby mosques, as well as clothes and caps usually worn by Muslims in the area, which the Hindutva activists were going to wear to sneak into and attack the mosques and gurudwaras. The only thing still needed was explosives. The making of bombs in a house owned by an old RSS activist – one who supposedly also dealt in firecrackers, at that – seemed like the perfect plan.

Of course, the story neither begins nor ends in Nanded. Since 2003, at least five, and perhaps six, Hindutva-related explosions have taken place in central Maharashtra alone, in Parbhani, Purna, Jalna and Nanded. Malegaon also witnessed a bomb blast last year, killing 40 people, with strong indications of a Hindutva hand behind it. (The final picture will emerge after an ongoing investigation by the Central Bureau of Investigation finishes.) Beyond the geographical similarities, the details of the attacks were uncanny: each took place between 1:45 and 2:00 in the afternoon, just after Friday prayers, at the most prominent mosque in town. (The bomb that went off in Nanded in 2006 exploded on 6 April, a Thursday, but was apparently meant to be set off at an Aurangabad masjid the following day.)

At the same time, this cannot be dubbed a Maharashtra-centric phenomenon. Madhya Pradesh's former chief minister, Digvijay Singh, has publicly admitted to the involvement of various groups and individuals affiliated with the RSS in similar acts in his state. As for the rest of the country, no systematic study of saffron 'terror' has yet been undertaken. One reason for this could be the thin line that separates the different *anushangik* (affiliated) organisations of the RSS, thereby making it possible to move from the 'legal' to the 'illegal' without great effort. Indeed, there is every possibility that funds collected from the Hindu diaspora for philanthropic work might also have been channeled to further 'terrorist' activities.

Nonetheless, culturally integrated practices are being utilised to arm certain sections of the Hindu community. Back in 2001, Rajasthan's then Chief Minister, Ashok Gehlot, revealed that up to four million *trishuls* – six to eight inches long and sharp enough to kill – had been distributed by the Bajrang Dal to Hindu households across the country. Meanwhile, in 2002, a group in Orissa, under the district Shiv Sena unit, formed the first-ever Hindu suicide squad, aimed at countering Muslim 'extremism' in Jammu & Kashmir and elsewhere. More than 100 youths, including some women, are said to have joined the group.

Hindutva Collusion

Nanded's population is made up of around 500,000 Hindus, 200,000 Muslims and 100,000 Sikhs. The town has seen a significant amount of communal tension in the past, which spiked following the demolition of the Babri Masjid in December 1992. In more recent years, this tension seems to have also spilled over into surrounding towns such as Parbhani, where, in November 2003, motorcycle-borne attackers hurled bombs into the midst of a large congregation of Muslims assembled for Friday papers. Although the identities of the Parbhani bomb-throwers were never traced, forensic tests following the Nanded blasts revealed that the accused were part of the same group of Hindu militants that had executed the attack in Parbhani.

Following the April 2006 blasts in Nanded, an odd silence ensued – in the local and national media, as well as in the local and national governments. There was also a disturbing lack of sincerity on the part of the investigating agencies in pursuing the case, despite appearing to have gathered significant evidence of the involvement of district and state leaders of the RSS and Vishwa Hindu Parishad (VHP). As investigations by the People's Union for Civil Liberties (PUCL) and other rights organisations have made clear, the district administration even saw to it that news of the blasts did not receive wide coverage. After the initial excitement, district officials also allegedly pressured the local media not to follow the case any further.

The lackadaisical reaction also spread to those involved in local and national investigations. Local police made contradictory statements, and failed to make arrests in the initial stages. Despite the sensitive nature of the Nanded case, the Central Bureau of Investigation (CBI) expressed its "inability" to conduct the subsequent investigation. In response to a case filed by some social organisations against the tardiness of the investigations, the CBI filed a suo moto affidavit explaining that it was "overburdened" and had "limited hands to deal with such cases". The cumulative effect of the half-hearted – or wholly obstructionist – initiatives, at both the state and central level, showed the kid-glove treatment being meted out to India's new breed of Hindutva militants. Secular activists questioned whether the reaction would have been similar had the explosions taken place in a minority-dominated area, and the involvement of some 'fanatic' Islamic group been detected.

The cavalier manner in which the probes of the Nanded blasts were undertaken may have prepared the ground for a stepping-up of similar activities in the area. On 10 February 2007, at little after midnight, biscuit boxes being hauled by 28-year-old Pandurang Ameelkanthwar in another area in Nanded exploded, killing him instantly. His cousin, Dnaneshwar Manikwar, sustained massive burns and died six days later. Ameelkanthwar had been a former *shakha pramukh* (branch head) of the Shiv Sena, and was also associated with the Bajrang Dal. He hailed from an area in Nanded called Rangargalli, a known hotbed of rightwing Hindu outfits.

A mere 'fire-related accident' was how state officials subsequently reported the incident. But preliminary findings of a civil-society inquiry suggest that Ameelkanthwar and Manikwar died due to handled planted explosives. Neighbours near the explosion also told the team that there had been a third person present at the time, who had also been injured but has been unaccounted for in subsequent reports.

These eyewitnesses also said that a police officer, who went on to be part of the official investigation, supervised the seizing and spiriting away of critical evidence from the spot. In their report, the civil-society investigators state that the Maharashtra police, particularly the superintendent and inspector-general, appeared to be in "undue haste to close all possibilities of a possible liquid-substance-driven explosion, preferring to quote oral findings of forensic experts from Aurangabad who are reported to have told them that it was a petrol-ignited fire." Among other evidence, this conclusion is brought under serious suspicion by the fact the explosion threw the iron shutter of a nearby godown to a distance of 40 feet – an extremely long distance for a fire set off by burning gasoline.

The civil society team also refers to a "nexus between some police officials and the rightwing Hindu outfits". According to the probe's findings, Nanded Police Inspector Ramesh Bhurewar, who was leading the investigation of the 2006 Nanded blast, was also in charge of the investigation into the Parbhani blasts in November 2003. During the course of the long investigation he had not made a single arrest. A First Information Report was only registered after a legislator raised a question in the state assembly. But following the Nanded blasts in April 2006, the accused admitted to having placed the bombs at Parbhani as well. As such, the civil-society report concludes: "The Nanded and state police are hence guilty of underplaying crimes wherein members of the minority community are the victims, causing a loss of face for the state police."

In their conclusion, the fact-finding team demanded that the central government keep a close watch over investigation into this increasing incidence of Hindutva 'terror' activities. They also asked for independent investigations into them under a team of neutral officers; and impartial, public inquiries into the Nanded, Malegaon, Parbhani and Purna incidents, in order to ascertain whether state intelligence and police agencies

Directorate of Panchayats and could manage to get a stay order from it. When the locals learnt about it, they attacked the building at night and demolished the structure.

She knew many of the people involved in the midnight demolition of the mosque and the madrasa, many of them young kids, who often saluted her when she passed them by. But all that is passé. In that dark night last year when the structure she had built single handedly came under attack, she realised how it is possible to make monsters out of ordinary peace loving people

At that point of time nobody could have said that this 'spontaneous' attack was part of a larger game plan of the rightwing forces, especially the Hindutva brigade. With police badly equipped to deal with such situations and an administration led by the Congress Party, itself suffering from a 'paralysis of willpower', the ensuing communal violence in Curchorem-Savordem provided a field day for these people.

Recent events in the same area have once again demonstrated how the forces of hate and communal disharmony are out to create new social divides in the area. The alleged desecration of temples at Cuchorem-Cacora near Panaji, and the police suspecting it to be the job of miscreants out to create communal tension, has rekindled memories of the March 2006 communal riots in Savordem and Curchorem. It is known how rightwing organizations, especially the BJP, had then incited trouble in the area after demolishing a structure which housed a mosque and a madrasa. Fact finding reports on the violence had specifically named a BJP leader and a candidate for the Assembly elections for instigating the violence.

The way Siddh Dev Mutt and Rakhandev temples, which are five kilomentres away from each other were plundered – with robbery being not the motive – and the way locals immediately came out on the streets, has left the law and order people worried. A senior police officer told the media that "...the incident was well planned" (*Indian Express*, 6th April 2007). Considering that elections to the Assembly are scheduled later this summer, events of a similar nature are not unexpected. While the people in power need to be extra-vigilant to prevent recurrence of such incidents in future and the law and order machinery needs to be geared up to face any untoward incident, one notices the state majority community in the use of weapons; and spreading rumours to widen communal splits. About the shakhas that the RSS organises under the rubric of physical training, Justice Venugopal said that the aim appeared to be "to inculcate an attitude of militancy and training for any kind of civil strife".

It was only in 2004 that the Terrorism Research Centre (TRC), a US-based institute, declared the RSS a 'terrorist organisation', lumping it together with a host of jihadi and secessionist outfits, including the Lashkar-e-Toiba, the United Liberation Front of Asom (ULFA) and the Hizb ul-Mujahideen. This new listing came close on the heels of an internationally embarrassing incident for the Hindutva-wallahs, wherein Gujarat Chief Minister Narendra Modi was denied a visa to travel to the US. These two slaps in the face left the Sangh Parivar bosses seething although it took more than eight months for the Parivar to formally react to the TRC's assessment. But this was not the first time that Hindutva organisations had earned international opprobrium. In 2002, secular activists in the US brought out a thoroughly researched report called "Funding Hate". For the first time, this document exposed how funds collected in the US by the India Development and Relief Fund (the IDRF, an umbrella organisation floated by the Hindutva brigade) were directly sponsoring sectarian violence in India.

Cover-up

One potential reason for the inability of the powers-that-be to establish a connection between Hindu militants and acts of terror in India could be the near absence of non-Hindus in the central government's various intelligence wings. Whatever the reasons, this dearth is shocking. Barring the Intelligence Bureau, which has around 12,000 personnel and only a few Muslim officers, none of the other intelligence departments have even a single Muslim officer between them. From 1969 until today, neither the Research and Analysis Wing (RAW) nor the National Technical Research Organisation (NTRO) has hired even one Muslim officer. (Following the Malegaon blasts, S M Mushrif, a retired Indian Police Service officer, publicly disparaged the Intelligence Bureau for having long been the source of "unsubstantiated rumours" due to "deep-seated bias" against the Muslims.) The state of affairs has inevitably led to what can be dubbed the government's rather monochromatic presentation of the menace of terrorism in recent years, with sole responsibility for attacks almost immediately placed on various Islamist groups, regardless of evidence.

Despite a 'secular' coalition currently holding the reins of power at the Centre and in many of India's state administrations, there have been depressingly few sincere attempts to move beyond the post-9/11 mythology and the rhetoric of the 'war on terror', which demonises Islam. So pervasive is this perspective that it is difficult to decipher any qualitative difference between the 'secular' Congress and the 'communal' BJP in their responses to any act of 'terror'. Instead, even as we have been witness to the dilly-dallying of the Congress following the Nanded and Malegaon blasts, the same Congress-led government had no qualms in targeting Muslims as a community after the July 2006 bomb blasts in Bombay. (In the immediate aftermath of the Bombay attacks, an anti-terrorist squad singled out the Muslim community for suspicion, and immediately began 'combing' operations.) The Maharashtra state administration has also shown its anti-Muslim bias in times of tragedy. Even while attesting to their sadness over the Malegaon blast, state officials saw to it that victims, the majority of whom were Muslim, received just a fifth of the compensation received by the victims of the Bombay blasts of 1993 – the majority of whom were Hindu.

The fallout of this situation has been the administrative failure to address terrorism unleashed by Hindutva activists and formations. One possible reason for the government's ostrich-like position could be that, due to electoral considerations, nobody has wanted to displease the majority Hindus. While it is true that Hindutva groups are not currently in a majority at the Centre, the impact of Hindutva nonetheless transcends its strength in government. Note the inability of 'secular' groups to bring criminal cases against the likes of communal leaders like Shiv Sena supremo Bal Thackeray, and the champions of Hindutva: Praveen Togadia, Lal Krishna Advani or Narendra Modi. Indeed, the present-day Congress itself is a faint shadow of its Nehruvian avatar: after all, it 'discovered' the idea of 'soft Hindutva' two decades ago, in a bid to further its hold on the reins of power.

Hindutva Charities and IT Tribunal

The Sangh Parivar and its front organisations never had it so good. It is getting character certificates for good conduct from the top functionaries of the government and from commissions/ bodies which have been constituted by acts of parliament!

Close on the heels of the National Commission on Minorities's acceptance of dagger distribution by the Parivar as 'Trishul Deekshas' which are part of 'religious ceremonies', comes the news that the Income Tax Department has certified it as basically a 'charitable organisation' (and not a 'communal society' as one of its own orders had earlier characterized it).

Recently the Income Tax Appellate Tribunal, Delhi Bench provided relief of Rs 55.37 lakhs to the VHP for the assessment year 1993-94. A bench comprising its senior members dismissed the Department's own appeal and accepted the submission of the VHP that it was a "charitable organization". In this submission the VHP had appealed to the Tribunal that it could not be held responsible for the unlawful activities, if any, carried out by some of its members and any others during the demolition of the Babri mosque in Ayodhya in Dec.1992 (*The Hindu* 20th July 2003). Taking a very legalistic view the Bench also pointed out that the participation of the office bearers of the VHP and the others was a matter sub-judice as it was before the Court and nothing need be said at this stage.

Bal Thackeray's 'Big Heart'

Is it possible to draw any political inference from the new bonhomie between the 'secular' Congress and the 'communal' Shiv Sena which was witnessed during the recent elections for the post of President? A conservative reading of the support extended by Shiv Sena for Ms Pratibha Patil, breaking its two decade old alliance with the BJP, can mean that after some tantrums from both sides the old alliance would be on track.

But considering that politics is a game of immense possibilities, it is enlightening to note the options which have opened up before all the players in the state. Perhaps it has something to do with Thackeray's new found love for Sharad Pawar or the Congress' s smart move to decrease its dependence on the Maratha patriarch. Certainly some people would say that it would be political harakiri for the Sena Supremo to permanently break his alliance with the BJP, and all the talk of Marathi *Manush,* and the bonhomie with the Congress is just another pressure tactic to compel the BJP, which is trying to dominate the alliance in the aftermath of recent splits in the Sena, to be more compliant. Whatever might be the case, one thing is certain: it would not be easy for the two saffron parties to declare that they plan to reopen a new leaf in their relationship. Options in the state are more fluid than before.

The recent meeting between Bal Thackeray and Vilasrao Deshmukh and RR Patil at 'Matoshree', the house of the Thackerays, does give an indication that the new found bonhomie is here to stay for some time. "You have a big heart" Vilasrao Deshmukh is learnt to have told Balasa-

The memory of the poor, hapless Kashmiri fruit seller, who was paraded as the kingpin of the bomb blasts in Delhi last year, must still be fresh in people's minds. Presented as the 'prize catch' by senior police officers before the media, he was later declared innocent by the same police. One can bet that none in the police fraternity lost even one night's sleep over brutalizing an innocent man and putting him and his near and dear ones to tremendous mental as well as physical torture.

The most recent case showing the modus operandi of the police in a poor light is related to the four year old attack on the Raghunath temple in Jammu. Four innocent persons had to languish in jail for such a long period for no fault of theirs. The courts have finally absolved all the accused of any charges and have advised the police to properly use its minds in handling sensitive cases of such nature.

The list is definitely endless.

It is no surprise that the images of Md. Afroz or for that matter the hapless Kashmiri fruit seller or the innocents nabbed in the Raghunath Temple case readily come before the mind's eye whenever 'guardians of law and order' reach over roof tops to make some grandiose announcements. The recent claims made by the ATS (Anti Terrorism Squad) of Maharashtra state in case of the Malegaon bomb blast, (8th September '06) seems to be no exception.

Malegaon, a city of around 7 lakh people, 75 per cent of whom are Muslims, saw death descending on innocent citizens on the very day of *Shab-e-Barat.* A day when Muslims visit the graveyards of their loved ones, clean and decorate the graves and spend the night there, and read special prayers for the occasion. But who from Malegaon and adjoining areas would have imagined that the day to remember the departed ones would turn out to be the last day for some of them and would maim many among them for the rest of their lives? The two blasts, which occurred at two different places in the city killed around 31 people and wounded more than 250 of them.

Residents of the city shudder to think of how they should save themselves from such horrors. The only comfort in the otherwise gloomy scenario was that there had been no repeat of 2001- the year when the city witnessed large scale rioting. This time round, despite provocation, there was no communal flare-up. The 'Communally sensitive' town remained calm. Instead one could see new bonds of solidarity getting forged between the two communities who for various reasons have remained in an adversial relationship with each other.

Considering the nature of the crime, in which fanatics planted bombs in crowded areas in the city expecting to see people killed in large numbers and communal flare-ups to follow, it is clear that there was meticulous planning behind it. The question naturally arises, who could have benefited from a growing communal divide? It can be safely assumed that it should be a fanatic group that believes in and propagates a religion-based ideology.

Leave alone the radical media, even a conservative newspaper like the *Times of India*, instead of unleashing its usual tirade against the 'omnipresent Jihadi terrorists', carefully captioned its write up 'Bajrang Dal or Lashkar' (9th September, Updated at 12.311 jrs. IST) while discussing the bomb blasts in Malegaon. In the particular write-up it specifically mentioned the modus operandi adopted by the Bajrang Dal in blasts at Parbhani's Mohammadi Masjid and mosques at Purna and Jalna earlier this year. Of course it did not rule out the possibility of the involvement of Lashkar in this particular case.

The first official confirmation of sorts that the Sangh Parivar organizations could have a role in the blast came from the Prime Minister himself. Emphasising the need to investigate the functioning of the Hindu right wing formations he clearly stated that he could not confirm or rule out the possibility of the involvement of Bajrang Dal in the bloody act at Malegaon. He made this calibrated statement en route to Havana, while going for the NAM summit.

"Bajrang Dal continues to be under the scanner." "There is no reason to rule them out. We still haven't found anything to prove that Bajrang Dal is not involved," a senior officer said. "The Hindu fringe group is under investigation in Malegaon because of the role of its activists in various bomb blasts." ('PM doesn't rule out Bajrang role', Josy Joseph, Wednesday, September 13, 2006 00:50 IST, *DNA* India)

It was at this juncture that, when even the Prime Minister himself had clearly stated that he could not confirm or rule out the possibility of the involvement of Hindutva extremist formations in the bloody act at Malegaon, a concerted campaign was taken up for spreading unsub-

Goa

Communal Tinderbox Waiting to Explode

Curchorem, a city in South Goa district, part of Quepem Taluka, with a population of 25,000, and neighbouring Savordem, have today come to define what shape Goan polity could take in the future. In fact the simultaneous vandalisation of two temples in the area, at a five kilometers distance from each other, and the planned mobilisation of people belonging to a particular community, who came out on the streets immediately to protest the incident, has sent shivers down the spine of the police.

As of now, security has been beefed up after this deliberate attempt to create a communal divide. But taking into account a weak Congress Party regime in the state, which has yet to emerge from its internal bickering, the marginal status of the secular forces, and an aggressive BJP, which is gearing itself for the coming elections, it is not possible to guarantee that communal peace would be maintained.

The demolition of a mosque which housed a madrasa, is still a fresh memory for Samshad Begum Anarbi. She had got the structure built on her own, with of course community members coming forward to extend financial help. In fact, the idea had been to build a mosque and a madrasa together where people could pray and young children could study Arabic. The whole structure was built on a government land, which came under the Twenty Point Programme.

On February 24, last year the Savordem panchayat issued a notice in which they stated that the structure is illegal and would be demolished within seven days. Samshad Anabi immediately approached the and social formations were interned but most of the leading opposition figures were also put behind bars.The suspension of democratic rights, the clampdown on the press and the forcible sterilisation campaigns, supposedly to control family size, were few of the gory aspects of the whole episode.It is also a fact that the declaration of Emergency gave rise to an underground resistance which was joined in by various shades of opinion.

Looking back it is clear that if people would not have put up resistance at various levels, the cause of democracy could have suffered further damage. And it is in the fitness of things that a true believer in democracy would make special attempts to express one's gratitude to all such people who had to face detention during this period.

But is it proper to extend this honour to even those people who exhibited tremendous cowardice during the period of detention or expressed willingness to serve the 'emergency regime' if they were released from jail? While making any plan to honour the real fighters one needs to take into consideration this fact as well.

Any justice loving person would abhor the very idea of 'honouring' such cowards who 'preferred to crawl when they were asked to bend'. Individuals apart, as an organisation the Rashtriya Swayamsevak Sangh (RSS) and activists of its plethora of affiliated organisations proved to be 'pioneers' in tendering an apology. Time and again the not so glorious role of the Sangh Parivar and its affiliated organisations during the Emergency comes under scanner.

Today the Sangh Parivar may want us to believe that it led the democratic upsurge during "India's Second Freedom Struggle" (as they call the anti Emergency struggle in the Sangh Literature), it may wax eloquent about the way thousands of its activists were interned by the Indira regime but that will not hide the fact that its leaders were found to be wanting during that crucial period.

An irony of the situation is that while this period is frequently invoked in our political discourse, scholars of Indian history have not found it fit to examine it in a thorough manner. Discussions about it normally gravitate towards Indira Gandhi's authoritarian personality and the damage to democratic institutions at that time. It is natural that this personification of the darkest period in Indian democracy leads us

As a recap it may be useful to add that everyone is aware of how the police targeted the entire Muslim community in the immediate aftermath of the recent blasts in the local trains in B'bay. (July 2006) People are also familiar with the dilly-dallying tactics adopted by it in the Nanded bomb blasts case involving RSS/Bajrang Dal activists, which resulted in the deaths of two of its activists while manufacturing bombs (April 2006). The partisan role played by the same police in the 1992-93 post Babri Mosque demolition riots has been well documented by the Srikrishna Commission.

The state administration has also not failed in showing its anti-Muslim bias even in times of tragedy. While shedding crocodile tears over their plight, the official machinery saw to it that the victims in the Malegaon blast, majority of whom were Muslims, received less compensation (1/5 th) as compared to victims of the Mumbai blast, majority of whom were Hindus. (Iqbal A. Ansari, *The Milli Gazette* online, 14th Sept 2006).

The institutional discrimination against the Muslims has become very obvious. Whereas the police had maintained high vigilance in patrolling the town during the Ganapati festival which ended on 6th September, it failed to provide similar security on Shab-e-baraat, Friday, 8th September. On this tragic day there were no police patrolling or security measures in place.

Mubasshir Ahmed, a freelance journalist from Malegaon, explains one important aspect of the lapse in the security of ordinary citizens which has largely gone unnoticed. ('Malegaon's Date with Terror: 9/8', 6 November, 2006, www.countercurrents.org):

> The security at the Muslim cemetery was specifically discussed in the local Peace Committee meeting just before Shab-e-Barat. So grave was the concern that the committee members in fact discussed whether the policemen should be posted in plain clothes or in khaki inside the premises of the cemetery. A proposal to restrict the influx of beggars was also discussed – they should be restricted till the Sulaimani Masjid which is located 250 metres away from the blast site. There was no implementation on these proposals.'

A fact finding team consisting of Justice (retired) Hosbet Suresh, Prof. Shekhar Sonalkar, Jatin Desai, Suresh Khairnar and Nandini Chavan visited Malegaon on October 1-2, 2006 and met a cross section of the people, including top police officials. The said team was sent to Malegaon at the behest of the Centre for the Study of Secularism and Society (CSSS) and Vikas Adhyan Kendra (VAK) to find out the details. Its enquiry report 'Concerned Citizen's Inquiry Report of Malegaon Bomb-blasts' concludes with these observations:

> The police appear quite sluggish in its investigation as compared to its action role after Bombay bomb blast. After our discussion with police officer Shri Rajvardhan it appears that the police is convinced that Bomb blast was carried out by Muslims (with the involvement of SIMI). The police is not taking seriously the allegations by the Muslim leaders of Malegaon that some Hindu organizations could have been involved. Mr Rajvardhan said that more than 300 Hindus were interrogated but it is being done rather secretively, if it's at all being done. He fears that if he actively pursues Hindu organizations in this respect there will be backlash by Hindus and communal Harmony, which the police is trying hard to maintain, will be disturbed, and again Muslims will suffer. We did not have hard evidence to interrogate Militant Hindu organizations he said. But when it comes to Muslims, it seems police has no such fear and they are detaining some Muslims for interrogation, especially those who have a SIMI past. But those detained so far are poor Muslim power loom workers. Muslim leaders alleged that why police is not arresting main brain behind it, why is it arresting poor unknown power loom workers? The police on the other hand says that how can we reach the main brain without interrogating those through whom this work was done.

In one of his perceptive write ups 'Malegaon Blasts – Partisan Approach and Biased Police' leading secular activist Asghar Ali Engineer tells us:

> ...[I]n case of Malegaon it appeared, as the police is hardly interested in catching the culprits. Most of the human rights activists and Muslim leaders from Malegaon felt that the bombs could have been planted by some extremist Hindu organisations like the Bajrang Dal.
>
> The Malegaon Muslim leaders maintain that in Nanded in the month of April 2006, before Malegaon blasts, there was explosion in the house of a RSS activist Laxman Rajkondwar in which two persons were killed,

inconvenient it may be. The 'holier than thou' Sangh Parivar too cannot escape scrutiny.

If Mr Nitish Kumar is really sincere about honouring the fighters against Emergency, then first and foremost he needs to reorganise the very committee which he has constituted to chalk out the modalities to give pension to Emergency detenus and ask its present head to put in his papers. It is well known that Sushil Kumar Modi, who heads the committee, has been part of the Sangh Parivar ever since his school days. A person who owes allegiance to an organisation which had directed its activists to give an undertaking to escape the Emergency regime cannot be expected to do justice to the task given to him.

In fact it would be an insult to the broad majority of the one lakh forty five thousand detenus (only a few thousands belonged to the Sangh Parivar) who faced heavy odds inside the jails to further the cause of democracy.

One still remembers that during the NDA regime controversy had erupted after there were allegations on the floor of the Parliament that Prime Minister Vajpayee wrote letters of apology to Ms Indira Gandhi during the days of the Emergency. The Parliament was debating the no confidence motion against the Vajpayee regime then. According to PTI, while the spokesperson of the BJP had termed it "the biggest lie of the year", Lok Sabha Speaker Manohar Joshi deemed it necessary to examine the contents of a letter purportedly written by Vajpayee, which was sought to be read out by RJD leader Raghuvansh Prasad Singh in Lok Sabha during the debate on the no-confidence motion.

Coming back to the pension issue for Emergency detenus, Nitish Kumar has to decide whether he wants to really honour the true fighters or insult them by adding names of fake warriors in the list.

May 2007

To cut the long story short, it all started when the VHP did not file its returns for 1993-94 as the Centre had banned the VHP declaring it an unlawful organisation. After the return was filed the Assessment Officer (AO) denied to it the exemptions meant for charitable organisations. The AO held that as members of the VHP were involved in the Babri Mosque demolition, it is not an exclusivly charitable and religious organisation but "a communal society" .The VHP went in appeal to the Tribunal which reversed the AO's order.

This is not the first time that the Income Tax Department people have gone out of their way in allowing the VHP to maintain a veil of secrecy over its fund raising efforts. In 1990 the then Assistant Commissioner of Income Tax, Mr Vishwa Bandhu Gupta, had issued a summons to four top leaders of the VHP that they filed their income tax returns and also submit details of earlier years. But the aftermath of this Order was unprecedented. Within 24 hours of issuing this notice not only was the said Order withdrawn but Mr Gupta was immediately transferred and later suspended as well.

The question naturally arises as to what has been the basis for the Income Tax Department's somersault on the matter and its paeans on the 'charitable work' of the VHP when one of its own senior officers had bracketed it as a 'communal society'? Is it just a matter of interpretation of income tax rules and a realisation of an 'earlier folly', or an extraneous pressure from the powers that be, which compelled the IT sleuths to change their tune?

Every peace and justice loving person in India considers the demolition of the Babri mosque on 6th December 1992 and the consequent communal riots in the country which claimed thousands of lives as one of the darkest chapters in the history of independent India. It is also a fact that the movement to 'liberate the Babri Mosque', as it was called by them, was initiated and led by one of the front organisations of the Sangh Parivar, namely the Vishwa Hindu Parishad, along with numerous other front organisations of the Hindutva brigade. One still remembers how the VHP began with the Ram Janaki Yatras during the early eighties and raised tempers on the 'gross injustice meted out to the Hindus'. It is also well known that the Hindutva brigade put its might behind the movement to counter the Mandal initiative in the late

> against one another. The Ahle-Hadees obey the Qur'an strictly; their women wear the much-maligned naqab.
>
> Tearing it off, throwing it on the faces of male relatives who are the accused, trampling it under foot, and threatening that this would happen to all the women in the family, what could be the consequences of such action by the police on the victims and the community?
>
> A substantial number of SIMI and Ahle-Hadees followers are educated. At least five of those arrested, and many of those "picked up" (for questioning, often for days, with no record of their detention), are professionals.
>
> First-timers at police stations, they initially felt incredulous and indignant, and finally helpless and bitter at the way they, their parents and their religion have been humiliated, for no 'crime' other than being related to a SIMI member, or being active members of a mainstream Muslim sect.
>
> Have such tactics been used to investigate another blast in April, where two Bajrang Dal boys died while making bombs inside an RSS activist's house in Nanded? How widespread were the links of that conspiracy, given that fake beards and moustaches were found at the site? The ATS has been uncharacteristically discreet here.
>
> If having once been a member of SIMI makes you a terror suspect, what does that make members of the Bajrang Dal, which openly instigates violence against minority Indians? What is certainly suspect is the July 11 investigation.

A news item appeared in a prominent Bombay daily in the second week of October. Captioned 'Malegaon Muslim body gets threatening letter' it informed:

> A prominent Muslim organization of Malegaon, which was rocked by multiple blasts killing 31 persons more than a month ago, has received a threatening letter, police said here. The letter in Hindi, sent by 'Sangh Parivar and Bhavadiya Bramhan Sangh', has been addressed to Jamaitul Ulema and was posted from nearby Vajirkhede village, three km from Malegaon in Nasik district, they said. Police, however, did not reveal the content of the letter. A case was registered against unidentified persons on Tuesday night after the letter was handed over to police by the

> organisation which received it, police said. Police is investigating the origin of the letter. (*PTI* Wednesday, October 11, 2006, 22:07 IST).

It is incomprehensible why, till date, secrecy has been maintained about the contents of the letter.

We are also not yet clear on the whereabouts of the two people who purchased the two cycles in Malegaon which were used in the bomb blast. In the initial stages of the investigation police had released sketches of the two persons who were from some Hindi speaking area. Even a layperson would say that they would be able to shed some light on the conspiracy.

Even a cursory glance at the news on the case makes it clear that, contrary to the claims of the police, there are still many unanswered questions.

Of course as far as vital clues are concerned none is more important than the allegations that a dead body with a fake beard was unearthed at the blast site. It would be opportune to quote Radhika Koppikar of *Outlook* (13 September 2006, Web only) at this juncture:

> That the investigators should so blatantly rule out involvement of any Hindutva outfit is cause for concern. .... the fact remains that the cops are not chasing some clues. Take the case of "fake beard" as it has come to be known here. A tailor Aqeel Ahmed Ansari who works near the Bada Kabristan told cops and bystanders that he had picked up a body from near one of the bicycles and handed it over to volunteers in the ambulance, that this body did not have the lower part of the torso and its beard had come off in the ambulance. The suggestion being that it was a fake beard and therefore the body of a perpetrator. Coincidentally, the two hospitals that conducted post-mortems said that they had together handled 30 bodies and none was without the lower half.

People who are familiar with the communal situation in Maharashtra very well know the significance of a 'fake beard'. In Nanded the police had discovered fake beards, as well as dresses and caps normally worn by Muslims, in a raid on a deceased Bajrang Dal-RSS activist's house in the aftermath of the bomb blast in April.

Certainly there is a need to look afresh at the conspiracy in which blood of innocents was once again shed. Certainly there is a need that the whole investigation be handed over to some Special Task Force

Pension to the Victims of Emergency

Keep Out the *nikkerdharis* in Bihar!

Nitish Kumar government's proposal to give pension to the Emergency detenus has raised a hornet's nest. While leaders like Lalu Yadav have called it a 'publicity stunt', many other political activists have advised him to refrain from such emotional issues and to concentrate instead on governance and real issues of the people. Of course, despite criticism of various sorts Nitish Kumar does not seem to be relenting and in one of his recent *Janata Darbars* he advised his opponents to change their mindset to see the importance of this plan.

Of course it is not for the first time that such a proposal has been put forward by a political party. People would rightly remember that during Mulayam Singh Yadav's much debated Chief Ministership of UP which ended recently, a similar plan was initiated and more than five thousand such people were duly honoured with the title 'Loktantra Senani' (fighters for Democracy).

The question naturally arises as to what would be a correct position vis-a-vis this proposal of Nitish led government in Bihar. Should it be a simple 'Yes' or 'No' or can one qualify one's position with a few caveats.

There is not an iota of doubt that the internal Emergency clamped by the Indira Gandhi regime on 25th June 1975 to save itself from the impending crisis brought on by unfavourable decisions of the highest court and the growing mass discontent was one of the darkest chapters in the post-Independence trajectory of democracy in India. Not only thousands and thousands of people belonging to different political

Bal Thackeray's 'Big Heart'

Is it possible to draw any political inference from the new bonhomie between the 'secular' Congress and the 'communal' Shiv Sena which was witnessed during the recent elections for the post of President? A conservative reading of the support extended by Shiv Sena for Ms Pratibha Patil, breaking its two decade old alliance with the BJP, can mean that after some tantrums from both sides the old alliance would be on track.

But considering that politics is a game of immense possibilities, it is enlightening to note the options which have opened up before all the players in the state. Perhaps it has something to do with Thackeray's new found love for Sharad Pawar or the Congress' s smart move to decrease its dependence on the Maratha patriarch. Certainly some people would say that it would be political harakiri for the Sena Supremo to permanently break his alliance with the BJP, and all the talk of Marathi *Manush,* and the bonhomie with the Congress is just another pressure tactic to compel the BJP, which is trying to dominate the alliance in the aftermath of recent splits in the Sena, to be more compliant. Whatever might be the case, one thing is certain: it would not be easy for the two saffron parties to declare that they plan to reopen a new leaf in their relationship. Options in the state are more fluid than before.

The recent meeting between Bal Thackeray and Vilasrao Deshmukh and RR Patil at 'Matoshree', the house of the Thackerays, does give an indication that the new found bonhomie is here to stay for some time. "You have a big heart" Vilasrao Deshmukh is learnt to have told Balasaheb Thackeray. The Sena chief's prompt reply is worth noting: "I have a big heart indeed, but people fail to understand this."(*Indian Express*, July 19, 2007).

Even if no radical realignment of forces takes place, one thing is certain: the last glimmer of hope of the Bombay riot victims for justice has withered away forever.

It will not be so easy to obliterate the fact that officially close to 1,000 people were killed in those riots and 1,00,000 displaced during the organised mayhem which visited the city during December 2002 and January 2003 in the aftermath of the demolition of Babri Mosque. But it is equally a reality that despite the Srikrishna Commission recommendations no action has been taken against any guilty police officers, nor any politicos.

The continuous denial of justice to the riot victims was focused on in an editorial in *Outlook* (26 September 2006) last year. It had tried to counter pose the euphoria present among a section of the middle class over the verdict of the designated TADA court in the bomb blasts case and the conspiracy of silence about the Bombay riots. It said:

> ...Even as the CBI, Mumbai police and governments pat themselves on the back, and citizens demand death penalty for all the Memons – four of the family have been convicted, three acquitted – there has been no conviction in any of the thousands of cases registered during and after the post-Babri riots from December 7, 1992, to January 21, 1993.

In fact, Justice Srikrishna, who had been asked to enquire into the causes that led to the Bombay riots, had even specifically mentioned in his report:

> One common link (between the riots and the bomb blasts) appears to be that the former appear to have been a causative factor for the latter. The serial bomb blasts were a reaction to the totality of events at Ayodhya and Bombay in December 1992 and January 1993. The resentment against the government and police among a large body of Muslim youth was exploited by Pakistan-aided anti-national elements. They were brainwashed into taking revenge and a conspiracy was hatched and implemented at the instance of Dawood Ibrahim.

But the most damning indictment was reserved for the Sena Supremo himself who according to Justice Srikrishna

> ...[l]ike a veteran General, commanded his loyal Shiv Sainiks to retaliate by organised attacks against Muslims.

Of course, he had no sweet words for the people in power either and the callous manner in which they handled the situation:

> Even after it became apparent that the leaders of the Shiv Sena were active in stoking the fire of the communal riots, the police dragged their feet on the facile and exaggerated assumption that if such leaders were arrested the communal situation would further flare up, or to put it in the words of then Chief Minister, Sudhakarrao Naik, "Bombay would burn"; not that Bombay did not even burn otherwise.

Few months ago the *Combat Law* team had looked into how the Srikrishna Commission report was ultimately dumped. (*Combat Law* June-July 2007). It pointed out that no significant action had been taken against the 31 police officers – from the rank of the deputy commissioner of police to constables – indicted for their role by the Commission.

The petitioner Shakeel Ahmad (and Jyoti Punwani), who had filed a PIL in the Supreme Court to look into the actions taken against police officers, found to their dismay that "most of the officers against whom Justice Srikrishna passed severe strictures were in fact promoted. Many were granted anticipatory bail. All were released on bail with the public prosecutor often not arguing for their detention."

The case of RD Tyagi, a joint-commissioner of police at the time of the riots, who, according to Srikrishna Commission, was not at all justified in killing the nine unarmed and innocent bakery workers on January 9, 1993, is a case in point. He "merrily continued in service and retired as DIG. He has also been discharged from a case that was initiated against him. He was appointed to this high post by the Shiv Sena-BJP government at the instance of Bal Thackeray."

August 2007

Goa
Communal Tinderbox Waiting to Explode

> Curchorem, a city in South Goa district, part of Quepem Taluka, with a population of 25,000, and neighbouring Savordem, have today come to define what shape Goan polity could take in the future. In fact the simultaneous vandalisation of two temples in the area, at a five kilometers distance from each other, and the planned mobilisation of people belonging to a particular community, who came out on the streets immediately to protest the incident, has sent shivers down the spine of the police.
>
> As of now, security has been beefed up after this deliberate attempt to create a communal divide. But taking into account a weak Congress Party regime in the state, which has yet to emerge from its internal bickering, the marginal status of the secular forces, and an aggressive BJP, which is gearing itself for the coming elections, it is not possible to guarantee that communal peace would be maintained.

The demolition of a mosque which housed a madrasa, is still a fresh memory for Samshad Begum Anarbi. She had got the structure built on her own, with of course community members coming forward to extend financial help. In fact, the idea had been to build a mosque and a madrasa together where people could pray and young children could study Arabic. The whole structure was built on a government land, which came under the Twenty Point Programme.

On February 24, last year the Savordem panchayat issued a notice in which they stated that the structure is illegal and would be demolished within seven days. Samshad Anabi immediately approached the

Directorate of Panchayats and could manage to get a stay order from it. When the locals learnt about it, they attacked the building at night and demolished the structure.

She knew many of the people involved in the midnight demolition of the mosque and the madrasa, many of them young kids, who often saluted her when she passed them by. But all that is passé. In that dark night last year when the structure she had built single handedly came under attack, she realised how it is possible to make monsters out of ordinary peace loving people

At that point of time nobody could have said that this 'spontaneous' attack was part of a larger game plan of the rightwing forces, especially the Hindutva brigade. With police badly equipped to deal with such situations and an administration led by the Congress Party, itself suffering from a 'paralysis of willpower', the ensuing communal violence in Curchorem-Savordem provided a field day for these people.

Recent events in the same area have once again demonstrated how the forces of hate and communal disharmony are out to create new social divides in the area. The alleged desecration of temples at Cuchorem-Cacora near Panaji, and the police suspecting it to be the job of miscreants out to create communal tension, has rekindled memories of the March 2006 communal riots in Savordem and Curchorem. It is known how rightwing organizations, especially the BJP, had then incited trouble in the area after demolishing a structure which housed a mosque and a madrasa. Fact finding reports on the violence had specifically named a BJP leader and a candidate for the Assembly elections for instigating the violence.

The way Siddh Dev Mutt and Rakhandev temples, which are five kilomentres away from each other were plundered – with robbery being not the motive – and the way locals immediately came out on the streets, has left the law and order people worried. A senior police officer told the media that "...the incident was well planned" (*Indian Express*, 6th April 2007). Considering that elections to the Assembly are scheduled later this summer, events of a similar nature are not unexpected. While the people in power need to be extra-vigilant to prevent recurrence of such incidents in future and the law and order machinery needs to be geared up to face any untoward incident, one notices the state government itself suffering from 'paralysis of will power'. With internal bickering within the ruling Congress Party on the upswing and a senior leader of the Party, Churchil Alemao, showing signs of rebellion, one does not see any signs of improvement in the political situation.

The most disturbing part of the whole scenario is that even after a year since the rioting at Curchorem-Sanvordem, forget about the filing of charge sheets in a time bound manner, the investigations into the disturbances have not moved ahead at all. Day by day the faint hopes that the guilty would be brought to justice are fading away. It needs to be mentioned that while the rest of India has been witness to the flaring up of communal tensions now and then, nobody expected that even in Goa the small minority of Muslims would come under such an organised, vicious attack at the hands of the Sangh Parivar and its affiliated organisations. The rioting at Curchorem-Sanvordem shook Goan society to its foundations.

The March disturbances had also witnessed the introduction of a new element in the communal divide: Hindutva organisations had been able to win over a section of the Christians to target the Muslims. In its perceptive write-up 'Communal Violence in Goa: Neros in Khaki' *Gomantak Times* (Weekender, Panjim, March 5, 2006) had specifically mentioned: 'A controversial senior office bearer of BJP was heard saying "It is high time that Hindus and Christians join hands to kill the Muslims". Despite all this, no BJP leader was arrested or warned for igniting the crowd and creating communal tension!'

One could also find the rumour spreading machinery of the Hindutva brigade in full swing then. They had tried to rationalise the violence unleashed by the Hindutva cadres by claiming that armed people belonging to the minority community from Bhatkal and Hubli – parts of Karnataka – had reached the place. Not just the fact finding team, but even senior police officers, had debunked this propaganda. Anyone could ask the question that if people from the minority community were really armed, then, instead of retaliating or attacking the mob, why had they rushed back home, while many others took shelter in the mosque at Curchorem? Secondly, not a single vehicle, of those which were damaged or destroyed, had a Karnataka registration. All vehicles belonged to people from the minority community who were residents of Goa.

Commenting on the communal disturbances in March, Sujay Gupta in his Open Edit (*Gomantak Times*, 7/03/06) clearly stated:

> This is a strange war where there aren't two groups fighting each other. There is one assaulter – the Hindu fundamentalists co-opted into the BJP – and one assaulted – the community of Muslims. ... Given the manner in which things unfolded, the attack on the Muslims was premeditated. The disputed structure was demolished by a Hindu mob that had no jurisdiction over a disputed structure. They are not the "authority", the police is. This was the first real attack. How can the majority community which has initiated the task of affecting violence, have the gumption or gall to blame the minorities or the police for the violence?

The ascendance of the communal forces in Goan polity is now visible to everyone. Over the past few years, Goa has witnessed several incidents which have a communal tinge to them. In a public meeting held on 5th March 2007, noted social activist Ramesh Gauns underlined the challenges before the secular movement in a perceptive manner. Mentioning the reported clash at the Sirvodem mosque, and wondering whether it was truly a coincidence that this occurred exactly one year after the Sanvordem-Curchorem violence, he posed a question before the audience as to whether there were more sinister designs at play. He mentioned the case of Tariq Battloo, the alleged terrorist, who had been arrested just a few days after the previous communal violence, as another suspicious 'coincidence', which indicates that an impression is being sought to be created by fascist forces that minorities are responsible for communal disorder.

It does not need a lot of wisdom to comprehend how things may unfold in the near future. An ascendant Hindutva brigade, a lack lustre Congress, and the absence of a strong people's movement to unite people cutting across communities and castes, it should not come as a surprise if the situation deteriorates further.

One just wishes that the secular forces across the country get ready to go that extra mile to avert such a situation.

April 2007

Hindutva Charities and IT Tribunal

> The Sangh Parivar and its front organisations never had it so good. It is getting character certificates for good conduct from the top functionaries of the government and from commissions/ bodies which have been constituted by acts of parliament!
>
> Close on the heels of the National Commission on Minorities's acceptance of dagger distribution by the Parivar as 'Trishul Deekshas' which are part of 'religious ceremonies', comes the news that the Income Tax Department has certified it as basically a 'charitable organisation' (and not a 'communal society' as one of its own orders had earlier characterized it).

Recently the Income Tax Appellate Tribunal, Delhi Bench provided relief of Rs 55.37 lakhs to the VHP for the assessment year 1993-94. A bench comprising its senior members dismissed the Department's own appeal and accepted the submission of the VHP that it was a "charitable organization". In this submission the VHP had appealed to the Tribunal that it could not be held responsible for the unlawful activities, if any, carried out by some of its members and any others during the demolition of the Babri mosque in Ayodhya in Dec.1992 (*The Hindu* 20th July 2003). Taking a very legalistic view the Bench also pointed out that the participation of the office bearers of the VHP and the others was a matter sub-judice as it was before the Court and nothing need be said at this stage.

To cut the long story short, it all started when the VHP did not file its returns for 1993-94 as the Centre had banned the VHP declaring it an unlawful organisation. After the return was filed the Assessment Officer (AO) denied to it the exemptions meant for charitable organisations. The AO held that as members of the VHP were involved in the Babri Mosque demolition, it is not an exclusivly charitable and religious organisation but "a communal society" .The VHP went in appeal to the Tribunal which reversed the AO's order.

This is not the first time that the Income Tax Department people have gone out of their way in allowing the VHP to maintain a veil of secrecy over its fund raising efforts. In 1990 the then Assistant Commissioner of Income Tax, Mr Vishwa Bandhu Gupta, had issued a summons to four top leaders of the VHP that they filed their income tax returns and also submit details of earlier years. But the aftermath of this Order was unprecedented. Within 24 hours of issuing this notice not only was the said Order withdrawn but Mr Gupta was immediately transferred and later suspended as well.

The question naturally arises as to what has been the basis for the Income Tax Department's somersault on the matter and its paeans on the 'charitable work' of the VHP when one of its own senior officers had bracketed it as a 'communal society'? Is it just a matter of interpretation of income tax rules and a realisation of an 'earlier folly', or an extraneous pressure from the powers that be, which compelled the IT sleuths to change their tune?

Every peace and justice loving person in India considers the demolition of the Babri mosque on 6th December 1992 and the consequent communal riots in the country which claimed thousands of lives as one of the darkest chapters in the history of independent India. It is also a fact that the movement to 'liberate the Babri Mosque', as it was called by them, was initiated and led by one of the front organisations of the Sangh Parivar, namely the Vishwa Hindu Parishad, along with numerous other front organisations of the Hindutva brigade. One still remembers how the VHP began with the Ram Janaki Yatras during the early eighties and raised tempers on the 'gross injustice meted out to the Hindus'. It is also well known that the Hindutva brigade put its might behind the movement to counter the Mandal initiative in the late eighties. At present the whole matter of the demolition of the mosque is sub-judice and many of the leading lights of the VHP, Bajrang Dal, and the BJP are facing charges for hatching a criminal conspiracy to demolish the mosque. The Liberhans Commission is investigating different aspects of the whole episode and is shortly expected to give its opinion.

The nineties and the first years of the new millennium have also been witness to what Sumit Sarkar has called the "mass communalism" of the VHP. The growing attacks on Christians in different parts of the country leading to the burning to death of Graham Staines and his sons by extremists belonging to the Hindutva fraternity, the hate speeches delivered by the Singhals, Togadias and the Dharmendras, and the Dagger Distribution Ceremonies organised in different parts of the country under the leadership of the VHP and its sister organization, Bajrang Dal, and the pogrom organised in Gujarat in the aftermath of the tragic Godhra incident etc. – all these incidents/ campaigns have been directly and indirectly linked to the VHP and its parivar. So much so that the Chief of the Gujarat VHP, the octogenarian litterateur Mr Keshav Shastri, even gave details of how the VHP had prepared a list of the Muslim shops and establishments and accepted that 'his boys were involved' in the pogrom (Interview to Ms Sheela Bhatt on rediff.com).

It is a fact that the VHP has been a key player in the expansion of the base of the Hindutva brigade since its formation in 1964 and in providing a support base for BJP victories in the electoral arena. It has been very innovative in expanding its influence among the middle and the lower classes. The experience of late eighties and nineties shows us how it helped spread the appeal of Hindutva far and wide. It not only organised the sadhus and the sants, the most parasitic as well as the most revered strata of Indian society, under Dharam Sansads and the Ram Janambhoomi Nyas and several other outfits, but also claimed for itself the status of 'sole representative' of the Hindus.

Last November some secular and democratic Indians working/ settled abroad brought out a report 'Stop Funding of Hate' (www.stopfundinghate.com) which focused on the overseas funding network of the Sangh Parivar. This report, rich in facts, prompted many leading companies to stop contributing to the IDRF, a front organisation of the Hindutva brigade which collects funds from individuals and companies for 'development work' inside India. The campaign organised around this report succeeded in bringing out two simple facts about the overseas operation of the Sangh Parivar: 1) That the Sangh Parivar uses the guise of 'development' and 'relief' work to raise funds for its operations from overseas (despite trying to portray itself as an entirely domestic operation) and 2) That these funds are deployed to advance its intolerant Hindutva ideology and to propagate hatred against religious minorities. The success of the campaign 'Stop Funding Hate' compelled the Sangh Parivar to come out with a rebuttal of the charges levelled against it, although such rebuttal did not cut much ice and was largely ignored in the mainstream media.

It could be naïve to assume that the Tribunal people are ignorant of the acts of commission and omission engaged in by the VHP and other members of the Sangh Parivar, or that the senior members of the Tribunal genuinely believe that the activities of the VHP are benign and worthy of a 'charitable organisation' .

Perhaps they have taken a cue from '*Lauh Purush*' Advani's habit of giving clean chits to the members of the Hindutva brigade from time to time. More likely the clean chit represents the clout and influence that the Hindutva brigade wields in the institutions of the State.

August 2003

Pension to the Victims of Emergency

Keep Out the *nikkerdharis* in Bihar!

Nitish Kumar government's proposal to give pension to the Emergency detenus has raised a hornet's nest. While leaders like Lalu Yadav have called it a 'publicity stunt', many other political activists have advised him to refrain from such emotional issues and to concentrate instead on governance and real issues of the people. Of course, despite criticism of various sorts Nitish Kumar does not seem to be relenting and in one of his recent *Janata Darbars* he advised his opponents to change their mindset to see the importance of this plan.

Of course it is not for the first time that such a proposal has been put forward by a political party. People would rightly remember that during Mulayam Singh Yadav's much debated Chief Ministership of UP which ended recently, a similar plan was initiated and more than five thousand such people were duly honoured with the title 'Loktantra Senani' (fighters for Democracy).

The question naturally arises as to what would be a correct position vis-a-vis this proposal of Nitish led government in Bihar. Should it be a simple 'Yes' or 'No' or can one qualify one's position with a few caveats.

There is not an iota of doubt that the internal Emergency clamped by the Indira Gandhi regime on 25th June 1975 to save itself from the impending crisis brought on by unfavourable decisions of the highest court and the growing mass discontent was one of the darkest chapters in the post-Independence trajectory of democracy in India. Not only thousands and thousands of people belonging to different political and social formations were interned but most of the leading opposition figures were also put behind bars.The suspension of democratic rights, the clampdown on the press and the forcible sterilisation campaigns, supposedly to control family size, were few of the gory aspects of the whole episode.It is also a fact that the declaration of Emergency gave rise to an underground resistance which was joined in by various shades of opinion.

Looking back it is clear that if people would not have put up resistance at various levels, the cause of democracy could have suffered further damage. And it is in the fitness of things that a true believer in democracy would make special attempts to express one's gratitude to all such people who had to face detention during this period.

But is it proper to extend this honour to even those people who exhibited tremendous cowardice during the period of detention or expressed willingness to serve the 'emergency regime' if they were released from jail? While making any plan to honour the real fighters one needs to take into consideration this fact as well.

Any justice loving person would abhor the very idea of 'honouring' such cowards who 'preferred to crawl when they were asked to bend'. Individuals apart, as an organisation the Rashtriya Swayamsevak Sangh (RSS) and activists of its plethora of affiliated organisations proved to be 'pioneers' in tendering an apology. Time and again the not so glorious role of the Sangh Parivar and its affiliated organisations during the Emergency comes under scanner.

Today the Sangh Parivar may want us to believe that it led the democratic upsurge during "India's Second Freedom Struggle" (as they call the anti Emergency struggle in the Sangh Literature), it may wax eloquent about the way thousands of its activists were interned by the Indira regime but that will not hide the fact that its leaders were found to be wanting during that crucial period.

An irony of the situation is that while this period is frequently invoked in our political discourse, scholars of Indian history have not found it fit to examine it in a thorough manner. Discussions about it normally gravitate towards Indira Gandhi's authoritarian personality and the damage to democratic institutions at that time. It is natural that this personification of the darkest period in Indian democracy leads us to a blind alley and the socio-economic factors which led us to this juncture and the real role of the various organisations remain uninvestigated. The result is that forces like Sangh Parivar have been able to construct a mythology of their alleged bravery during that tumultous period.

It can appear incomprehensible to a layperson that while the activists of the Sangh Parivar were in jail its leaders in the words of Tapan Basu et al "revealed a curious duality". Tapan Basu, Pradip Datta, Sumit Sarkar and others in their early nineties monograph *Khaki Shorts and Saffron Flags* (Orient Longman, 1993) explain how the RSS reacted. RSS attitudes under the Emergency revealed a curious duality, reminiscent of the 1948-49 days.

> While the RSS was banned and Sangh Supremo Deoras was put behind bars, he like Golwalkar in 1948-49, "..quickly opened channels of communication with the Emergency regime, writing fairly ingratiating letters to Indira Gandhi in August and November 1975 that promised cooperation for lifting a ban (on RSS). He tried to persuade Vinoba Bhave to mediate between the RSS and the government, and sought also the good offices of Sanjay Gandhi. (p.52)

Bapurao Moghe, in an article in the Sangh mouthpiece *Panchajanya* (July 24, 1977) had also acknowledged that such letters had been written by the Sangh supremo. Lawyer and political commentator A.G.Noorani in his book *The RSS and the BJP* (Leftword, 2000) tells us that these letters "...[w]ere placed on the table of the Maharashtra Assembly on October 18,1977." He adds: "He wrote to the prime minister, first, on August 22 congratulating her on her speech on Independence day ('balanced and befitting to the occasion') and begged her to lift the ban on the RSS. He next congratulated her 'as five judges of the Supreme Court have upheld the validity of your election'" (November 11,1975).'(p. 31) It may be added that though Ms Indira Gandhi had won the case it was not on the basis of merit but by a constitutional amendment with retrospective effect. In these letters he repeated his plea for the release of RSS detenus and lifting the ban on the organisation. He also underlined that the RSS 'has no connection with the movements' in Bihar and Gujarat. Deoras ends these letters by offering the services of 'lakhs of RSS volunteers...for the national upliftment (Government as well as non government).'

A point which may skip attention is that in these letters the Sangh supremo Deoras was concerned with the RSS alone. And to save his organisation from the onslaught of an autocratic regime he was ready to declare that if the ban is lifted his men would be at the service of the regime. He does not ask for the release of all detenues, nor does he ask her to lift the Emergency. It seems the only problem which the RSS supremo was concerned with was that his organisation was banned; otherwise whatever the Indira regime was doing was good.

When Ms Indira Gandhi refused to budge from her stand, the Sangh supremo shot another letter (July 16, 1976) in which he congratulated her for 'your efforts to improve relations with Pakistan and China' and also declared that she has been given some wrong information about his organisation.

It needs investigation to see whether some sort of agreement was reached between Deoras and Ms Indira Gandhi through the mediatory efforts of the likes of Vinoba Bhave, but one thing that is clear is that the RSS workers were instructed to give an undertaking to secure their release from jail. The undertaking went like this:

> Shri ... detenu class ... prison agrees on affidavit that in case of my release I shall not do anything, which is detrimental to intenal security and public peace... I shall not do anything prejudicial to the present emergency. (*Sanghachi Dhongbaji*, Baba Adhav, Pune,1977).

According to leading socialist activist Baba Adhav, Deoras had himself acknowledged at a press conference in Delhi that he had written two letters to Indira Gandhi. Madhu Limaye, a towering figure of the socialist movement spent 19 months in three jails which were in RSS areas and knew of the RSS detenues' letters of apology.

It is understandable that the Hindutva Brigade which has built its *weltanshauung* around the twin concepts of 'bravery and cowardice' would like to forget this past episode, when instead of demonstrating uncompromising defiance it had preferred to cringe. They very well know that if this is not done the whole edifice of the Hindutva politics can come crumbling down. But history, as they say, does not forgive and forget. It keeps excavating and bringing out the past, howsoever inconvenient it may be. The 'holier than thou' Sangh Parivar too cannot escape scrutiny.

If Mr Nitish Kumar is really sincere about honouring the fighters against Emergency, then first and foremost he needs to reorganise the very committee which he has constituted to chalk out the modalities to give pension to Emergency detenus and ask its present head to put in his papers. It is well known that Sushil Kumar Modi, who heads the committee, has been part of the Sangh Parivar ever since his school days. A person who owes allegiance to an organisation which had directed its activists to give an undertaking to escape the Emergency regime cannot be expected to do justice to the task given to him.

In fact it would be an insult to the broad majority of the one lakh forty five thousand detenus (only a few thousands belonged to the Sangh Parivar) who faced heavy odds inside the jails to further the cause of democracy.

One still remembers that during the NDA regime controversy had erupted after there were allegations on the floor of the Parliament that Prime Minister Vajpayee wrote letters of apology to Ms Indira Gandhi during the days of the Emergency. The Parliament was debating the no confidence motion against the Vajpayee regime then. According to PTI, while the spokesperson of the BJP had termed it "the biggest lie of the year", Lok Sabha Speaker Manohar Joshi deemed it necessary to examine the contents of a letter purportedly written by Vajpayee, which was sought to be read out by RJD leader Raghuvansh Prasad Singh in Lok Sabha during the debate on the no-confidence motion.

Coming back to the pension issue for Emergency detenus, Nitish Kumar has to decide whether he wants to really honour the true fighters or insult them by adding names of fake warriors in the list.

May 2007

Political Hindutva

> A report prepared by one of the national secretaries of the BJP Mr Prabhat Jha analysing the election results for UP, provide enough proof of the pathetic situation in which the party finds itself today. This report would be presented before the national executive meeting of the BJP to be held in last week of June and much fireworks are expected there. (*Dainik Bhaskar*, 12 June 2007)

Media personnel bearing sympathy with the Hindutva cause – who are in decisive positions at various levels – have an extraorinary ability for deflecting the attention of the public from the pathetic situation in which the Sangh Parivar finds itself today – morally as well as organisationally.

Whether the Parivar is sermonising on character building going tatters *a la* the Babubhai Kataras or the Bangaru Laxmans or the Dileep Judeos, or the Party with a difference tag becoming a joke or the 'disciplined' infighting at various levels becoming a public spectacle, these pen/bytepushers make feverish attempts to maintain the aura intact.

Of course there are moments when it becomes next to impossible for them to push the real issues under the carpet or present a rosy picture of the disorientation in which the parent formation and its affiliated organisations find themselves today. Interestingly, recent results to by-elections in different states or assembly elections to UP and Goa have helped bring the issue to the fore. And it is becoming obvious that the countdown has finally begun for political Hindutva – the ideology of hatred and exclusion formulated by the Savarkars and the Golwalkars.

A report prepared by one of the national secretaries of the BJP, Mr Prabhat Jha, analysing the election results for UP, (*Dainik Bhaskar*, 12 June 2007) provides enough proof of the pathetic situation in which the party itself finds today. This report would be presented before the national executive meeting of the BJP to be held in the last week of June, and much fireworks are expected there.

The 56-page report, copies of which have been sent to the senior leaders of the party, tries to undermine the gravity of the situation. It tells us that the party lost elections to 17 seats merely by a margin of 2,000 plus votes. But figures presented in the report themselves reveal that it received five percent or less votes in 40 seats. There have been six seats where it got less than 2 per cent votes.Out of 89 reserved constituencies, its candidates won merely seven seats. But the parties most pathetic performance has been visible in the 81 seats where it stood fourth or fifth. Of course on four seats it went down to sixth or seventh number. If one compares its present performance to the last elections held in 2002 where its candidates were either in number one or number two positions in 297 segments, when it had gained only 88 seats, its downward march becomes more blatant.

Interestingly an important point which did not receive the attention it deserved as far as the UP debacle was concerned pertained to the role of Modi, the man in waiting for the top post in the BJP. It is worth noting that Narendra Modi addressed 17 meetings in UP, and most of the seats here were lost by the BJP. Also these elections were held under the direct supervision of the RSS as the parent organisation had felt that the BJP at times takes a sloppy attitude towards Hindutva – the *raison d'etre* of the Parivar. Many of the RSS pracharaks were sent to the state to streamline the party at the district level. The intervention of the RSS in the whole campaign was evident also from the way in which an incalcitrant looking Yogi Adityanath was tamed or how the fiery Sanyasin Uma Bharati was asked to withdraw her candidates from the fray supposedly to 'save Hindu Unity'. It is clear that all these feverish efforts could not fetch any extra seats and the BJP had to remain satisfied with half the number of seats it had earlier held (93 to 50).

Of course the lack of transparency with which the Sangh Parivar functions also became clear once the results were out. Despite the fact that Sangh had supervised the elections and helped BJP to finetune its strategy for polarising the voters on communal lines, the RSS mouthpiece did not lose a minute in blaming the state BJP for its poor performance, for not being 'Hindutva' enough during the campaigning. It also added a 'pearl of wisdom' to its analysis by claiming that Mayawati's victory is essentially a victory of their ideology. One was reminded of the famous Aesop's fable which tells us of a dog walking under the bullock-cart and thinking that it is he who is carrying the load.

Of course analysis of the UP debacle would not be the only worrying thing which the BJP leadership would be addressing in its national executive meeting. UP fiasco – where all the top bosses of the BJP and their near and dear ones had to bite the dust, and the home district of the party president Rajnath Singh could not return even a single BJP candidate to the assembly – has been followed by defeat in Goa where despite strong anti-incumbency trends in the air, the BJP faced a second consecutive defeat.

Anyone could see that the Hindutva brigade had pulled all stops there to come to power. As is clear from the results, the BJP will have to continue to sit in the opposition with reduced number of seats (14) than its tally in the last elections (17). The desperation with which the BJP had tried to wrest power from the ruling coalition can be gauged from the fact that it had stayed out of 7 constituencies to allow rebels of the Congress to have a free run against the Congress. Apart from forging alliance with all sorts of dubious people, it had also tried to act smart by trying to sell the 'clean image' of the former Chief Minister Manohar Parrikar. But the most disturbing acts which the Hindutva organizations had engaged in pertained to their attempts to polarize Goan society on communal lines.

In the first week of April news of vandalisation of two temples in an area only five kilometers away from each other, and the planned mobilization of people people belonging to a particular community which came out on the streets immediately to protest the incident, sent shivers down the spine of the police. The alleged desecration of temples at Cuchorem-Cacora near Panaji, and the police suspecting some miscreants out to create communal tension, had even rekindled memories of the March 2006 communal riots in Savordem and Curchorem. It is now history how right wing organisations, especially the BJP, had incited trouble in the area then after demolishing a structure which housed a mosque and a madarsa. Fact finding reports on the violence had even specifically named a BJP leader and a candidate for the Assembly elections for instigating the violence. (Ref : 'Goa :Communal Tinderbox Waiting to Explode' (www.countercurrents.org 10 April 2007)

But not content with this planned vandalisation of temples the mischievous elements belonging to the Hindutva brigade had tried to foment communal tension in Marmagoa after the alleged harassment of a hindu girl by two youth belonging to the minority community. (May 2007). They had tried to terrorise the minority community in and around Marmagoa continuously for two consecutive days, and the local administration had turned a blind eye towards their activities.

Apart from the drubbing it received in UP as well as Goa, the BJP has allso come a cropper in two hotly contested by-elections which were held in states where it is part of the ruling arrangement, namely Karnataka and MP. As has been rightly noted by analysts the defeat of the BJP candidate in Ullal (Dakshin Kannada) by a comfortable margin of 8,000 votes, in the recently held byelections to the Karnataka assembly has definitely added to the worries of the coalition which is ruling the state since more than a year. Coming after the defeat faced by the coalition in the Chamundeshwari byelection, this second consecutive defeat has definitely impacted the morale of the coalition partners, namely BJP and Janata Dal (S).

While the Janata Dal (S) has tried to save face by saying that a sympathy factor helped Mr Khader of the Congress win the elections, the state leadership of the BJP has tried to wriggle out of the situation by saying that the Congress tried to create fear about the BJP in the minds of Muslims (who incidentally comprise 52 percent of the population).

It is a different matter that the BJP wanted to conveniently forget the manner in which it tried to foment communal trouble with due help from the local administration and a partisan state ministry. All its attempts to terrorise the minorities by giving free rein to the affiliated organizations of the Sangh Parivar had received condemnation from different quarters of the media. Commenting on the byelection result an editorial in the *Deccan Herald* (June 6, 2007) under the heading 'Vote for Secularism' rightly underlined:

> Ullal by-elections were held in the backdrop of communal riots which rocked the district for nearly 2 months recently. The local BJP leaders, including a minister, allegedly had a hand in fuelling the trouble. The people of both communities especially minorities suffered a great deal but police remained passive spectators.Mr Kumarswamy did not even show the courtesy of visiting the riot hit areas and home minister MP Prakash showed reluctance to act against police officials who had failed to function properly.

While experiments in hardline Hindutva seem to have come to a naught in this keenly fought election in the southern state, the way the BJP lost its bastion Shivpuri (MP) in the recent by-election to the assembly must have sent more alarm bells ringing. This despite the fact that the Hindutva brigade is moving in this state in a planned manner to consolidate its base and further marginalise the minorities. It need be told that there have been more than 117 communal flareups since BJP came to power in the state. Many districts witnessed riot or riot like situation for the first time in post-independence history. And the modus operandi is similar : free play to the lumpens of the Hindutva brigade and a saffronised administration turning a blind eye towards all such acts.

UP, Goa, Karnataka and MP – states where the political environment and ethos cannot be said to be similar – all are underlining a single feature in so far as the future prospects of the BJP are concerned. With progress of time India of the 21 st century would have less and less space for formation(s) based on exclusiveness and hatred. All such formations would be faced with the same predicament : shrinking base and a disoriented cadre which would engage in sporadic violence from time to time.

Vijay Singhvi (*The Tribune*, 13 June 2007) in his op-ed piece 'BJP's Shrinking Base' observes :

> Young minds in India have changed their aspirations, ambitions, their idioms and their way of thinking about life and the future. The modern mind is not taken in by the BJP's now already stale mantra of minorityism, pseudo-secularism and the national security state. The global

> economic movement has demolished the state boundaries into an unrecognisable shambles, that has in turn affected the definitions and understanding of patriotic fervours on which the Sangh Parivar has built its entire edifice of the Hindu Rashtra.

Anyone familiar with the RSS brand of politics and with the changes in the national-international situation can understand that the 'Jurassic Park' mentality of Hindu Rashtra envisaged by the Hedgewars-Savarkars-Golwalkars does not have any future in today's India. It is bound to fail. Of course that does not mean that their journey into oblivion would not be accompanied by untold sufferings of the masses and Gujarat-like 'successful experiments' littered with blood.

With onset of time it would become further difficult for the BJP to gain new social support to its side even as the traditional support base gets further dwindled. It took four decades for the Congress to suffer shrinkage of its vote base. The BJP which claims for itself a different *Chaal*, *Chehera* and *Chintan* (could be roughly translated as 'movement, face and thinking') achieved it in less than a decade.

June 2007

Experiments in Indoctrination
Rajasthan and Karnataka

Would you believe that in many of the school textbooks in the state of Rajasthan the great woman-saint Meerabai or Sant Kabir find no mention, but there are detailed descriptions of Rani Padmini and others who committed *Johar* (self immolation in groups) when their kingdoms came under attack from enemies?

Is it proper that the tribesmen who supposedly helped Ram in his battle be referred to as "vanya jatis" with "heen mansik avastha" (low mentality), or that the Rajasthani saint Ramdev be referred to as a person who "even after being born in upper caste made contacts with the untouchables"?

Would it be correct to mention Indian culture varyingly as "Arya sanskriti", "Bharatiya sanskriti" and "Hindu sanskriti" and the Mughal rule as foreign rule?

These are some glimpses from the textbooks prescribed for Hindi language and social studies by the Rajasthan Board for Secondary Education for Class X students. They are full of such erroneous and sectarian ideas, which are humiliating for Dalits, Adivasis, minorities, women and every other secular person. It was in the fitness of things that activists associated with the civil liberties movement demanded immediate withdrawal of these books. In a press conference they made it clear that there exists a "preponderance of sentiments, as preached and practiced by the Rashtriya Swayamsevak Sangh (RSS) in these books. (*The Hindu*, 13th December 2006).

The latest controversy over textbook writing in this Hindutva ruled state reminds us of many such controversies which emerged around the NCERT textbooks when followers of this ideology happened to be masters of India's destiny not quite sometime back. One such textbook published during those times even avoided mention of Gandhi's killer Nathuram Godse on some flimsy grounds. The authors of these books had no qualms in glorifying Hitler. The portrayal of the Nazi leader, Adolf Hitler, as "hero" and a "Nationalist", and as a man who stood for socialism and nationalism in these NCERT books was questioned in Parliament as well. The silence of the text books on the cold blooded massacre of Jews under his regime had also become a cause of concern then. ('Furore in LS over TOI report on NCERT', *PTI,* Monday, April 28, 2003 03:24:05 p.m.).

Some time then an interesting announcement had also appeared in a section of the media which incidentally did not receive the attention it deserved. It said that the BJP-led government had decided to open special 'Brahmin schools' supposedly for the popularisation of the Vedas. Through the good offices of a central minister, the UNESCO was persuaded to dole out Rs 5 crore for this scheme. Under this scheme, 15 Brahmin schools were to be opened in different parts of the country. To encourage meritorious Brahmin students, students were to be given scholarships also. The rationalisation behind the founding of these schools was simple: they were purportedly an effort to counter the religious education being imparted through the madrasas!

Whether it is textbooks or the building of institutions conducive to the popularisation of their agenda, one can see that the Sangh and its affiliated organisations are very clear about passing off political agendas as knowledge.

As Prof Romila Thapar had explained in one of her speeches "...[S] ome of the organizations that constitute the Sangh Parivar have, since their inception, used education to forge this identity. It is in some ways ironic that these organizations took education as a means of ideological imprinting far more seriously than those who were committed to the values of an independent, modern society. This method of creating an identity through doctoring history is familiar to us from the treatment of history in Pakistan and Bangladesh as well, although the identities thus forged are different."

The recent developments in Karnataka where the BJP is sharing power with a 'secular' Janata Dal demonstrate the seriousness with which the Parivar takes up the issue of recasting textbooks in their own image. Although the move to obliterate the great Tipu Sultan's name from Kannada textbooks, at the behest of the state education minister who used to be a Sangh Pracharak, backfired, it nevertheless exposed their intentions. For the Education Minister of the state the alleged neglect of Kannada language by Tipu Sultan was reason enough that the great ruler be obliterated from Karnataka's history.

For him it hardly mattered that Tipu was a ruler who was much ahead of his times, who was an apostle of Hindu-Muslim unity, fond of new inventions, and innovator of the world's first war rocket. He was so inspired by the French Revolution that despite being a ruler he referred to himself as Citizen and even planted a tree of 'Liberty' in his palace.

In fact for these Hindutva influenced people it was a minor matter that Tipu sensed the designs of the British and tried to forge a broader unity among the domestic rulers, and even tried connecting with the French and the Turks and the Afghans to undermine the hegemonic designs of the British. It did not matter to them that he died in the battlefield fighting the British.

Of course the Hindutva brigade's attempt at changing history to suit its political agenda does not end here. The latest is that they have decided to help the villagers of Rajasthan write histories of their own villages. One can imagine the kind of history that would get manufactured.

January 2007

'Character Builders of the Nation' and Mr Shekhawat

There will be a Gujarat-like situation in Rajasthan if the State Government did not stop its 'appeasement of Muslims' and 'anti-Hindu' policies. Bhairon Singh Shekhawat, former Rajasthan Chief Minister, Gangapur on 23 April (*The Hindu*, 30 April 2002).

Bhairon Singh Shekhawat, present incumbent to the Vice-President's seat, would not have imagined in his wildest dreams that his suspension from the Sikar Estate Police way back in 1947, allegedly for accepting bribe/misconduct, would be communicated to the public at large sixty years later. Perhaps he, and the mighty 'Parivar' to which he belongs, should be blamed for this unnecessary exposure of his personal life. A perusal of the old records, as evident from write ups and news items in the Rajasthan press, tell us that although he was later reinstated he sought premature retirement within a year of this reinstatement.

Today this facet of his personal life is public knowledge – thanks to the mud slinging campaigns that have characterised the elections to the top post of the Republic, namely the President of India. As the campaign heats up one can expect more damning exposures relating to his personal and political life in the scoop hungry media.

There is no doubt that the Advanis and Shouries, who were patting themselves on the back for taking the initiative to excavate the past of Ms Pratibha Patil, were not expecting that they would be paid in the same coin. Now it seems that the 'moderate' Shekhawat will have to do a lot of explaining to save himself from further embarrassment.

Perhaps one of the most damaging details of his political career could be the case of one Shalini Sharma who happened to be very close to Mr Shekhawat when he was the Rajasthan Chief Minister. This lady, who was made a vice-president of the State Social Welfare Board by the then Shekhawat regime, was later caught in a high profile prostitution racket and it was discovered that she supplied women to powerful BJP ministers. The racket was having a smooth run with the Vice President of the State Social Welfare Board herself overseeing the 'operations', but the whole thing came to light because of a young teacher. This young teacher, who worked in one of Shalini's schools and who herself was a victim of this game, gathered courage to report the matter to the police. Today Shalini and her husband are languishing in jail, but the rest of the world has a right to know who else from the BJP hierarchy were involved in this business.

Another serious charge which awaits Mr Shekhawat is the manner in which he 'shielded' his son in law Narpat Singh Rajvi, who was allegedly involved in the fudging of land records when Shekhawat was Chief Minister in 1994-95. Enquiries later revealed that Mr Rajvi had claimed compensation for about 600 acres of land that did not belong to him. According to a story in *Outlook* ('Monsoon Mudslinging', 9th July 2007)

> ...[N]arpat Singh Rajvi – currently industries minister in the Vasundhara Raje government – had claimed compensation in lieu of land, acquired for the Indira Gandhi Canal in Bikaner district, which actually did not belong to him. The matter figured for several days in the state assembly, when Congress MLA Surendra Vyas raised the matter. A revenue inquiry established that Rajvi's father, who had been a tehsildar in his time, had manipulated land records to show Rajvi as owner of a substantial chunk of agricultural land in Bikaner's Momewala village. The controversy centred around the fact that the land records predated Rajvi's birth.

Of course, the slew of charges against Mr Shekhawat does not end here. Way back in 1992 a MLA from Rajasthan had written to the Home Minister, SB Chavan, that Shekhawat's nephew was involved in tampering of land records. The *Outlook* report also tells us that prior to the assembly elections in the year 2003, Mr Shekhawat made many pre-assembly election flights to different places in Rajasthan 'on state aircraft'.

The people of the country would certainly like to know why the perpetrators of the massacre of Dalits at Kumher, which occurred in early 90s, still remain unpunished despite his being in the Chief Minister's chair for a large part of the 90s.

The citizens of the nation would also like to know why the idol of Manu, the author of *Manusmriti* – the religious text of the Hindus which condemns the dalits and women to a secondary status – still occupies an honourable place in the precincts of Jaipur High Court, and why he did not remove this idol installed there, in the first place, at the behest of Acharya Dharmendra, a fire spitting leader of the Vishwa Hindu Parishad.

While the 'monsoon mudslinging' could continue for a while, the more troubling aspect of l'affaire Shekhawat is the manner in which this one time RSS pracharak helped transform Rajasthan into another 'Hindutva Lab in the making.

It is clear that the three time Chief Minister of Rajasthan (22 June 1977- 16 Feb 1980, 4 March 1990-15 Dec 1992 and 4th Dec 1993-29 Nov 1998) and leader of the Opposition for a considerable portion of the remaining period, Bhairon Singh Shekhawat, can be said to be a central figure in the growth of the BJP-RSS in the state. If today the state appears to be a bastion of Hindutva politics where minorities are under increasing attack, where society can openly practice caste apartheid, and the bureaucracy finds itself highly communalized, his role in this transformation needs to be underlined.

One still remembers the November 1997 issue of *Communalism Combat* which detailed the growing violence against women in Rajasthan under the BJP rule, and how the then BJP Chief Minister, Bhairon Singh Shekhawat, and his Deputy Chief Minister, Hari Shankar Bhabhra, had justified incidents of rape, acid throwing and molestation. (*'Why talk of humans, even gods cannot be sure of a woman's character'* – Bhabhra).

Bhairon Singh Shekhawat's continued support for obscurantist values is evident from many actions. *People's Democracy* (22 September 2002) had underlined:

> Along with the ruling political elite, the administrative machinery too is permeated with a deep-rooted bias .When Roop Kanwar was burnt

> alive in 1987, top political leaders like Bhairon Singh Shekhawat and Rajmata Scindia and some state government officials had visited the site to offer their prayers.

The year 2001 was witness to the serious attempts on the part of the BJP-RSS to replicate the Gujarat model of Hindu Rashtra in the then Congress ruled Rajasthan. And the most ominous had been the 'Trishul Diksha Samarohs' organised by the Bajrang Dal through which such trishuls, which were in fact Rampuri knives, were distributed in lakhs. In a public meeting the then Chief Minister, Ashok Gehlot, had charged that more than 40 lakh trishuls had been distributed in different parts of the state. It was for everyone to see that government agencies, administration and the police had come under severe strain due to the well coordinated actions and campaigns by the RSS, Shiv Sena, VHP and the Bajrang Dal, which was aided and abetted by the parliamentary wing of the Hindu extremists, the Bharatiya Janata Party (BJP).

Teesta Setalvad had quoted a leading journalist in her write-up on communalisation of Rajasthan (Nov 2001, *Communalism Combat*):

> Nine years, in totality, of BJP rule has been used by the party leadership to successfully infiltrate echelons of the administration and the police," Sriprakash Sharma, senior journalist and editor of *Rashtradoot* told *CC*. "Even now, sections of the top cadre of the IAS and the IPS visit the former BJP chief minister Bhairon Singh Shekhawat and the latter publicly flaunts this as he did a few weeks ago at Diwali.

An editorial in the *Economic Times* two years ago (May 8, 2005), 'Rajasthan: A Gujarat in the Making', had rightly underlined the dangers present to the secular fabric under the BJP regime.

> The fog of communal venom hangs heavy over Rajasthan, no thanks to the brazen anti-minorityism being propagated by the Sangh Parivar over the past couple of months. The Vasundhara Raje government, which has the responsibility to protect the democratic-secular ethos of the Constitution, has reportedly been using every subterfuge to renege on its role.
>
> That is alarming. Rajasthan shouldn't become a second Gujarat. The Sangh Parivar has had considerable influence, traditionally, in the state's southern parts...

The other day Maulana Madni, who was with the Uttarakhand Congress till recently, and who had to quit his post because of pressures from the fanatic elements of the Hindutva brigade, went to meet Mr Shekhawat and declared his support for him for being the only fit candidate for the post. The Maulana even declared him to be a 'messiah of secularism'. Of course, this was not the first time that opportunist elements belonging to religious minorities had visited his house and declared their support for this candidature. Media was recently agog with news of a few such visits organised by people like Shahnawaz Hussain, one 'minority face' of the Party.

But all these certificates from a few opportunist leaders of the minorities cannot hide Mr Shekhawat's highly dubious role in making Rajasthan the second most important laboratory for 'Hindu Rashtra'.

Nobody can forget that Mr Shekhawat had no qualms in warning the state government to desist from 'appeasement of Muslims' if it wanted to avoid a 'Gujarat type situation' precisely when the genocide in Gujarat was on.

It is a disturbing sign that secular-democratic individuals/formations in the country have not bothered to put forward these aspects of Mr Shekhawat's personae before the general populace. It appears that they were taken aback by the attack unleashed by the Saffron Camp on the candidature of Ms Pratibha Patil. Perhaps they were not yet ready to emerge from the mesmerising influence which Mr Shekhawat allegedly had as 'impartial' speaker of the Rajya Sabha.

Leave alone Mr Shekhawat's candidature for the post of President, they did not even bother to question Mr Shekhawat's presiding over the birth anniversary celebrations of Golwalkar, the second Supremo of RSS, while he was still Vice President of India. They simply did not comprehend that by this act Mr Shekhawat had legitimised a known hate monger like Golwalkar and demeaned the office of the Vice-President of India.

It is well known that MS Golwalkar was a strong supporter of the ethnic cleansing perpetrated by the Nazis, which he openly glorified in his book *We or Our Nationhood Defined* (1939). He yearned for a *Manusmriti* like regime which condemned dalits and women to a secondary status, and opposed the making of our Constitution under the leadership of the legendary Dr Ambedkar, and had in fact contended that *Manusmriti* be made the new constitution of independent India. Golwalkar's highly dubious role at the time of partition during which he took the opportunity to instigate violence against the minorities is also a well known fact.

Of this Golwalkar, in his message to the special issue of *Organiser*, Shekhawat wrote:

> Shri Guruji was a staunch nationalist and an impassioned patriot who had contributed immensely in varied spheres of nation building activities with great distinction. A scholar of eminence, he symbolised the Sanatani ideals. Guruji dedicated his entire life for the enduring welfare of the country and the people. (March 26, 2006 *Organiser*)

In fact one finds a lot of commonality in the images of Vajpayee and Shekhawat, both 'moderate' faces of the BJP. While Vajpayee could adorn the high seat of Prime Minister with due support from some 'secular' formations, Shekhawat also aims to replicate this formula of success.

It is a different matter that when the occasion came a 'moderate' Vajpayee had no qualms in castigating the religious minorities. The world saw on television how (in Goa) Vajpayee, the then Prime Minister of India, had taunted and chided Muslims by declaring "wherever they are, they live separately", and nonchalantly asserted: "If a conspiracy had not been hatched to burn alive the innocent passengers of the Sabarmati Express [at Godhra], the subsequent tragedy in Gujarat could have been averted. But this did not happen." He then rhetorically asked: "But who lit the fire?"

Not to be left behind, Shekhawat had declared "There will be a Gujarat-like situation in Rajasthan if the State Government did not stop its 'appeasement of Muslims' and 'anti-Hindu' policies."

July 2007

The Yogi and the Fanatic

Would Eastern UP be the next Gujarat?

Gorakhpur, a district in UP bordering Nepal, which had made national headlines during the anti-colonial struggle for its various militant interventions, is today making news for altogether different reasons. Gone are the days when the imaginary of the nascent Indian nation had caught the imagination of the masses, gone are the days when the region was reverberating with anti-feudal and anti-British slogans. Today all that is passé. Today's slogans have a majoritarian slant and there is talk of building a Hindu Rashtra. There are attempts to make the area a citadel of a particular brand of Hindutva where the writ of only the local MP, who also happens to be the Mahant of a famous *mutt* belonging to the Nath tradition, runs.

This unfolding scenario became evident to the outside world when the 'firebrand' local MP, Yogi Adityanath, organised a three-day international conclave named 'Virat Hindu Mahasammelan' (22-24th December 2006) in Gorakhpur, which was attended by thousands of people. The participants included many leaders of the Sangh Parivar, but there was a significant presence of the local sadhus as well, and more than five hundred delegates from Nepal. Ranging from the Shankaracharya of Govardhan Peeth, Puri Swami Nishchalanand Saraswati, to the International President of VHP, Mr Ashok Singhal, or an ex-General of the Nepalese army, Keshar Singh and the ex Union minister Chinmayanand, the conclave had brought together a motley combination of religious sadhus and politicos and activists of the Hindutva brigade to discuss the 'challenges present before Hinduism.'

The congregation not only called for 'declaration of Nepal as Hindu State and restoration of monarchy there, but also resolved for the construction of a grand temple in Ayodhya, "liberation" of the Kashi and Mathura shrines, and a ban on cow slaughter. It also criticised the Indian Government's stand on Nepal and said no political party was taking Maoists' activities there seriously. The Mahasammelan also deliberated on the 'pathetic' condition of the Hindus in Nepal and the alleged activities there of the ISI of Pakistan, which was 'spreading its network to create disturbance in India'.

The Mahasammelan was organised parallel with the three day national executive meeting of the Bhartiya Janata Party, billed as the 'party's grandest show of unity and strength in recent times'. And while the BJP in its executive meeting seemed to initially waver on the agenda of construction of Ram temple at Ayodhya, the Mahasammelan, which was in a sense a show of defiance by its own party MP, focused precisely on the agendas which the BJP seemed to be going soft on for reasons of immediate political exigencies. It is a different matter that at the end of its meeting the Party itself discovered the 'merits' in raising these contentious issues.

The question naturally arises as to whether the 'party with a difference', which swears by discipline, has decided to tail its own 'defiant' MP, or is the Mahasammelan a part of a wider game plan of the Hindutva brigade which has tasted the 'success' of this model in this part of UP – a model which has the potential of making it another 'Hindutva laboratory'? Anyone can see that at a time of declining fortunes of the Hindutva forces the activities of Yogi have brightened its prospects miraculously in this part of eastern UP.

It was a marker of things to come that when Gujarat was burning in the aftermath of Godhra, with the ire directed at minorities, Gorakhpur was not far behind. Many parallel instances of terrorization of minorities, of razing their houses to the ground, all under the leadership of this 'firebrand' leader, have come to light. Loud proclamations of turning Gorakhpur into a Godhra-Gujarat were also heard. In a post-Godhra bandh here a leader of Hindu Mahasabha, considered the right hand man of Yogi, had openly declared: "If only Yogiji permits us we will repay a hundred per each." The local MLA, Dr Radha Mohan Das Agarwal, in his speech, reported widely in newspapers, had defiantly declared: "Gorakhpur is a Hindu Rashtra. Yogijee is both its President and Prime Minister."

II

The weekly *Outlook* (Hindi) in its issue of 24th February 2003 ('Yogi: Danger to BJP', Yogesh Mishra) unambiguously stated "… [t]he similarity of Gorakhpur and Gujarat does not stop at the identity of their initials. On a closer look yet more similarities have begun to appear...If there is Modi there, here is an upcoming hero 'Yogi'."

In fact the said write-up focused on a similar international gathering of the Vishwa Hindu Mahasangh, which was also held at Gorakhpur (February 2003). It would be opportune to add that this is the same Mahasangh which had organised the latest Mahasammelan referred to above. A point worth noting about the February 2003 Mahasammelan was that all the top leaders of the RSS had made themselves available for it. Despite his ill-health the ex-supremo of the RSS, Rajjubhaiyya, as well as International working president of the VHP, Mr Ashok Singhal, had made it a point to participate in the programme. Ashok Singhal was so overwhelmed by the success of the meeting that he declared Yogi as the new symbol of the Hindu youth.

The power which Yogi wields over the top brass of the BJP was evident once again a few months later when the then Deputy Prime Minister, LK Advani, accepted Yogi's invitation to Gorakhpur in a move that upset the state BJP leaders. These leaders were miffed when Adityanath opposed the BJP candidate in the 2002 assembly elections. By this swift move the Mahant forced other BJP leaders to attend his durbar and to pay obeisance.

What is so significant about Yogi that has rendered him the connoisseur of all eyes in the Hindutva brigade?

Adityanath Yogi who became the youngest legislator in the 12th Lok Sabha at 26 (1998), and got re elected twice after that, has helped change the situation in and around Gorakhpur in a qualitative manner. It is the unique nature of his intervention which has made it possible to carve out alliances cutting across castes by raising economic demands, and on the other hand, enabled him to emerge as a kind of 'Hindutva Robinhood' who would 'relieve the Hindus of their sufferings'. He has been able to successfully widen the base for Hindutva forces. In this process he has been greatly helped by his long association with the Gorakhnath *peetham*. His anointment to the Mahant's post in the Nath peeth, which has been very popular in this region for centuries and enjoys respect among mainly the subaltern classes, has definitely helped him in this 'mission'.

While the 'credit' for transforming this area into a different sort of bastion for Hindutva politics may be given to Yogi, yet it should be noted that the process of the gradual Hindutvaisation of this *peetham* began soon after independence and gained momentum in the '80s with the beginning of the Ramjanambhoomi movement. It is a marker of the changed ambience that Gorakhpur city witnessed a communal flare up last year (2003), and today the city and the adjoining areas have come under what is known in the lexicon of statecraft as 'communally sensitive zones'.

Gorakhpur is one of the few areas in UP where the BJP escaped the ignominy of being defeated. The 34 year old Mahant Yogi Adityanath won the seat for the third time in succession during the 2004 elections to the Parliament. It is also noteworthy that for four consecutive terms before that his guru and the earlier Mahant to the Gorakhnath Peetham, Mahant Avaidyanath, had occupied this seat. Could we then surmise that the BJP organization here is strong, and is what saved the BJP from the ignominy of defeat? The answer is "NO". A BJP public meeting at Gorakhpur on the eve of the elections, with such known personalities as Kalyan Singh (the prodigal son who had returned) and Rajnath Singh present had proved a disastrous flop. The reason was that Yogi Adityanath had kept himself away from the meeting on the specious excuse of going to Delhi for medical treatment for one of his relatives, and without his co operation the BJP simply could not mobilize people effectively.

Also, during the election campaign Yogi had characterized the BJP as a party speaking in two voices, and had appealed to people to oppose it. Yet, the BJP not only did not expel this MP, but did not even issue a show-cause notice to him. On the contrary, the Yogi continued to enjoy the blessings of the seniors in the RSS and the BJP without any hassles for himself.

III

> Nautanwa, Maharajganj: Ram Bharat, a dalit living at Kadjahiya Tola, Chandanpur has alleged that just because he would not quarrel with his Muslim neighbour, workers of the *Hindu Yuva Vahini* instigated somebody to pick up a quarrel and had manhandled him. (*Hindustan*, 5 October 2003)

A key feature of the Hindutva experiment engaged in by Yogi is to always keep Muslims in focus and win over the dalits and backwards to his side. In order to organise the dalits against the Muslims he has made it a policy to interfere in all small or big quarrels between them, and has endeavoured to give these a communal tinge. There are no two opinions that Yogi has succeeded in instigating anti-Muslim feelings in Gorakhpur, Deoria, and from Siddharthnagar to Baharaich. The geographical layout of Gorakhpur has also helped him. At one end it abuts Ayodhya and on the other Nepal. In line with the RSS campaign, the bogey of ISI training camps on the Indo-Nepal border is also raised by Yogi. Local newspapers regularly carry propaganda of increase of ISI activities through the *madarsas* on the Indo-Nepal border, or of 'clandestine relations between the ISI-Maoists'. Needless to say these are all figments of their feverish imagination.

The Uttar Pradesh PUCL, and another organization, INSAAF, in their enquiry report, '*UP Ab Gujarat ki Rah Par*' (UP Now on the Path of Gujarat), had given a long list of deeds that set Yogi out to become a mini-Modi. On the basis of this report, a result of on the spot investigations into the incidents at Mohan Mundera, Nathua and Turkmanpur, a representation was also made to the NHRC (5th July 2002) inter alia describing how Yogi gives lurid communal colours to what is after all just a criminal misdeed; how the police and the administration adopted a purely defensive posture during the attacks which engulfed the Muslim population in terror and insecurity. The unfortunate fatal attacks on Muslims at Mohan Mundera (District Kushinagar) on 19th June

2002, at Nathua (PS-Pipraich) on 23rd June, or again on 25th June 2002 at Pande Hata (Gorakhpur), are links in the same chain. It may be mentioned that on account of provocation of alleged rape of a backward class girl by an anti-social element who happened to be a Muslim, a mob of thousands of people attacked the Muslim locality, setting their houses on fire. Hindutva terrorists had a hand in it. There are reports that after heaping destruction on the Muslims at Mohan Mundera the mob descended on Nahua (PS Piparaich, District Gorakhpur) where, following the harassment of a dalit Hindu girl, there were some incidents of stabbing. The mob set fire to three Muslim houses there. This was preceded by a public meeting, and when people gathered in sufficient strength the locality was challenged, and the attack mounted. However, in this case a complaint has been filed against the members of the Hindu Mahasabha and the rowdy Deepak Agarwal, a right hand man of Yogi.

IV

October 2005 witnessed a communal flare up in Mau, eastern UP, on the eve of the Durga Puja celebrations. It saw the killing of nine innocent people and hundreds wounded. While the negative role played by the local MLA, Mukhtar Ansari, during the riots, and the lethargy exhibited by the law and order machinery in controlling the situation, were reported and became public knowledge outside the immediate areas, the aggressive role played by Yogi Adityanath was not much talked about.

In their report on the Mau situation after the riots, Saajhi Duniya, a group of intellectual and social activists, rightly noted (www.sabrang.com) this fact:

> Whatever is happening in Purvanchal is occasionally discussed but there is no serious initiative to analyse the same. For last one decade the aggressive activities of heir of Goraksha Peeth and BJP MP Yogi Adityanath to organize Hindus was clearly reflected in the riot in Mau. During the last decade the Yogi has made this entire area, specially the area known as Gorakhpur during the times of Britishers, his laboratory. ...
>
> The maximum influence of the Yogi is in the districts of Gorakhpur Division (Gorakhpur, Deoria, Kushinagar, Mahrajganj) and Basti Divi-

> sion (Basti, Sant Kabir Nagar, Siddharthanagar). Now he is spreading his wings in Azamgarh Division. Mau is a part of this division.
>
> Yogi functions through different organizations which he calls cultural organizations. Included among these organizations are Hindu Yuva Vahini, Hindu Jagran Manch, Sri Ram Shakti Prakoshtha, Gorakhnath, Purvanchal Vikas Manch, Vishwa Hindu Mahasabha and Hindu Mahasabha. The main functionary of all these organizations is only Yogi Adityanath...the most vital organization for Yogi is Hindu Yuva Vahini. This organization comprises mostly unemployed youth, small level criminals and the youth struggling for identity. For them any small event involving Muslims becomes very important. As soon as they receive the information of such an event, the workers of Hindu Yuva Vahini reach there as the messengers of Yogi and later Yogi himself reaches. Most of their acts are destructive like arson, destruction of property and beating. A lively example is Mohan Mundera episode in Kushinagar. Here a Muslim boy raped a Hindu girl and the girl died during treatment. After 3 days when Yogi came to know about this, he reached there with his Vahini workers. The property of all the 72 Muslim families was looted. Their houses were put to fire. Masjid was damaged. Police remained a neutral witness. There are several such examples.

The report also provided details on how Yogi tried to aggravate an already inflammable situation. It tells us:

> When Yogi's effort to go to Mau with his workers, after the riots started, did not succeed, then he held a meeting at Dohri Ghat itself where he was stopped. This polarized Hindus and it affected the elections of district panchayat membership also. Not only this, it also emboldened the supporters of Yogi in Mau, and the wrong message of mass scale massacre of Hindus was sent to the places outside the district. When Yogi Adityanath came to Lucknow in connection with a programme recently, he not only repeated the falsehood that Hindus were being massacred in Mau but also gave a warning of revenge.

Delineating the inferences from the riot it said:

> This riot of Mau is the biggest and the most fearsome of all the riots, which have taken place here. For the first time the rioters organized themselves on such a large scale and executed violence in a systematic manner. The loss has also been maximum.

> According to the people of Mau it is also for the first time that during the riot schools and hospitals belonging to the minority community were vandalized, and large scale attacks on Mosques were carried out. This is a great cause for worry.
>
> What was limited to discourses is now translated into actions. Eastern UP is sitting on a communal volcano. Anything may happen any time here. The riot in Mau and the violence in the neighboring areas clearly indicate this. Soon after the riot in Mau there were immediate attempts to incite communal violence in Ballia, Ghazipur, Azamgarh, Deoria, Meerut and Agra.

V

It is really surprising that the 'Yogi Phenomenon' which represents a significant addition to the Hindutva arsenal and which has helped further its hate agenda so aggressively has not received the proper attention it deserves. Apart from stray newspaper reports or articles in some mainstream magazines focusing on particular events one has yet to come across a serious appraisal of the growing assertion of the forces of Hindutva in this area. If the RSS-BJP 'division of labour' can be construed as the first way in which Hindutva has unfolded itself, and the Shiv Sena's experiments in Maharashtra which have won over a significant section of the OBCs to its side can be considered a second strategy of Hindutva, the Gorakhpur experiments definitely qualify as a third successful initiative to further Hindutva politics.

It combines in itself many a significant features which would have ramifications for the country as a whole. One can clearly see that not only has Yogi been successful in winning over a section of dalits and backwards to Hindutva politics by demonizing the Muslims, but he has also very cleverly ensured the gradual Hindutvaisation/ Brahminisation of a mainly 'subaltern' peetham.

The most puzzling as well as the most dangerous aspect of this phenomenon in eastern UP is that the Sangh Parivar has been able to achieve (to use Gramsci's concept) a 'hegemony' of sorts among a large section of the Hindus.

It is time one wakes up to this strange situation where we have 'little' fascists who are popular as well. It is time we are able to shed our old straight jacketed understanding of fascism and see for ourselves how a Yogi can double up as a fanatic-fascist and a democratically elected leader, something true of Narendra Modi, as we well know.

It is important to look into this fact with utmost urgency because the recent National Convention of BJP has demonstrated the growing fascination for Narendra Modi within the Sangh Parivar. And it is logical that such elements would rather prefer similar faces elsewhere as well. And despite his public infractions Yogi is the best bet for them in the Eastern part of UP.

2007

Ayodhya: Mutts of Crime

Ayodhya, the city which has rather defined the contours of our polity in recent times, has achieved the status of remaining in the news for all kinds of things. And the recent meeting of Sadhus belonging to various akharas, who shared the platform despite innumerable differences among them, is a case in point. Despite being in adversarial relation to each other, many of them had come together supposedly to fight 'their common enemy', namely the scourge of terrorism. Many of these saffron robed sadhus made fiery speeches, but one could easily see that there was no attempt at introspection, nor any attempt to comprehend the growing metamorphosis of many mutts as centers of crime or the conflation of the criminal and the communal.

The personnel of the Special Task Force of the Uttar Pradesh Police had a tough time in Ayodhya when they recently visited the different mutts. Gone was the bonhomie witnessed earlier when they were greeted in a royal fashion on their earlier visits. This has something to do with the job they had in hand.

In fact the STF people were on the lookout for some persons, including some sadhus, who were allegedly involved in a bank robbery. A team of robbers had looted Rupees ten lakhs from the Grameen Bank in Gonda, and the police had discovered that it was members of the Mahant Arun Sadhu gang who were allegedly involved in the operation. Police also had definite leads which revealed that the same gang was also involved in many other cases of kidnapping and extortion. The modus operandi of the particular gang was simple: commit a crime and take refuge in temples to escape from the clutches of the police. ('Police Search Temples Looking for Bank Robbers', *The Hindu*, May 11, 2008).

The depredations of the Mahant Arun Sadhu gang reminded one of an earlier flare up when rival groups of mahants had tried to slug it out in public for control over temple trusts. A write-up in a prominent daily (*The Telegraph*, February 3, 2005) had provided graphic details of the fight.

> On Monday night, rival groups of Deoram Das Vedanti and Nrityagopal Das opened fire near Ramballabh Kunj temple, injuring the former, police said. Deoram is in hospital.
>
> Tension was simmering between the authorities of the temple's Janki Jivan Trust, believed to be cash-rich, and Nrityagopal's Mani Ram Das Chavni Akhara over the Trust's control.
>
> The rivalry spilled over after a meeting on January 31, when the two rival chief priests came to blows, prompting their associates to draw out double-barrel guns and fire. Deoram, an accused in an old criminal case, was hit in the shoulder.
>
> Earlier, in 2001, Nrityagopal had survived a bomb attack in the ongoing dispute over the Trust.

These were the same days when the police in Lucknow had said that they were looking for another Mahant, Shyam Shukla alias Shyam Maharaj, who had played the role of kingpin in the abduction of a Kanpur industrialist, Ravinder Kedia, and two of his associates. Kedia was released only when he paid a ransom of Rs18 lakh.

For close watchers of the Ayodhya situation, the disputes over temple trusts can be construed as a routine affair. The Faizabad police had earlier been directed by its higher-ups to remain vigilant over these increasing cases of rivalries between temple managements, infiltration of such establishments by criminal elements, and the free flow of arms among Mahants and their associates. It is not surprising, therefore, that there should be a clamor for gun licenses among different temple trusts. From figures available till three years ago it is evident that at least 350 Ayodhya residents, most of them temple-trust heads, have acquired licensed arms.

Rivalries between temple trusts have even led to killings. In 1994, mahants Ram Pratap Das and Prem Narayan Das were killed following a clash over land. The year before, a temple priest was murdered at Janki Ghat. In 1995, another priest, Ram Arghya Das, was murdered, followed by the murder of Ramkirpal Das in 1996.

Certainly, all those already worried about how the majoritarian forces have vitiated the composite ambience of the historic city have cause for further worry. The criminalisation of the saffron fraternity has become a further threat to peace in the city.

A seven-year-old study by Kanhaiya Bellary reveals a few interesting facts about the *mutts* in Ayodhya and Bihar. ('Mutts of Crime', Kanhaiya Bhelari, *The Week* Magazine, Cover Story, Nov 23, 1997):

> Tradition binds them to austerity, but opulence is their way. They are sworn to celibacy, but marry they do and have children. Attaining salvation is their ultimate goal, but for property they aim. In politicians they trust and on criminals they rely. They are the mahants (head priests) and sadhus of the thousands of mutts in Ayodhya and other parts of eastern Uttar Pradesh and Bihar .The mutts, there are no fewer than 8,000 in Ayodhya and about 7,000 in Bihar, are an industry by themselves, with some like the Gorakhpur Temple in Uttar Pradesh raking in offerings worth Rs 50,000 each day.

According to him "More than 40,000 'holy men' live in the *mutts* in Ayodhya. Of them more than 60 per cent of the mahants and over 25,000 sadhus are from Bihar. Most of them are Bhumihars or Brahmins, and they fight over *mutt* property. Kishore Kunal, IG of the CISF, even said that the Bhumihar mahants of Ayodhya's *mutts* had hired a number of criminals from the Begusarai belt of Bihar to establish their supremacy among the sadhus in Ayodhya...Police records show that in the last 10 years at least 150 mahants or sadhus have been killed in eastern Uttar Pradesh and Bihar because of ownership disputes. In Ayodhya alone, 20 sadhus have been killed in the last seven years...There is little that even the police can do about the unholy goings-on in the *mutts*."(*The Week Magazine*, Cover Story, Nov 23, 1997).

During the times of the United Front government when Uttar Pradesh was still under President's rule, the district administration of Faizabad had prepared a list of sadhus having criminal cases against them and they found 86 sadhus living in *mutts* in Ayodhya, who had such cases against them.

The same study explained the difficulties faced by law enforcing agencies in curbing the activities going on in many such *mutts*. A senior police officer had explained 'Raiding a *mutt* means inviting the wrath of the Hindus.' One can surmise how VHP and other affiliated organizations of the Sangh Parivar which have tremendously benefited from their Ayodhya agitation, have thus legitimized a process where criminality in the garb of spirituality can easily gel with politics of hate propagated by them.

It is true that as long as faith rules over reason in the minds of the people, the criminals are bound to exploit the situation to their benefit. A nuanced look at the unfolding situation would also reveal that there is a lot of overlapping between the two, or one can say the conflation of the two trends in very many places.

People like Ramvilas Vedanti, Chairman of the Ramjanmabhoomi Trust in Ayodhya, who is famous for making inflammatory speeches against Muslims and the secular fraternity, in a sting operation done by *CNN-IBN* had appeared as past master of money laundering and tax evasion in the sting operation. (*CNN-IBN* Posted Monday, May 07, 2007 at 08:11) He had even shared a secret with the interviewer that he has formed a separate trust to facilitate his work of converting black money to white money for a commission.

Titled 'Godmen turn Conmen, Taxman red' a write-up on the group website had provided details of the sting operation. (*CNN-IBN* Posted Sunday, May 06, 2007 at 20:30. Updated Monday, May 07, 2007 at 02).

> The investigation caught these gurus – Pilot Baba, a former Indian Air Force officer, Vedanti Maharaj, former BJP MP and Guruvayur Surya Namboodiri, who claims to be an astrologer – on camera and showed how they used their positions to launder money by bargaining like experienced conmen. The Vishwa Hindu Parishad – to which Vedanti owes his affiliation – seemed eager to distance itself from the Baba. VHP Vice President Giriraj Kishore said Vedanti was not a part of the VHP and also blamed the media.

One still remembers that the government had then even promised 'swift and strict' action in this case which had shocked the entire country. As things stand it is clear that despite prima facie evidence, neither were the individuals booked under relevant laws, nor were the accounts of the Trusts sealed.

And like many other such places Ayodhya continues to fester with criminals doubling up as Sadhus or vice versa.

The famous poet Majaz, whose birth centenary is being celebrated, had rather swiftly captured the changing reality of such holy places.

Masjidon main maulvi khutbe sunate hi rahe,
Mandiron mein barhaman ashlok gatey hi rahey
Ik na ik dar par jabeen-i-shouq ghisti hi rahi
Aadamiyat zulm ki chakki mein pisti hi rahi
Rahbari jaari rahi, paighambari jaari rahi
Deen ke parde mein jang-i-zargari jaari rahi.

(The mullah and the pundit and their ceaseless sermon
Man bowed before each one of them but did he learn
The great messiahs came claiming divinity.
Their religions, mostly ruses for plunder turn by turn.)

Nepal Has Done It

To paraphrase Mao, one can say that Nepalese people have finally stood up!

They have finally broken the shackles of the centuries old monarchy which had become a symbol for everything that is rotten in Nepalese society. Continuous palace intrigues which reached a pinnacle in the massacre of the earlier king and his entire family, a thoroughly reactionary social-economic agenda, and a continuous obeisance to external pressures had led to a situation where broad masses of the Nepalese people seemed condemned to live a life of misery and suffering.

A key part of the victory of the Nepalese people is also the manner in which they have dealt death blows to the proponents of Hindu Rashtra and shown that these forces are not invincible. The leaders of the democratic upsurge have resolved to work for building a Nepal which is secular, democratic, and inclusive and just, where every community is assured of equal participation in the running of the country. Given the key role of the Maoists in the unfolding scenario and their track record, one can vouch that Nepal stands on the threshold of tremendous possibilities.

It is a different matter that for the RSS and its affiliated organisations – whose 'model Hindu Rashtra' has collapsed before their very own eyes – it is a dark moment which they would like subverted.

I

Jaswant Singh, the ex foreign minister of India, who also handled the finance portfolio for quite sometime, could not hide his displeasure at the recently held meeting of the BJP executive.

He called it a 'negative development' and a 'danger to India's security' and said that 'as a believer in Sanatan Dharma' he felt 'humiliated' and as a Hindu, he felt 'diminished over the ouster of a Hindu king.'

Jaswant Singh is not alone in expressing a negative opinion on the end of the 250 year old monarchy. In one of his recent outbursts, Mr Ashok Singhal, the President of the Vishwa Hindu Parishad is reported to have compared Jihadists and Maoists who would together bring further calamity to the tiny country.

It was only expected that all such outbursts from the BJP and its allied organisations would be immediately rebuked by the Nepalese leaders as interference in the internal affairs of Nepal. Rambahadur Thapa, a senior leader of NCP (Maoists), in fact did characterize these utterances as 'anti-Nepal' and an 'intervention in the internal affairs of the country'.

Why does Mr Singh feel so perturbed over the end of a regime which had concentrated all power in the hands of a small caucus centred around the King, and which had denied basic human rights to a vast majority of Hindus, and which had condemned the followers of other religions to a secondary status? Does it also have something to do with the emergence of the NCP (Maoists) as the single largest party in the new republic, and that this has led to the emergence of the most diverse and representative parliament in the world today? Independent observers have noted that the newly elected Nepalese parliament has more than one third of women and an other one third representation is from the different ethnicities and oppressed castes.

Do Mr Jaswant Singh and others of his parivar think that while their formation should benefit from participating in the electoral-democratic process, for the Nepalese people only monarchy provides the best solution?

II

Other hotheads from the Sangh Parivar were equally vociferous in their denunciation of the changes in Nepal. They in fact organised a meeting in Balrampur in the immediate aftermath of the Nepal mandate and chalked out a plan for the restoration of the 'Hindu Rashtra'. Yogi

Adityanath, 'Bal Thakre', the "Narendra Modi" of Purvanchal (Eastern UP), was in the forefront in planning the meeting.

A report of the said meeting makes clear what transpired there:

> Tulsipur(Balrampur), April 25: The World Hindu Federation (WHF) adopted an aggressive line against Maoists in Nepal in its three-day general council meeting at Devipatan temple in Balrampur. The federation has proposed to form a global task force to restore Nepal's status as a "Hindu Rashtra".
>
> Nearly 75 delegates from Nepal, led by WHF's international president General *(retd)* Bharat Keshar Simha, are in Balrampur to attend the meeting.
>
> General Simha, who was a former honorary Resident Ambassador of Nepal in various countries, is also the Nepal King's honorary ADC.
>
> Simha said: "If Maoists can take up arms, why can't religious people like us?"
>
> Asked about the future role of the king in Nepal's politics, Simha told *The Indian Express*: "We don't bother about the king's support. Our aim is to restore Nepal's status as a Hindu Rashtra."
>
> The latest issue of the WHF's mouthpiece, *Dharma*, carried a message from King Gyanendra. "We are confident that the general council meeting will, through its deliberations, contribute to the preservation and promotion of the rich Hindu ethos. I wish every success in achieving its noble goals for the greater good of humankind," the king's message said.
>
> In his address as the president of WHF, General Simha wrote: "We were confident that there was complete consensus regarding Nepal's status as a Hindu Kingdom. But when Nepal was declared a secular state unilaterally by the interim government, there was no effective protest or opposition from any international quarter." General Simha blamed the Indian government for patronising Maoist leader Prachanda. "The formation of seven parties' alliance that includes the Maoists was possible because of the efforts of the Government of India," he said.
>
> The Nepalese delegates felt that their organisation should not highlight the issue of King Gyanendra. "We all were king's men. But the situation demands that we should support the restoration of Nepal's status as Hindu Rashtra. Hindu Kingdom and Hindu Rashtra are integrated

with Hindu religion," said Vishnu Prasad Sapkota, a resident of Nepal's Deodhar Dham. Another Nepalese delegate Deen Badhu Aryal said the main agenda of the federation was to get the sympathy of world Hindu community for the Nepal cause. "We want support from India-based pro-Hindu organisations," he added.

There are a few Nepalese who blame the king for the loss of the country's status as a Hindu nation. "The king had a team of wrong advisers. He failed to get the support of Indian leadership. His predecessors had always maintained good relations with Indian leadership. Raja Mahendra was close to Indira Gandhi," Dr Tulsi Tirki recalled.

Gorakhpur MP and president of WHF's India chapter Yogi Adityanath, who has organized the meeting, said that the emergence of Maoism is a serious threat to India's security. "Our policy makers had ensured that India should not share direct borders with China. They preferred Nepal, Tibet and Bhutan as buffer states. China can now expand its base in Nepal in the name of Buddhism after Nepal ceased to be a Hindu Rashtra," he said. Claiming that the WHF is prepared to fight with Maoists in Nepal, he said, "Whatever language the Maoists understand we will reply in the same language." On Saturday, the WHF will declare the name of its new president. "We prefer a young leader to head the organisation," said one of the office-bearers of WHF.

III

Both, the displeasure articulated by Jaswant Singh and the above mentioned meeting with its meticulous planning to 'restore Hindu Rashtra', go to show the special relationship enjoyed by the Sangh Parivar with the (now defunct) monarchy. To be very frank, it was a relationship which benefited both parties. While the Monarchy enabled the Sangh Parivar organisations to spread their network in the Himalayan kingdom, despite it bringing them in conflict with local religious heads who did not support their *weltanschauung* (world view), on their part the BJP and other Sangh Parivar organisations provided crucial support to the beleaguered monarchy on very many occasions.

It is now history how Ashok Singhal, the VHP working president, in a conference of Hindu leaders from across the world held in Kathmandu, had exhorted all Hindus to follow the monarch of Nepal. He said: "It is the duty of 900 million Hindus the world over to protect the Hindu samrat (king)...God has created him to protect Hindu dharma." In this conference these leaders had deified King Gyanendra as the world's only Hindu monarch. Mr Singhal had also then proposed to organise a world Hindu meet in New York in the coming year under the leadership of King Gyanendra (*Indian Express*, January 23, 2004). He added that the New York gathering would project Hindus as a global power...with the Nepal king leading the way.

It did not matter to Mr Singhal then that with his utterances he was showing loyalty to the King of another country, something derided by his one time leader and RSS ideologue Golwalkar. In his monograph *Bunch of Thoughts* Golwalkar had castigated Muslims, Christians and Communists as the country's main enemies for their "extraterritorial loyalty". It is worth noting that the secular formations and individuals in this part of the world did not try to put him on the defensive over such a sensitive issue.

Apart from the mutual support they derived from each other the 'Hindu Rashtra' in Nepal under the rule of the king served a deeper ideological purpose for the Sangh Parivar. It acted as a 'model' for the Sangh Parivar's own project of nation building. The internal social-cultural situation in Nepal under the monarchy suited its purpose well.

IV

For the Sangh Parivar and its affiliated organisations Nepal was the only nation in the world where the `one nation, one people, one culture' *weltanschauung* of the Hindu rashtra was already in place. The monarchy in Nepal had made religious conversion an offence and the slaughter of the official national animal, the cow, could be punished with 18 years of rigorous imprisonment. The state had also imposed its own version of 'sanatan dharma' on the people of Nepal.

Under this Hindu rashtra, the autocratic rules still persisted in the Himalayan kingdom. Its constitution made the Hindu way of life a basic part of Nepalese life. It stated: "Nepal is a multiethnic, multilingual, democratic, independent, indivisible, sovereign, Hindu and Constitutional Monarchical Kingdom". The richest people in this Hindu rashtra were the royalty, priestly class and the outsiders. The monarchy was so privileged that, according to the constitution "... No question shall be raised in any court about any act performed by His Majesty".

In order to preserve its Hindu character, conversion to any other religion was prohibited. Until 1963, the Nepali state upheld Hindu jurisprudence--formally at least. In view of this ban on conversions 90 per cent of the population was stated to be Hindu. Despite the constitutional guarantee of no discrimination based on caste, the age-old stranglehold of this institution continued. 'Untouchables', who constitute 22 per cent of the Nepalese population, were its greatest victims. For centuries, Nepal's untouchables have had to stay out of Hindu temples, refrain from drawing water at village wells and have even had to change their children's names just so that they could get an education. The status of Dalits and backward communities was the same as it was in India 100-125 years ago.

This Hindu rashtra had become the single biggest supplier of people to other countries. The system trained young workers and soldiers for other countries. Statistics of persons leaving this 'Ram Rajya' on account of poverty and migrating in search of jobs are really mind-boggling. These are the hard facts pertaining to Nepal under the monarchy.

Sudheendra Sharma, a social scientist who has written extensively on the religions of Nepal, rightly underlined that "...cultural isolationism from India meant that Nepal was also shielded from influence of the 19th century Hindu renaissance. Furthermore, within the territorial bounds of the nation-state, this policy meant aggressive Sanskritisation and cultural integration of hill ethnic communities based on an orthodox Hindu framework."

It is widely known that Nepal was ushered into a constitutional monarchy as a consequence of a people's movement against the partyless panchayat system in 1990, when a new constitution was adopted by the parliament. But very few people are aware that when the constitution of 1990 was written, there was pressure to make Nepal an officially secular state like India. It could be called the only key demand which was put forward by the Dalits, tribals, women and people from other faiths like Buddhism.

The pressure generated was so great that at one point of time the members of the constitution committee even had to concede to the demand that Nepal will not be declared a Hindu state. This demand created dissensions within the constitution committee as well. However, in the end, the views of the Hindu establishment won the day, and the constitution was decided in favour of making Nepal a Hindu country.

All that is *passe* now. And, despite all the pious wishes and attempts of the BJP leaders and Sangh Parivar organisations, the model Hindu Rashtra has finally been given a decent burial. Nepal is now a secular democratic republic with Maoists at the helm of affairs. Perhaps the agony and pain experienced by the likes of Jaswant Singh and other Hindutva acolytes could be compared to the shock and disbelief experienced by people – who believed in justice and progress – over the dissolution of the Soviet Union.

Of course it needs be underlined that the Sangh Parivar and its affiliated organisations made some last ditch efforts to save the monarchy despite the overwhelming majority in Nepal being opposed to it. When the Terai region in Nepal witnessed violent agitations recently the role played by Hindu extremist organisations also came under a scanner. Mr Bharat Bhushan had specifically commented on this aspect in one of his write ups in *The Telegraph:*

> Nepalese political observers also point to the role being played by Hindu extremist organizations from India in fomenting trouble in the Terai to save the king. A high-ranking Rashtriya Swayamsevak Sangh representative from Nagpur is believed to have held a meeting in Gorakhpur with several royalists, including Upendra Yadav and members of the Sadbhavna Party. The role played by the local Indian MP, Mahant Avaidhyanath, is also being questioned by some in this regard. ('Royalists Fish in Terai Trouble', 29th January 2008)

But as things unfolded before us we saw that all their not-so-pious wishes and attempts failed to stop the wheels of history in Nepal. A new Nepal is before us.

V

To conclude, the recent developments in Nepal do signify a qualitative shift in the Nepalese polity. They have demonstrated that people united can defeat machinations of the Hindutva brigade and can put a stop to US interventions. The question before us is whether people who yearn for genuine democracy and secularism in this part of the world are ready to learn from the experiences of the Nepalese people who with their actions have vindicated the age old dictum that 'People United Shall Always Be Victorious'.

It is a popular perception that Nepal and India share a very special relationship. There is lot of eulogisation in the media about the free flow of citizens across the two countries and the commonality of cultural ambience in both the countries. The Gorkhas of Nepal who essentially work as mercenaries in the Indian army – participating wholeheartedly in the all the wars of the Indian state – are also lauded for their bravery.

It is rarely mentioned how this 'special relationship' has benefited ruling classes of both countries. On the one hand Nepal has provided cheap labour in very many forms here, and on the other hand the free flow of people from poverty stricken Nepal has acted as a safety valve for the ruling classes of Nepal who could lord over their fortunes in a medieval manner.

The Nepalese people's unity has demonstrated that things can be changed for the better and it is not beyond possibility that the 'special relationship' could benefit the people on both sides, with ruling classes being put on the margins.

The question is if Nepal has moved forward on the path, should India remain far behind?

July 2008

One India, Two Peoples

It is difficult to say what will happen next.

Whether the police and security forces would understand their folly and would release Tariq Ahmad Batloo unconditionally or whether Delhi police who have branded two of their earlier contacts Irshad Ali and Mohammad Marouf Qamar as 'Al Badr Terrorists' would make amends for their steps? Whether media would engage in a deep soul-searching about its complicity to join the powers that be in making 'terrorists' out of innocent people? Nor is it possible to predict when the 'terrorisation' and 'stigmatisation' of particular communities would end, nor when the division of peoples into Holy Cows and Scapegoats would end.

It would not be an exaggeration to say that the future of India as a republic is at stake here.

Kafka in Goa: How Tariq Ahmad Batloo was 'Declared' a 'Terrorist'

Has anyone heard the tragic and rather unbelievable story of Tariq Ahmad Batloo, the Kashmiri trader, who is languishing in one of those 'high security prisons' in Kashmir meant for 'dreaded terrorists'?

In fact Batloo's arrest in Goa last year had made headlines where it was claimed that he was arrested while getting off the Mangala Express carrying a 'kilo of RDX, grenades and detonators in his suitcase' and had planned to 'set off bomb blasts in Goa'. When the case came up for hearing in the court the cops neither had a ticket to prove he had traveled on the said train, nor could they produce the RDX or grenades which he was supposedly carrying on the day. There were many other loopholes in the case and when it became evident that it was a frame-up and Batloo was picked up a full week before his 'official' arrest, he was acquitted by the judge.

But that was not the end of his tragic story. *The Herald*, a respected daily in Goa, in its editorial 'Making of a Terrorist' had given details of the aftermath of his acquittal (Panjim, 15 July 2008):

> Battlo, accompanied by his brother and cousin, was having a shave at a barber's when police picked them up and took them to Vasco police station. They were instructed to take the very next flight out of the state. Police were at the airport, questioning them, as well as photographing and filming them, and making calls on their mobile phones. As soon as they reached Delhi and collected their bags, they were surrounded by men in plain clothes who took Battlo away. Two days later, J&K police said they caught him in his 'hideout' in Jammu, on the same day that he left Goa. He has been booked in an old 2005 case against someone else, and now faces the prospect of spending a few more years in jail, until another court realises that it wasn't possible for him to reach Jammu on the same day he left Goa at 5.45 pm and reached Delhi at 8.30 pm, and acquits him from those charges as well.

Perhaps Tariq Ahmad Batloo's saga reminds one of the classic novel *The Trial* by Kafka where an ordinary citizen is ranged against forces much beyond his control. *Herald* had rightly concluded:

> The strange case of Tariq Ahmed Battlo – the man who was released by a Goa Fast Track Court only to be seized by plain clothes policemen outside the New Delhi airport and whisked away in a car, after which Jammu & Kashmir policemen claimed he was arrested from a 'hideout' in Jammu – will probably come back to haunt us all.

For anyone who is a close watcher of the 'terrorism' scene in the country it would be difficult to believe that the case of Tariq Ahmad Batloo is an exception. There is a growing list of innocent persons from the minority community who have been apprehended under some pre-text or the other, branded as 'terrorists', tortured for months together to extract some confession from them, and ultimately booked in some case to spend the prime time of their lives behind bars. *Tehelka*, the

English weekly, recently did a series of articles in its July-August (2008) issues which highlighted the plight of innocent Muslims who have had to bear the brunt of police highhandedness under the pretext that they belonged to some 'terrorist' organisation.

One can cite any number of cases where the long arm of the Indian state has reached out to pick up innocent people in order to cover up their incompetence in providing security to citizens. After each bomb blast or a surprise violent act, arrests are made, organisations named, but in most such cases the police and investigative agencies are not able to prove their claims. And they have in their kitty enough 'strong laws' which enable them to put behind bars for months together anyone, without a semblance of legal hearing taking place.

"Coimbatore Blasts: A Police Fabrication: SIT"

In a significant instance, during the last week of March, the Special Investigation Team (SIT) from Tamilnadu discovered that the cases registered against five Muslim youth in Coimbatore had been fabricated by the police (*The Milli Gazette*, 1-15 April 2008). July 2007 had witnessed the arrest of five youth – Haroon Basha, Malik Basha, Ravi alias Tipu Sultan, Bolo Shankar alias Theequrrahman and Shamsudheen – on the basis of some "secret information" received by them. The police version of the story referred to a conspiracy by this group to plant bombs in various hospitals in Coimbatore, supposedly to increase the influence of 'Manitha Neethi Pasarai' (MNP), a human rights organisation. It was also announced that the police had seized pipe bombs from the accused. As is always the case a section of the media carried stories based on the police version.

When MNP's claim, that the whole episode was a fabrication by the police, gathered broader support the government was forced to start a fresh enquiry into the case by the SIT. The SIT officials even recommended action against the cops – namely, Intelligence Assistant Commissioner Rathina Sabhapati and his associates – who had arrested the five youth belonging to 'Manitha Neethi Pasarai' (MNP), a human rights organization, to malign the group.

It is worth emphasising that as a result of the CID report, Rathina Sabhapati was demoted and transferred to another place.

In fact it had been a rather shocking revelation for the SIT that the whole exercise of the arrest of these innocent youth and the "seizure" of explosive materials planted earlier by the cops themselves was part of a joint effort on the part of Rathina Sabhapati and Inspector Elankovan with due support of senior officers. Basically it was an exercise to malign the MNP.

Delhi: Tihar Jail

The act by the Coimbatore police pales in significance in comparison with a case involving the Delhi police, in the heart of the capital city. The case pertains to two persons, namely Mohammad Marouf Qamar and Irshad Ali, residents of Bhajanpura (Delhi) and Sultanpuri (Delhi), who were working as informers for the Special Cell of the Delhi police. It has been more than two and a half years that they have been languishing in the Tihar Jail on false charges of being "Al Badr terrorists" – all for their refusal to continue working for the Special Cell which now desired them to work as moles in a militant camp in Kashmir. They were first kidnapped by the police and later shown as having been nabbed from the Mubarak Chowk bus stop on GT Karnal road in North Delhi on February 9, 2006 with two kgs. of RDX and pistols. Later it was revealed that Qamar had been abducted from his Bhajanpura residence on 22 December 2005, whereas Irshad Ali went missing from his Sultanpuri home on December 12. Oblivious of the fact that the Special Cell people had themselves kidnapped the duo, the family members of both lodged a complaint with the police about their sudden disappearance.

Later Qamar and Ali both moved Delhi High Court and in protest against police harassment asked their lawyer Sufiyan Siddiqui not to file any bail application. When the matter came for hearing the holes in the case became evident as their counsel produced records of calls between them and Special Cell officials before their "arrest", which proved that they had been police informers. Interestingly statements of Special Cell officials also contradicted each other. As it invariably happens, the police claimed that they had been nabbed from a J&K bus in the capital with RDX, but could not produce any tickets of the journey. Nor did the driver or conductor of the particular bus know anything of the matter. Besides, the Special Cell did not carry out any search of these "dreaded terrorists", nor did they disclose in the charge sheet as to where from they had received the arms and explosives.

The CBI enquiry made it clear that the Special Cell's version "did not inspire confidence" ('Some Respite for Police Officers who 'framed' Informers', *Hindustan Times*, 6th August 2008). It also agreed to the fact that the "duo were victims of a conspiracy hatched by the Special Cell in collaboration with the IB officials". Justice Suresh has asked the CBI to proceed against the guilty officials.

One can just imagine that if this is possible in the national capital itself, under the full gaze of the media, what may not happen elsewhere. Of course, considering the tremendous importance of the media, which is considered a 'watchdog of democracy', such incidents can become routine if stakeholders in the media itself become open to sidestepping the institutions of democracy and take upon themselves the job of 'investigating' such 'terror related crimes' and pronounce 'judgement' on that basis.

Media: Don't Swallow It!

Gauri Lankesh, a senior journalist from Karnataka, and editor of a Kannada weekly *Lankesh Patrike* had in an article (*The Milli Gazette*, 16-31 March 2008) demonstrated how the media itself joins the bandwagon in demonising particular communities and specific sections of society and metamorphoses into a 'legitimate tool' in their 'terrorisation' and 'stigmatisation'.

In her detailed write-up she discussed details of a case where three young men were arrested in Hubli and Honnali towns on charges of vehicle theft (Riazuddin Ghose, Mohammad Abubakar and Mohammad Asif). Perhaps because all three belonged to the minority community, 'within a day of their arrests, police sources leaked to the media that they suspected that the trio might be involved in planning terrorist attacks all over the country'.

The police leak was enough for all sorts of speculative stories in the print as well as electronic media where the reporters provided juicy and spicy details about the 'terrorist trio's plan' to blow most of Karnataka's key buildings. All these reports, which were sourced to 'police officials who did not want to be named', contended that these three young men 'had links up to Osama Bin Laden and down to the local 'sleeper cells' of LeT or SIMI'. The men were also suspected of conducting arms training in forests, flying the Pakistani flag, possessing RDX, distributing arms and weapons to 'sleeper cells', recruiting hundreds of youth to terrorist organisations, possessing AK-47s etc.

One report which appeared in the *The Hindu*, can be summed up thus: 'The fact that one of the arrested youth claimed before the magistrate that his human rights have been violated by the police made the magistrate suspect that he was no ordinary youth....On the basis of this assumption, the magistrate instructed the police to subject him to a thorough interrogation. And that was when the "terrorist links" were revealed.'

The hyper activity in media – which even published news of 'arrest' of a number of students when the police had not done so and which also reported that "religious books and material" were seized from the trio (as if carrying religious literature itself is a crime ?)- led to a situation where the three 'accused in bicycle theft' were depicted as among the most dreaded terrorists of recent times.

The caution expressed by a senior police officer, Mr Shankar Bidri, while talking to a TV channel fell on deaf ears. He had said: "So far no proof has been unearthed to label these youths as terrorists. The media is indulging in blatant fabrication of news. What if their case too turns out to be another Dr Mohammad Haneef case? Let us not turn into terrorists those who are innocent."

Of course there is another sinister method by which the media goes that extra mile in 'stigmatising', and 'criminalising' individuals under false pretexts. The highly mischievous manner in which *The Times of India* carried a defamatory report on Bangalore technies is a case in point. Under the caption 'New Network of Terror Technies Comes to Light' (28 Feb 2008) it tried to put every Muslim individual who is working in the I.T sector under suspicion. The report by a ND Shiv Kumar claimed that 'Bangalore appears to have turned into a hub of radical technies. Under the banner of Muslim Information Technology Professionals Association, these technies in the city are said to be networking and aiding radical groups.' Apart from spreading such baseless canard against a particular community, the report also singled out a few persons whose contribution to the whole IT industry is widely recognised. And this included Mr KM Sherif. The mischievous report even mentioned that the police are looking for KMSherif, imputing that he is absconding.

KM Sherif, an IT professional of 25 years standing, who has worked with Wipro and Sun Microsystems and who is at present Chief Executive Officer of a reputed IT firm, could not have ever imagined that such a slanderous piece on him would be carried by the *TOI*. He has filed criminal proceedings against *The Times of India* for defamation and has even sent a legal notice to the owners and publishers, and editor of the paper. In a moving letter he explained the current situation:

> ...An environment has been created where the press can imply any random person to be a terror suspect, and the so-called terror suspects are immediately judged by the press and fascist sections of society to be terrorists with no due process available to them. In most cases, the people who are thus implicated have no backing or support and are isolated by the society and thus are doomed even when they are innocent.

It is not difficult to imagine how such reports inflict irreparable damage to the careers of minority students who are aspiring for entry into the IT industry and also to those who are already working in IT firms.

Interestingly, the same media which is ready to go the extra mile when it comes to the issue of 'Jihadi terrorism' (or 'Fassadi terrorism' – to quote MJ Akbar) seems to develop cold feet when they clearly see the involvement and participation of Hindu terrorist groups in violent act(s). The blasts in Kanpur (24th August 2008) which occurred in a private hostel run by a retired employee MSS Mishra, which clearly involved Bajrang Dal activists, is a case in point. It took more than three days for the *Indian Express*, the *Hindustan Times*, *The Hindu*, or for that matter, *The Times of India*, to report an incident which exposed a big conspiracy hatched by the Hindutva brigade to foment communal riots. In the words of a senior police officer, the explosives gathered by the duo 'were enough to blow half of Kanpur'. Interestingly the Hindi newspapers were more forthright in reporting the incident. Even a newspaper like *Dainik Jagran*, which is considered close to the Hindutva brigade, covered the explosion immediately.

Bajrang Dal Bombers

> It is official. The Sangh Parivar members have now joined in plotting terrorist attacks. On Sunday afternoon, a bomb accidentally went off in Kanpur killing a former Kanpur city convener of the Bajrang Dal and his associate while they were assembling a bomb in a private hostel room. (*The Mail Today*, 26th August 2008)

Sharadanagar, a rather non-descript locality in Kalyanpur, Kanpur, has suddenly made national-international headlines, thanks to a bomb-explosion in one of the private hostels run by a retired employee of KESKO, Mr Shiv Sharan Mishra. Mr Mishra had built this private hostel, which had nine rooms and 14 students stayed in the hostel, and Rajiv (his son) had kept one room with him.

The explosion witnessed the deaths of Rajiv alias Piyush S/O Mr SS Mishra and Bhupinder Singh Arora, a friend of Rajiv and ex-convener of the city Bajrang Dal, in the explosion, with serious injuries to two others. The bomb explosion was so massive that there were cracks in all the walls of the hostel and bomb splinters reached 50 metres from the spot of the explosion.

It is reported that Piyush, who worked as complaint officer in a mobile company in Lucknow, came home with Bhupinder and asked the residents of the hostel to vacate the rooms on the pretext of checking the electric wiring. As soon as the occupants left the hostel, a massive blast occurred. Recovery of a timer device and prohibited explosive raw material show that a major terror plot was being hatched there.

Bhupinder ran a photo studio in the Sarvodaya Nagar locality of Kanpur and his shop was close to the city's popular JK temple, police said. According to the police the explosives were meant to explode during Sunday's celebrations. On Monday the police recovered some crude hand grenades, lead oxide, red lead, potassium nitrate, bomb pins, timers and batteries from the spot. The police felt that the quantity of explosives stored there was enough to destroy quite a large area.

The most notable fact about the perpetrators of this conspiracy, who died in the explosion, is that both belonged to the Bajrang Dal, the 'storm trooper' wing of the Rashtriya Swayamsevak Sangh. The leaders of the Bajrang Dal have conceded that the two 'worked with the organisation' some time ago and one of them happened to be the convener of the city wing.

Considering the grievous nature of the crime, and the fact that a major tragedy was in the offing, it was expected that the state government with necessary help from the central government would try to unearth the real conspirators behind the plan. It is a positive sign that the police have recovered mobiles of the two men and can now, if they so wish, take the case to its logical end.

But even as leaders of the city Bajrang Dal have conceded that the perpetrators were members of their organisation 'who have stopped working for it since sometime', the police in the city is 'still investigating their details'. There is a strong indication that the police may turn the focus of the investigation to Babbar Khalsa to save the real perpetrators of this act. In a report of the incident which appeared in *Dainik Jagran* a Hindi daily (25th August 2008) one gets an idea as to which way the wind is blowing in this case. It tells us that 'The name of Babbar Khalsa Force has cropped up in the conspiracy to wreak havoc in the city. The ATS members dropped hints to this effect.' It further adds 'according to ATS sources, Bhupinder was related to Babbar Khalsa Force and police has seized two of his mobiles'. It is conveniently omitted that Bhupinder Singh was once the City Chief of Bajrang Dal.

There is also a strong possibility that the powers that be would 'individualise' the crime and would not move beyond the facade. Such apprehensions with regard to the polity and the state apparatus are not unjustified. We have been witness to the cavalier attitude of the police as well as the intelligence agencies when a terrorist act committed by Hindu fanatics comes to light.

In a press conference held in Delhi ('Setalvad raps CBI on Nanded terror', 29th August 2008, *Mail Today*) leading social activist Teesta Setalvad and filmmaker Mahesh Bhatt reported the "massive cover-up operation" launched by the CBI on the Nanded terror incident which similarly saw deaths of two youths of the Bajrang Dal in 2006. According to them the CBI did not apply "sections of criminal conspiracy or booking the Bajrang Dal accused under the Unlawful Activities (Prevention) Act" while submitting a charge sheet this March in court.

They further add:

> The CBI charge sheet filed in March 2008 in the Nanded case is eyewash. The CBI has watered down the entire terror trail and links to terror training grounds of Bajrang Dal youth in Maharashtra – the Bhonsla School in Nashik and Nagpur – have not been explored. The Mumbai anti-terrorism squad (ATS) charge sheeted 11 persons for criminal conspiracy but the CBI did not even consider the possibility of a conspiracy – it has, in fact even diluted the ATS case.

Victims as Perpetrators!

Friday the 22nd happened to be an important day in so far as it underlined the manner in which minorities are viewed and dealt with by the state and the civil society in today's India.

A three day 'People's Tribunal on the Atrocities Committed against Minorities in the Name of Fighting Terrorism' was inaugurated on this day at Hyderabad. Organised jointly by different civil society organisations the tribunal intended to bring victims from 10 states to depose before an eminent jury of judges and lawyers and journalists.

The People's Tribunal sought to question the manner in which terrorist incidents/acts are treated in the country and 'only people from one community are arrested, only organisations of one sort are blamed and motives too similar are rattled most of the times. Facts like members of all communities getting killed, including of the community being blamed for the act, or the same community's place of worship having been targeted simply go unquestioned.'

The day also saw a protest demonstration at Churchgate, Bombay under the auspices of 'Awami Bharat and the Dalit-OBC Intellectual Forum' against the manner in which Ken Heywood, a key suspect in the Ahmedabad terror attack, who had sent the terror mail just five minutes before the attack happened, was allowed to escape the country.

Demanding that 'Ken Haywood should immediately be recalled to India and a thorough investigation be carried out, as he seems to be a key person in the planning and execution of the Ahmedabad and other terror attacks' the invite for the demonstration implied the possibility of 'Haywood being an undercover CIA operative with the task of fomenting terror so as to destabilise India and spread fear and insecurity, and pushing India further into the US-Israeli camp.' The concerned citizens' demonstration at Churchgate Railway Station sought to question the manner in which 'A person who was under the constant glare of the media and who even had police security posted outside his residence' was allowed to leave the country. It was rightly said that 'The very fact that even his passport was not confiscated speaks volumes of our "intelligence" agencies.'

The deponents in the tribunal comprised two categories of people: people who were arrested by the police on flimsy charges and then let off due to lack of evidence, and relatives of people who are in jail under similar charges. All those who deposed belonged to the Muslim community. A few of the deponents also submitted copies of documents pertaining to their cases. The jury which comprised eminent judges, social activists and journalists issued its interim report which emphasised that a large number of innocent young Muslims have been or are being victimized by the police on charges of terrorism in gross violation of the law. The People's Tribunal showed how the police, intelligence agencies and even the judiciary are constantly compromising civil liberties and constitutional rights all over India. It seems that the Indian state has become an apparatus that willfully ignores the basic human rights of minorities in the country. It rightly emphasised that it is the collective responsibility of society 'to ensure that the merchants of terror are punished but at the same time society has to take care that deep rooted prejudices do not develop against certain sections – so much so that these sections start wondering whether they are part of this society or not.'

The tendency on the part of the police to rush to the press immediately after nabbing some person and doling out the stories of their success and the progress of the investigations also came in for heavy criticism. The media inadvertently or because of malice towards particular communities also reproduces this police version ad verbatim.

Interim recommendations of the People's Tribunal are worth some consideration: Human Rights Commissions at the state as well as central level taking up such matters sincerely, courts becoming more cautious in granting police or judicial custody considering the fact that alleged confessions of the accused can also be doctored, courts awarding compensation for the destruction of life and reputation of persons acquitted by the courts, trial courts being provided with medical officers who can immediately examine an accused complaining of torture in police or judicial custody, police not be allowed to get blank papers signed by the accused, members of Bar Associations seeking to prevent lawyers from representing accused persons be hauled up for Contempt of Court for interfering with the administration of justice. The most important recommendation was addressed to the Indian government, namely that it sign the International Criminal Court Treaty known as the Rome Statute which has been signed by most countries.

All Beaten Bears?

The saffrons know how to peddle their 'achievements' and denounce their 'opponents'. And when Narendra Modi's anti-terrorist squad, with due help from other state governments, officially 'cracked the case' of Ahmedabad blasts and arrested its 'masterminds' there was no stopping them. Senior leaders of saffron dispensation described the 'success' of the Modi regime in solving the case within a fortnight and attributed it to the 'no nonsense approach of the Party' towards terrorism.

But despite all the brouhaha over this 'spectacular achievement' and despite receiving congratulatory messages from many quarters, one notices public skepticism about the claims made by the government. Sheela Bhatt (rediff.com, 26th August 2008), who recently did a story 'highlighting how the Gujarat police force cracked the Ahmedabad blasts conspiracy and how they were going about building an airtight case against the terrorists', gave vent to this feeling. According to her 'the biggest stumbling block before the Gujarat police' is the general disbelief or public skepticism 'over its claim of having cracked the case.'

But before coming to the grand disjunction between claims by the Gujarat government and the people's perception about it, it would be opportune to underline an important conclusion on the part of the government which has largely gone unnoticed. As per the Gujarat government's claims it has not only got evidence against the planners and executioners of the bomb blasts in Ahmedabad and Surat, it also has definite insights into the conspiracy aspect of the blasts in the Samjhauta Express and in Jaipur. The import of this is that (to quote Ms Sheela Bhatt):

> In other words, what the Gujarat police is claiming is that the blasts in Hyderabad, Bengaluru, Jaipur, Ahmedabad and probably Samjhauta Express were conceived, planned and executed by the militant faction of the Students Islamic Movement of India formed after 2005.
>
> That also means the usual suspects – like Pakistan's Inter Services Intelligence, Lashkar-e-Tayiba or HUJI of Bangladesh – can't be blamed for some of the recent blasts that have killed more than 200 innocent Indians...
>
> A senior Bharatiya Janata Party leader in Gujarat, whose party is in power in the state, says, "We have not found any external links to SIMI in the execution of the blasts in Ahmedabad and Surat.

It remains to be seen how palatable this would be to the ideologues of the RSS-BJP whose *weltanschauung* rests on the twin pillars of Pak bashing and stigmatising Islam.

The general public skepticism could be discerned at two levels.

The police force in the country is laced with tremendous power and little accountability which has made it too complacent. Normally as they can pick up any bear and parade it as a self-confessed tiger, they have little drive or motivation to go after the real tiger(s). This situation results in appalling intelligence failures and breeds incompetence and corruption within the force. In one famous judgment in the fifties Justice AN Mulla castigated it as 'the biggest organised goonda force in the country'.

In the case of terrorism related investigations the police force acquires further immunity thanks to the special laws drafted for special conditions. If under normal law confession before a police officer is not admissible as evidence, under such laws such confessions are admissible. It follows that terrorism related investigations which are considered special always face credibility problems in this part of the world.

As regards Gujarat the memories of Sohrabuddin and Kausarbi encounter killings are still fresh about how the police force from the two states – Gujarat and Rajasthan – had coordinated the killings and presented them as encounters with Lashkar-e-Toiba operatives planning to eliminate Narendra Modi and other senior leaders. Later it was revealed that the controversial Gujarat IPS officer and "encounter specialist" DG

Vanzara, now under arrest for the death of Sohrabuddin in November 2005, and his team of trigger happy police personnel had killed at least 15 people in the past few years in nine encounters on the alleged grounds that they were plotting to kill the Gujarat chief minister Narendra Modi and other senior BJP leaders. He had also arrested scores of "terrorists" on similar charges.

The public skepticism has another important dimension.

People have not forgotten that blasts in Ahmedabad evoked contradictory reactions from the mainstream parties. A senior leader of the BJP, Ms Sushma Swaraj, had blamed the Congress party for the blasts which, according to her, wanted to divert people's attention from the controversial means adopted by it to win the vote of confidence. As opposed to Ms Sushma Swaraj, a senior Congress leader and ex Chief Minister of MP, Mr Digvijay Singh, had asked why blasts occur whenever the BJP is in trouble. He had also said that he had enough proof to show that the RSS and its front organisations had been involved in bomb making in earlier events. People noticed that this was the first time that mainstream political parties had moved away from the usual 'SIMI' or 'Pakistan bashing' to blame other forces. As rightly noted also by historian Amaresh Mishra in one of his write-ups in *The Milli Gazette* this was the first time that the political nature of the bomb blasts and the politics underneath it was coming to the fore.

It is now history how the scenario dramatically changed once the central government lost its case against SIMI in the Special Tribunal appointed by it to justify the ban, and the government had to rush to the Supreme Court to get a stay order. Suddenly one fine morning we were told that Narendra Modi's police (whose role in the 2002 carnage is well known now) have ultimately cracked the case and that police in different states had shown exemplary co-ordination in nabbing the accused. Just the day before as we had been waiting with bated breath for news of the interrogation of Ken Haywood – the key link in the whole case – by the ATS in Bombay (with a 'lookout notice' issued against him), we discovered that he has already fled the country.

The powers that be told us that in fact Indian Mujahideen and SIMI are the organisations which had perpetrated the dastardly acts. The proof is purportedly again a 'confession' made by the head of SIMI, Safdar Nagori, arrested in Madhya Pradesh in March.

Where Do We Go From Here?

...It is difficult to say!

Would the police and security forces understand their folly and release Tariq Ahmad Batloo unconditionally? Would the Delhi police, which has branded two of its earlier informers Irshad Ali and Mohammad Marouf Qamar as 'Al Badr Terrorists' make amends for their actions against them? Would the media engage in soul-searching regarding its complicity with the powers that be in making 'terrorists' out of innocent people? One cannot say. Neither is it possible to predict when the process of 'terrorisation' and 'stigmatisation' of particular communities would end.

As of now there seems to be no end to the phenomenon of the long arms of injustice picking up scapegoats from some sections of the Indian population and on the other hand treating others as 'holy cows' and protecting them despite their reprehensible crimes against the people of the country.

It would not be an exaggeration to say that the future of India as a republic is at stake here.

August 2008

Phoney Jihadis, Real Culprits

Ramvilas Vedanti, a senior leader of the VHP, refuses to remain out of controversy for very long.

If last year he was caught in a sting operation by CNN-IBN, alongwith many leading stalwarts of the spiritual world, 'explaining how he changes black money into white albeit with little bit of commission', this year he made headlines when he issued 'death sentence to Mr Karunanidhi supposedly for 'insulting Lord Ram'. One still remembers how he asked Muslims to 'vacate' the *Parikrama* area of Ayodhya after the 'terrorist attack in Ayodhya' on the specious argument that their presence in the area creates a feeling of insecurity. It is true that if one were to create a rating for making provocative statements Vedanti, like his more famous colleagues in VHP, would not bevery far behind.

But the latest controvery is a bizarre one.

On 30th August he lodged a complaint with the Faizabad police alleging that he is receiving death threats from SIMI and Al-Qaeda. The district administration promptly provided him with additional security and his mobile phone was placed under electronic surveillance to track down the miscreants. And lo and behold! Forget Al Qaeda or SIMI, to everyone's dismay the police caught Ramesh Tiwari, city president of Bajrang Dal in Katra, and Pawan Pandey, a local convenor of Hindu Yuva Vahini from Katra in Gonda district.

The duo told the police that since their Guruji (Ramvilas Vedanti) was not getting Z category security as enjoyed by VHP leaders like

Ashok Singhal and Praveen Togadia, they took this step 'after Guruji gave us the consent'. It was obvious that Vedanti did not press the police to take any legal action against them and the duo was promptly released. (*Indian Express*, 15th Sept 2008).

One can just imagine the mayhem followers of Vedanti could have created and how they could have polarised the whole atmosphere along communal lines if the police had not shown alertness.

It is worth emphasising that recently a group of sadhus led by Mahant Yugal Kishore Shastri, who is a Mahant of Saryu Kunj temple which is adjacent to the disputed Ram temple in Ayodhya, demanded legal action against Vedanti. A memorandum signed by 100 sadhus has been despatched to the Chief Minister's office demanding immediate arrest of Vedanti 'for conspiring to create communal violence in Ayodhya and adjoining areas.' It is also learnt that since Vedanti, an ex MP is also contemplating to contest the elections from Gonda, he was keen to create a riot type situation there.

A look down memory lane reveals that there was nothing 'creative' in the complaint lodged by Vedanti with the local police. In fact he was just copying one of his own colleagues from the Ram Mandir movement

It was only last year that Anil Chamadia, a leading journalist, media critic and social activist, in his column on media affairs in the Hindi magazine *Kathadesh* provided details of a similar case when Mahant Nrityagopal Das of the Ramjanambhoomi Nyas supposedly received a threat 'at the hands of the Al-Qaeda.' The newspapers also took up the case of the threat received by him in a big way, claiming there was failure on part of the government to provide security to 'patriots'. Along with a forty-line news item about this 'threat', a separate box item was added giving details of Ashok Singhal's and Praveen Togadia's reaction to the whole affair.

Mr Purushottam Narayan, a leader of the VHP, even claimed that a 'threat to the Mahant is a challenge thrown by Al-Qaeda before the whole Hindu society which necessiates 'unity of Hindus at every level'.

The very next day truth about the whole affair was out. Santosh, one of the disciples of the Mahant was arrested in Haridwar and he revealed that he had himself written this letter as his Guruji (Nrityagopal Das) was not getting Z category security as enjoyed by VHP leaders like

Ashok Singhal and Praveen Togadia. It is worth noting that the newspaper which had printed the 'threat received by Nrityagopal Das did not deem it necessary to publish the denial of the charges.

One can just go on citing examples where close associates of the saffron brigade engage in conspiracies which go to stigmatise particular communities and strengthen negative attitudes towards them.

While the followers of Vedanti or Nritya Gopal Das tried to utilise and further buttress the threat posed by the likes of Al Qaeda or SIMI, their brethren in the Hindutva brigade have no qualms in engaging in real terrorist acts by assuming fake identities resembling a member of theminority community.

The Nanded bomb blast on 6th April 2006, which killed two activists of Bajrang Dal, has demonstrated how these Hindu terrorists engage in meticulous preparations to fake their identity. The fake beards and clothes worn by the minority community recovered from the houses of the perpetrators of the act demonstrates the modus operandi of these fanatics.

September 2008

Silent Emergence of Hindu Terrorism

I

What is common between Kathmandu, the capital of Nepal, Thane and Vashi which happen to lie in Maharashtra, Tenkasi, which is part of Tamilnadu, and Indore which lies in Madhya Pradesh? Apropos there seems to be no commonality, although a close look at stray incidents of violence in these places brings forth a pattern which has serious import for the manner in which (non-state) terrorism is viewed in this country. It is disturbing that the media, which calls itself 'watchdog of democracy' and which has no qualms in stigmatising the minority community on unfounded allegations of 'terrorist acts', has suddenly gone mute as the perpetrators of terrorist acts in all these cases belong to the majority community.

It needs be remembered that Kathmandu – capital of the newest Republic of Nepal – witnessed bomb explosions outside the Birendra International Centre where newly elected members of the constituent assembly had assembled for the oath taking ceremony. Although nobody was killed and only few faced minor injuries, it was a clear signal that elements opposed to the momentous changes in the Nepalese polity were involved in the attack. The local police immediately blamed Hindu fanatics for this cowardly attack.

Observers of the Nepal situation did not lose sight of the fact that pro-monarchy Hindutva forces had even resolved to take up arms for the restoration of the *Hindu Rashtra*. A meeting was held by them in the immediate aftermath of elections to the constituent assembly and was attended by sympathetic elements from both the countries. It had been organised under the aegis of *Vishwa Hindu Mahasangh*, an international organisation of Hindus, in Balrampur (India), which was presided over by the 'firebrand' BJP MP Yogi Adityanath.

If Kathmandu witnessed bomb explosions as a violent reaction to the victory of the Republican forces in Nepal, Indore, the erstwhile capital of the Holkars, witnessed firing by activists of Hindu organisations in full public view. They had assembled there after a rally as part of the celebrations to commemorate the coronation of Chhatrapati Shivaji. Shivaji Maharaj, as he is popularly known, was a great secular ruler of the 17th century in Western India who fought with the Mughals. The firing incident which was covered by the media took place under the watchful eyes of the local police which remained a mute spectator and did not even deem it necessary to file a report on this thoroughly unlawful act. The brazenness of the participants in these celebrations was evident also from the fact that they even handed over the guns to the kids present there who also fired in the air.

Of course this was not the first time that such a firing incident had taken place. A few months ago marches (*Path Sanchalan*) were organised in different parts of Madhya Pradesh under the aegis of different Hindu organisations owing allegiance to the RSS. These *path sanchalans* were also marked by firings at the culmination of the rallies. And as expected there were no police complaints. Nobody questioned how the lathi wielding *swayamsevaks* suddenly metamorphosed into gun wielding Machos out to silence 'anti-nationals'. Considering that many areas in MP, especially Malwa, have always had a strong presence of the Hindutva forces, one can surmise what led to such 'spontaneous sounding' firing incidents.

At a press conference held in Indore city (23 rd April 2008), the former chief minister of MP and Congress general secretary, Digvijay Singh, had rightly analysed the precarious communal harmony situation in the state. He had demanded that "...[l]ike SIMI, Bajrang Dal should also be banned because this RSS outfit, along with some other allied organisations, indulges in bomb making and giving training in making of bombs. He said that he still sticks to his earlier accusation of making of bombs by Bajrang Dal. He said that RSS has retreated after they accused him of slander." (*The Milli Gazette*, 1-15 June 2008).

Perhaps the former Chief Minister was alluding to the discovery of a bomb making factory in Nanded (Maharashtra) at the house of an old RSS activist, which saw accidental deaths of two Bajrang Dal / RSS workers (April 2006). Five other members of the terrorist group were also arrested by the police. The episode revealed a well-thought out plan to start a communal riot. Apart from maps of mosques in the area, the police had discovered fake beards and dresses normally worn by Muslims in the area. Further interrogation of the other accused in the case also made it clear that the same group was responsible also for other incidents – namely Parbhani, Jalna, Purna – in Maharashtra, where Muslims had come under mysterious attack at the time of Friday prayers.

Despite a formally secular government in power in the state, the police did not care to unearth the wider game plan hatched by the top echelons of the Hindutva brigade. It is common knowledge that the more than 80 years old 'cultural organisation' and its affiliated fronts maintain a strict hierarchy, and any violent actions on the part of local activists are simply not possible without the involvement of the top bosses of the 'Parivar'. The police neither used any strong law to apprehend the real culprits, nor tried to oppose the bail applications moved by other members of the Hindu terrorist module.

And today, according to informed sources, the whole issue of the bomb making factory and the busting of a Hindu terrorist module lies buried under the hubris of government apathy and connivance of a section of the bureaucracy.

II

> The arrest of *sevaks* of the *Sanatan Sanstha*, a religious group that is behind the *Hindu Janajagruti Samiti* for planting bombs in theatres at Thane and Vashi adds a new dimension to terrorism. Seven people were injured when one of the bombs planted by the *sevaks* exploded in the parking lot of Thane's Gadkari Rangayatan theatre on 4 June. Ramesh Hanumant Gadkari, Mangesh Nikam, Santosh Angre and Vikram Bhave, the four bombers, are all full-time activists

> of the *Sanatan Sanstha,* living in ashrams run by the organization. Police say that they had planted a bomb outside a mosque or dargah on the Pen highway last Diwali, to check its intensity, but it did not explode. Nikam had earlier set off a bomb in the house of a family in Ratnagiri that had converted to Christianity, and was on bail awaiting trial. ('Terror's New Face', *Herald,* Panjim, 19 June 2008)

Has western India – especially Maharashtra, Goa – slowly and silently emerged as the epicentre of a different sort of terrorism? The bomb explosion in Nanded in April 2006 at the house of a RSS activist and busting of a Hindutva terrorist module, and a repeat of a similar explosion in February 2007 in the same city which also witnessed two deaths, could be said to be two major incidents that mark the emergence of homegrown Hindutva terrorism. It is no mere coincidence that four major stalwarts of the idea of Hindutva – Savarkar, Hedgewar, Golwalkar and Bal Thackeray – hail from this area. And the dilly-dallying adopted by the powers that be vis-a-vis these explosions in Nanded was a clear signal to these forces that they can move ahead with impunity.

The recent events in Thane, Panvel and Vashi demonstrate that hard line Hindutva groups, which have secretly and surreptitiously built a wide network of active and sleeper cells, are ready to go quite far to make their presence felt. Taking advantage of the freedom from scrutiny by police and the intelligence establishment, many such new outfits have sprung up. They have been indoctrinating lakhs of people through their agenda of hate and exclusion under the cover of 'spiritual gatherings' and distribution of spiritual literature. ('Quietly, hard line Hindu outfits build a network across Maharashtra, Goa' (*Indian Express,* June 23, 2008). Terrorist acts committed by these groups in the above mentioned places and their capacity to indulge in similar acts elsewhere is an indication that unless dealt with firmly they might well spread their tentacles elsewhere as well. And the day would not be far when Hindutva terrorist networks are able to reach all nooks and corners of the country.

On 31st May 2008, while the show of the much debated play 'Amhi Pachpute' was on at the Vishnudas Bhave auditorium, Vashi, (Maharashtra), unknown to everyone, a show of another kind was also on outside the hall. Thanks to the alertness and presence of mind shown by those present a bomb placed by some miscreants was spotted, and a bomb squad immediately rushed in and neutralised the bomb. A major disaster was averted. Yet, the police neither felt the need to interrogate the leaders of the 'Hindu Janjagruti Samity', which had been organising a series of protests against the play, supposedly for 'hurting religious sentiments of Hindus', nor did it venture to move beyond questioning its 'usual suspects'. It is likely they would also have closed the file after some time citing 'lack of any clues', had not another incident soon occurred, in fact within four days.

The venue had now shifted to Thane, another city in Maharashtra, and the location was the basement of the 'Gadkari Rangayatan Auditorium' where another show of the same play was on. Unlike Vashi, here the bomb explosion could not be averted and a few people were injured.

It was clear to even a layperson that these incidents were linked and an organised group was behind these incidents. In acknowledgement of the gravity of the situation the 'Anti Terrorism Squad' of the Bombay police was given responsibility for investigating the case.

The ATS was successful in nabbing Ramesh Hanumant Gadkari (Age 50) and Mangesh Dinkar Nikam (Age 34), full time activists of the 'Hindu Janjagruti Samity' and 'Sanathan Sanstha', from Panvel (15th June 2008), and the very next day it caught Vikram Bhave and Santosh Sitaram Angre, charging each one of them with masterminding the bomb explosions in Vashi and Thane. It came to light that these terrorists had also been involved in another bomb explosion in Panvel four months ago, during a film show of 'Jodha Akbar'. (20 February 2008).

The Sanstha denied any knowledge of these incidents and claimed that the activists might have carried them out at their own initiative. It is obvious that these protestations of innocence should not be taken at face value. The police must thoroughly investigate the affairs of the *Sanatan Sanstha* and the *Hindu Janjagruti Samity*, both of which have been registered as charitable organisations in Goa. Certainly these organisations cannot evade responsibility when the literature widely distributed by them calls for 'elimination' of 'evildoers' and claims that it is the 'religious duty' of all Hindus to combat and counter 'enemies of Hinduism'.

The editorial in *Herald* further adds:

> ...[S]anatan Sanstha and the Bajrang Dal, two Hindu fundamentalist organisations that are both linked to bomb blasts, are the main constit-

uents of the broad joint front called the Hindu Janajagriti Samiti, which has been holding public meetings all over Goa claiming Hinduism is in danger, and making provocative speeches.

III

According to a write up in the *Indian Express* (June 18, 2008): '...the arrests were enough for Deshmukh to point fingers at the possibility of Hindu groups being involved in subversive activities too. "Normally, when such incidents take place a particular community is suspected," the Chief minister said in a statement late on Monday. "But the arrest of two people belonging to a Hindu organisation proves that such suspicions are baseless. Criminals do not belong to any religion."'

Investigations into the antecedents of the arrested activists revealed that they have had trysts with bombs and violence in the past as well. The Chief of Maharashtra's Anti-Terrorism Squad told media persons that "Various members of these organisations are being questioned. If their role is found in the planning or execution of these incidents, we will certainly write to the centre and seek that they are banned." (*Indian Express*, 23 rd June 2008).

As of now it is difficult to predict how things would unfold, but notable fallout of these explosions and the consequent arrests is that there is at last a broader awareness of the activities of these Hindu extremist groups which work like wheels within wheels, and are quietly mobilising Hindus on a cocktail of Ramrajya, Hindu Dharma and "dharmakranti" – religious revolution. As mentioned both Hindu Janjagruti Samity and Sanatan Sanstha are registered in Goa as charitable organizations, even as they are linked to these activities. A new outfit Dharmashakti Sena was also floated by them in 16 towns and cities of Maharashtra on Gudi Padwa day this April. Pictures of its inaugural rally in April show young men dressed in military fatigues. According to *Herald*:

> Defense of Hinduism is one of the biggest themes in the literature and meetings of the HJS and the SS. [In] The massive 44-volume compilation titled 'Science of Spirituality', published by the Sanatan Bharatiya Sanskruti Sanstha and 'compiled' by Dr Jayant Athavale, founder of the Sanatan Sanstha, Hinduism is consistently portrayed as being under threat from the forces of Christianity and Islam, aided and abetted by

> the 'so-called secularists', who are seen as traitors to Hinduism. The volumes have titles like 'Protecting Seekers and Destroying Evildoers' and 'Reinstatement of the Divine Kingdom'. Defending the faith against the various purported threats by allegedly anti-Hindu forces is stated to be the primary duty of all true believers. The nature of this 'defense' is spelt out in great detail. It involves identifying those who work against 'dharm', making lists of such people, and then moving to 'eliminate' them. It is claimed that all this is part of 'spiritual practice'. (Panjim, 22 June 2008).

Interestingly all talk of Hindu Unity in the worldview of HJS falls at the altar of caste and other regressive practices in our society.

> Believers are exhorted to guide offenders away from the path of incorrect practice. The volumes in the series support the regressive and obscurantist practices of the past, including the caste system, talking repeatedly about the proper role of various castes in society. (ibid.).

While curbing the activities of these organisations or banning them would demand extra efforts on part of the government, as of now there are very many things which can be done to stop their vicious, hate filled ideas from reaching a wider cross-section of society. The contents of their literature are sufficient for this.

> For an organisation which is so ultra-sensitive about the slightest imagined insult to Hinduism – imagined or real – the literature of the Sanatan Sanstha is rife with attacks on other religions. Priests are depicted with horns, indicating that they are devils. There are frequent references to the Bible, alleging that it promotes incest and other immoral practices. In September 2004, 'Sanatan Prabhat' carried a statement saying that the body of St Francis Xavier should be destroyed. It has also carried other scurrilous articles about Goa's patron saint. In November 2005, 'Sanatan Prabhat' published an article, 'Mohd. Paigambar: An incarnation of Tripurasur [an 'asur' or demon]', which led to rioting in Miraj town of Maharashtra, and the imprisonment of the editor of 'Sanatan Prabhat'.
>
> After having created an ideological framework which creates a fundamentalist mindset and makes it the 'duty' of the true seeker to defend the faith against all those who are projected as attacking it, it is disingenuous of the HJS and the SS to disclaim responsibility for the acts engaged in by their members. Ex-members of these organisations talk

> about the cult-like atmosphere that is created, with unquestioning obedience being stressed. Members are then brainwashed into believing that Hinduism is under siege. Against this background, and with all the talk about 'defence' and 'elimination of evildoers', it is hardly surprising that adherents begin to explore ways of taking direct action to defend the faith. In this regard, the philosophy of the HJS and the SS is not all that different from the philosophy of terrorists, whom they claim to oppose. (*Herald*, Panjim, 22 June 2008)

Of course, if the government is serious about curbing these extremist organisations, it can start with filing criminal proceedings against the 'bible' of the HJS itself – namely the 'Science of Spirituality' under section 153(a) and (B) and related clauses on grounds that it promotes disaffection and disharmony between different communities.

But would it be proper to say that only western India is witness to the silent emergence of Hindu terrorism, or is the phenomenon gradually acquiring a national spread?

IV

> Here is a news report which shows that Hindutva terrorism is not confined to western India.
>
> The special police team, led by Deputy Inspector General of Police, Tirunelveli Range, P Kannappan has arrested three persons in connection with the Tenkasi RSS office bomb blast case.
>
> The investigations revealed that the blasts were planned to provoke a backlash between two groups of different and dominant communities in Tenkasi. Speaking to reporters at Tenkasi on Monday, Inspector General of Police, South Zone, Sanjeev Kumar said on January 24, there was a bomb blast at the RSS office and an auto, parked inside the new bus stand at Tenkasi, was destroyed.
>
> Following this, special teams were formed to nab the accused. Investigations revealed that S Ravi Pandian (42), a cable TV operator, S Kumar (28), an auto driver, both from Tenkasi, and V Narayana Dharma (26) of Sencottai had planted 14 pipe bombs in the office of Ravi Pandian.
>
> ...Moreover, the bomb blast inside the new bus stand was planned to divert the police investigation, said Sanjeev Kumar.

('3 arrested in Tenkasi bomb blast case', Tuesday February 5 2008 08:12 IST, *Express News Service* (*New Indian Express*))

S Ravi Pandian (42), a cable TV operator, S Kumar (28), an auto driver, both from Tenkasi, and V Narayana Sharma (26) of Sencottai today represent the less reported phenomenon of Hindutva terrorism. For all practical purposes till 23 rd January they remained activists of Hindu Munnani – an affiliated organisation of the RSS – engaged in what they deem to be 'patriotic' work.

Today they are the new face of 'terrorism' unleashed by the Hindutva brigade.

But not only these three 'musketeers', one should add names of four more people who were apprehended on 5th February, identified as A. Balamurugan (20), S Velmurugan (18), A Murugan (24), all hailing from Tenkasi and Maasaanam (20) of Shencottai. They have been arrested for assisting S Pandian in making bombs and detonating them at the RSS office and the town's new bus stand. According to *The Hindu* (6 Feb 2008), the police even recovered bombs and detonators from them.

Given the hierarchical nature of the Sangh Parivar outfits, these blasts could not have been triggered without the knowledge of its top brass in Tamilnadu.

Thanks to the painstaking efforts of Mr Kannappan, DIG Tirunelveli range, who did not fall prey to the usual stigmatisation and terrorisation of the religious minorities, and his thorough investigations into the incident (24th January 2008) which involved bomb blasts at the RSS office in Tenkasi and another one at the bus stand, the culprits could be apprehended.

It is now learnt that the Sangh Parivar organisations which fared miserably during the last elections were keen that Tenkasi does a 'Coimbatore', their calculations being that they would get sympathy votes. One may recall that this is the 10th anniversary of the Coimbatore blasts, which had seen deaths of innocent people.

A report filed by MH Jawahirullah (www.twocircles.net) says:

According to Sanjeev Kumar, IG, South Zone, the bomb blast inside the new bus stand was planned to divert the police investigation. DIG of Police Kannappan said the trio tested the capacity of the bombs

> at Papanasam before executing the plan. Since the bombs contained substances like ammonium nitrate, electric detonators, batteries and timer devices, the explosion was possible within 30 to 40 seconds, said Kannappan. The Investigation is still going on. The Police said 14 pipe bombs were assembled and the operations began from July last year.

There are reports that the Tirunelveli Police has indicated that the explosives used in Tenkasi are similar to those used in the Mecca Masjid blast at Hyderabad. It is incumbent that in the light of these revelations in the Tenkasi blasts the CBI should reinvestigate the Mecca Masjid blasts and other blasts which took place in different parts of the country.

V

> General Secretary of the Congress Party, Mr Digvijay Singh, has attacked Chief Minister Shivraj Singh Chauhan and the RSS on the recovery of arms in Shyampur, District Sihore. While releasing to the press the letter he has written to the Chief Minister, Mr Singh categorically stated that members of the RSS are engaged in sending swords and knifes to instigate communal violence. The two miscreants from Shyampur, who were found to be in possession of arms and were duly apprehended, belong to the RSS. The letter specifically mentions that since the accused belong to the RSS the Chief Minister would not take any action in this matter. You are under pressure from the RSS also, he wrote. Mentioning his earlier letter Mr Singh said that Mangilal and Phool Singh were arrested for delivering 24 swords and four knifes at Satyanarayan Bhati's house on 16th March. These two persons belong to the RSS. Within a few days of the recovery of arms, minorities in Narsinhgarh and Talen (Rajgarh) came under attack and five people from both sides lost lives.
>
> The Congress leader mentioned a letter written by Sihore S.P. which says that despite attempts by the police the two accused have refused to divulge information about the source of these arms. To conclude, the point one would like to emphasise is whether it is possible to link Tenkasi with Vardha, or Nanded with Ahmedabad, or for that matter Sihore, in our own atomised world view or not ? ('Sangh Sends Swords and Knifes' *Bhaskar,* Hindi Daily, 19 July 2007)

The arrests of Hindutva terrorists from Thane and Panvel was followed by a controversial editorial in *Saamna* – edited by Bal Thackeray

– in which he praised Hindu organisations involved in the blast, but asked them to make better "Hindu" bombs instead of the low intensity bombs, to match those made by "Islamic Terrorists", and explode them in "mini-Pakistans" in India. It also said that to save Hindus, Hindutva organisations need to form suicide squads much on the lines of Islamic terrorist organisations. According to the editorial, "Islamic terrorism" was "flourishing" in the country and to counter it, "Hindu terrorism" of the same power should be created.

It is quite natural that the provocative utterances should have received condemnation from a broad spectrum of political opinion – with many parties demanding prosecution of Bal Thackeray. But inadvertently this served a dual purpose. On the one hand it helped deflect the attention of the concerned people from the silent emergence of Hindu terrorism and on the other hand it was a tacit acknowledgement of its existence and growth.

Considering the danger it presents to communal harmony it is time that, apart from strategising against what is known us *Jihadi* terrorism, we also focus our attention on the terrorism which is being unleashed in the name of the majority community, namely Hindu terrorism. It is time the security establishment makes a radical departure from the prevalent understanding of terrorism, the polity gathers enough courage to face this reality and to make a fresh beginning, and the civil society at large breaks itself free from its community specific prejudices. Only then would it be possible to rein in the scourge of terrorism.

The words of advice from senior journalist Prem Shankar Jha would be opportune at this moment. In a write up for *Outlook* (May 26, 2008), immediately after the Jaipur blasts, he said:

> ...An effective anti-terrorist strategy requires us to look even more deeply into ourselves. The police and security agencies only mirror the prejudices of the majority community and these have become more pronounced in the past two decades. Why has no one in office ever formally expressed regret for the terrible pogroms that have scarred the face of our society – from the [19]93 Mumbai killings to the [20]02 Gujarat massacres? Why are Indian courts suddenly handing out death penalties by the dozen, with a predisposition to singling out minorities? Indeed, so great has been the bias and so quixotic the rulings that it has

provoked Amnesty International into making a scathing criticism of the Indian judiciary.

India's war against terror has just begun. But security forces cannot fight on their own. If our political leaders and the public don't do their part, we will find ourselves losing.

A balanced approach would enable us to look at facts with an open mind and would also help us look at minor details or minor clues to reach the perpetrators of such acts. Is it not disturbing that while India is witnessing terrorist actions in different parts of the country in most of the cases the security people have not been able to make any headway in the investigations? Leave alone catching the real perpetrators of such acts they are targeting a specific community en masse. There have been countless stories of violations of human rights of very many people which have been very well documented by different citizens groups.

Take the instance of the Jaipur blasts. A story appeared in the newspapers of one Vijay who was immediately spotted after the Jaipur blasts, telling the police the name of his other (lady) accomplice, both supposedly responsible for the blasts. Nobody has heard of Vijay since then.

Take the instance of the Malegaon blast. A few victims told the police that a body with a fake beard was recovered from among the dead bodies. Considering that the issue of fake beards was raised prominently in the context of the Nanded bomb blasts, the security agencies could have fine tuned their investigation to incorporate this angle, but they continued in the old manner. And, remarkably, they did not bother to question the hospital people or investigate the denial of this fact in the hospital, despite the contradictory eye witness accounts of fake beards.

It has been about a month and a half since the tragic Jaipur blasts, yet the police is not any wiser. According to the *Times of India* (27th June 2008) "...But as days have passed, suspect sketches, clues and leads once touted as vital have proved worthless and loudly proclaimed theories proved thin. Rajasthan police went on a manhunt in the city's shanties where Bangladeshi immigrants are holed up. They came back empty handed." It also adds that "Investigators are not ready to name HuJI as a definite suspect any more and only say its role and that of some Pakistan based terror outfits have not been ruled out."

The fate of other bomb explosions is no different. The Hyderabad Mecca Masjid blast is being probed by the CBI for almost a year now and nothing concrete has emerged.

Would it be proper to assume that the police or the security establishment have simply decided that after some perfunctory attempts following such incidents they should just move on, leaving a spate of cases unresolved?

In fact, there is an urgent need to transcend the habit of stigmatising or criminalising a particular community for all the ills of our society and to go beyond the stereotyped branding of terrorism. Perhaps it is necessary to ask those questions which have not been asked so far.

For some time now many Urdu papers have been voicing suspicions on involvement of Israeli-US agents in some terrorist actions. Given the proximity of the Hindutva lobby with Israel, it is also being said that secret Hindu terrorist organisations are receiving training in Israel. Apparently these Hindu organisations are sending groups of cadres to Israel for agriculture training. But it is being said that under the cover of this alibi the Israeli Special Forces have been training the Hindutva cadres on bomb handling and fabrication techniques.

The correspondence between a terrorist action and its likely beneficiaries need also to be matched. One thing is certain: such terrorist actions can only increase communal polarisation (although it is to the credit of the people that there have been no communal flare-ups in any part of the country after such acts, despite provocations from the majoritarian elements) and would help keep India in the US ambit. The US has already made a mess in the mid-east and would find it profitable to build a strong US-Israel-India axis in order to maintain regional hegemony. It views with suspicion all regional cooperation between India and its neighbouring countries, especially from the mid-east. It has consistently opposed the Iran-Pakistan-India gas pipeline.

Many commentators have written that the Jaipur blasts went on to benefit the BJP in the Karnataka elections which followed. Can it then be a possibility that some stray Hindu terrorist group at its own level executed the plan so that another member of the Hindutva family reaps its benefits?

VI

Any peace and justice loving person would say that the question of (non-state) terrorism needs to be revisited. While our concern about the growing network of *Jihadi* terrorism is justified and we should not slacken our struggle against its criminal, anti-people activities/ manifestations, it should be recognised that our approach towards the whole question of terrorism has remained imbalanced, or at best partial. One can cite incident after incident where the involvement of the RSS, Shiv Sena, or one of their affiliated organizations, can be clearly demonstrated in acts which are considered 'terrorists actions' in today's parlance. Today 'Islamic Terrorists' or 'Maoists' are the usual suspects in the eyes of the media or the intelligence people. The same can be said about the mental image of terrorism in the minds of most people.

Should we not remember what can be characterized as the first act of terrorism in independent India?

Most people would agree that the killing of Mahatma Gandhi by a Hindu fanatic, Nathuram Godse, constitutes the first terrorist act in independent India. Godse, a Maharashtrian Brahmin, was associated with the Hindu Mahasabha at the time of Mahatma's assassination and had made his initial forays in the world of politics with the RSS. It is now well known how the Hindu fanatics planned the murder of the Mahatma, and how the likes of Savarkar and Golwalkar were held responsible for creating the ambience of hate which culminated in the gruesome act.

If one adds to this similar other episodes in the trajectory of independent India--like the death of Indira Gandhi killed by her Sikh bodyguards, or the killing of Rajeev Gandhi who fell to a suicide attack by a Tamil Hindu woman, or for that matter the demolition of the 500 year old Babri mosque by the marauders of the RSS-VHP-BJP-Shiv Sena – and closely follows the debates and new information, one would realize that the 1984 'riots', (actually genocide of Sikhs mainly perpetrated by Hindu lumpen elements instigated by the then ruling Congress Party), the emergence of the Khalistani terrorists movement or the five year old Gujarat genocide, they all involved the RSS and its affiliated organisations.

Compare all these major episodes in the history of Independent India with the mental images that people have of them. You would agree that the dominant mental image identified with terrorism is of one or the other religious minority.

The question naturally arises as to why this is so despite the participation of the Hindutva organizations in many a gruesome incident, and the role played by them in instigating riots being exposed by many a commissions of enquiry, and despite their own admissions before the camera about the planning which went into the Gujarat pogrom (courtesy *Tehelka* sting operation). The Hindu fanatic who doubles up as terrorist has not penetrated our consciousness or become part of our social common sense. To re emphasise, one is not being soft towards the likes of Lashkar-e-Toiba or Jaish-e-Mohammad, whose activities are definitely condemnable, but only asking, why is it that every terrorist act in any part of the country is attributed to the minorities, while other equally dangerous outfits belonging to the majority community are allowed to go scot free?

Perhaps there is no simple answer to this query. One will have to delve deep into our past, take a dispassionate look at the anti-colonial struggle and also the tragic phase of partition riots. We will have to discern the threads of our present, understand for ourselves the role of different actors and ideologies to find tentative answers. In a multi religious, multilingual country like ours the complexities are immense. We find ourselves in a situation where the 'communalism' of the majority community is easily construed as 'nationalism', while every assertion by the minority communities even on genuine demands tends to be given a 'communal' tinge. It follows then that 'terrorism' unleashed by the majoritarian forces is easily disguised as justified 'pent up anger' against the minorities.

Despite these odds, and that forces of hate and exclusion appear more organised today, we can feel heartened that there have been a number of occasions when people have shown that they will not fall prey to any divisive agenda.

August-October 2008

Malegaon To Modasa Blasts

> The write-up in the *Indian Express* (23 October 2008) says what human rights groups and other secular political formations had been saying, that the coordinated bomb blasts in Malegaon and Modasa was a handiwork of Hindu terrorist groups. Sources in Maharashtra Police reveal that they were allegedly carried out by Hindu Jagran Manch, an Indore based extremist group which is close to Akhil Bharatiya Vidyarthi Parishad – the student wing of the RSS.

The police revelation that the bomb blast that killed their little daughter Farheen and four other innocents was planted by Hindu terrorists is not going to bring back the smile on the face of Wahiuddin. Saba Parveen still repents that she sent her younger sister Farheen to Bhikku Chowk to buy some pakoras. Little did she know that she would never again get to see her 10 year old sister, a class V student, alive.

The blast at Malegaon's Bhikku Chowk, has literally shattered the family of Shaikh Liaquat Wahiuddin, Farheen's father, who lives just 100 feet away from the Chowk near the Kasbapada masjid. The father of three daughters and two sons, and his wife, saw all hell break loose soon after the bomb blast.

The couple fainted when they reached Wadia hospital and saw their own daughter, who had suffered severe burns in the blast, lie lifeless.

The latest bomb blasts in Malegaon have seen four deaths, when a motorcycle parked near the old SIMI office, which was laden with explosives, exploded, killing four people on the spot. It is worth noting that the people living in the vicinity of the Chowk had informed the police about this unclaimed motorcycle, stationed there for hours together. But the police did not bother to turn up and reached the place only after the blast.

It is not difficult to imagine the palpable anger which exists among people there with regard to the police callousness and the insensitivity of the administration. People of this town, which has significant numbers of Muslim population, have not forgotten the treatment meted out to them by the police and the administration when there were similar blasts in the city during their religious congregations, killing 40 people in 2006. Despite enough hints about the involvement of Hindutva terror groups in the perpetration of these acts, where a torso with a fake beard was also identified, ultimately it was some Muslim youths who had got booked for this crime, and they are still languishing in jail. A CBI enquiry, ordered after a great deal of popular pressure and intervention of civil rights groups, claims to have reached a dead-end.

In a meeting with Baba Siddique, the 'guardian' minister of Nasik, representatives of different Muslim organisations in Malegaon gave vent to their feelings of disgust and deep hurt over the developments. Angry community leaders asked the minister "You blame SIMI for blasts in temples, you blame SIMI for blasts in market places, you blame SIMI for blasts in Masjids. The latest blast has taken place just below the SIMI office. Now whom will you blame?"(*Mail Today*, Oct 3, 2008).

It is to the credit of the police officers belonging to the Anti Terrorist Squad of Maharashtra led by Mr Hemant Karkare – who was instrumental in nabbing the activists of Sanatan Sanstha and Hindu Janjagruti Samiti for the bomb blasts in Thane, Vashi and a few other places in Maharashtra (June 2008) – that they shied away from blaming some or the other Islamic terrorist organisation for the blast. Thanks to their professionalism they could apprehend the real culprits soon.

The perpetrators of the bomb blast, who had packed a motorcycle with nuts, bolts, nails, ball bearings and three kilograms of explosive material, near a mosque, below a SIMI office and at the time chosen by them – on the eve of Eid – had definitely had the local police and the ATS groping in the dark initially. The Hindu terrorists had also tried to hoodwink the police by putting some Islamic stickers on the two wheeler.

According to the report in the *Indian Express*:

> The breakthrough, they said, came when they traced the origin of the two-wheeler used in Malegaon. The vehicle used was a LML Freedom brand, although some of its parts had been cannibalized from other vehicles and the chassis and engine number had been erased.
>
> But with this brand out of production, dealer records and help from forensic experts led the probe to Gujarat, the sources said. The motorcycle was allegedly owned by a man with "ABVP background" there, while the attackers belonged to the Hindu Jagran Manch with its headquarters based out of the office of an NGO in Indore.

In fact from the beginning the police were sure of one thing – that the blasts in Malegaon and Modasa in Gujarat were a coordinated effort, as both occurred at around 9.30 PM in Muslim dominated areas. ATS chief Karkare had even expressed that the Gujarat and the Malegaon blasts were similar in nature.

In fact past such incidents show that bikes have been favourite instruments of the Bajrang Dal to attack Muslims. Narco tests of those involved in the Nanded bomb blasts (April 2006), which saw deaths of two Bajrang Dal activists, had clearly revealed that 'mysterious blasts' in Parbhani in 2003 and Jalna (2004), which involved perpetrators on bikes throwing bombs at the congregation and fleeing, were actually the handiwork of a terror module of the Bajrang Dal itself.

A detailed write-up in the *Indian Express* ('Hindu Extremist Groups on Radar In Malegaon Probe, Sagnik Chowdhury, 1 st October 2008) reiterated the line of thinking of the ATS officials as far as this particular blast is concerned. "A day after the Maharashtra police said it could not rule out the possibility of Hindu extremist hand in Monday's blast in Malegaon, investigators are revisiting the crude bombs that were planted in auditoriums on the outskirts of Mumbai earlier this year." The ATS is planning to question the activists of Hindu Janjagruti Samiti, Sanatan Sanstha and other stray Hindu extremist organisations for their possible involvement in the act. The 1020 page charge sheet filed by the ATS in September against the members of these organisations for their terrorist acts is an added reminder for it to pursue the case in a balanced manner.

A deeper analysis of terror strikes since 2006 also reveals that there are at least five such terror strikes which targeted minorities and their religious places and they still remain unresolved. A report filed by Aman Sharma (*Mail Today*, October 3, 2008) provides details of these blasts and the status of investigations. The Jama Masjid blast (14 injured, April 2006 – Friday), where low intensity, crude bombs were placed in a polythene bag, is still pending with the Delhi police, and no outfit has been named. Malegaon (40 killed, September 8, 2006 – Friday), which saw four bombs outside mosques on Shab-e-Barat, where RDX-ammonium nitrate bombs in boxes on bicycles was used, still remains unresolved. The investigation in the Samjhauta Express blasts (66 killed, February 19, 2007), where six bombs were planted inside the Indo-Pak Samjhauta Express, has also not shown any progress, nor any organisation has been named. The case of Mecca Masjid blasts (11 killed, May 18, 2007 - Friday) where two bombs were planted inside Mecca Masjid in boxes, is also pending with CBI. The enquiry into Ajmer Sharif bomb blasts (3 killed, October 11, 2007 – Friday), where two bombs in tiffin boxes were used and where ammonium nitrate bombs were triggered by mobile phones, has also not made much head way. The case, still pending with Rajasthan police, has also not named any organisation.

Considering the kind of communal common sense that pervades in the functioning of the police and the media in our country it is difficult to predict what will happen next. The investigations into the recent Kanpur blast (24 August 2008) which saw deaths of two RSS activists, Rajiv Mishra and Bhupendra Chopra, while making ammonium nitrate bombs, is an example worth studying. While the police took two of their colleagues for narco analysis, it did not even bother to question their alleged mentors – one of whom happened to be a Professor in the IIT with an RSS background. Their colleagues – Sunil Dixit and Subodh Dixit – had (to quote *Mail Today*, 19 Sept 2009) "...even accused the police of treating the Sangh Parivar mentors of the two alleged bombers with kid gloves." They say "the ideological mentors of Bhupendra and Rajeev – Awadh Bihari, provincial general secretary of Vishwa Hindu Parishad and Prof Vishwas Kulkarni, a professor of Physics at IIT Kanpur and also the vibhag sanchalak of RSS, Kanpur zone – have not been questioned."

October 2008

Hindutva Terror in Karnataka

> A Karnataka dacoit with links to a radical Hindu rightwing group has confessed to having carried out the Hubli district court bombing of May10, 2008.
>
> The blast took place as the first phase of polling for the Karnataka Assembly elections was on – in a magistrate's courtroom where cases against top SIMI leaders including Safdar Nagori were scheduled to be heard two days later. ('Dacoit with Hindu Outfit links behind Hubli blast', *Indian Express*, January 13, 2009)

Does anybody remember the bomb blasts in Hubli (Karnataka, May 2008) courts last year when preparations were on for the coming state assembly elections? These blasts which took place on a holiday did not witness any casualty although they extensively damaged the court premises. But the most important part played by these blasts was the atmosphere it created in favour of the BJP.

As it always happens after such mysterious blasts, many innocents belonging to the minority community were illegally detained and quite a few among them also booked for their 'role' in the blasts. The police had promptly claimed that 'sleeper cells belonging to LeT and SIMI' had executed the blasts.

One still remembers how the Sangh Parivar had tried to exploit the bomb blasts in its favour. The former Deputy Prime Minister, LK Advani, had even used the bomb blasts case to attack the Congress-led UPA government at the centre for 'soft-pedalling the issue concerning terror' and holding it responsible 'for the increase in terrorist activities in the country'.

The Hubli Bar Association had followed the example of several other bar associations in different parts of the country by immediately passing the 'unanimous' resolution that they would not defend any 'terrorists' supposed to be involved in the blasts. And when a conscientious lawyer named Ibrahim Jalagir tried to file a bail application on behalf of the detained he faced organised attack. His office was vandalised and he along with his colleague were badly beaten by these hoodlums.

Now, when the BJP government is firmly in the saddle and the accused in the bomb blasts case have already spent months behind jails, has come news which is certainly not soothing to the ears of the saffron commanders. The IGP of North Karnataka, Ragavendera Auradhkar, recently addressed a press conference telling the media that the mysterious bomb blasts which had struck the Hubli courts last year were the handiwork of a criminal gang led by one Nagraj Jambagi.

According to the IGP it was the same team which had planted a bomb on the Belgaum-Hubli highway last year. However, this bomb had failed to explode as it was raining heavily. After high drama, the bomb squad had finally retrieved the bomb. In fact Nagraj had also led a gang involved in seven murder cases in North Karnataka and several cases of abduction. Interestingly the police had stumbled upon this gang while investigating the murder of a Bagalkot businessman.

Reporting about the incident, *Mail Today* writes (13 Jan 2009):

> Hindutva terror has struck Karnataka. The Karnataka police arrested nine persons with Sangh Parivar links for allegedly setting off a bomb in the court of the junior first class magistrate in Hubli May 2008. They were also accused of planting a live bomb on the Dharwad-Belgaum road. This points to the presence of Hindutva terror suspects in the state.
>
> The police had initially blamed SIMI for both the Hubli court blast and the planting of the live bomb.

Police have also seized live bombs, gun powder, lethal weapons, Rs 11.08 lakh in cash, gold, silver and two motorbikes from them. Apart from Nagaraj Jambagi (24), a resident of Heggur Plot in Bilagi taluk, the arrested persons include Ramesh Pawar (24), Basavaraj Diggi (22), Manjunath Binjawadagi (19), Deepak Govindakar (28), Lingaraj Jalgar (24) – all from Bagalkot; Basavaraj Rugi (20) of Honakuppi village in Gokak taluk; Hanamanth Sainasakali (22), and Channabasappa Hunasagi (35) of Indi taluk in Bijapur.

Although the police are not forthcoming about the political connections of the group, or in sharing the important information about its alleged Sri Ram Sena connections, anyone familiar with the Hubli-Dharwad region would have many other details about the gang of criminals, their political affiliations and their other deeds.

Many residents of Bagalkot have been witness to the *Trishul Deekshe* ceremony in the area wherein many of the arrested had wholeheartedly participated. For the uninitiated it may be told that VHP international secretary Praveen Togadia had popularised this trident-wielding programme as part of mobilising Hindus. Nagaraj Hollbasappa Jambagi, the gang's leader, has also been closely associated with Sri Ram Sene (SRS), a 'saffron front'.

A social worker from Hubli told *Mail Today* (Jan 13, 2009) that the '[b]ombings were part of an effort to set up a militant Hindutva organisation.' "Jambagi is the right hand man of SRS chief Pramod Mutalik (known as Karnataka's Togadia), who is setting up a Rashtra Raksha Army. He does not believe in the police or the armed forces. His people are given weapons training. There are several such groups here. They had a five-day training camp in Koodala Sangama recently."

It may be known that Pramod Mutalik happened to be the former Convener of the South India Unit of the Vishwa Hindu Parishad and of the Bajrang Dal. He was dismissed in 2005-06 following inflammatory speeches made by him on the Baba Budan Giri issue and is presently the founder and National President of the Rashtriya Hindu Sena and of the Shreerama Sene, active in Karnataka. Mutalik had recently affiliated himself with the Shiv Sena of Bal Thackeray.

A few months ago when Karnataka witnessed anti-Christian violence Shreerama Sene had publicly claimed credit for the attacks and desecrations of Christian churches, schools and convents, and thereafter for the attacks on protesting Christian youth, women and children.

This open violence had led to Christians blocking the streets in protest against police complicity and inaction against the fanatics.

The dilly-dallying on the part of the administration has also led to a strong demand 'to arrest the National President of SRS Pramod Mutalik'.('Hubli court blast: Demand to arrest Shri Ram Sena chief', SO News service, Tuesday, 13 January 2009):

> Koppal: There was a strong demand in Koppal by All Progressive Confederation (Pragati Sanghatana) demanding the state to arrest the National president of Shri Ram Sena, Pramod Mutalik, immediately whose organisation is responsible for the blasts carried out in Hubli court.
>
> Speaking on the occasion, the State president of Karnataka Sauharda Vedike, Basavraj Suli Bhavi, said that Pramod Mutalik is responsible for creating an atmosphere of disharmony and hatred in the state. He is a liability in a peaceful state and his organization can cause a lot of harm in the society. His organization is involved in Hubli court blast and a failed attempt to blast the NH Bridge in Dharward. It is very much possible that the Shri Ram Sena is positively involved in this.
>
> He also expressed his anger that only the activists are arrested and not the chief of the Shri Ram Sena. It should be noted that Pramod Mutalik was an activist of Bajrang Dal earlier, and later he left that organisation to form Shri Ram Sena. He also had declared that he will form a suicide bomber squad for which he has already enrolled many of them.

With pressure building for his arrest, Pramod Mutalik has flatly denied any knowledge of Jambagi and his gang. Much on the lines of his Sangh veterans, who were put on the defensive when their links with Sadhvi Pragya and others in the Malegaon bomb blast case became apparent, he declared that this gang does not hold SRS membership, although he promised legal aid to the accused. It is of course known that none of the organizations of the Sangh Parivar network maintain membership registers, a factor that enables them to dissociate the 'parent organisation' from any wrong doings by members of associated organizations. Pramod Mutalik was simply following this practice, although he was ready to 'start an agitation to defend them'.

Indian Express (13 Jan 2009) says that, according to IGP Auradkar, Jambagi had procured the bombs from one Hanumant Sainsakali, a 22 year old technical diploma student from Indi on the Maharashtra border. It is worth noting that investigations in the aftermath of the bomb blasts in the Hubli courts had shown that the bomb was similar to the one used in the May 18, 2007 blast at Hyderabad's Mecca Masjid.

One needs to also remember that when the Malegaon investigations began the involvement of Hindutva terrorists in similar incidents had also come under scanner. The Mecca Masjid blasts, as well as the blasts in Samjhauta Express which had remaind unsolved, were further investigated. Although, initially, the ATS Maharashtra had not found any connection between the Karnataka and Malegaon blasts, as of now there seems to be a qualitative change in the picture. A Karnataka connection to the Malegaon blast is also being explored.

As we go to the press a team from ATS, Maharashtra is camping in Karnataka to hunt for one Pravin Mutalik. A report filed by a reporter of the *Times of India* tells us that (*TOI*, January 18, 2009, 'ATS team in Karnataka to nab suspect') Mutalik could be 'one of the three bomb planters in the Malegaon case.' It quotes the ATS: "As per our investigation Mutalik was very much present in Malegaon along with wanted accused Ramji Kalangasara and Sandeep Dange." Mutalik has been termed as technical expert.

There is no denying that Hubli, which is a small town situated 425 km northwest of Bangalore, and which has been famous for many stalwarts of Hindustani and Karnataka classical music living in its environs, is a pale image of what it has been. No lover of classical music would have imagined that a day would come when they would be witness to music of a different kind.

As things stand Huballi (Hubli's new name, the name Hubballi literally means "Hu" – flower and "Balli" – creeper in Kannada.) has become a strong link in the emerging pan Indian network of Hindutva terror.

2009

Between 'Spiritual' and 'Criminal'

Kiritbhai, a famous religious preacher, recently found himself embroiled in a controversy of his own making.

Forget his long speeches laced with religious songs and the devotees getting all exhilarated. This time it was the turn of Kiritbhai himself to listen to music albeit of a different kind.

It was ironic how he rushed to the Bombay police complaining of the fraud committed on him by a couple calling themselves Jhunjhunwalas. In his complaint to the police the religious preacher is reported to have told them that this fraudster couple won his confidence and then took a loan from him and just vanished.

It was the turn of the police officers to be amazed when they discovered that Kiritbhai, who preached a life of simplicity and a turn away from the 'material world' had loaned 35 million rupees to the fraudster couple. This was no small amount and it seems they duly alerted the Income Tax people to find out for themselves the source of this income

As things stand today while the Bombay police is trying to locate the fraudster couple, the income tax people have also become active! For the Income Tax sleuths the query is simple: how come a religious preacher with no recognisable source of income, and who preaches virtues of a spartan life, could amass wealth to the tune of crores which could be loaned at interest? And if one were to believe a section of the media Kiritbhai seems to have become incommunicado. When *News Today* a Hindi eveninger from Indore (March 30, 2008) tried to contact Kiritbhai to know his version of the chain of events, he refused to talk on the issue and claimed that he was 'right now in Bengal'.

If Kiritbhai had not rushed to the police and had decided to maintain silence on the 'fraud committed on him', nobody would have been any wiser on the role monies play in the spiritual world of jet riding sadhus and globe trotting *Bapus*.

Of course, considering how cases against the high and the mighty are hushed up it is not difficult to predict what would happen next in this particular case. One fine morning one may hear that Kiritbhai himself has 'decided' (or one should say been 'advised') to withdraw the case to save himself from further embarrassment claiming that it was a pure case of miscommunication.

Our recent past saw a similar case of cover up when *CNN-IBN* and *Cobrapost* had aired an expose which showed godmen laundering money, in the name of God, all for a commission (*CNN-IBN* Posted Monday, May 7, 2007 at 08:11). The government had then even promised 'swift and strict' action in this case which had shocked the entire country. Ramvilas Vedanti, Chairman of the Ramjanmabhoomi trust in Ayodhya, who is famous for making inflammatory speeches against Muslims and the secular fraternity, had appeared as a past master of money laundering and tax evasion in the sting operation. He even shared the secret with the interviewer that he had formed a separate trust to facilitate his work of converting black money to white money for a commission.

Since it was time for the UP elections and some of the godmen -who were caught on the camera – had never tried to hide their proximity to the Hindutva brigade, the expose had obviously assumed political overtones. To offset the damage to its image, the BJP had questioned the authenticity of the sting operation, while the VHP had as usual raised the pitch that Hindus were being victimised.

> Titled 'Godmen turn Conmen, Taxman red' a write up on the group website had provided details of the sting operation. (*CNN-IBN* Posted Sunday, May 6, 2007 at 20:30 Updated Monday, May 7, 2007 at 02:00)
>
> New Delhi: Spiritual gurus, *babas*, Godmen – they are known by many names and are often the repository of a collective religious faith in India.

> But the faith has been maligned and many who claim to be God men, promising to rid lives of evil are nothing short of evil themselves.
>
> After a *CNN-IBN-Cobra Post* investigation revealed the ugly side of some of the most popular Godmen, sharp reactions have been pouring in.
>
> The investigation caught these gurus – Pilot Baba, a former Indian Air Force officer, Vedanti Maharaj, former BJP MP and Guruvayur Surya Namboodiri, who claims to be an astrologer – on camera and showed how they used their positions to launder money by bargaining like experienced conmen.
>
> The Vishwa Hindu Parishad – to which Vedanti owes his affiliation – seemed eager to distance itself from the baba. VHP Vice President Giriraj Kishore said Vedanti was not a part of the VHP and also blamed the media.
>
> "People like Vedanti are not worthy of being a part of VHP. Also, I think a section of the media is out to malign us. Otherwise what was the need of Shankaracharya being arrested? All this is being done to bring bad name to Hindus. This has nothing to do with religion. Vedanti is not part of any organisation," Kishore said.

As to bringing these Godmen under law, it was clear that criminal proceedings could have been initiated against them. In a tete with the CNN-IBN correspondent Shiv Pujan Jha spoke with the former income tax commissioner Vishwabandhu Gupta. Mr Gupta had strongly emphasised on bringing these Godmen under the law. According to him it was a

> ...[f]it case for criminal proceedings. Two of the biggest religion mafias are the Ram Janmabhoomi Nyas and the Vishwa Hindu Parishad amongst the Hindus. They have 10 bogus trusts floated from the same address. The names are there (in our record) and so are the addresses. They are getting money from 50 countries abroad and are also getting tax exemptions. There are no accounts as well. You see, this is a big menace. We have calculated and found that religious leaders annually earn $3 bn which is about Rs 10,000 crore-Rs 15,000 crore worth of money. What they do is they get land at throwaway prices. During the last government, 11 including that Sadhvi Ritambhara – whatever her

> qualifications are – got a fantastic (sic) piece of land at a throwaway price for the services that she heads today. They have fraudulent names, addresses, existences and expenditures. They use it for spreading communal hatred. Money has been used by Bajrang Dal cadres in Gujarat to purchase Motorola, we have got receipts for that. *(See:* CNN-IBN Posted Sunday, May 06, 2007 at 20:30 Updated Monday, May 7, 2007 at 02.00)

On the dilly-dallying by the state over this expose, Brinda Karat, leader of CPI (M), had demanded action against the seven godmen who had 'admitted involvement in havala operations on a television programme' (*The Hindu*, 26 May 2007). In a letter sent to Home Minister Shivraj Patil she had categorically said: "These gentlemen run Trusts and charitable foundations which are used as cover for their nefarious and illegal activities. They have cynically misused and made a mockery of the faith of those who have become their devotees. They have made crores through a racket of helping tax evaders. But equally important, the routes they have provided for conversion of black money into white can easily be used [by] terrorist organisations and anti-national elements to fund their activities".

History bears witness to the fact that no action was taken against the erring 'Godmen' despite strong prima facie evidence against them.

Perhaps friends of Kiritbhai may ask the government to emulate the approach adopted last year.

April 2008

More on Character Builders

> *Na taala toota na tijori, Phirbhi BJP mukhyalaya se dhai karod chori* (Neither the lock was broken nor the safe, Still 2.5 crore rupees were stolen from the Party headquarters.) A SMS which was circulated widely in the journalist community.

What is the weight of 2.5 crore rupees if one decides to have the whole amount packed in the denomination of Rs 1, 000 notes? It is exactly 31 kilograms.

Please do not get surprised by my correct reply. I just wanted to share a few details of the 'theft' at the head office of the main opposition party, namely BJP, which have appeared in different newspapers.

According to the treasurer of the party there is no cause for worry and only when the 'ankeshan" (auditing) is over would it be possible to say anything definite on it. The latest news is that the amount supposedly missing from the coffers has been reduced, without any explanation of course.

From a recap of the reports one can say that only the notes of Rs 1,000 denomination have been found missing from the party's treasury. The notes of Rs 500 denomination have been left untouched. Certainly this is not a matter that the chartered accountant or any of her/his assistants can deliberate upon or throw light on. The only sane advice they can give to the party would be to call the police and get the 'missing' amount traced.

It is also learnt that the party has roped in private detectives to solve the case. The only meaning one can derive from this fact is that the party itself does not believe in the version presented by the treasurer and would prefer to find out the truth on its own. Perhaps the best way would have been to entrust the job to any federal investigating agency, which would also have helped dispel any misgivings about the lack of transparency in the party. But one is sure this is not going to happen.

Another notable feature of the 'theft' is that it was leaked to the press by some insiders. Why would insiders of a 'party with difference' engage in leaking secret information to the outside world, particularly such information as would bring the party in further disrepute? They could of course be some very genuine people who want to clear the 'Augean stables' at great risk to the reputation of the party, or they could be an 'aggrieved party'--people left to defend themselves after the 'vanishing act' of the notes.

Whichever the case, the 'theft' at the party headquarters has left many people red faced and the top bosses were compelled to cancel/ postpone an urgent meeting. The theft has once again brought into sharp public focus the inability of the BJP to showcase itself as a party that is 'different'. Recently in an interaction with the RSS, the BJP leaders were advised to behave like 'good boys who can behave responsibly'.

The whole episode of the 'missing' money has rekindled memories of similar exposures. The great scamster Harshad Mehta – who had mesmerised the chattering classes for quite a while with his 'Midas Touch' image – had once alleged that he had bribed the Prime Minister's Office to get his work done. One still remembers the speculative articles in newspapers accompanied by illustrations which argued that it was impossible to pack and deliver such an amount without getting noticed or caught at the high security gate.

With regard to this particular case people are asking that if the said amount really went missing why no one noticed a bag or packet of some 31 kgs. being passed out through the gate.

This episode reminds one of a similar incident at the party head office when the then President of the party, Mr Bangaru Laxman, was caught on camera 'accepting' a bundle of notes from an 'arms dealer'. He was also seen telling the journalist who was present there as the agent of the arms dealer 'to come with dollars next time'. There is no point in repeating the aftermath of the *Tehelka* exposures which demonstrated how defense deals are managed. Bangaru Laxman saw his unceremonious exit from the top echelons of the party with immediate effect and the RSS declared him to be a 'failed swayamsevak'. Later the party declared that Mr Bangaru Laxman was accepting donations for the party itself.

Of course as far as matters of financial wheeling and dealing are concerned, the involvement of people brought up in the Sangh tradition is numerous. While the world at large witnessed visuals of Bangaru Laxman accepting wads of notes from a fraudulent arms dealer (thanks to the sting operation done by *Tehelka*), it was also noticed that the biggest contingent of MPs who faced expulsion due to similar sting operations, belonged to the Sangh lineage. People who wear their Sangh lineage on their sleeves had no compunction in occupying land meant for Dalits for years together (Venkaiah Naidu) or making a beeline for plots at prime locations in Delhi under fictitious trusts. It is a different matter that the RSS still has the audacity to call itself an organization committed to character building.

The world has not forgotten why the ex-spokesperson of the RSS M.G. Vaidya (who is considered a 'think-tank' in the RSS parlance and expresses views which are still considered very much akin to the RSS patriarchs) had to resign from his post all of a sudden even as the NDA was in power, when media exposed the dubious role played by his son and daughter in law in a financial company. Perhaps the best such example from the Sangh hierarchy is that of Madan Das Devi, who liaisons between the BJP and the RSS. Tavleen Singh, a journalist said to be close to the RSS, in a signed article 'Rashtriya Swayamsevak Sangh' (*Indian Express*, 2003) had given details of Devi's son's involvement in the Petrol Pump Scam.

Interestingly, this 'moral degeneration' of the leaders of the Sangh Parivar is not a recent phenomenon. Balraj Madhok, a senior leader of the Bharatiya Jana Sangh, provides details in his autobiography on the lifestyles of senior leaders. In his *Zindagi Ka Safar*, published in three parts, he presents vivid descriptions of how senior leaders functioned then and how the top bosses of the RSS, namely Golwalkar, dealt with the issues involving moral turpitude.

Balraj Madhok writes:

> Some time back when I was the President of the Jana Sangh, Jagdish Prasad Mathur, in-charge of the Central Office, who was staying with a senior leader at 30, Rajendra Prasad Road, had complained to me that the leader had turned that house into a den of immoral activities Everyday new girls were brought there. Now water is flowing above our heads. So as a senior leader of the Jana Sangh I have dared to bring to your notice this fact. I have had some information on the character of the leader, but that the situation had deteriorated so much, I did not know. (Balraj Madhok, *Zindagi Ka Safar – 3: Deendayal Upadhyaya Ki Hatya Se Indira Gandhi Ki Hatya Tak*, Delhi: Dinmaan Prakashan, 2003, p.22).

He further provides details about Golwalkar's reaction to the whole episode. Madhok had discovered then that the senior leadership of the RSS was bent upon making this particular leader the President of the Bharatiya Jana Sangh. Discussing his meeting with Golwalkar, he writes:

> After listening to my talk he kept quiet for some time and then said –'I am in the know of the weaknesses of the character of these people. But I have to run an organization. I have to take everybody together, so like Shiva I drink poison everyday. (ibid, p.62)

The latest disclosure by Mr Shekhawat that the main reason for the reverses faced by the party in Rajasthan is that tickets were not distributed, they were sold to the highest bidder, has definitely made their task of projecting themselves as 'different' even more difficult.

Coming back to the matter of the 'theft' at the party office, a question needs to be clearly asked: If the party cannot manage even its own coffers properly, then how can it manage the coffers of the nation if it comes to power?

January 2009

'Hindurashtra' in Delhi

Protest by Hindutva organisations against construction of a mosque in Rohini Sector 16, Delhi...Prayer by the Muslims not allowed by Hindutva forces on 26.6.2009 and those who were coming for the Namaz were beaten up and chased back...Hooligans marched in the street to look out for Muslims... Women also participated in large numbers... Timely intervention by the police...19 arrested...Appeal to maintain communal harmony by citizens groups.

According to reliable sources, a piece of land was allotted by the DDA to the 'Dargah Islamiya Intezamiya Committee' for a mosque in the area in North-West Delhi to cater to the longtime demand of the minority community. In fact people from Rohini have either to go to Badli or Avantika, if they have to offer Namaz on any day. Based on reports appearing in *Rashtriya Sahara, Roznama Sahara* (27 June 2009) and others.

I

Wahid bhai, who is nearing his sixties, is feeling low since the last few days.

A doctor by profession, he is suddenly contemplating shifting from his own flat in Rohini to his paternal home in the Jama Masjid area. In fact it was only a few years ago that he had purchased this flat despite opposition from his other relatives.

To be very frank the recent developments in his neighbourhood have left him completely devastated. He had not imagined that many of his own neighbours – who were regular visitors to his house as well as clinic

– would raise slogans which were offensive to the whole minority community.

In this part of Delhi people owning allegiance to his faith – who were not in significant numbers – had to travel quite a few kilometres just to offer Namaz on special occasions. And during the time of Ramzan when people fasted for the whole day, it became more difficult to do so. Sometime back the government had agreed to the proposal put forward by a local organisation for a mosque and had granted a piece of land in the area. Many community members in the area had contributed wholeheartedly and a token amount was deposited with the government in lieu of the piece of land.

Wahid bhai shivers to think if the police had not shown enough alertness what could have happened on that particular day when people had gathered there to offer Namaz.(Friday, 26th June 2009).It was a mere coincidence that he was away on that day and had gone to meet his relatives in another part of the city. Although he had noticed how the Hindutva forces had become hyperactive to stop the construction of the mosque, it was beyond his comprehension that they would resort to violence. He was also told that the fanatic elements had also attacked a man in his own hair cutting saloon. And the most tragic part of the whole episode was that many youth from a poor neighbourhood, which housed many victims of the tragic 1984 riots, were also to be seen in the melee. The only silver lining to the otherwise disturbing situation was the manner in which a few ordinary wo/men stood their ground and resisted the lumpens who were attacking people, and talked of unity of all religions.

II

As of now there is calm in the area but it seems deceptive. Police is vigilant and is taking extra precaution but mischievous forces may again become active. Nobody can deny that they are keen to keep the pot boiling. It was no coincidence that a temple 'came up' suddenly one night on a piece of government land, near the mosque itself. And a 'bhandara' was also organised at this temple, supposedly to mobilise people. This temple was in addition to many other illegally constructed temples which have come up in recent times in the area (Rohini Sector 15, 16,

17 and others) by encroaching on public land. A few of these temples have even proved to be money spinners for their promoters.

For outsiders the manner in which communal forces have become active in a middle class dominated area of Delhi may seem incomprehensible. But close watchers of the situation know of the desperation in the ranks of the pro Hindutva forces when the results of the elections to the parliament were declared. To the surprise of all, this area which used to be a stronghold of the saffrons registered more votes to the Congress candidate vis-a-vis the saffrons. And thus, apart from the national context where the saffrons faced humiliating defeat, the sense of vengeance among them had an added local context.

However, can it be said that this is for the first time that Delhi has witnessed such majoritarian attempts to deny to minorities even the constitutionally guaranteed right to freedom of religion? It was only last year that a church in Delhi was attacked by the Hindu Right ('Delhi church attacked 2 weeks ago, cops mum', *Times of India*, 4 October 2008).

> New Delhi: The fanatical Hindu mobs have struck in the Capital. And the police has kept it under wraps. A good fortnight ago, a mob attacked a handful of Christian families at the Peeragarhi Relief Camp and demolished the frontal portion of the Christian prayer hall in the camp.
>
> This camp in west Delhi is barely 15 km from Parliament House. To this day, this group of Christians is holding weekly mass with police protection. The families say they are living in constant fear of local miscreants allegedly owing allegiance to "some religious organisations" who accuse them of carrying out "forced conversions" and threaten to "take away" their daughters unless they "mended their ways".
>
> The mob had struck on September 16. Despite repeated attempts, the community has not managed to get a FIR registered for what they call "vandalism" and police describe as "regular land dispute".
>
> Ezik Malik, the priest-in-charge of the prayer hall says that a day before the actual demolition, he had got a call from an unidentified caller saying that the roof of the hall had collapsed.

> "We promptly went to rebuild it when suddenly this mob of 500 reached the place carrying saffron flags and sticks. They started pelting stones that left six people injured. There were anti-Christian slogans and then they demolished part of the hall. Policemen just looked on. On hindsight I realised that they had damaged the roof to create a situation that could later be used as an excuse for unrest." He added that despite repeated attempts the local police station refused to lodge a FIR but gave the community protection.
>
> ...DCP (west) Sharad Aggarwal denies any religious angle in the unrest. "It was entirely a land dispute," he claimed. "The Christians were trying to extend the prayer hall beyond the boundary wall which is when locals objected. There was an agitation but everything was under control because we were right there when it happened. There was no demolition and we have given them police protection."
>
> The MCD, which is the sole body that can carry out demolitions, is not aware of any unauthorised construction here. MCD commissioner KS Mehra said he was unaware of the incident. A MCD spokesman, however, said that the police or anyone else is not authorised to carry out demolitions. "We carry them out and ask for police protection," he said.

A similar piece of news was reported from Dilshad Garden, Delhi when thirty Hindutva extremists had disrupted the prayer service of St. Sebastian Church on February 23, 2008 in Dilshad Garden. Fr. Antony William, the priest of the church had told the Christian Legal Association that they had prior information that local goons might attack the church, and had requested police protection for the Sunday worship service. However, the attack came after the worship service concluded and the constable had left the premises. The Hindutva extremists, who had been hiding in a nearby temple, came to the church and started shouting anti Christian slogans. The miscreants resorted to stone pelting at the vehicles belonging to the congregation members. Nobody was injured in this incident. The concerned police station was duly informed and a case was registered under Section 427 of the Indian Penal Code.

III

It need be noted that a day after the incident in Rohini, many citizens and political groups in the area organised a meeting to take stock of the situation and decide on an appropriate response to the machinations of these anti-human forces. They have already sent a memorandum to the higher authorities – signed by many residents of the area as well as few resident welfare associations – communicating to them that they do not approve of such actions by the fanatic forces to vitiate the atmosphere. They have also demanded that administration maintains extra vigilance so that these mischievous forces are not allowed to raise their head again.

The said memorandum can also be said to be an open appeal to all people/formations yearning for secularism and democracy.

Is it not high time we understand that the political defeat of the BJP in an election does not necessarily mean the social defeat of the ideas of Hindutva? And the recent developments in Rohini suggest that such forces can utilise every opportunity to polarise social divisions and capitalise on them politically.

One still remembers the famous poem by the legendary poet Gorakh Pandey '*Is saal Danga bahut hua, bahut hui hai khoon kee baarish, agale saal achchhi hogi fasal matdan ki*' (This year there were many riots, much blood got spilled, next year it would reflect in voting).

June 2009

Welcome Mossad!

> In 'The Real Trade of CIA and Mossad,' Paul J. Balles, a retired American professor and free lance writer says: "CIA in America and Mossad in Israel should have been prize winners as terrorists, because in dozens of situations around the world they have indulged their love of instilling fear in innocent people. If the bombing, invasion and occupation of Iraq were not terrorism at its worst, it is only because the death of 4098 Americans is a more important statistic than the deaths of hundreds of thousands of innocent Iraqi civilians." (Quoted in *Mainstream*, Vol. XLVI No. 48, Terrorism Inc.: 'Nexus between CIA and Mossad' by Shyam Chand, 16 November 2008)

The discussion and debate generated by the bloody terror attack in Bombay allegedly carried out by the dreaded Lashkar-e-Toiba still continues. While relations between India and Pakistan have reached a new low, the only saving grace of the unfolding situation is that the war of words did not transcend the level of rhetoric and the ruling elites of both countries showed wisdom in not precipitating the matter further. Considering the growing people to people relations between the two countries, and a significant section of the Pakistani people having expressed words of sympathy after the terrorist attack, one just hopes that relations between the two neighbours become normal in near future.

Of course, as far as Mossad- the notorious intelligence agency of Israel – is concerned, the terror attack had a very 'positive fallout'. One finds appreciative mention in the Indian media as well as in political circles of Israel as role model for 'being successful' in 'curbing the terrorist menace' within its own borders.

Interestingly, all these media people, ranging from the Barkhas to the Arnabs, have not bothered to find out how this more than fifty years old organization, formally responsible for intelligence collection, has in actuality been engaged in 'counter-terrorism', covert operations, paramilitary activities and political assassinations. One could say that this negligence is part of the general amnesia with regard to Israel's role in international politics. They do not want to take a critical or dispassionate look at its 'myth of success' vis-a-vis the Palestinian militants, nor do they want to know the extent of terrorism engaged in by this agency against the legitimate struggles of the Palestinian people.

It needs be remembered that Mossad was formed on December 13, 1949 as the "Central Institute for Coordination", on the recommendation of Reuven Shiloah to the Prime Minister, David Ben-Gurion. In March 1951 it was reorganized and made part of the Prime Minister's office, reporting directly to the Prime Minister. Mossad's former motto can be translated, in softer words, as "For by wise counsel thou shalt wage thy war" – a quote from the Bible (Proverbs XXIV, 6). To reflect Mossad's public 'coming out' this motto was recently substituted by another Proverbs passage: "Where no counsel is, the people fall, but in the multitude of counselors there is safety." (Proverbs XI, 14)

It is a marker of the growing legitimacy of Mossad that it found respectable mention recently when top industrialists from Karnataka met with Mr Yediyurappa, the Chief Minister of the state. The delegation was led by Ms Kiran Mazumdar Shaw of the 'Biocon' fame and the Infosys CFO, Mohandas Pai. The delegation met with the Chief Minister to convey their concern about the deteriorating security situation in the state. According to a report published in *DNA*, they were categorical in their demands: "AK-47s, grenades and other modern weaponry and equipment are needed. Military patrolling should also be arranged." The Biocon CEO suggested creating a well-equipped crack anti-terrorist squad in Karnataka. The possibilities of getting them trained by Israeli secret service Mossad should be explored, she said. (*DNA*, Sunday, November 30, 2008, 01:51 IST)

For any close observer of the bloody track record of Mossad this sanitisation of the agency was disturbing.

The changed ambience in the country vis-a-vis the infamous intelligence agency is no doubt due to the growing proximity of the Indian and Israeli regimes on the issue of 'counter-insurgency'. Apart from seeking arms it is clear that India also sought help from the Israeli Defence Force in Kashmir. A senior commander of the Israeli army Maj. Gen. Avi Mirzahi even paid an unscheduled visit to Kashmir '...to get an up-close look at the challenges the Indian military faces in its fight against Islamic insurgents. Mizrahi was in India for three days of meetings with the country's military brass and to discuss a plan the IDF is drafting for Israeli commandos to train Indian counter terror forces. Under the proposed agreement, the IDF would send highly-trained commandos to train Indian soldiers in counter terror tactics, urban warfare and fighting in guerrilla settings.' (Sep. 14, 2008 Yaakov Katz, *The Jerusalem Post*)

Again, only a few months ago Defence Minister, Pranab Mukherjee, in a written reply in the Parliament, had made the startling revelation about the growing military and strategic relationship between the two countries. In fact it was reported that India had concluded defence contracts with Israel worth $2.76 billion between 2002 and 2005. Looking at these figures it is apparent that Tel Aviv is the second largest supplier of military equipment to Delhi after Russia.

The logical fallout of the new found love for the Israeli regime, and the attempts to imitate its 'success' in reining in the 'extremist' elements, is that no section of the Indian media reported that Mossad was found propping up 'Islamic terrorist' groups in the mid-east.

Some time ago a 'splinter group' of Al-Qaeda was found to be involved in a terrorist attack in Yemen. As happens in all such attacks, innocent people were killed and property worth billions of Rupees was destroyed. With its efficient handling of the case, the Yemenese police was successful in nabbing the culprits. But police officials and the people in power were in for a surprise when they discovered that the splinter group had been propped up by Mossad, the dreaded intelligence wing of Israel's Zionist regime.

> A terrorist cell busted in Yemen last month after a suicide attack on the US embassy there had links with an Israeli intelligence agency, the

> state-run Saba news agency reported. The report, quoting an unnamed source, said investigations and data retrieved from a computer seized from the cell, showed there was correspondence between the Islamic Jihad group's deputy leader Bassam Abdullah Fadhel Al-Haidari and an Israeli intelligence agency. Dubai, Oct 8 (IANS)

The question naturally arises, was it for the first time that Mossad had propped up an 'Islamic terrorist' group? *The Week*, a leading newsmagazine in the subcontinent had done a special story way back in 2000 ('Aborted Mission: Investigation: Did Mossad attempt to infiltrate Islamic radical outfits in south Asia?' by Subir Bhaumik, February 6, 2000, http://www.the-week.com/20feb06/events2.htm) showing how the Indian intelligence agencies had nabbed a group of Islamic radicals in Kolkatta airport for their 'suspicious' looking activities and discovered to their dismay that this group was going to Dhaka on a special mission at the behest of Israel.

> On January 12 Indian intelligence officials in Calcutta detained 11 foreign nationals for interrogation before they were to board a Dhaka-bound Bangladesh Biman flight. They were detained on the suspicion of being hijackers. "But we realised that they were tabliqis (Islamic preachers), so we let them go," said an intelligence official. They had planned to attend an Islamic convention near Dhaka, but Bangladesh refused them visa. Later, seemingly under Israeli pressure, India allowed them to fly to Tel Aviv.

According to Indian intelligence officials

> *...[T]el Aviv "exerted considerable pressure" on Delhi to secure their release. "It appeared that they could be working for a sensitive organisation in Israel and were on a mission to Bangladesh," the official said. "The Israeli intelligence outfit, Mossad, is known to recruit Shia Muslims to penetrate Islamic radical networks."....*
>
> *"It is not unlikely for Mossad to recruit 11 Afghans in Iran and grant them Israeli citizenship to penetrate a network such as Bin Laden's. They would begin by infiltrating them into an Islamic radical group in an unlikely place like Bangladesh," said intelligence analyst Ashok Debbarma. The pressure exerted on India by Israel for the release of the men, and the hurry with which they were flown back suggested an aborted operation.*

> *Mossad watchers say the operation was possibly blown off by "unwelcome intervention" in a friendly country, and they decided to pull out.*

The 'aborted mission' in India reminds one of the 'Operation Susannah', better known as 'Lavon affair', way back in 1954 when the nascent Israeli state witnessed a power struggle between Prime Minister Moshe Sharret and Defence Minister Lavon. In an article written after the Mumbai terror attack, a south African scholar Saber Ahmed Jazbhay (*Media Monitors,* 1 December, 2008) provides details of the action by Jewish terrorists when they blew up British and American targets in Egypt. In fact

> [t]he intention was to blame it on the Egyptian regime headed at the time by Gamal Abdel Nasser but the affair was blown and the ring leaders, all Jewish were apprehended and a few were hanged whilst those who survived the usual prison ordeal were forgotten about in Egyptian jails. It was only in 2005 that the Israelis acknowledged involvement when President at the time, Moshe Katsav, honoured the nine Israeli agents who were involved. (For further details refer 'The Dispersion of Egyptian Jewry: Culture, Politics. and the Formation of Modern Diaspora' by Joel Beinin http://www.escholarship.org/editions/ view?docId= ft2290045n;brand=eschol view?docId=ft2290045n;brand=eschol)

Considering the long history of the dreaded Mossad in engaging in all sorts of covert operations, including exporting 'Islamic Jihad' of a certain kind, would it be asking too much that the new apologists of the agency revisit its more than fifty years old history and then decide?

December 2008

Can the Saffrons Bounce Back?

The BJP would bounce back in the near future much on the lines of a Shav *(dead body) metamorphosing into Lord Shiva.* Mohan Bhagwat, RSS Supremo talking to media in Delhi

There are rare moments in the trajectory of a modern democracy when one is witness to the apparent implosion, albeit in a slow motion, of a political party. Today, the right-wing Bharatiya Janata Party (BJP), the principal opposition party in India, which was yearning to reach the citadels of power just a few months ago, presents such a spectacle. With two consecutive defeats, in the 2004 and 2009 parliamentary elections followed by the factional bloodletting which is now reaching its pinnacle, the 'Party With a Difference', as it described itself, presents a pale shadow of its earlier self. It is a sign of the tremendous crisis faced by the party that, for the first time in its 29-year old history, the top leadership of its parent organisation, the *Rashtriya Swayamsevak Sangh* (RSS), had to recently intervene to put the house in order. Apart from the newly-appointed RSS supremo Mohan Bhagwat, a number of other senior leaders congregated in the capital to hold consultations with the top brass of the BJP to find a solution to its seemingly intractable problems. The latest news is that the BJP President, Rajnath Singh, and leader of the opposition, LK Advani, have been 'persuaded' to relinquish their posts. A search is on for possible successors.

In fact the expulsion of Jaswant Singh, supposedly for writing a book on 'Partition', merely a day after RSS Supremo Mohan Bhagwat's interview to a TV channel about curbing factional squabbles within the BJP, was an indication of things to come. Despite being one of the founders of the Party, who has held important portfolios like finance and external affairs under the Vajpayee dispensation (1998-2004), he was neither issued a show cause notice nor did the leadership of the party deem it necessary to give him audience.

As of now, the warring factions within the party – represented by the likes of followers of LK Advani like Arun Jaitley, Sushma Swaraj, Venkaiah Naidu, and that of Rajnath Singh – appear to have formally buried the hatchet to show a united face, and to keep the RSS in good humour. There are, however, enough indications that this will prove to be a transient phase, undoubtedly giving way to further factional fights in the near future. It is clear that in the currently unfolding post-Vajpayee, post-Advani scenario (two 'Swayamsevak' stalwarts who ruled the roost for more than fifty years), none of the second rank leaders want to remain embroiled in the latent intra-party power struggle. Ranging from Rajnath Singh himself to the likes of Ananth Kumar, Narendra Modi, Arun Jaitly, Sushma Swaraj, and Shivraj Singh Chauhan, the leaders have been found engaged in acts from time to time, which have impacted the party in a negative manner. The question naturally arises, what does future hold for the party? Will it be able to rise from the 'ashes', to quote Mohan Bhagwat, or will it crumble into a marginal player like its earlier avatar, the Jansangh. Ultimately, an accurate assessment of the evolving situation is possible only if we understand the underlying party dynamics leading to its present predicament.

Dissenters Unwelcome

It goes without saying that the roots of the turmoil within the BJP go much deeper than the two reasons – the party's consecutive defeats at the hustings and the 'free for all' which has ensued at the top – analysts are presenting. In hindsight, one can see that things would not have come to such a pass if the party leadership, including its mascot and projected prime minister, had accepted moral responsibility for the resounding defeat and relinquished their posts. Perhaps it could have paved the way for serious introspection at different levels, helping to reinvigorate the party.

Interestingly while the central leadership was allowed to go scot free for its acts of omission and commission, the same yardstick was not applied to the state level leadership. Anyone could see that neither LK Advani – who led a very personalised election campaign to reach the highest pinnacle of power – nor Party President Rajnath Singh – who failed miserably to steer clear of controversies – engaged themselves in serious self-criticism. Nor did they show any readiness to relinquish their posts or facilitate a real churning in the party. On the other contrary, the central leadership had no qualms in compelling state leaders to resign their posts owning moral responsibility for the disaster. Despite support of the majority in the state legislature BC Khanduri was asked to step down from the post of Chief Ministership of Uttarakhand, and Vasundhara Raje, the ex Chief Minister of Rajasthan is being pilloried to leave her post.

The BJP's two greatest weaknesses have been its inability to attract new social forces, especially the youth, to its side and its inability to project an accommodation agenda acceptable to other political formations. These are two sides of the same malaise: the party's failure ultimately to present an inclusive, forward looking vision in tune with the changing times. The party's inability to steer a course independent of the exclusivist RSS, which has been legitimising indiscriminate violence against the minorities as a kind of 'final solution', has also made its position more vulnerable.

Scholars, including Lord Meghnad Desai and Amartya Sen, have always entertained a hope that the BJP would one day remove the albatross (RSS) from its neck and evolve into a mainstream right wing party – in the mould of those in Europe – ready to function in a multi religious and multi cultural scenario. There is a resonance of this idea within the BJP itself, largely among the moderates or the modernisers. For them, it is important that the party appear to be putting aside 'ideological issues' which sound 'sectarian' and 'divisive' to focus on issues which attract the middle class and the young. They are essentially interested in the broad electoral alliances. Another section, in contrast, wants to show that the umbilical cord with the RSS is intact. Indeed, this group prefers greater intervention by the RSS in the functioning of the party, in the strong belief that the BJP should emphasise that it is a Hindu Party committed to Hindu interests.

Apart from this tension about identity politics, there is also a divide brewing on the direction the economy should take. Interestingly, a majority of the party members are happy to embrace the path of neo liberal reforms initiated by the Congress. Only a minority promote the Swadeshi agenda put forward by the RSS, but apart from the rhetoric associated with swadeshi there is little evidence of seriousness on that. Another little discussed aspect of the BJP's evident failure to attract new voters has to do with the public perception of its six year performance in government at the Centre, from 1998 to 2004, on issues of governance, transparency and accountability. Its image took a public beating when many of its stalwarts – schooled in the RSS mould since childhood – were caught on camera in sting operations accepting wads of cash [*Tehelka* Sting Operation, 2001; Cobrapost-Aaj Tak Operation, 2005.]. The irony of this, considering the RSS's regular paeans to 'character building', was not lost on the people.

Other factors have also contributed to the present chaos in the party. To begin with, there is complete absence of any real internal democratic mechanism to choose a party leader acceptable to ordinary party workers as well to the general voting public, although here the Congress is no better. In addition, RSS interventions to resolve complex leadership positions within the BJP contribute to increasing interference by the Swayamsevaks in its activities as well. The influence of RSS Pracharaks, who have no accountability to the people and have a 'Jurassic Park' mindset vis-à-vis India's future, can only complicate matters further. The increasing stranglehold of the RSS also stifles other voices within the party. The parent organisation has always maintained that the 2004 and 2009 defeats resulted from the dilution of the Hindutva agenda in the BJP. No dissenting voices are allowed on this issue.

Societal Woes

In this impending post-Vajpayee, post Advani phase, the party will be all the weaker with the loss of these two faces of Hindutva – one 'moderate' and the other 'hard line'. Indeed, the two leaders could have helped facilitate a forging of alliances as they did during 1998-1999, which brought the party to the centre stage of Indian politics. Is the BJP now condemned to remain in wilderness for the foreseeable future? Broadly speaking, there are two countervailing factors which could prove a blessing in disguise for the saffron party. The first has to do with the neo liberal economic reforms and its continuing impact on the broad masses of the people marked by their further pauperisation. The second has to do with the social, cultural and intellectual bases of communalism which still remain intact.

In India, with its billion plus people, the track record of the state as well as the civil society vis-à-vis management of such inter-communal conflicts has been rather pathetic. Forget the fact that the secularism enshrined in the constitution is infringed upon by various forces, the state itself is found to be wanting at various levels in dealing with communal flare-ups. With the ascendance of majoritarian formations on the national scene, violent conflicts on communal lines have rather seen a quantum jump, and alongside a gradual deterioration in the overall response of the state in curbing the same.

To understand the gravity of the situation one has only to glance at some old figures related to communal conflicts. 'Study by the Bureau of Police Research and Development, a Union Home Ministry body, says that between 1954 and 1996, almost 16,000 people lost their lives in 21,000 incidents of rioting, while over one lakh were injured. Only handfuls have been held accountable.'(Communal Riots, *India Today*, July 21, 2003).

As noted in an editorial comment in the 29 August issue of the *Economic and Political Weekly* "...[t]here is an inherent contradiction between neo liberal economic reforms, which continue, and the UPA's social agenda. At present this contradiction is well under control but can unravel at any point. The UPA's strategy of "reforms with a human face" will then come under strain and could engender conditions for the re- growth of revisionist politics. The BJP may be down, but it is surely not out of Indian politics for a long time." On a side note, it may be remembered that the earlier avatar of the BJP, the *Bharatiya Jan Sangh,* as well as the RSS, benefited greatly from the anti-Congress movements of the sixties and seventies, all campaigns which emerged on the issues of corruption, price rise and growing unemployment among the youth. A similar possibility cannot be discounted in the current context.

The Congress Party, which deftly unseated the BJP in the 2004 elections by stitching together a 'secular coalition' and has been able to pull off an encore in 2009, has never attempted to take the 'anti-communal struggle' beyond the *Sarva Dharma Samabhav* discourse. In fact, instead of adopting an uncompromising position on the issue of secularism to defang the hard Hindutva of the Sangh Parivar, it has had no qualms in rediscovering the virtues of soft Hindutva on different occasions.

Close observers of the Congress recall with horror how Congress embraced the path of soft hindutva in the eighties and thus facilitated the rise of the 'hard hindutva' forces. Whether it was the issue of Meenakshipuram conversions or for that matter the genocide of Sikhs in 1984 or the opening of the gates of Babri Mosque, supposedly to 'free' Ramlalla, one could discern the growing ascendance of the majoritarian forces within the Congress at the cost of secularism.

The meeting of the National Integration Council (August 2005) which was held after a gap of 13 years also underlined the fact that the government has yet to emerge from the mindset dominant during the past NDA government. The agenda papers circulated before this gathering in a way tried to peddle a convenient lie which is very dear to the Sangh establishment. They clearly stated that forcible and fraudulent conversions (to Christianity) are the main cause of civil unrest in tribal and other rural areas.

The manner in which the then state government led by Virbhadra Singh, Congress, had adopted a bill making religious conversions a criminal offence, and the move by the AP government two years ago to introduce the idea of exclusive religious zones around Tirupati and other 'sacred' places, all had the trappings of a soft Hindutva line.

It is obvious that no strategy for a reversal of the agenda for a communal and majoritarian construction of society and polity has been brought forward in this interregnum. No experts are needed to predict that without any perceptible change in the 'majoritarian middle ground' of Indian politics – a space marked by great expression of religiosity, emphasis on maintaining group boundaries, lack of awareness about blatantly communal events and minimal approval of minority interests, among other things – the material basis for the emergence of communal forces with a new vengeance will always remain.

September 2009

SECTION 2

Logic of Caste in New India

Silence of the Lambs
Untouchability and India's (D)urban Elite

Untouchability is abolished now and its practice under any form is prohibited. (Constitution of India, Article 17)

Despite the constitutional mandate, untouchability is prevalent in 12 states – Andhra Pradesh, Bihar, Karnataka, Gujarat, Kerala, Madhya Pradesh, Maharashtra, Orissa, Rajasthan, Tamilnadu, Uttar Pradesh and Pondicherry.

It is prevalent in a mild form in 6 states –Jammu and Kashmir, Punjab, Haryana, Himachal Pradesh, Goa and Delhi and in the Union Territories. (Maneka Gandhi in Parliament, July 1998)

To those aware of the the scourge of untouchability in India, details of the kind furnished by Maneka Gandhi before Parliament are not shocking. But judging from recent developments it appears that there are many, particularly among the more influential sections of the intelligentsia, who either do not know or do not particularly care about the persistence of such a nauseatingly undemocratic practice. There is no denying the fact that despite half-a-century of constitutional measures untouchability continues in myriad ways and forms. In many places Dalits, to date, are denied entry into temples or served tea in 'special' glasses in hotels and restaurants or are not allowed to draw water from government wells situated in areas where dominant castes reside. Dalit women are driven to prostitution through religious customs like the Devadasi system or are forced to do menial and 'polluting' jobs like scavenging as a hereditary duty enjoined on them by lowly birth. And it is a sign of the durability of this system that despite many superficial changes, partly under constitutional duress and partly induced by the compulsions of modernity, it has managed to maintain intact the core function of insulating caste purity from caste pollution.

Why does the need arise at this point to recapitulate these details of a system that pervades Indian society and violates the country's Consitution every day in numerous ways – a system which, in the words of Dr Babasaheb Ambedkar, imposed itself not as a "division of labour but as a division of labourers"? These seemingly well known facts bear urgent repetition precisely because of the reluctance displayed by members of the Indian intelligentsia and the government to use available opportunities to tackle a problem that shames the nation. The issue of caste apartheid or caste discrimination, especially dalit oppression, has now become the focus of attention as a possible agenda at the proposed Durban World Conference against racism, racial discrimination, xenophobia and related intolerance, to be held in August-September 2001 under the auspices of the United Nations. The conference has been timed to mark humanity's successful victory over apartheid a decade ago and also to chalk out a strategy to do away with the vestiges or remnants of a similar nature. This has given rise to a debate among India's intellectuals, activists and some politicians, about the inclusion or exclusion of the issue of caste oppression, and especially dalit oppression, at the Durban conference.

The debate has been going on at several levels and has raised questions of various kinds. One of the main disputes relates to defining the agenda of the conference. Whereas there are many who would like the conference to move beyond formal proclamations on racism and engage in serious discussion about discrimination based on "occupation" and "descent" as well, as part of the agenda of the conference, India has taken an intransigent position on the question of dalits. Although it is ready to discuss the Romas of Europe and the Burakus of Japan it has officially expressed strong reservations about the inclusion of dalit oppression on the agenda.

This position is at variance with the South Asian neighbours, especially Nepal and Sri Lanka. Both countries are ready to include caste oppression as part of the discussion. It may be noted that in Nepal, dalits in the mid-hills and tarai plains are said to constitute 22 per cent of the population which is about the same as the Indian figure. Nepal is candid in its admission of the problem. What stops India from doing likewise? What is even more intriguing is that it was India, an initial signatory to the Convention on the Elimination of Racial Discrimination (CERD), which had taken the initiative for the inclusion of discrimination based on "descent" at one of the earliest CERD conferences. In effect, India is backtracking on an earlier commitment.

The position taken by the Indian government is that caste oppression is an "internal" issue of the country. This has given rise to the second question in the ongoing debate, namely, what, in such social circumstances, constitutes an "internal" issue of any country and what is an issue that lends itself to "external" scrutiny. The obvious discrepancy between internationalising the issue of race apartheid, in which India took a vanguard position, and sweeping the problem of caste discrimination under the domestic carpet, as a matter to be dealt with internally, seems to have escaped the government.

This in turn has raised a third and fundamental point of debate: what constitutes a nation and what is the nature of the relationship between the nation and its citizens? Does national interest mean the interests of the broad masses of the people or are the basic rights and interests of some sections to be dispensed with in the interest of protecting the nation's dignity.

An unfortunate fourth point has also emerged in this debate and revolves around the peripheral and largely academic question of the similarity and difference between race and caste. That this point is being discussed at length, despite its complete irrelevance to the issue at hand, indicates the extent to which trivial issues are being used by motivated individuals to sidetrack the debate and mislead the ill-informed. A cursory glance at the draft documents of the conference makes it adequately clear that the issue is not as complex as it has been made out to be.

Given the vigour of the ongoing debate what is disturbing is that a majority of the Indian elite has adopted an ostrich-like attitude. Their unconscionable silence amounts to nothing less than tacit support for the government's specious argument that caste oppression as an "internal" matter of India cannot be raised in international fora. The silence is most starkly evident in the political sphere because it, in effect, represents the convergence of attitudes of the far right, the centrist formations and the mainstream left on the issue. Most political parties have by and large refrained from taking a clear-cut position over an issue which is linked to the real empowerment and dignity of fully a fifth of the Indian population – who, for thousands of years, have been denied that most basic right, the right to live like human beings.

Because of this abdication of responsibility by the more influential sections of civil society, it has been left to a minority – consisting of dalit organisations, some NGOs, and a handful of radical political formations – to question the government's credentials and commitment to the socially oppressed. This small combine has pointed to the stealthy manner in which the government has gone about dealing with the issue. It has kept Parliament in the dark, and it has not consulted the National Human Rights Commission (NHRC), a statutory body constituted by an act of Parliament. Perhaps it is the government's view that dalits do not merit parliamentary discussion and civil safeguards. This is how the government deals with an "internal" issue.

Increasingly, the debate over the inclusion of dalit oppression on the agenda of the UN conference is being dominated by the question of the similarity and differences between race and caste. Dalit activists have denounced the narrow definition of caste that dominates the sophist arguments of those who oppose the linking of caste oppression with race discrimination. Such definitional nit-picking is quite pronounced in the arguments put forward by Professor Andre Beteille, a prominent Indian sociologist, who resigned in May this year from the committee constituted by the Prime Minister for drafting India's response at the UN conference. According to him "Race is a biological category having distinctive physical markers whereas caste is a social category. The consequences of this will be to add more divisions in Indian society. We have enough divisions based on language, religion and caste, which we have to address. So we don't need to fabricate or invent yet another based on race."

This seems to be the position that India wants to adopt at the UN conference. Beteille's academic opinion that caste is not race can always be debated at leisure. What is important at the present moment is the simple fact that both racism and casteism are social categories with political ramifications. And this aspect of both problems does not afford us the luxury of leisurely debates. Beteille's stand also completely neglects the proposed ambit of the conference. The draft document of the conference specifically takes into consideration "discrimination" based on "occupation" and "descent". But Beteille is not the only one raising irrelevant objections. Professor Dheerubhai Sheth, a well-known political scientist, while noting, in the *Jansatta* of 12 June 2001, the benefits that will accrue to the dalits if the issue comes up for discussion at the conference, concludes by raising the spectre of the abolition of affirmative action if caste is equated with race. Leading columnists in Indian publications have also put forward similar arguments.

Why Internationalise Caste Oppression?

It is precisely because of the indifferent silence and the vociferous opposition that dalit activists want the problems of caste prejudice to be raised at international fora like the UN so that global pressure can be brought to bear on the Indian government to protect lower castes. This has become an important issue because of the actions and intentions of the Government of India. At the 57th session of the Commission on Human Rights, Savitri Kunadi, India's permanent representative at the United Nations, clearly outlined the government's stand that the caste system does not fall within the purview of racial discrimination. It was not surprising therefore that the organisers of a Global Conference against Racist Oppression and Caste Oppression in New Delhi in March 2001 had to face official wrath. The Indian government refused permission to many foreign delegates to participate in the conference. Doubts are now being raised in many quarters about whether the Indian government will permit organisations and individuals who have been championing the dalit cause to even attend the Durban conference.

In addition to all this is the long history of the Indian government's responses to international bodies on the issue of caste and race. From the document titled Perspective of UN Treaty Bodies on Caste, it is clear that in recent years United Nations Human Rights bodies have underlined the existence and persistence of caste-based oppression in India and many South Asian countries. They have also emphatically drawn attention to the fact that numerous national level legislations have failed to protect dalits from discrimination.

It has taken a long time for the dalit problem to be recognised so openly. Though India ratified the Convention on the Elimination of all forms of Racial Discrimination (CERD) in 1969, it was not until 1996 that the CERD Committee made its first explicit reference to caste-based discrimination, "untouchability" and scheduled castes. But the Government of India was quick to respond. In its 1996 state report to CERD, the Government of India took the position that caste discrimination did not fall within the purview of CERD because caste was not the same as race and the term "descent" in Article 1 referred exclusively to descent based on race. This was not an argument that CERD found persuasive. In its concluding observations on the Government of India's 1996 state report, CERD opposed this position stating that though caste may not be equivalent to race it nevertheless fell within its purview under Article 1 of the Convention.

According to the CERD document A/51/18 Donas339-73, "The Committee states that the term 'descent' mentioned in Article 1 of the Convention does not solely refer to race. The Committee affirms that the situation of the scheduled castes and scheduled tribes falls within the scope of the Convention." Interestingly, the history of CERD reveals that when the draft of the CERD did not include the term "descent" in Article 1, it was the Indian government which had insisted on including it. Today, the same government opposes the inclusion of caste based discrimination, in CERD and the World Conference against Racism (WCAR), under the term "descent".

There is an arresting lack of congruence between the Government of India's position and the views contained in the Constitution and the various commissions and committees of inquiry instituted by it. A statement released by academics, jurists and civil society groups after the New Delhi conference in March, demanding the inclusion of caste issues in the Durban agenda shows quite clearly how the Indian Constitution looks at the whole issue of caste and race. According to the statement, "...Article 15 of the Constitution of India which outlaws discrimination based on grounds of religion, race, caste, sex or place of birth, treats caste at par with race as a prohibited ground of discrimination. Article 17 while declaring the abolition of untouchability has in effect accepted the existence of caste based discrimination and its effect of untouchability as racial discrimination." Article 341 of the Constitution states that "The president may with respect to any state or Union territory and where it is a state after consultation with the Governor thereof, by public notification, specify the castes, races or tribes or parts of or groups within castes, races or tribes which shall for the purposes of this Constitution be deemed to be scheduled castes in relation to that state or union territory, as the case may be." According to the statement it can be construed that "...according to the Indian Constitution the concept of SCs is inclusive of the concept of race."

The March 2001 New Delhi conference also looked at a few of the judgements relating to discrimination against Dalits and inferred that many of these judicial decisions recognise caste "as a prohibited ground of discrimination not only at par with race but also as a form of racial discrimination. The different definitions of caste adopted by the several decisions of the Supreme Court of India show that for the purposes of treating caste as a prohibited ground of discrimination, caste is race in the Indian context [K.C. Vasantkumar vs. State of Karnataka 1985 (supp.) 1 SCR 352]... The 9 judge Constitution Bench in the case of Indira Sawhney vs. Union of India [1992 (supp) 3 SCC 217 at 714] defines caste in the following terms: "a caste is nothing but a social class – a socially homogeneous class. It is also an occupational grouping, with this difference that its membership is hereditary. One is born into it. Its membership is involuntary.' In another judgement the same Supreme Court described 'caste discrimination to be more atrocious than racial oppression'."

The National Human Rights Commission has observed in the case of a dalit atrocity in Devaliya, Amreli district, Gujarat (No. 14/6/99-2000) "... [D]evaliya is only a tip of the iceberg of the atrocities flagrantly committed with impunity on the Dalits in the country. Their total dependence on daily earnings is the root cause of their being subjugated to indignities. Due to education and marginal cultural development, when some youths either assert the right to equal treatment or attempt to protect the dignity of their person or of their women or resist the perpetration of the practice of untouchability or atrocities being committed on Dalits, they are often branded as Naxalites and extremists, they are implicated in false crimes and killed in false encounters." The observations of the NHRC echo the conclusions of various commissions and committees formed by the government from time to time to look into the cases of atrocities against dalits.

In the light of the unanimity of opinion expressed by various bodies of the state there can be no justification for the exclusion of caste from the agenda of the forthcoming UN conference on racism. If the matter has to be dealt with internally there have to be appropriate instruments and the necessary will to accomplish the tasks. Unfortunately, the existing instruments do not inspire confidence. There have been instances when the courts have been less than sensitive to the question of caste oppression. The judgement in the Keezhavenmani massacre (Tamil Nadu 1969) in which 44 dalit women and children were killed in cold blood by the local dominant castes as a punishment for demanding better wages is just one instance. The final judgement of the court in this first organised caste massacre in independent India is shocking. All the accused were allowed to go scot free on the dubious assumption that "...since they are upper caste people it appears impossible that they would have gone walking to the hamlets of the dalits." Given such an approach, by the government, consistently, and the judiciary, intermittently, it seems unlikely that treating the dalit problem as an "internal" problem will yield any meaningful progress.

It is necessary for civil society organisations to take the lead in placing the issue before the world if a government that makes so much of its contribution to South African democracy and the Palestinian cause looks the other way when 200 million dalits are abused and reviled within the country's borders. The forthcoming 53rd session of the UN Sub-commission for the Promotion and Protection of Human Rights ought to play a catalytic role in the emergence of such a campaign.

The 52nd session of the Sub-commission, which convened to prepare the agenda for the Durban conference, adopted a unanimous resolution recommending that "The world conference focus inter alia on the situation of racism, racial discrimination, xenophobia, related intolerance and ethnic conflict, and other patterns of discrimination such as contemporary forms of slavery that are based on race, colour, social class, minority status, descent, national or ethnic origin or gender, including topics such as: a) the link between forms of slavery and racial and other discrimination based on descent. b) the implications of multiple identities (race, colour, descent, minority status, national or ethnic origin, gender..." India was also a party to the decision of that Sub-commission's meeting. The same meeting entrusted an expert member from Sri Lanka to prepare a working paper on forms of discrimination based on occupation and descent with special reference to South Asia. He was also to identify those communities which suffered such discrimination, the judicial and legislative measures adopted to ameliorate their conditions, and make future recommendations. The 53rd session of the UN Sub-commission will be held in August to discuss the paper.

What will be the Indian representative's stand at that meeting? Can India transcend its alleged "national" interests and be ready to discuss its "internal" matter at a world forum with an open mind? Or will history repeat itself and policymakers and self-serving intellectuals continue to claim that letting others comment on the plight of Indian dalits will be an affront to the nation's sovereignty? Perhaps they need to be reminded of the words of Sarveshewar, the famous Hindi poet of the sixties, "...a nation is not just a map on a piece of paper..."

July 2001

Inverting Dalit Consciousness

...Here on the slopes of the hills,
Facing the dusk and canon of time
Close to the gardens of broken shadows
We do what prisoners do
We cultivate hope

Mahmoud Darwish, Palestinian Poet

Introduction

Gujarat Genocide 2002 – The 'successful experiment' led and conducted by the saffrons as a sequel to the tragic Godhra massacre has already seen more than 2000 deaths, lakhs of people uprooted from their homes, millions of people losing hope for a just and peaceful life, and a majority of more than billion plus population of the country getting a shock of their lives. And now with a highly emboldened 'lunatic fringe' of the saffrons itching for a similar showdown in other parts of the country, and with the growing communalisation of the civil society serving as a backdrop and the limitations of the secular intervention already visible, it cannot even be said that this was the last 'experiment' of its kind.

This 'first' televised 'riot' (if one goes by the popular parlance, otherwise essentially it was a genocide) has many other 'firsts' to its credit. It has not only helped erase the fictitious line which allegedly separated the 'lunatic fringe' and the 'moderate' elements within the Parivar, it also demonstrated a clear 'method in madness', an art[1] which these zealots have perfected over the years through many such not so glorious experiences. The only factor which can be construed as some consolation is that this planned and well organized violence against the minorities, by and large, remained restricted to the 'model state' of the Parivar, proving once again that the state government connived and colluded with the marauders.

Even if the embers have seemingly died down, the fire still smoulders. With a friendly government in power, and the Ayodhya time-bomb ticking away ominously, many more "Gujarats" could recur from time to time merely to ensure that this highly unpopular regime can polarize "Hindu" votes and sentiments to reap benefit in elections.

In Search of Answers ...

There can be no two opinions that the developments in Gujarat since the end of February 2002 have largely taken us unawares. All of us who swore by the common heritage of the different religious communities in this country, who upheld the secular traditions of the people, who till the other day maintained that riots were just misdeeds perpetrated by a gang of criminals only serving some unscrupulous politicians in league with some stray fanatical religious groups have a Pandora's box opened before us. It is a fact that neither did we foresee how the communal, fascist elements could 'perfect' or 'plan' the art and science of making a riot, nor the massive participation of people from all walks and strata of life in this bloody pogrom against the hapless minorities. Our failure appears all the more poignant when we remember that before 'Gujarat' was perpetrated similar frenzy had been witnessed when Indira Gandhi was killed, and again when Babri Mosque was demolished. The entire nation was plunged into the worst communal riots since independence. It appears all the more stark when we look back to see how 'Sikhs' were demonised as 'enemies of the people' in the early eighties, and how very glibly and subtly Muslims substituted Sikhs in these campaigns during the nineties.

Of course there are many other related questions. How did the 'land of Gandhi' metamorphose itself into the 'land of Godse', and how could Gujarat become a successful 'laboratory' of the Sangh Parivar for its experiments in 'social engineering'? Why is it that despite so many religious saints and *mutts*, ranging from Swadhyaya Andolan to Murari Bapu's hegemonising of the spiritual realm of the people, a significant chunk of the Hindu population collaborated in some way or the other with the marauders? How is it that a large section of the middle class not only supported the storm troopers of the Parivar when they descended on the innocent Muslims, but also had no qualms in participating in the loot and plunder of establishments owned by them? What prompted the women to participate in the pogrom at many levels and in myriad forms? Why is it that the more prosperous regions in Gujarat witnessed more violence whereas a relatively backward area like Saurashtra, and one of BJP's strongholds at that, was comparatively calm? What has been the role of the NRI Gujarati communities in the events that unfolded in their 'mother' country? Of course the most surprising and disturbing phenomenon in this entire episode has been the large scale participation of dalits and tribals in many areas in this 'retribution campaign against the Muslims'.

While appreciating the fact that quite a few academicians as well as activists are trying to come to grips with many of these questions, a point worth underlining is that somehow the whole phenomenon of the participation of the 'subalterns' in this pogrom did not receive the attention it deserves. Barring a few exceptions[2] and some stray journalistic writings, neither the participation of the dalits nor the silence maintained by a few dalit networks over this phenomenon has caused any significant ripples in the intelligentsia.

There could be many reasons for this. It is possible that the horrific nature of the unfolding tragedy has kept a large body of the intelligentsia hooked to analyzing the overtly communal politics being played out by the Parivar and its social ramifications. Another possible reason could be that many of the committed intellectuals might have simply considered the whole phenomenon in purely economic terms as is their wont and could have arrived at some simplistic conclusions not worthy of further debate and discussion. A third possible reason could be the 'absence' of the dalits as a category in theoretical frameworks of many of the analysts.[3]

It is not that there has been lack of information on this score which might have sort of made their participation invisible. Beginning with the controversial interview of the state chief of VHP Mr Kashiram Shastri, a well known Gujarati litterateur, to the cyber magazine Rediff.com many reports filed by various media persons thereafter revealed the role of the dalits and the tribals in this mayhem at many places.[4]

That dalits and tribals were used by the Sangh Parivar people in the genocide of Muslims in Gujarat is also borne out by the reports published by democratic minded citizens or organizations.[5] These reports underline the fact that in many a case where FIRs have been filed for the carnage it is the poor dalits and tribals who have been made scapegoats by submitting their names in the cases although they were not the only ones who participated in the riots, and were certainly not among those who planned or led the killing mobs. The local leaders of the Sangh Parivar or other local elite have seen to it that the names of the upper caste-class supporters are excluded from the reports so that they can be saved from getting implicated in the court cases .

Of course before elaborating on the negative role of the dalits and the tribals in these bloody developments in Gujarat some points need to be noted in order to arrive at a balanced picture. First and foremost, their role in the genocide was not an all Gujarat phenomenon and was confined to a few districts only. There were many instances when they risked their lives to save their Muslim neighbours from the marauders.[6] Rather they played a key role in maintaining a semblance of sanity in the otherwise dark atmosphere which prevailed when the Hindutva storm troopers descended on the streets. Ram Rahim Nagar, a large jhuggi cluster in Ahmedabad inhabitated mostly by poor dalits and Muslims stands as a towering testimony to the spirit of communal harmony which was precariously maintained despite agents provocateurs on both sides. Secondly, apart from the Muslims it is dalits who, as a community, suffered most casualties and loss of property in this tragic bout of killings.

It has also been reported that in tribal dominated districts like Sabarkantha, Dahod, and Chhota Udeypur which witnessed many a gruesome massacres of innocent Muslims, the tribals, despite being instigated to 'teach the Muslims a lesson', by and large abstained from sexual assaults against their womenfolk.

Even so the question naturally arises as to what prompted them to join the bands of Hindutva rioters? A report filed by the *Outlook* reporter (July 1, 2002) 'Poisoned Edge: The Sangh exploits dalit and tribal frustration to recruit soldiers for Hindutva's "war" rightly raises the question: "Of all the disturbing facts that emerged from the post-mortem of the communal carnage in Gujarat, the most baffling and alarming is the large-scale participation of Dalits and tribals in the rioting. Independent observers, researchers and social activists are agreed that their involvement was unprecedented. Never before was the divide between the Dalits and Muslims so pronounced and so violent. Even more shocking: tribals, who have little in common with mainstream Hinduism, brandished weapons, looted and killed as they violently avenged the 'attack on Hindus'."

Neo-militants: Dissecting the Dalit Psyche

There are basically three types of reactions which have to be looked into for understanding the participation of the 'subaltern classes' in this genocide. The first and foremost reaction is on classical lines which sees the dalits as lured by money, liquor and political prospects and used as jehadis by the Hindutva forces. There have been reports of rumours being propagated that the government itself had sent orders that the Muslims be taught a lesson, and thus the illiterate and innocent tribals were instigated and provoked to participate in the genocide .The images on television which showed police connivance in the whole pogrom added fuel to the fire. It is clear that this whole 'understanding' about their participation smacks of the inherent biases which the non dalits entertain about the 'incapability of the subalterns to exercise wisdom', which in turn further strengthens the well entrenched stereotypes.

The second reaction focuses on economic factors which helped deteriorate the harmonious relations between the dalits and the Muslims. In an article written in *Frontline* (12 May 2002) Dione Bunsha, while discussing Hindutva's growing base, dwells upon what labour researcher Jan Bremen has to say on this ". ..who attributes it to globalisation and the manner in which capitalism has grown in the State. The informalisation of Ahmedabad's workforce following the closure of its textile mills resulted in the pauperisation of the workers. Sections among these marginalised workers, mainly dalits, are part of the Sangh Parivar's lumpen elements.[7] A discussion with a famous trade union leader from Ahmedabad, Mr Dwaraka Nath Rath, also promotes this viewpoint.[8]

An altogether different type of reaction to the entire gory episode is provided by the likes of Kancha Illiah, a dalit-bahujan scholar. While acknowledging that a gap does exist between the dalits and Muslims in many parts of the state, he indirectly blames the Muslim elite for this state of affairs and asks them to make special efforts to bridge the gap. In his article 'Dalit, OBC and Muslim relations' (*The Hindu*, 29 May 2002) he has put forward this position in no uncertain terms. According to him "The Muslim intelligentsia failed to establish a rapport with the Scheduled Castes, the Scheduled Tribes and the OBCs at the ground level." He adds "…The Muslim intelligentsia must also be held responsible for showing indifference to the issues of caste and untouchability... In the case of Islam there is not only no investigative tradition, there is no social service tradition with a sense of social interaction before someone embraces Islam. Muslim intellectuals must learn from Christian missionaries and work among Dalits, Adivasis and OBCs so that a relationship of trust is established. All oppressed must learn to work for each other's liberation and build social bondages among them. That is the best way to prevent another Gujarat."

It is true that all these explanations while trying to depict reality as they perceive it are not able to unravel the complex phenomenon of neo-militancy among the 'subalterns' which prompted them to join the marauders of the Sangh Parivar.

These still do not explain what sort of real/imaginary interests of the subalterns were served during the unfolding dynamic of the riot-like situation which the fifty plus years of independence have not delivered to them, as they continue to live lives of poverty and ignorance, full of insult and humiliation, exploitation and oppression for a majority of them. Is it not surprising that during all these fifty plus years of history of independent India the dalits never once launched a similar militant struggle, and on a similar scale, to fight their subhuman condition? How is it that the same dalits who have been the target of all the casteist, especially the Hindutva, since the early eighties anti reservation riots in Gujarat have gradually found a common cause with them?

Empowerment of a different kind?

It is clear that these recent developments in Gujarat are a classic case of the submergence of the dalit identity in the 'larger canopy' of Hindu identity as defined by the Sangh Parivar. It is worth noting that this phenomenon of 'Dalit empowerment of a different kind' or the confluence of dalit identity with the Hindu identity has uncanny similarity with the aftermath of Babri Mosque demolition which witnessed large scale participation of women, especially Hindu women, in the riots and which posed quite a few uncomfortable questions before the women's movement. To quote Tanika Sarkar and Urvashi Butalia "...Politically and methodologically this assertive participation of women in right wing campaigns, pulled down many of our assumptions... in a state of crisis... for we have always seen women as victims of violence rather than its perpetrators ..."(*Women and the Hindu Right*: ed.Tanika Sarkar and Urvashi Butalia, Kali forWomen, 1995, p.3). Any sympathetic observer of the phenomenon of the Dalit assertion, which in the late 80s and early 90s, to some extent at least, acted as a countervailing force to the growing communalisation of the state machinery and civil society, is similarly baffled now.

A survey of the chequered history of Gujarat of the last 100-odd years, spanning both the pre-independence and post-independence eras, throws up a couple of facts which can be said to be symptomatic of Gujarat. The first and foremost of these is the relative absence of any significant social or cultural movement and the continuing dominance of the conservative wing in the struggle for independence. Prior to October 1960 Gujarat was part of a bilingual state, the Bombay Province. The two parts were separated after a prolonged agitation for the reorganisation of states on linguistic basis. Compared with the 'Maharashtra' experience the 'Gujarat' part of the then Bombay province did not have a strong trade union movement or a well entrenched social cultural movement. (A notable exception could be said to be the work of Swami Dayanand Saraswati, the founder of Arya Samaj, who was born in Gujarat. Of course one should not fail to underline the controversial role Arya Samaj played in its attempts at 'reforming' Hindu society. No sane person can condone the strong anti-minority overtones in its work and the essentially revivalist nature of this movement. It is another matter that such a movement also did not have any support base in Gujarat.) Certainly there are historical reasons behind this state of affairs but it is high time the role played by the different actors and players is also put under microscope. The manner in which the leadership of Gandhi influenced Gujarati life was noticeable. He had a multi dimensional impact on the polity and the social setup in the state. History is witness to how his intervention nipped in the bud the possibility of a militant labour movement when the historic strike of the Ahmedabad textile mill workers was on. The formation of 'Mazdoor Mahajan' based on his trusteeship principle proved to be the death knell for the nascent militant workers movement.

In Maharashtra, starting from the one led by Mahatma Jyotiba Phule in the 1840s culminating in the emergence of the greatest leader of the dalits Dr Babasaheb Ambedkar, taking up of issues of caste annihilation and the liberation of women as part of social-cultural movements, helped accelerate the process of rejuvenation and reinvigoration of Marathi society from within. The 'Gujarat' experience, on the other hand, did not show any turmoil on that scale. A cumulative impact of all these factors was that the task of restructuring of Gujarati society from within remained unaddressed, in turn leading to the growing dominance of various socially conservative forces maintaining their stranglehold over civil society in the state. With the marginalizing of the radical or socially progressive forces the situation became quite conducive for all sorts of status quoist forces to grow and branch out within different walks of life.

Of course this does not mean that there was no churning at all within the Gujarati society or that it did not exhibit any dynamism in its confrontation with British rule. It would be more opportune to say that it had its own specificities which gave its dynamism a different tone and tenor. A close analysis of the Gujarati society reveals the uniquely enterprising and the industrious nature of the Gujarati elite, evident also in pre- British times. Surat and a few other ports had carved a niche for themselves as leading trading centres even during the Mughal period. The arrival of the British gave a new fillip to this entrepreneurship. It is not surprising that even today there is a significant presence of the

Gujarati immigrants in the commonwealth countries in general and the United Kingdom in particular.[9]

But by and large even after the departure of the British and ushering in of the era of independence Gujarat could not make a decisive break with this unfolding dynamic. The early seventies did witness a strong student youth 'Navnirman movement' against corruption and nepotism which compelled the then Chief Minister of Gujarat, Mr Chimanbhai Patel, to resign However, that was last of the broad movements for 'secular' aims as far as the state was concerned. The status quoist and opportunist policies of the Congress, which involved the formation of a 'KHAM' alliance (Kshatriya, Harijan, Adivasi and Muslim), coupled with the counter mobilisation of the other upper castes and upper classes by the Sangh Parivar outfits in the state, resulted in the first anti- reservation riots of their kind in the state in the early 80s. The anti-reservation riots were of such magnitude that dalits were targeted in 18 out of the 19 districts in the state. It need be underlined that the Sangh outfits were involved in this targeting of the dalits. Dionne Bunsha in her article 'The Hindutva Experiment' (*Frontline*) rightly notes "…However, by the mid-1980s, the BJP changed its stand towards Dalits in a bid to co-opt them. Realising the largeness of the number of Dalits and Scheduled Tribe and OBC persons in the State, who together account for 75 per cent of the population, the BJP started attempts to unite all castes under the Hindutva plank. It corrected its anti-reservation stand and was able to reap the gains of this move. When riots broke out in 1986 during Ahmedabad's annual Jagannath rath yatra, the BJP managed to garner the support of the OBCs and Dalits. This marked a shift in its support base."

It is interesting to note that the absence of a strong dalit movement in the state (which in neighbouring Maharashtra had carved out a niche for itself in the form of the Dalit Panthers party and numerous dalit writers) made the task easier for the Hindutva forces who were making shrewd moves to co-opt the dalits. While Gujarat did witness the formation of Dalit Panthers, much on the lines of neighbouring Maharashtra, the 'panther experience' did not strike root here because of lack of conducive environment While the dalits in Maharashtra, especially its radical sections, had intensified their struggles against Brahminism and had been able to influence the social-political milieu in a significant manner, here in Gujarat the search for an alternate identity was through getting co-opted in the Hindutva identity.

Similar parallel processes could be seen unfolding in the tribal dominated areas and districts of the state. In these areas the Vanavasi Kalyan Samiti, one of the organisations belonging to the Sangh Parivar, has been active for quite some time. K Balagopal, the well known civil rights activist, in his much discussed 'Reflections on 'Gujarat Pradesh' of 'Hindu Rashtra" (*EPW*, June 1, 2002), rightly points out that the activists of the Samiti are engaged in 'hinduising' the tribals, and are gradually and silently becoming successful in directing their wrath against the Christians and the Muslims. In their case too one notices their search for an alternate identity getting co-opted in the 'Hindu' identity as defined by the Sangh Parivar, i.e., "in the specific hate- filled sense in which that term is understood by the Sangh Parivar" A Congress adivasi MLA is quoted as having said: "The search for an identity that has accompanied the growth of education among the adivasis has been filled by the Sangh Parivar". A (Muslim) Principal of a College explained the ferociousness of the tribals in these terms: "The new convert to Islam is always more ferocious in defending the religion than the traditional Muslim, and the same could be happening to the adivasis."(Both references *EPW*, June 1, 2002).

Conflation of Identity: Enter the Hindutvaised Dalit

It is a contrast of epic proportions that whereas the phenomenon of dalit assertion was making its presence felt in the national politics and had become one of the defining features of the polity of the nineties, the politics of 'hindutva' was worming its way into these oppressed sections in Gujarat. The submergence of this subversive identity in the cesspool of *varnashram* could be considered a slap in the face of the struggle for dalit emancipation.

Whereas the grammar of Indian politics was getting redefined by the contours of new aspirations of dalits and the other oppressed sections, the Hindutva forces were successful in not only skirting the real issues of social justice but also assimilating the emergent rebellious voices in their 'war cries' against the 'demons' in their' model' state. The decade which witnessed the emergence of a party representing dalit assertion (BSP) sharing power on equal terms with the BJP in the biggest state in India had as a countervailing feature the participation of a significant sections of the dalits in the project led by the same fascist -Brahminical forces in Gujarat. Analysts have noted with concern the participation of the dalits from Gujarat in the Ram Janambhoomi movement, including in the operation of the demolition of Babri Mosque.

The question naturally arises as to why those deprived and depressed sections of Indian society, especially Hindu society, who are condemned to live a life of subhuman existence, wanted to imitate their social oppressors and to prove that they could also be seen in the same image. The process of Sanskritisation, elaborated by the famous sociologist MN Srinivas, partially explains the dalits' penchant for becoming 'Hindus'.

The caste system, as is obvious, is essentially a system of social hierarchy based on the twin concepts of purity and pollution, sanctified and legitimised by religion. In relation to the whole process of social mobility there are only two options open before the lower castes. They can either reject or renounce the whole edifice of religion which sanctifies this system and strive for an alternate identity, or they can strive to climb the social hierarchy by imitating the way of life and ritual of the dominant castes. MN Srinivas rightly explains: "The caste system is far from a rigid system in which the position of each component caste is fixed for all time. Movement has always been possible and especially so in the middle regions of the hierarchy. A low caste was able in a generation or two, to rise to a higher position in a hierarchy by adopting vegetarianism and teetotalism and by sanskritising its ritual and pantheon. In short, it took over, as far as possible, the customs, rites, and beliefs of brahminism, and the adoption of the brahminic way of life by a low caste seems to have been frequent though theoretically forbidden.[10] Of course the attempts by the lower castes to sanskritise themselves have never been peaceful and there were often clashes between the upper and lower castes if the lower castes tried to sanskritise themselves.

The entry of the British and the changes they wrought in Indian society and the consequent fifty plus year history of independent India did open up possibilities of challenging the Brahminical system based on *varnashram dharma*. But as regards Gujarat, considering its peculiar trajectory and the overall dominance of conservative forces in the political as well as social-cultural spheres, it becomes clear that the possibility of revolt or rebellion against the Brahminical system and the striving for an alternate identity was already foreclosed for the dalits and other oppressed sections.

As evident from the strict hierarchy in the Congress and its paternalistic approach towards dalits, the aspirations of the newly educated dalit youth could find few takers in them. And, as opposed to the Congress, the Sangh Parivar with its plethora of organisations and the politics of Hindutva which suited their quest for an identity proved an ideal bet. And so when there was a churning in the various strata of oppressed sections, the absence of a strong democratic movement, coupled with the near total absence of a transformatary social cultural movement, facilitated the communal forces actions to make inroads in the dalit-tribal psyche.

The growing dominance of the highly regressive and reactionary Hindutva politics appears more striking if we consider the simple fact that Gujarat is supposed to be an 'advanced state' of the Indian Union, recognised for its progress in the economic spheres. It has a well developed middle class. In so far as foreign direct investment is concerned it stands at number two in being able to attract foreign investment. The enterprising nature of the Gujarati elite is also noticeable in that many of the *noveau riche* from the farming sector have made inroads in the urban sector. The dividing line between the industrial elite and the farm elite is getting blurred day by day.

Of course this elaboration of the dynamic Gujarati society would be incomplete if we do not focus on the 'other' Gujarat which exhibits the underlying social tensions not normally visible. Apart from the overtly visible violence, the invisible violence takes up myriad forms. The 2001 Census reveals that the latest sex ratio in urban Gujarat is 879 females per 1000 males, the lowest figure in the last hundred years. It is evident that in the private sphere, violence is being perpetrated within one's own family in the form of foeticide and infanticide. If one considers the sex ratio in the population category of 0-6 years here too the state of Gujarat has fared badly as this ratio has decreased from 928 in 1991 to only 878 in 2001.

Politics of Hindutva and Dalits: The National Context

It is true that the post Godhra 'neo-militancy' witnessed in a significant section of the dalits and the tribals was quite unique and had its genesis in the specific circumstances which obtained in Gujarat. It has been reported that a few dalit networks active in Gujarat did not find it fit to even condemn the participation of dalits in the pogrom against Muslims.[11] But can it be said that the 'communalization of the dalit-tribal consciousness' or the channelizing of dalit assertion for the Brahminical-Fascist project of the Parivar is specific to Gujarat alone? Sadly, it has to be said that the answer is a big 'no'.

Ranging from the 'clean chit' given by Ms Mayawati to the politics of retribution experimented by Narendra Modi and providing a helping hand to Advani and Co to save them from the Babri Mosque demolition case to the exercise in 'cohabitation' engaged in by the likes of Ramvilas Paswan till recently, there are numerous examples of dalit assertion becoming tied to the project of Hindutva as a result of political expediency. Few people know that Namdeo Dhasal, a leading dalit poet and one of the pioneers of the Dalit Panther movement in the early seventies, who even led the revolt of the dalit youth against the compromising leadership of the Republican Party of India in its post Ambedkar phase, is these days a leading light of the Shiv Sena. The activities of organizations like the Hindu Munnani in the dalit bastis of Chennai and the brutalisation of the Khatik community in Kanpur under a Kala Baccha (since killed) for use in the communal conflagrations during the Ram Janambhoomi movement are also part of the same process.

One could even say that the whole phenomenon of dalit- backwards assertion of the nineties, which helped check the growth of communal fascism at various levels, ended in a whimper with a significant part of this dalit-backwards swell submerging itself in the 'kamandal' politics. This despite the bitter fact that the Sangh Parivar never even made a pretence of disowning the Chaturvarna system largely responsible for the plight of the dalits, nor apologised or missed any opportunity to castigate Dr Babasaheb Ambedkar for his (according to them) 'pro-British' opinions. It has also opposed the policy of reservations under one pretext or the other.

One hardly needs underline the immense potentialities in the phenomenon of dalit assertion in today's caste ridden polity. It is undeniably a step forward in the democratisation of Indian society and has caused real churning in the polity dominated by Brahminical values and traditions still strong despite fifty plus year experiment in electoral democracy. The impressive intervention of BSP under Kanshi Ram in the national politics reflects this churning. The success achieved by BSP has certainly encouraged emergence of similar experiments in different parts of the country.

There are evidences also of another kind of groundswell among the various dalit castes. They are organizing themselves under the banners of their respective caste and sub-caste for achieving their rights. Consequently their guns are trained, apart from the Varna system, on the so-called rich dalit castes, or the creamy layer within them, as well, whom they perceive to have monopolised a large part of the reserved posts. The Mahar/neo-Buddhists vs. Matang and Charmakar debate in Maharashtra, and Mala vs Madiga in Andhra Pradesh are symptomatic of this rising trend. So much so that in Andhra Pradesh the dispute between the Malas and the Madigas, both listed under the scheduled category, gave rise to a militant agitation of the Madigas. The Madigas under the banner of Madiga Reservation Porata Samity launched a statewide militant mass movement for caste-wise categorisation of reserved seats in educational institutions and jobs etc so that extremely depressed castes which could not avail of the quota for historical reasons could avail of it now.

It is indeed ironical that at a time when the issue of dalit assertion has got acceptance even in the mainstream polity a counter tendency has emerged which seems to fracture their new found identity. One could also perceive the whole process as an explosion of identities hitherto suppressed by the hegemonic caste and class structure of society. In the beginning of the 70s the term dalit denoted a broad, homogenous fraternity. This is no more the case. If you just say dalit you are making an incomplete statement. It would be necessary to also specify whether he is a Mala or a Madiga or a Matang or a Charmakar. This process has thrown up new 'icons' from among the different castes and the sub-castes as well. There is also a danger of the old leaders who earlier claimed pan dalit status being reduced to their 'own' caste leaders. The emergence of

Avantikabai Pasi in UP or the famous author Annabhau Sathe in Maharashtra as new leaders of the Matangs underlines this ground reality. Incidentally, Mr Sathe remained a Communist Party worker all his life and was a leading light of the Progressive Writers Movement. Nobody would have imagined that in his lifetime he would be projected as the leader of 'his caste', and a saffron alliance in power would present his selected writings before the people.

It is worth noting that within the dalit movement, especially among its intelligentsia, there are three sets of opinions as far as alliance with the saffrons is concerned. One stream of opinion advocates such an alliance on tactical grounds and says that such temporary unity would be beneficial in the longer run. Essentially its argument revolves around the inherent contradictions between the upwardly mobile backward caste people and the dalits, especially in the countryside. They feel that at the turn of the 20th century dalits are primarily oppressed by these new kulaks largely coming from the backward castes, and that their alliance with an upper caste party like the BJP can save them from this onslaught. They clearly say that 'social fascism' (as represented by the emergent kulak leadership) is more dangerous than 'communal fascism'. They even turn out statistics to show the number of dalits killed at the hands of the kulaks in different parts of the country.

The other stream, while categorically opposing any alliance with the saffrons even for a shorter period, advocates that dalits should search for their 'natural allies' who, according to them, can only be the leftists of various hues. According to them the fascist project is essentially aimed at the restoration of the Brahminical order and nothing should be done to sanctify such a medieval project.

The third stream advocates equidistance from both 'communal fascism' and 'social fascism'. It talks of developing a strong dalit movement on its own steam, arguing this is the only path to becoming a key player in the polity.

What Next?

The 'successful experiment' in Gujarat has posed a challenge to all those who still believe in and practice secularism and are fighting for a more humane and just society at various levels.

The weaknesses of the left and other secular forces are evident and there need not be much burning of midnight oil trying to fix responsibility on individuals or formations. The progressive forces have to acknowledge that their weaknesses and failures have led us to this situation where a significant section of the real, would-be leaders of 'revolution' as perceived by them has joined ranks of forces that are their real enemies. But this is not for the first time that such a thing has happened.

Some things need to be done if we want to avoid a Gujarat-like recurrence in the near future. First and foremost there is a need to thoroughly review and critique how we have understood and practiced secularism, and to widen the secular space in our society which is not only a multi-religious but also a multi-caste and multi-racial society. Nobody can deny that all of us, from the liberal intellectuals to the ultra-left radicals, have basically focused our attention on the state which had guaranteed us secular governance All our efforts hinged exclusively on the state and we depended entirely on the administrative machinery for enhancement of secularism. Mr Sumanto Banerjee, in one of his excellent articles titled 'When the 'Silent Majority' Backs a Violent Minority' (*EPW* March 30, 2002), written in the midst of the ongoing genocide in Gujarat, rightly points out: "… There is a growing tendency among the left and secular parties to depend on the state administration, instead of mass education and mobilisation, to resist communalism." Such an abdication of the responsibility of political education along secular lines, he argues, can only sacrifice the 'silent majority' to the political indoctrination of the religious fundamentalists – whether of the Hindu or the Muslim variety. "It is clear that we only left the vast social space or the civil society space for the reactionary or conservative formations in the society including the RSS or the Jamait people." Achin Vanaik, a leading radical scholar of our time, in his monograph written in the mid- nineties, asks the secular forces to distinguish clearly between a secular state and the task of secularisation of our society. It should be clearly understood that the real meaning of secularism is not only that religion be ousted from the functioning of the state but also be separated from the normal functioning of social life of the majority of people.

Secondly, we should strike a proper balance between the political-economic work and the social-cultural work. A cursory glance at the routine practices of various left or secular political formations in this country makes it abundantly clear that while enough emphasis is given to the political-economic work, by and large the task of social-cultural intervention is left unattended. In a backward society like India this imbalance in approach results in various regressive and conservative forces gaining strength.

Thirdly, as a major component of this social, cultural work we should strive to launch mass movements for doing away with caste based discrimination leading ultimately to the annihilation of caste and for the destruction of patriarchy. Mass campaigns also need to be launched for doing away with different regressive institutions and practices which are prevalent in our society.

Fourthly, as a part of strategic preparations for the radical transformation of our state and society we should build parallel institutions of people on issues of daily concern which can act as rudimentary centres of parallel power. In a country like India which is basically a limited democratic state these parallel institutions carry special significance.

Certainly all these proposals do not purport to be a comprehensive list of the do's and don'ts. But we need to understand that if we rectify our narrow understanding and correct our practice the current anti-human, fascist political project of the Hindutva brigade would meet the same fate which visited their predecessors. Of course it is going to be a long battle and we cannot expect immediate victories.

References

1. With the confessions of a few senior leaders of the Parivar coming out in the open, with them giving details of the preparedness which existed prior to the Gujarat genocide, it has been proved beyond doubt that the 'spontaneous reaction' to the heinous Godhra killings was engineered by the higher ups in the Parivar. It need be noted that Professor Keshavram Kashiram Shastri, 96 year old Chairman of the Gujarat unit of the VHP, told rediff.com that the list of shops owned by Muslims in Ahmedabad was prepared on the morning of February 28 itself -Quoted in *Mainstream*, March 16, 2002. Even Nanaji Deshmukh, a man belonging to the Parivar, had the nonchalance to say that the post Godhra killings were orchestrated.

2. Notable among them is 'Reflections on 'Gujarat Pradesh' of 'Hindu Rashtra', K Balagopal, *Economic and Political Weekly*, June 1,2002.

3. Urvashi Butalia, feminist scholar, put it quite aptly in one of the meetings in Delhi organised around the issue of inclusion of caste discrimination in the Durban conference. While discussing her book on partition she said that during her painstaking work it had not even occurred to her that she should explore the status of the dalits.

4. *Outlook* (Date: 1/7/2002) 'Poisoned Edge: The Sangh exploits dalit and tribal frustration to recruit soldiers for Hindutva's 'war''.

5. 'Act Two', People's Union for Democratic Rights, Delhi, 2002.

6. *Outlook* (Date 1/ 7/ 2002). 64-year-old Anand Parmar, a social activist, was at the receiving end when he tried to dissuade a dalit mob from rioting in Ahmedabad. Stones were pelted at his office and he was threatened with dire consequences. But undaunted, he has once again resumed his work. Says he: "Our fight is against unemployment, illiteracy and poverty. We have no business rioting."

7. *Frontline* (Cont.) Dionne Bunsha, Bremen says in a recent essay: "Gujarat could be understood as an experiment for trying out what will happen to state and society under a policy regime which does not attempt to harness the most brutal consequences of a market-led mode of capitalist production. The total eclipse of Gandhian values... has also led to the shrinking of social space. The disappearance of a climate leaning towards social democracy and tolerance has been accompanied by an increase in communal hate politics." Tracing the roots of ghettoisation, Bremen says it accelerated after the decline of the Mazdoor Mahajan Sangh founded by Mahatma Gandhi. He likens the economic boycott and targeting of Muslims to the initial phase of the Nazi regime.

8. According to Dwarakanath Rath, a left activist and trade union leader, in 'old' Ahmedabad there are quite a few bastis where dalits and Muslims have been living together for decades, many of whom worked in the sprawling textile industry in Ahmedabad. With the gradual slump in the textile industry the world over and the technological changes which occurred at the shop floor more than 90 thousand workers have lost their jobs in the last twenty years and at present less than 20-25000 workers are employed there. Growing insecurities in the lives of the unemployed who are engaged in some odd jobs and the lack of any alternative arrangement to help them, accompanied by the loosening of the bonds of solidarity which existed between the poor of both the communities when they were working together, have provided a fertile ground for all sorts of real or virtual identity based organisations to flourish among them.

9. For more on this see 'The Pathology of Gujarat', Achyut Yagnik, *Seminar,* 2002.

10. MN Srinivas, *Social Change in Modern India*, (Orient Longman: Hyderabad, 1996).

11. *Outlook* (July 1, 2002) 'Poisoned Edge: The Sangh exploits dalit and tribal frustration to recruit soldiers for Hindutva's "war"'. The role of NGOs working with tribals and dalits has also come under scanner after the riots. Interestingly, Gujarat-based NGOs working under the National Campaign for Dalit Human Rights (NCDHR) boasted of being the biggest and the most influential contingent at the World Conference against Racism in Durban last September. But throughout the communal violence, their silence has been rather inexplicable. Many have been pointing an accusing finger at organisations like the NCDHR. Says human rights activist and Jesuit priest, Cedric Prakash: "The organisations that boast of championing the cause of dalits and tribals failed to even condemn the riots. Their moral stand is weakened in places like Gujarat where the dalits have turned perpetrators of violence against Muslims."

February 2003

Subverting the *Shudra-Atishudra* Revolution?
Hindutva and Bahujanwad in Uttar Pradesh

Introduction

The third experiment in cohabitation engaged in by the party of the Hindutva and the Bahujan formation has also met an untimely death. The BSP-BJP government in UP led by the 'Dalit ki Beti' Ms Mayawati has been replaced by the one led by the 'Dharati Putra' Mulayam Singh Yadav. While the party of the Hindutva has declared that it has been betrayed by the Bahujan formation and has therefore decided to teach a lesson to their erstwhile friend, the indomitable leader of the Bahujan formation, Ms Mayawati, has announced that she will not take rest until she dethrones the Hindutva formation from the citadels of power in Delhi.

It is worth noting that within a span of mere eight years the Bahujan formation has already entered thrice into a power sharing arrangement with the Hindutva formation at the state level, and if the first experiment continued for a period of four and half months, the second experiment went on for a period of six months, while the third experiment has had the longest existence, that of one year and some months. The complex interplay that this involved can be gauged from the fact that during the same period the Bahujan formation actually played a key role in the defeat of the Hindutva formation at the centre.

Of course the alliance of these formations and its convoluted trajectory has always left analysts wondering. Can it be called a tactical alliance on the part of the Bahujan formation, or is it sheer opportunism dictated solely by the urge for power sharing? Certainly no simple answers are possible in the given situation.

It is time we looked at the genesis of the Bahujan formation, the rationale provided by it to further its alliance with a "Manuwadi" formation, and also how this has helped or hampered the Hindutva combine and impacted upon the short term and long term prospects of the project of dalit emancipation.

Enter the Bahujans!

'Bahujan', the term coined by the great social revolutionary of the 19th century, Mahatma Phule, to differentiate the broad masses of the 'shudras and atishudras' from the 'shetjis and bhatjis', and which remained dormant for decades in post independent India, has returned with a vengeance. Ranging from the polity to civil society, and from the media to the academia, its presence is being acknowledged everywhere, and the concerns exhibited by them have suddenly acquired a new resonance. Gone are the days, the mid eighties, when political pundits looked askance and ridiculed its first presence on the streets, when people carrying blue flags were seen across north India with their slogans '*Vote Hamara, Raj Tumhara, Nahin Chalega*', '*Jiski Jitni Sankhya Bhari, Uski Utni Bhagidari*', or '*Tilak, Tarazu aur Talwar, Inko Maro Jute Char*' in public meetings .

Today we are witness to a party bearing this name catapulted to the centre of national politics, one that is the fourth largest political party in Indian polity. Other formations in the political arena are also seen vying with each other to either reformulate their agendas in order to co opt this new development as part of real politik, or are desperately in search of alliances with this formation so that they are not left on the margins by this upsurge.

With communal fascist bloody politics of the Sangh Parivar as a backdrop and the neo liberal economic policies accelerating the process of marginalisation of the people, this whole phenomenon of dalit assertion in the discourse of the Bahujans has added a new vigour/vitality to the otherwise grim scenario and a new dimension to the dynamics of the polity at the fag end of the 20th century.

Of course the phenomenon of the rise of the 'bahujans' in a span of less than ten years and its ability to redefine the grammar of Indian politics has also brought in its wake fresh doubts, questions, apprehensions about the future direction of the Ambedkarian project in post Ambedkar times. Concern is also being expressed whether the radical transformatory potential of the Ambedkarian project would thus get dissipated in the electoral morass. It is also being asked whether getting political power without regard to the means and methods adopted can really bring about dalit emancipation. Recounting Ambedkar's constant refrain on the possible 'Hindu Rashtra/Rajya' and its negative impact on the dalit situation doubts are also being raised over the 'necessity' of the 'tactical alliance' with the party of Hindutva, even if for a short period. It is being noted that the lack of sympathy/empathy with left politics ingrained in this 'bahujan' phenomenon[1] has for the time being scuttled all possibilities of dialogue between the various shades of left formations and the rising tide of dalit assertion.

Of late Uttar Pradesh has emerged as a key centre of the unfolding dynamic of 'Bahujan politics'. With the decline of the Congress and the consequent marginalization of upper castes from the top echelons of power in the state, UP is today, to paraphrase Mr Kanshi Ram, the 'laboratory of a Bahujan Raj'. It is also worth noting that in the same period UP has evolved as an epicentre of the Hindutva Brigade led movement for the 'liberation of Ramjanambhoomi' and has also become a fertile ground for what is known in popular parlance as the 'forward march of the backwards'.

It is time for a dispassionate look at the going ons in this state: the juggernaut of Bahujanwad, its critical engagement with the polity and society in general and with the forces of Hindutva in particular.

But before coming to the actual unfolding of Bahujanwad it would be opportune to understand the short term and long term agendas of the forces of Hindutva served by their engagement with the Bahujan phenomenon.

Fear of the Shudra Revolution?

The measure of its success in uniting such victims of Brahminism can be assessed from the fears of RSS. The annual reports of the RSS released on 15th

March 1985 devoted a full para to the success of the BSP in uniting the oppressed and exploited caste groups and securing brotherhood against them... In the eyes of RSS such a success of the BSP is the greatest danger to the Hindu fundamentalist. Kanshi Ram (*Oppressed Indian*, April 1985).

Bahujan Samaj Party is one of the real problems for RSS in north India. Balasaheb Deoras (Quoted in *Illustrated Weekly of India*, Aug 14, 1988)

There is today an urgent need to build up moral and spiritual forces to counter any fall out from an expected Shudra revolution. MV Kamath, *Organiser*, 1 May 1994 p.6, commenting on the SP-BSP victory in UP elections

Hindutva is in many fundamental aspects akin with Brahminical Hinduism. Like Brahminical Hinduism, which holds together under its canopy a plethora of sects and opinions a system of graded inequality based on purity and pollution properly in place and its core values/agendas intact, Hindutva has also demonstrated tremendous flexibility and innovativeness in cobbling together alliances of outfits which may be working at cross purposes with each other but have no qualms in sticking together against its common enemies. While at the level of its own organisations it has evolved numerous formations--from the 'missionary' RSS to the 'lunatic fringe' Bajrang Dal – it has skillfully extended this experience of welding them together in the field of polity.

It will be a study of sorts to unravel how it has been able to rope in both the 'secular' Chandrababu Naidu on the one hand and the 'fascist' Shiv Sena on the other, or the Dravidians at one end of the spectrum along with the Badals and Chautalas, to expand its political influence and widen the appeal of its agenda. For that matter the party of Hindutva has also maintained a love-hate relationship with the party of the Bahujans, namely the Bahujan Samaj Party. Its third experiment for power sharing with the BSP might have been over recently, and the party of the Bahujans might have taken a vow to unseat it, but it is fact that the party of the Hindutva has been well served by its alliance with the Bahujan formation.

As far as the latest, recently ended alliance with the Bahujan formation is concerned, the unfolding UP scenario which emerged after the last assembly elections with the hung assembly, provided Hindutva with a unique opportunity by which it could arrest its downslide and simultaneously gain further stability for the coalition government at the centre which it led. For a party which had slid down to the third position from the number one position within a span of just five years in the heart of the Hindi heartland because of serious inner party squabbles and misgovernance and which saw its fortunes dwindling in other states as well, there were not many options that it had.

Thus, despite opposition for such an alliance from an influential section within the BJP at the state level, it preferred to become a junior partner in the 'bahujan' led government. But apart from the short term power sharing benefits, and a possibility of reaping electoral dividends in future elections, there were few other important considerations as well which did not have that much of an immediate import.

It is clear that the Hindutva brigade has always denied agency for the subaltern classes, especially the *shudras* and *atishudras*. Time and again they have demonstrated their admiration for the *Manusmriti* (the religious code of conduct revered by the upper caste Hindus which legitimised and sanctified the inhuman status accorded to the *shudras* and *atishudras*) and their disdain for any type of autonomous dalit movement. It may be noted that the mouthpiece of the Sangh Parivar had opposed the formulation of the constitution on a secular basis and had even advocated the acceptance of *Manusmriti* as India's constitution. The hatred of the Hindutva forces towards any autonomous movement of the dalits was one of the causes which prompted the founders of the RSS to establish the organisation.[2] Hindutva's diabolical game vis a vis the rising dalit consciousness is apparent from how they have treated Ambedkar, one of the greatest leaders of the oppressed and exploited and a pioneer of the autonomous dalit movement.

It is a fact that during his lifetime and even after his demise Ambedkar was an anathema to the Hindutva brigade. The Hindutva ideologues were never comfortable with Ambedkar's uncompromising struggle against Hindu religion and the graded inequality legitimised and sanctified by the same and his call to the oppressed and depressed to come forward to 'capture political power'. The very fact that Ambedkar announced his decision to renounce Hindu religion in the thirties, which he ultimately implemented by accepting Buddhism in mid fifties, could never be digested by the Sangh fraternity. The Hindutva forces never lost an opportunity to denigrate him and his politics even during his lifetime. Their rallying together of all reactionary elements in opposing the 'Hindu Code Bill' which Dr Ambedkar piloted, and their attempts to soft pedal the protective discrimination guaranteed to the dalits and tribals when the constitution was being drafted, are two glaring examples which show the real intentions of the Hindutva brigade.[3]

A change in the approach of the Sangh Parivar towards dalits and Ambedkar was evident when they asked a dalit to conduct the *shilapujan* ceremony during the Babri Mosque 'Liberation' movement, and on the first anniversary of the Babri Mosque demolition day the programme organised in Ayodhya by the Sangh Parivar had a large portrait of Ambedkar apart from the stalwarts of the Hindutva brigade adorning the stage.

The Hindutva ideologues have rightly perceived that a broader anti upper caste front comprising the backwards, dalits and the minorities could prove to be their nemesis. Such a front would not only explode the myth of the 'monolithic Hindu identity', it also has the potential of becoming so formidable that it can marginalise their well cultivated Hindutva project once again. It is clear from the quotations above, in the beginning of this section, that they were quite apprehensive of the unfolding of the 'bahujan' project. Their fears seemed vindicated when they found that the SP-BSP alliance reached the top echelons of power in UP despite the largest post independence communal mobilization by the Sangh Parivar around Babri Mosque demolition (1993). And from day one their sole attempt was to drive a wedge in this alliance.

The third pertained to the consolidation of the unity of the dalits and its own mainly upper caste base against the resurgent middle castes or backward castes (a repeat of the truncated Brahmin-Harijan-Muslim axis forged by the Congress in its heydays) which could be extended to other states as well. The alliance with the party that had dalit concerns at the core of its existence was an attempt to also present itself in a 'positive light' to the dalit masses and help remove its own 'label' of 'A team of Manuwadis', peddled by the leaders of the 'Bahujan formation'. It was an endeavour, moreover, to co opt the rising dalit assertion, and to 'hindutvaise the militant dalit consciousness'.

Towards a 'Bahujan Raj'!

> Kanshi Ram's strategy and his larger understanding of social change are now considerably evolved. He no longer believes in the primacy of social reform. Rather, expenditure of effort on any object other than the capture of government power is seen to be superfluous. It is administrative power that will bring about desired social change. (Mendelssohn and Vicziary, 98:223)

Before coming to the nitty gritties of the alliance of the Bahujan formation with the forces of Hindutva and its overall impact on the politics of dalit assertion it would be opportune to take a look how the intervention of Kanshi Ram has impacted the post Ambedkar dalit movement .

The ups and downs of dalit politics after the death of Dr Babasaheb Ambedkar can broadly be divided into three phases – the rise and fall of the Republican Party, the emergence of the Dalit Panthers, and thirdly, the growing assertion of dalits for political power and their consequent refusal to remain satisfied with merely the education and job opportunities arising out of the policy of reservation. The impressive intervention of BSP in the national politics under Kanshi Ram underlines this third stage. It is noteworthy that while in the earlier two stages of the post-Ambedkar dalit movement, the aspect of 'social-cultural movement' and the unfolding of dalit politics in Maharashtra guided its orientation, in the third stage their role has been increasingly marginalised. The success achieved by BSP has encouraged the emergence of similar experiments in different parts of the country.

For Kanshi Ram the Bahujans comprise all those 85 per cent of the people ranging from the SCs, STs, OBCs and the religious minorities oppressed by the 'Brahminical social order'. It is noteworthy that strongly denouncing the (to quote Kanshi Ram) 'era of stooges' in post Ambedkar dalit movement 'who were enjoying at the feet of the Brahminicals', Kanshi Ram charted a path which aimed to 'make the Bahujan Samaj a ruling Samaj of India.'[4] It has been his contention that unless these 85 percent people are made 'the ruling samaj' atrocities against them cannot be stopped.

While at the social level the whole concept of 'Bahujanwad' has evolved in a manner that it has tried to weave an alliance of all people oppressed under the BSO (Brahminical social order), ensuring the dalit assertion as its core has enabled it to become a sizeable force, insofar as UP is concerned. In the political field the pioneer of this Bahujan politics has worked out temporary alliances with forces which have not been favourably disposed towards the dalits and the other oppressed.[5] A cursory glance at the political developments in UP in the decade gone by would make it clear that it entered into a pre poll/post poll alliance with three different formations. It formed a pre poll alliance with Samajwadi Party and thus enjoyed fruits of power, albeit for a fixed time (1993-95). With the fall of this government, because of withdrawal of support by the BSP, there emerged the possibility of a government led by Mayawati herself, with due support from BJP. This first experiment in government formation lasted four and a half months.

When the elections to the next assembly were held the BSP entered into a pre poll alliance with the Congress in which it was a senior partner in the alliance (1996). After the elections the BSP entered into an alliance with BJP for the second time, when Mayawati was made Chief Minister for a period of six months and it was decided to put the post on rotation. After her turn as Chief Minister of UP was over, the BSP withdrew support to the Kalyan Singh ministry on charges of soft pedalling the SC-ST Act. BSP's third alliance with BJP in UP fructified last year when she occupied the Chief Minister's chair for the third time, an experiment that ended abruptly in Aug 2003.

While the BSP's alliance with Samajwadi party, which helped trounce the BJP from the seat of power, was a one time affair and its pre poll alliance with Congress in 1996 was also not repeated despite attempts for the same from the Congress side, this was the third time that BSP opted to go in for an alliance with BJP at the state level. It is worth underlining that despite aligning thrice with the BJP in UP, the BSP played a key role in the defeat of the Vajpayee-led government at the Centre when the 'no confidence motion' against the government was moved by the combined opposition in the 12th Lok Sabha.

What can be said to be the main consideration of the BSP in forming an alliance with the 'A team of Manuwadis'[6] namely the BJP?

As already mentioned, the key factor in BSP politics is the Bahujan's, especially the dalits' assertion for political power. The oft quoted quotation of Ambedkar, "Dalits will have to become the ruling community" is freely used by the BSP and its supremo Kanshi Ram in this connection.

It is clear that for the BSP 'Bahujanwad' is an attempt to build a counter hegemony to the Brahminical Social Order (BSO) and is derived from the perception that through political power alone is a qualitative change possible in the lives of the Bahujans. And as Mr Kanshi Ram has time and again underlined he has no hassles in forming and breaking alliances even with "Manuwadi" formations if it serves the purpose of installing a Bahujan regime, albeit for some short period.[7]

The short term and long term impacts of such an alliance on dalit consciousness in particular and the dalit liberation movement in general are enormous.

Unleashing the Dalit Agenda

> *Ladke Lenge PM CM, Arakshan se Lenge SP, DM.* Slogan raised in BSP rallies

As mentioned earlier the first experiment in alliance of BSP with BJP had ended in four and half months supposedly because the 'aggressive pushing of dalit agenda' by the BSP rang the alarm bells in the BJP camp. The second experiment lasted just six months when BSP itself withdrew support to Kalyan Singh for soft pedalling the dalit atrocities Act and the third experiment in cohabitation had an abrupt ending within a span of a year and a few months.

A brief overview of these experiments would give an idea of how the agenda of 'Bahujan Raj' with dalit concerns at its core unfolded itself in UP.

One can broadly classify the measures undertaken by the BSP while in power in three broad categories.

Legal measures – Strict implementation of laws especially those focusing on dalits; special attempts to put an end to the atrocities on dalits;

help in distributing land to the dalits which was due to them, broadening the ambit of reservation etc

Social-Cultural measures – Formation of Ambedkar Udyan; installation of Ambedkar's statues; holding of fairs in the name of Bahujan warriors and saints.

Strict administration – It has also been an attempt of Ms Mayawati to give the impression of a no nonsense, tough administrator through frequent postings of bureaucrats, and promoting her supporters in the bureaucracy to replace upper caste officers.

Incidentally the assumption of power by Ms Mayawati in 1995 with BJP's support had many firsts to its credit. It meant not only that a dalit woman had become the Chief Minister of the largest state for the first time, but also that she was a member of a political formation which was not dominated by upper castes and had a dalit agenda at its core. In the long span of more than fifty years of Indian democracy dalits have occupied the chair of Chief Ministership only thrice. The earlier three chief ministers, namely in Andhra, Rajasthan and Bihar, all belonged to formations which were more or less dominated by the upper castes or the rising middle castes.

Ironically it was also for the first time in the history of independent India that a formation proclaiming the legacy of the Ambedkarian project had entered into an alliance with a Hindutva fascist formation which had consistently opposed all independent assertion by the dalits and had tried its best to 'stall the shudra revolution'.

Her first stint of power, albeit for a period of four and half months only, demonstrated the 'distinctness' of the intervention of the bahujan formation in the overall polity. Carving out of new districts and renaming them to evoke 'bahujan' associations, similarly renaming universities, holding 'Periyar Melas' – evoking the heritage of a persona non grata insofar as the Sangh Parivar is cocerned, special emphasis on the development of Ambedkar villages where the population of the dalits was around 30 per cent, creating grants for dalit children to attend classes, allocating 27 % of the state budget for the OBCs, and permitting the benefit of reservations to low caste Muslims were some of the measures undertaken by her regime. It was also during this period that Mayawati government did not permit the VHP to organise an important function at Mathura in September 1995 which would have precipitated communal tensions. This she did despite the fact that her government was receiving support from the BJP.[8]

Interestingly, the installation of Ambedkar statues all over the state, which received a new impetus with the assumption of the Chief Minister's chair by Mayawati, had begun during the first SP-BSP government itself. The growing dalit assertion which manifested itself through this symbolic action led to conflict at various places between the dalits and the upper or dominant castes. According to *India Today* (10 April, 1994, p. 56) over a period of four months sixty incidents linked with the installation of statues led to 21 casualties among the dalits.

When Mayawati assumed power as Chief Minister she announced an Ambedkar Udyan to be built in an area of 28 acres in Lucknow, dedicated to Bharat Ratna Dr Ambedkar.

The second period of alliance with the BJP started in the year 1997 when the electorate did not give a clear mandate to any party and the state had to be put under President's rule for six months. The BSP-BJP shared power for the second time with an agreement that they would rotate the post among themselves. In many ways this was a continuation of the BSP's efforts to strengthen its base and the BJP's effort to retain its dwindling support. The BSP began from the point when it had been forced to relinquish power and systematically resumed the projects it had undertaken during the first alliance, and gave a fresh impetus to the older projects by implementing all schemes and enforcing laws which would benefit its core base of dalits. An interesting feature of this period was the special attention to land rights of the dalits.[9] Attempts were made in this period to give them the "pattas" which had been allotted, but not actually given to them (number of beneficiaries 1, 58,000 who were given 1, 20,000 acres of land). Special campaigns were taken up to give new "pattas" to the dalits (number of beneficiaries 81,500, land distributed 52,379 acres). Two additional features of this campaign were to stop the process of eviction of dalits from the village land which they had occupied (number of beneficiaries 20,000, land involved 15, 000 acres) and also regularise those "pattedars" who were more than ten years old.[10]

The third period of alliance with the BJP, which began last year and which came to an abrupt end in the month of August 2003, was initially marked by the eagerness of both parties to cater to each other's sensitivities with the aim of continuing the alliance, and not to take any precipitative action. Taking into consideration the apprehensions of the core constituency of the BJP, mainly the upper castes, a Government Order directed that the SC-ST Act should be used only in cases involving rape and murder of dalits. It is worth noting that the earlier two alliances were marked by the strict implementation of the SC- ST Act, and the non implementation of this Act now became a ground for Ms Mayawati to withdraw support to Kalyan Singh who was to continue as Chief Minister for a period of six months. Kalyan Singh's by and large soft pedalling of the activities of the 'lunatic fringe' of the Sangh Parivar during this period should also be noted.[11] It was also during this period that Ms Mayawati invited Mr Advani to participate in a BSP rally, and instead of issuing a fresh notification in the Babri Mosque demolition case, transferred the case to Rae Bareilly branch of Sessions Court. Bajrang Dal was freely giving arms training to the 'militant Hindu Youth', Praveen Togadia, the International General Secretary of the VHP was not prohibited from organising 'Trishul Deeksha Samarohs' a number of times in various places, and the stray incidents of violence against the Christian missionaries went on unabated. And the government instead of taking any stringent action against them focussed instead on the activities of gangs/groups associated with the oppositional formations. While there were no restrictions on the activities of the "lunatic fringe" of the Hindutva brigade, the voices of the secular and democratic forces were being continuously stifled.[12]

It cannot be denied that all these moves were part of a well thought out strategy which the BSP had planned in advance. Mayawati's giving clean chit to Narendra Modi after the Gujarat genocide, and her campaigning for Modi in Gujarat in the last assembly elections, acted as a 'curtain raiser' for things yet to come.

Apart from its softness towards the communal forces, the Bahujan formation was also engaged in gradually de-emphasising its 'Bahujan' identity and embracing what it called the 'Sarva Jan' identity. Ever since the last elections Kanshi Ram and Mayawati have been emphasising the party's 'Sarva Jan' line and have quietly and subtly put its 'Bahujan' agenda on the backburner.[13] In the last elections to the UP assembly a slogan raised by the BSP also demonstrated its eagerness as well as compulsion to break out of its 'Bahujan' mould.

Hathi Nahin Ganesh Hai! Brahma Vishnu Mahesh Hai!

Literally translated it means Hathi (symbol of BSP) is basically Ganesh (a favourite god of Hindus) who is another reincarnation of the three gods of Hindus symbolising Creator, Defender and Destroyer.

One can see how a concerted attempt was made to win over the Hindus, especially the upper castes, and also communicate to them that the BSP is a formation which can accommodate everyone. In tune with this de-emphasising of its 'Bahujan' agenda, it also chose more people from the upper castes as candidates in the last assembly elections. The electoral outcome also reflects this change in emphasis: dalit MLAs comprise only a quarter of the total seats won by the BSP.

At this juncture it is difficult to say what will happen next.

Apparently the acts of commission and omission committed during the controversial Taj Corridor project precipitated the present low in the relationship between these two allies. Ms. Mayawati has resigned from her post and has vowed to oust the BJP-led coalition from the Centre. But things do not appear that simple. A vocal section within state BJP had consistently opposed going in for the alliance with BSP. It appears that this faction has got the upper hand in precipitating the present crisis.

As things stand today all plans of the BJP to extend the alliance with the Bahujan formation in the coming elections for five assemblies and extending it to other states for the next parliamentary elections have collapsed like a pack of cards. With the popularity graph of the NDA government taking a further dip, the BJP was found to be desperately in need of this alliance.

Looking Back

How does one evaluate the pluses and minuses of the trajectory of Bahujanwad in UP? The most complex question would be how does one look at BSP's "opportunist/tactical" alliance with the forces of Hindutva?

As already mentioned the advent of BSP on the national scene in general and UP politics in particular has become a harbinger of a new phase in the post Ambedkar dalit movement.

It is a fact that the BSP has not only helped reinvigorate the post Ambedkar dalit movement but has simultaneously widened its ambit in a qualitative manner. It is now a thing of the past that--with the growing fractionisation of the dalit movement after the demise of Ambedkar--the whole movement was in such disarray that dalit politicians or dalit parties rested content with playing (in the words of Prof Gopal Guru) 'guest actor' roles in the upper caste dominated parties.

BSP has not only had some success in getting out of the 'single caste' status of the earlier dalit formations or their 'guest actor appearances' on the political scene, it has also skillfully tried to weave together a formidable alliance of 'oppressed castes and religious minorities' while trying to keep the core agenda of dalit assertion intact.

A significant achievement of the unfolding juggernaut of Bahujanwad has been that it has demonstrated in the political arena that the whole idea of a homogenized Hindu majority, which the Hindutva fascists have been peddling for their immediate as well as long term ends, is a myth. It has also demonstrated that this Hindutva myth can simply be burst asunder if proper coalitions of castes are put in place.

It is also a fact that it has managed to break the stranglehold of the upper castes on UP politics which was the case till late eighties. The changed ambience in the state politics can be gauged from the fact that the BJP and the Congress, two upper caste dominated parties, are finding themselves in a blind alley and are now struggling to find their new bearings in the changed circumstances.

The political ascendancy of a formation claiming dalit agenda has not only helped raise the self esteem and self respect of the downtrodden in Indian society, it has also unleashed processes of their empowerment at the grassroots. Redefinition of the relationship between the erstwhile dominated and the dominant castes has taken various forms, ranging from the struggles over sites for statues of Ambedkar in public places to the fight over illegal occupation of lands allotted to the dalits.

There is also no denying that the practice of going in for pre poll or post poll alliances has been skillfully used by the bahujan formation to its advantage. In a span of just ten years it has gone in for alliances with three altogether different formations and has ensured that its mass base expands. It is worth noting that its alliance with the BJP has benefited it in no uncertain terms, not only in electoral terms but also in the arena of mass politics in general, whereas for the BJP the situation is getting from bad to worse.[14]

Of course the story of the unfolding dynamic of Bahujanwad or its engagement with Hindutva does not end there. There are a few issues in reference to which the Bahujan formation has either followed the beaten track or has failed to show the necessary vision to address them clearly or has shown extreme short sightedness.

A key question concerns the whole concept of 'Bahujan' itself and its perception in society. The idea, despite the immediate electoral successes, has has not taken roots and does not seem to be taking roots in social terms. For any such idea to take root there needs be a reinvigorating of the social-cultural aspect to the movement with a special focus on the anti caste struggle, which seems lacking here.

It is also clear that this has affected its long term prospects of continuing its struggle against Brahminism and has made it an ally with a communal fascist formation whose hands are soaked in the blood of the minorities. It has helped legitimise the most brutal force in Indian politics – the Hindutva Brigade – which is at present ruling the country.

It has willy nilly made the dalits appear as allies of the Hindutva Brigade and this is bound to have serious ramifications for the movement for social change in this country. Brushing aside the strongly voiced opinion of Dr Ambedkar regarding the unhappy prospects for the dalits and other oppressed in case 'Hindu Raj' became a reality, and in a reversal all those struggles which he and other leaders of the movement for dalit emancipation waged against Brahminism.

It is worth noting that a few intellectuals claiming Ambedkarian legacy have provided theoretical justification for the unity of BSP and BJP arguing that for the dalits 'social fascism' of the backwards is more dangerous than the 'communal fascism' of the Parivar. According to them the upper castes represented by the BJP are a declining force in rural areas and for the dalits, a majority of whom are still village bound, an alliance with them would provide immediate security. Of course, a few dalit activists have debunked this rationale and have provided statistics to show that in the preceding decade the dalits had primarily been under attack from the upper castes, especially Rajputs, than from the OBCs. They also claim that the talk of 'social fascism' being more dangerous than 'communal fascism' is merely a 'post facto justification' for the opportunist alliance and does not take into consideration the divisions within the ranks of the backwards or the dalits.

What Next?

It can be said that the post Ambedkar dalit movement is passing through one its most crucial phases since the death of Ambedkar. While it can be said that that there is a broader acceptance of the ideas of Phule-Ambedkar in the mainstream of society, and a greater appreciation of the struggle against Brahminism within the left movement, along with a sincere attempt to review and reconsider earlier mechanical understandings around caste and gender, the carriers of the legacy of Dr Ambedkar are finding themselves in a vortex for which they themselves are partially responsible.

The central question which needs to be addressed is how this 'vulgarisation' of Ambedkar's method came about in a movement which has historically understood the interconnections between political struggles and struggles on social-cultural and economic concerns. While it is true that Dr Ambedkar emphasised the need for making the dalits the 'ruling community', and often said that the question of untouchability is basically a political question, he did not in his practice ever create a Chinese wall between political and other struggles. For him all these struggles were part of the general transformation he fought for throughout his life.

In fact, contrary to Ambedkar's lifetime, in the 'Republican phase' of the (post Ambedkar) dalit movement the pendulum was tilted towards social-cultural movements. In its 'Bahujan' phase it has swung towards capture of political power regardless of the means adopted. While the earlier one sided emphasis on social cultural movements has been rectified, but this new agenda of capturing political power has meant that the momentum on the social plane has not been sustained. Various other aspects internal to the movement, especially gender concerns, and the creation of proper organisational mechanisms have been left unaddressed.

Will it be possible for them to correct course and retrieve the radical legacy of the Ambedkarian project once again? As things stand today it is definitely difficult to predict the outcome.

References

1. The apt description for the same can be had from one of Kanshi Ram's famous quotes: "The Congress and the BJP can be compared to white snakes in the green grass whereas Communists can be compared to green snakes in green grass."

2. In his "official" biography of the RSS, *Sangh Vriksha ke Beej*, Mr C P Bhishikar talks about the genesis of RSS. In his interaction with Mr Hedgewar the reasons behind the foundation of RSS were explained.

3. The disdain for Ambedkar was so ingrained in the RSS that none of the stalwarts or its activists bothered to even visit the Deeksha Bhoomi situated in Nagpur, where their own centre is located, till early eighties. Only in the early eighties, under the supremoship of Deoras, did the RSS have a rethinking on this matter, and reviewing its earlier policy decided to co-opt him in its list of 'pratahsmaraniya' (worth remembering in the morning). But the strategy was clever and varied. Ranging from attacking his thoughts (*Riddles in Hinduism*) to projecting him as a 'stooge of the British', to portraying him as 'anti muslim', it adopted many tactics from its kitty to present Ambedkar as a 'Hindu icon' opposed to Muslims.

4. Kanshi Ram has written a monograph on the same theme *Chamcha Age: Era of Stooges*, 1982, in which he has given details of the compromising nature of the post Ambedkar dalit leadership.

5. It can also be said that Kanshi Ram is the only politician in mainstream politics who likes to go in for 'frequent elections' and who has publicly declared that he has no qualms in entering 'opportunist alliances' if it strengthens the Bahujan's ascendance to power.

6. For BSP, the BJP and the Congress were the A team and B team respectively of the 'Manuwadis'.

7. "My aim is that BSP should move forward. At any given point, I'll enter into a tactical alliance with another party if I feel it will strengthen the BSP. And it is what I have done in the past. I did not enter into an alliance with the BJP because of any ideological common ground- in fact we are poles apart ...We

entered into an understanding with the BJP last year to increase the base of the BSP and when we feel we are not benefiting any longer, we'll end it ... I'm only looking for suitable ladder. Cited in the *TOI*, 21 Aug, 1997, quoted in *India's SilentRevolution*, Christopher Jafferlot.

8. For more details refer to *India's Silent Revolution*, Christopher Jafferlot, Permanent Black, 2002; *Dalit Assertion and Bahujan Samaj Party: A Perspective from Below*, Vivek Kumar and Uday Sinha, Bahujan Sahitya Sansthan, 2001.

9. All references in this section are from *Iron Lady: Kumari Mayawati*, Mohammad Jameel Akhtar, journalist, p. 88.

10. Sudha Pai and J Singh, in their article 'Politicisation of Dalits and Most Backward Castes,' *EPW*,7 June 1997, p.1358, also give details on how the Bahujan effect was unfolding itself, especially vis a vis land rights, while focusing on the developments in and around Meerut district, UP.

11. A significant exception to this practice was when Mr Togadia was not allowed to enter Bareilly in the mid of August 2003 and relations between the two formations were at breaking point.

12. It was quite symptomatic that last year the Student Youth Convention, organised under the auspices of AISA-AIYA at Faizabad on 10-11th May 2002 to commemorate the '1857 struggle for India's Independence' underlining communal harmony, was not allowed to take place and hundreds of its activists were jailed for weeks together. While there was no reining in of the Togadias, the noted Gandhian and Magasaysay award winner, Sandeep Pandey, is facing charges of sedition for holding a fast for communal harmony in Ayodhya. It is in tune with this new approach that despite early warnings from many quarters the state did not take any steps against the activities of the 'rebel' BJP MP from Gorakhpur, Mr Adityanath, which in turn cost it dearly because the city witnessed communal riots for the first time in post independence Indian history.

13. It can be said that the process of 'Sarvajanisation' of the Bahujan formation started only in 1998. During the 1998 and 1999 parliamentary elections the party distributed audiotapes welcoming the *savarnas* and also promising them due respect. According to *The Pioneer*, 20th Feb 1998, in a public meeting held at Basti, eastern UP, Mayawati clearly said that, "BSP is no more a caste based party because it had adopted the policy of *Sarvajan Hit* (welfare of all castes)... the party now wanted to take the help of all to remove the disparity prevailing in the society." Gone were the days when even before starting a meeting the '*savarnas*', if any present, were asked to leave the place immediately, and slogans were raised denigrating them '*Tilak, Tarazu aur Talwar, Inko Maro Jute Char* (One who is familiar with the north Indian lexicon can see that in this slogan

itself Tilak stands for Brahmins, Tarazu stands for the Banias and Talwar stands for the Thakurs/ Kshatriyas).

14. The BSP's progress in the UP assembly elections:

1	1989	373	13	9.83
2.	1991	386	12	9.2
3.	1993	166	67	11.2
4.	1996	299	67	20.06
5.	2002	403	98	23.0

Source: Chief Electoral Officer, UP, Lucknow.

2004

Calamity and Discrimination

> *[U]ntouchability, is a kind of disease of the Hindus...it is a mental twist... I do not know how my friend is going to untwist the twist which the Hindus have got for thousands of years unless they are all sent to some kind of hospital.* Dr BR Ambedkar, 1954, Quoted in Bhagwan Das, 95:53.

Water is said to be a great leveler. But even the ravaging flood waters which have created havoc in the districts of Barmer and Jaisalmer in Rajasthan failed to crack an age old structure – the walls between castes.

Reports coming in from different parts of the flood affected districts of Rajasthan have indicated how victims belonging to the Dalit castes were being hounded out of the relief camps by dominant castes who believe that their entry would 'pollute the sanctity of camps'. Leave alone accommodation, or the relief camp toilet facilities, dalits are being denied even food and water. The hatred towards the dalits runs so deep that even in the hour of common tragedy the dominant castes are vehemently opposing the drainage of water from the worst affected dalit majority Malwa and Kawas villages.

Confronted with the studied silence of the articulate sections of our society over these developments, dalit groups in Rajasthan have formed a monitoring committee to look into complaints of discrimination against dalits in relief and rehabilitation measures. This committee would also try to ensure that the Dalit victims who face caste discrimination are rendered justice and get a fair deal. (*The Hindu*, 13th September 2006)

This plight of the dalits in Rajasthan echoes a similar chain of events following the Tsunami which had killed thousands of people. One of the leading newspapers had then revealed it all. 'There's something even an earthquake measuring 9 on the Richter scale and a tsunami that kills over 1 lakh people can't crack: the walls between castes. ..' It presented details of how Dalits from 63 affected villages from Nagapattinam, Tamilnadu were facing the brunt of the powerful Meenavar fishermen (a Most Backward Class).

Here also dalits were being thrown out of relief camps, pushed to the rear of food and water lines, not being allowed to take water from UNICEF facilities and in some cases not even being allowed to use the toilet. (*Indian Express* January 8, 2005). Comparing the situation of the Dalits in Nagapattinam and Barmer, it was easy to infer that the dominant castes have rather shared notes with each other.

One thing is quite clear. May it be 'feudal' Rajasthan, or Tamilnadu which has a history of social reform movements, or Gujarat the 'successful model of a Hindutva lab' where dalits were pushed to the margins in the matter of post-earthquake relief – whenever the question of rendering relief to the dalits is concerned, even in the worst of calamities, there is hardly any difference in terms of the callousness and discrimination practiced.

In all such cases of caste discrimination, where the offenders of dalit human rights could easily be identified and prosecuted, the role of the state and its various agencies has always been found to be wanting. The unwritten consensus among the functionaries of the state is not to 'disturb the social equilibrium' at such a crucial juncture. A social activist present in Nagapattinam had indignantly told the reporter, "...No one is willing to take up the matter at the field level as this could complicate things."

The approach of the state and its agencies thus once again vindicates what any number of reports brought out by the National Commission of SC and STs have been repeating ad infinitum. The broad conclusion of these reports is that the different institutions of the state, ranging from the police to the judiciary, have rather preferred to look the other way or have connived with the powers that be in saving the guilty when dalits and other oppressed sections were humiliated or were subjected to violence. And one has no option but to concur with the view of the ex justice of the Supreme Court, Mr VK Krishna Iyer, that the laws formulated for the protection of dalits have effectively been turned into 'paper tigers'.

For an outsider it may appear surprising how the 'social nausea' (to quote Ambedkar) refuses to subside even in times of calamity. But for someone familiar with the Indian social fabric and its age old doctrine of exclusion legitimised and sanctified by the Brahminical ideology such behaviour is a 'routine matter'. There is need to understand that incidents of such nature (as witnessed in Barmer or Nagapattinam) demonstrate how this ideology of purity and pollution has permeated deep into the psyche of people. The outcome is a 'common sense' that defies rationality.

January 2005

Dalits: Law as Paper Tiger!

What to the American slave is your Fourth of July? I answer, a day that reveals to him, more than all other days in the year, the gross injustice and cruelty of which he is the constant victim. To him, your celebration is a sham; your boasted liberty, an unholy license; your national greatness, swelling vanity; your sounds of rejoicing are empty and heartless; your denunciations of tyrants, brass-fronted impudence; your shouts of liberty and equality, hollow mockery; your prayers and hymns, your sermons and thanksgivings, with all your religious parade and solemnity, are to him mere bombast, fraud, deception, impiety, and hypocrisy--a thin veil to cover up crimes which would disgrace a nation of savages. There is not a nation on the earth guilty of practices more shocking and bloody, than are the people of these United States, at this very hour. Frederick Douglass, former slave, 1852

Introduction

Does the cost of a 'goat' equal that of a human being? Whether drinking water from a public lake where even animals are free to visit should lead to a riot like situation, or the very interpersonal decision to marry a girl/boy of one's own choice should culminate in the killings of the couple at the behest of the community elders?

Any person who bears humane sensibilities and sensitivities would rather decry these 'medieval' responses towards fellow human beings.

S/he would find her/himself at wits end if s/he probes further and discovers that people affected by Tsunami engaged themselves in systematic discrimination against dalits who were similar victims. S/he would be aghast to know that the upper caste perpetrators of the Keezhavenmani massacre (1969) of 44 Dalits were allowed to go scot free by the judiciary on the specious plea that the 'Upper Caste Gentry would not have gone walking to the place'.

In any civilised country, all such exposures in the media would at the least have caused nation wide uproar, led to fresh stirrings in the nation's conscience, culminating in a process of self-introspection and possibly self-correction. But India presents itself as a peculiar case in the comity of nations. Here all such covert and overt violence against a part of the citizenry has received not only legitimacy, thanks to the purity and pollution based caste order, but has been sanctified by the religious scriptures also. One still remembers how one of the top leaders of the VHP had rationalised the killings of five dalits in Jhajjar four years ago by saying that the *Puranas* – the religious scriptures of the Hindus – accord precedence to a bovine vis-à-vis a human being.

Thus India, a country of billion plus people, whose leaders are pitching for a superpower status, and one whose people take pride in its ancient traditions and culture, and whose elite goes gaga over the booming sensex, presents a rather strange spectacle of a nation. If one decides to go by economic indices of growth alone we may get a rosy picture, but a closer look at the goings on within the society makes it obvious that there is a disjunction between the world of economics and the life worlds of its people. The core of the society bares its encounter with barbarism in abundance.

But before raising the follies of the nation and its people in a generalised manner, it would be opportune to take a close look at the alleged theft of a goat which got exchanged by snuffing out the life of a man in his teens recently.

Not playing a Goat!

> Lucknow: A teenaged dalit named Mukesh was beaten to death in Ferozabad district for daring to participate in Bhagwat Paath organised by the local Lodh Rajput community. The victim's brother and some relatives who came to the rescue of the teenagers were also assaulted. The incident took place on Tuesday night.
>
> Though the police confirmed that the provocation behind the murder was caste bias, the accused alleged that they had caught the victim while

stealing a goat. The police could arrest only two of the twelve named accused.

The above news appeared in the 15th June 2006 Lucknow edition of *Times of India*. Of course there was no follow up of the incident in the print or the electronic media. Rather it received the same fate as scores of other news, which are considered unimportant.

Imagine if one of those intrepid journalists were to decide to follow the story to see for her/himself how the event unfolded. What would be her/his observations?

To be very frank, the journalist would discover not single but multiple versions of the whole incident. For all practical purposes s/he would have to decide her/his presentation of the 'truth' depending upon her/his own location in the caste matrix.

The Lodh Rajputs, among the resurgent OBCs, who form the backbone of local power structures in many areas, would be hell-bent on proving the 'crime' of the deceased. Perhaps to garner further community support for the inhuman act committed by their own caste men, they may present a fresh slew of charges against him and perhaps vouch that he had also harassed the ladies of the community. They would be loathe to listen to any counter view to their argument that raised the issue of 'punishment' commensurate with 'crime', or of the role of institutions of justice delivery established by the republic more than 56 years ago to do the same.

The hapless dalits on their part would share their grief of how they had learnt of the tragic death of one of their dear ones, how the police had adopted dilly dallying tactics and how it had become a party in the stigmatisation of the whole dalit community. It does not require much acumen to prophesise that unless and until some powerful voice/s join the grief of the dalits, the brutal murder of Mukesh by the Lodh Rajputs would slowly lead to the blind alley of a 'closed file'.

The tragic prognosis of this incident may appear disturbing to any civilized person, but the fact of the matter is that the manner in which the troika of state-judiciary-(rest of) civil society unfolds itself in most cases of dalit atrocities, the fate is not unexpected or dissimilar. May it be a case of 'traditional' atrocities whereby the dalits are denied any rights whatsoever in Hindu society, or may it be the case of 'modern' resistance put up by the dalits, or simply a caste Hindu response to the changing situation of the dalits, the picture is same everywhere.

It was only last year that a dalit basti situated in Gohana (a town, which is hardly 100 kms from the capital) was attacked by a few hundred strong mob of mostly *Jat* youths. The marauders burnt down scores of their houses and looted their property in the daytime in the presence of two hundred strong police force posted near the *basti* with senior officers in attendance. The immediate provocation for the attack was the murder of a *Jat* youth allegedly by a few dalits who felt agitated when the murdered man along with his friends had passed obscene remarks against dalit women.

Another aspect of the attack was that the *Jat* youths were just 'implementing' the decision of the caste council (caste panchayat) which had given an ultimatum to the police to hand over the 'culprits' to them or face reprisal attack on the *basti*. To rub salt on the wounds, when the marauders left, the senior-most boss of the police in the region not only minimised the extent of plunder but also expressed satisfaction that there had been no loss of lives from either side.

It was clear to any impartial observer that the main 'grievance' of the Jats against the dalits was that many among them had refused to follow the 'community profession' of safai and had charted an alternate path of life and were refusing to tolerate humiliation any more.

Recently when a group of human rights activists visited the *basti*, they found to their dismay that out of the 23 upper caste accused in the case (while the actual number was in hundreds) till date only three could be apprehended, and they too were released on bail immediately. The CBI enquiry ordered into the case is moving at a snails pace and seven dalits are still languishing in jail, without any signs of bail, supposedly for being party to the death of the Jat youth.

Way to Injustice Paved With "Good Laws"

> Social justice minister Meira Kumar pointed out that the conviction rate in cases registered under the Protection of Civil Rights Act is a mere 3.75 per cent. Besides, 75 to 77 per cent cases of crimes against Dalits remain pending despite the existence of special and designated

> courts. Union home minister Shivraj Patil, who was also present at the conference, acknowledged that the system was not delivering justice and existing laws safeguarding the rights of backward classes may have to be changed or tightened. January 12, 2005, *The Telegraph*

The first Prime Minister of India Jawaharlal Nehru always sang paeans to the Unity and Diversity of the country. But he forgot to add that one institution which 'unites' the Indian people, spread over the subcontinent, is their strict adherence to the age old 'caste system'. It is a system based on exclusion and graded hierarchy and the only 'diversity' which it allows is in the nature of violence which is unleashed against the people who are considered at the bottom of the Caste Matrix.

Perhaps the plight of the dalits in Gohana or in Ferozabad would lead us to a query on presence/absence of appropriate laws to curb such offences against them. A person unaware of how the Indian polity functions may presume that the spurt in atrocities against the dalits is mainly due to the absence of appropriate laws. S/he is sadly mistaken.

The founding fathers of the Constitution had solemnly resolved *to secure to all citizens Justice: Social, Economic and Political, Liberty of thought, expression, belief, faith and worship, and equality of status and of opportunity, and to promote among them all fraternity, assuring the dignity of individual, and unity.* The Constitution emphasised that: *The state shall not discriminate against any citizen on grounds of religion, race, caste, place and birth or any form.* The Directive Principles of the Constitution underlined: *The State shall promote with special care the educational and economic interest of the scheduled castes/tribes and shall protect them from social injustice and all forms of exploitation.*

It is worth noting that in accordance with these Constitutional provisions a number of measures have been initiated by the government for providing protection to ex-untouchables (Scheduled Castes or SCs) and the tribals. These measures can be categorised under two broad heads: protective and developmental. Under the 'protective' head untouchability was legally abolished and its practice in any form forbidden by the Protection of Civil Rights (Anti-Untouchability) Act of 1955.

To protect those under the categories of SC and ST in a more effective and comprehensive manner a few other legislations were introduced. Policies of reservation and representation were adopted to improve the access and participation of these sections in the economic, educational and political spheres. The enactment of the Bonded Labour (Abolition) Act, 1976 or laws to curb child labour were part of the other major measures taken to make the protection of these sections more stringent and effective. The year 1989 witnessed the government enacting another act, namely the Scheduled Castes and Tribes (Prevention of Atrocities) Act to prevent atrocities against SC/STs. The necessity for enactment this Act had arisen because under the existing circumstances the Protection of Civil Rights Act (1955) and normal provisions of the Indian Penal Code were found to be inadequate to provide safeguards. The SC and ST (POA) Act, 1989 was pioneering in many ways. It provides for not only the appointment of special courts, but also punishment for neglect of duties by officials, forfeiture of property of the perpetrators, confiscation of arms from the dominant castes in the area, declaration of a particular area atrocity prone, and even asks for distribution of arms to the downtrodden etc.

But as Justice VK Krishna Iyer, the legendary human rights activist and a former Supreme Court Judge, puts it, all such 'half hearted legislation has proved to be impotent and ineffectual in practice'. He added that the aim behind these attempts was to have a 'more effective, more comprehensive and more punitive provisions of law' but 'the ruling classes saw to it that, at the functional level, the legislations were paper tigers' (All quotes from the 'Foreword' by Justice Iyer to a book '*Dalit Utpidan aur Vidhik Upchar*, by PL Mimroth, 2000, Delhi).

There have been innumerable reports detailing how the local police, in connivance with the perpetrators themselves, sabotages implementation of laws basically meant to protect the dalits and the tribals. It is noticed that instead of filing cases under the POA Act, it prefers filing cases under normal provisions of Indian Penal Code, which facilitates release of the accused on bail. It also facilitates filing of 'counter cases' against the victims, so that a compromise could be reached. The Third Report of the NPC (New Delhi: GOI, 1980, p.31) had rightly underlined how "[f]alse criminal cases are sometimes engineered merely for the sake of making arrests to humiliate and embarrass some specified enemies of the complainant, in league with the police for corrupt reasons."

A related phenomenon is how powers that be take steps to deter enlightened people from fighting for the constitutionally guaranteed rights of the dalits and the tribals. *Human Rights Watch Report* (Vol. 4, No. 15, June 1992) shares details of how *Criminalisation of Social Activism* in India takes place. In its much acclaimed report 'Broken People – Caste Violence against India's "Untouchables"'(1999) *Human Rights Watch* repeats how 'State agents have acted directly and forcefully against those attempting to claim their rights. Dalit activists throughout the country face charges as "terrorists", "threats to national security" and "habitual offenders..." (p. 153).

The 'Report on Prevention of Atrocities against Scheduled Castes' (NHRC, 2004, Delhi) rightly underlined how the 'state has failed in this respect' on 'several fronts'. These are 'failure to effectively implement the laws relating to atrocities against SCs and STs', which is 'reflected both in respect of preventing violence from taking place' as well as in the 'inability to punish perpetrators of violence after the crime is committed'; 'failure to act against its own agencies involved in the commission of violence'; 'failure to strengthen the watchdog institutions' etc. 'The failure of the state vis-à-vis mobilization of caste Hindus in favour of social democracy embedded in the constitution and various laws and state policies' can also be considered palpable, which has 'created ambivalence in its intentions and contradictions in its actions'.

The Sixth Report of the National Commission for SCs and STs (1999-2000 and 2000-2001) had expressed its deep sense of dissatisfaction over the way all these measures are implemented. While commenting that "...the number of cases registered under Prevention of Civil Rights Act and SC and ST (Prevention of Atrocities) Act has been showing downward trend", as a healthy development, it exposes the way this reduction in the number of cases is achieved.

> ...from its reviews with various state governments the commission is of the view that a large number of cases go unregistered, mainly because of the reluctance on part of the police officers to register the cases and also because of lack of awareness among the members of these communities about the provisions of these acts.

> In addition, there are delays in investigation, collusion with offenders and manipulation of witnesses and evidence which all contribute to reduce the effectiveness of these protective legislations." (See Preface, p.II)

In the same vein it tells us that in most of the states neither the meetings of the monitoring and vigilance committees are held regularly, nor are any special courts set up to deal with cases of atrocities on dalits. It also adds:

> The question of setting up exclusive special courts, particularly in the states having large pendency, needs serious consideration of the government. The rate of convictions in various states ranges from 5 to 10 percent and it is necessary to examine the reasons for such low convictions rates and for taking urgent corrective action... The apex court has held that the Special courts cannot directly entertain the cases under these acts, without following committal proceedings. It is, therefore, necessary to amend these acts suitably to authorise the special courts to admit cases under these acts directly.

One can go on mentioning the various schemes or affirmative action programmes run by the government supposedly for the empowerment of the dalits, and on the other hand also give details of the systematic manner in which conscious attempts are on to deny what is due to them. One would be surprised to learn that not only thousands of posts, which are meant for them especially, have been lying vacant for years together, but there are thousands and thousands of people belonging to the non dalit category who have manipulated jobs meant for these sections by procuring 'false certificates', and the concerned authorities are sitting over this despite repeated complaints by the aggrieved people. The seriousness of the phenomenon of false certificates can be gauged from the fact that the last two annual reports of the National SC and ST Commission (since bifurcated) have devoted a chapter each to discuss the gravity of the situation arising out of this.

This makes it crystal clear that the state has to show firm political will, get ready to make amends to ameliorate the situation and move beyond pious rhetoric, if it is serious about the commitments it made to the 'other people' exactly 54 years ago while promulgating the constitution. But one cannot expect that there would be any radical departure from the way in which the state has been functioning in this regard.

Of course before moving on to the unholy alliance between the state and (a section of) civil society it would be opportune to take a close look at the Gujarat experience.

A Close Look at the Gujarat Experience

The Gujarat Earthquake in the year 2001 and the consequent relief and rehabilitation programme was an eye opener to the outside world regarding the deep seated caste bias in the Gujarati community apart from the much talked about bias against the minorities. There were reports that at places the relief and rehabilitation work bypassed the dalits and the Muslims. There were also reports about the siphoning off of the relief material to the relief camps inhabited by the non-dalit or upper caste Hindus and how consciously the dalits as well as the Muslims were deliberately left out in many cases.

The organised genocide of Muslims in the year 2002 at the behest of the Sangh Parivar organisations which was aided and abetted by the Modi government was another occasion when the travails and tribulations of the dalits came under further scrutiny. While a section of the dalits' cooption in the Hindutva agenda and their metamorphosis as foot soldiers of the Hindutva brigade was duly reported, the *Varna* dominated media did not deem it necessary to emphasise some related facts. The genocide in Gujarat had also a little dalit blood accompanying it. The dalits lost 108 lives in Gujarat, 38 in the city of Ahmedabad alone. Quite a few of these deaths occurred due to the dalits resisting the Hindutva goons by siding with hapless Muslims.

Of course when one looks at how the Atrocities Act unfolds in the state, one sees the same shocking pattern which is evident at the national level. A conclusion of a detailed and systematic study of 400 judgements done by Vajibhai Patel, Secretary of Council for Social Justice corroborates this. It tells us that utterly negligent police investigation at both the higher and lower levels, coupled with a distinctly hostile role played by the public prosecutors, is the main reason for the collapse of cases filed under the Atrocities Act. It is worth noting that he has meticulously documented these judgements delivered under this Act since April 1, 1995 in the Special Atrocity Courts set up in 16 districts of the state. The study also blasts the common perception that the inefficacy of this law is due to false complaints being lodged or compromises between the parties. In actuality it is a complicit State that has rendered the Act toothless.

A write up in the *Communalism Combat* (March 2005) by Teesta Setalvad presents in a nutshell the main findings of the study:

In over 95 per cent of the cases, acquittals have resulted due to technical lapses by the investigation and prosecution, and in the remaining five per cent, court directives are being flouted by the government. Often while crimes under the IPC against the accused have been proved, offences under the Atrocities Act have not, suggesting a systemic bias against recording and establishing crimes under this law.

As a result of the attitude of the state police and the state public prosecutors, those accused under the Act for criminal acts like murder (for which life imprisonment is the sentence) and rape are being allowed to go scot-free.

Numerous judgements of the special courts set up under the Atrocities Act in Gujarat – which due to lapses in investigation and prosecution, have led to the acquittals of the accused – have passed strictures against the negligence demonstrated by both the police and the public prosecutors and even summoned time-bound 'action taken' reports. Often policemen have even resorted to giving false evidence to protect the accused while prosecutors have attempted to mislead the courts by arguing that the provisions of the Atrocities Act are not mandatory.

Under section 4 of the Atrocities Act, "Whoever, being a public servant but not being a member of a Scheduled Caste or a Scheduled Tribe willfully neglects duties required to be performed by him under this Act, shall be punished with imprisonment for a term which shall not be less than six months but which may extend to one year." In 95 per cent of the judgements studied by the CSJ, courts have passed strictures against errant police officials *invoking provisions of section 4 under the Atrocities Act,* but the government of Gujarat, instead of taking action against the erring officers, has honoured them with promotions.

The deliberate manner in which the state machinery connives with the perpetrators of the crime is evident in very many ways.

- Acquittal due to investigation by a lower officer: The atrocity rules of the 1995 Act make it mandatory that investigations of an offence should be carried out by either a DSP or an officer above his rank, who is supposed to send his report directly to the state DGP. In 95 per cent of the cases it is observed that the accused are acquitted merely on the ground that the investigation of the offence was done by an officer below the rank of DSP

- Acquittal due to non-inclusion of caste certificate by the police: The Act makes it clear that the caste certificate of the complainant issued by a competent authority be annexed to the complaint and produced by the police before the court. There have been several judgements when rape accused were allowed to go scot free merely because the investigating officer did not annexe the caste certificate of the complainant.

-Negligence by public prosecutors: The appointment of special public prosecutors to try cases is mandatory under the Act but the hostile role played by such SPPs to prosecute cases destroys the case. It takes years to reach the stage of trial and when the victim/complainant enters the witness box to depose, s/he does not know who the PP is. The CSJ has studied several judgements in which the courts have passed severe strictures against deliberate attempts by the special public prosecutors to avoid implementing the special provisions under the Act thereby vitiating the prosecution case itself.

The CSJ study rightly notes that 'an utter lack of commitment to this legislation and lack of political will by state governments to prosecute the atrocities committed under this Act have rendered this legislation meaningless.' It also says that 'the Scheduled Caste Welfare Department of the state government, created with the objective of providing social justice to Dalits and Adivasis, has glaring vacancies in key posts making the implementation of social justice measures even more difficult. There are over 300 vacancies in this state department, from the rank of district officer downwards in Gujarat alone.'

(Un)civil Society and its Silences

It is possible that all these details which expose the realities of the situation of the dalits in the state could be brushed aside as a story repeated ad nauseam. All talk of atrocities on dalits could be presented as another extension of the way in which the 'state in the third world' unfolds itself. But the key point is that caste atrocities, much like gender oppression or racial discrimination, have a specificity which transcends the binary of 'state as perpetrator' and 'people as victims'. In fact they implicate the partisan role played by the people themselves.

The 'Report on Prevention of Atrocities against SCs' prepared by NHRC (2004) presents details on how civil society in India presents itself in relation to the caste based order:

- Civil society becomes a distinct beneficiary of the caste based order, and helps perpetuate the existing unequal social relations and frustrates attempts to democratize society, because through the customary arrangements the dominant classes are assured of social control over people who can continue to abide by their commands without any protest.

- In fact civil society represents the deep divide in social values, where people themselves wish to enjoy all rights and privileges which a democratic liberal society offers them but is vehemently opposed to the same being granted to the scheduled castes.

- Civil society effectively undermines the authority of the state by obstructing the effectuation of rights and entitlements to all citizens and is complicit in perpetuating caste based inequalities, indignities and violence against SCs.

- Civil society reflects a deep seated ambivalence between obscurantism and modernity.

Of course the uncivil nature of civil society presents before us a unique challenge where the need then arises to go beyond the existing discourse on civil and constitutional rights and to address the failure of 'the largest democracy of the world' to go beyond mere form. We have to appreciate that it concerns the greater hiatus that exists between constitutional principles and practice and the corresponding ethical ones based on a diametrically opposed ideal. Everyone has to see that under the purity and pollution based paradigm which is the cornerstone of our caste system, inequality receives both legitimisation and sanctification. As caste inequality is accepted both in theory and practice, a legal constitution has no bearing on the ethical foundation of caste-based societies.

It was a manifestation of this real hiatus that when Bhanwari, a *saathin* from the Women's Development Programme, Rajasthan, was raped by some villagers, the trial judge acquitted the accused on the reasoning that "rape is usual" and an "upper--caste man could not have defiled himself by raping a lower-caste woman."

July 2006

Khairlanji
All Nero's Brethren

> *(They) were doomed to the flames and burnt, to serve as a nightly illumination when daylight had expired. Nero offered his gardens for the spectacle.* Tacitus (Roman historian and official, c.58 to 115 C.E.), *The Annals, Book XV*, C.E. 62-65

Dead bodies don't speak.

But for the near and dear ones it is always possible to reconstruct what must have bothered the dead person at that last moment of her/his life while her/his eyes still exhibited the yearning for life.

And if the death itself is a public spectacle in which people from their own neighbourhood, whom they knew very well, have joined the orgy, have brought other people there for the brutalisation of their bodies, then even someone living thousands of miles away can also read the last flashes of ideas flickering in the dead persons minds.

It is now part of public memory how Surekha Bhootmange, aged 45 years, a dalit (mahar) by caste, mother of two sons -Roshan and Sudhir – and a bright daughter Priyanka, who yearned to join the military, all four spent the last one hour of their lives. Ordinary looking people who had to pay a very dear price for standing up to the local dominant castes bent on snatching their small piece of land.

A few fact finding reports brought out since provide details of their gory end. They also tell us how the four bodies were dumped onto a cart and thrown in different corners of the village. But the worst was yet to come. Despite this public spectacle of murder and rape there was no movement in the village for quite some time. It appeared as if the state machinery had decided to side with the marauders. The loneliness of Bhaiyalal, Surekha's husband and Siddarth, her cousin brother was so acute that they lived in constant fear of death.

According to close watchers of the state, Khairlanji rather represents a climax of the deteriorating situation in a state which, despite its 'progressive' image, has systematically ingrained denial of justice to dalits and the other marginalised sections of our society as part of policy. May it be the ongoing social boycott of the dalits in Aarajkheda village, Renapur tehsil in Latur district, which happens to be Chief Minister's home district, or the similar boycott of dalits in village Yavati in Nanded district, the state has never tried to shed its partisan image vis-a-vis attacks on dalits.

The barbaric killings were followed by a systematic cover up operation with due connivance of the local police and administration. A village level panchayat was held immediately after the gory incident and it was 'decreed' that nobody would utter a word on it. The police officials also 'complied' with the request, and subsequently only cases under some vague sections of the Indian Penal Code were filed, such where bail is easier.

It is also alleged that the local MLA, who belongs to the BJP, was both instrumental in instigating the perpetrators and then helping them hush up the case. It is not surprising that the BJP-Shiv Sena leadership which is ever ready to put the ruling coalition on the mat has maintained complete silence over the incident. The Nitin Gadkaris and the Mundes and the Thakres have not even condemned the barbaric killings of the dalits. In fact to divert people's attention from the spontaneous and militant assertion of the dalits, the Bhandara district units of the Shiv Sena and Bajrang Dal have joined hands to raise a counter agitation on an emotive issue.

The Deputy Chief Minister, who also manages the Home portfolio, expressed satisfaction over the direction of investigation. Later, when the militant movement of the dalits compelled him to wake up from deep slumber he, instead of taking urgent steps to defuse tension, preferred to make some irresponsible statements. Instead of addressing the causes of the dalits' anger, he 'discovered' that their anger was a pointer towards growing naxal-dalit affinity.

While the state government and its machinery tried to sweep the issue below the carpet and the saffron Parivar in Opposition maintained a studied silence, the response of the leadership of the mainstream dalit movement was also not qualitatively different. Neither the factions of the dalit formations participating in the state government nor those which remained outside it made any efforts to raise the pitch over the incident. The conspiracy of silence on the part of the dalit leadership in the state was so blatant that when lakhs of people converged in Nagpur (2nd October) to celebrate the golden jubilee year of the historic conversion of dalits to Buddhism, none of them deemed it necessary to highlight the Khairlanji killings. Even according to conservative estimates 15-20 lakh people visited Deekshbhoomi during those celebrations which continued for a fortnight.

In the backdrop of the Khairlanji killings a demand has been raised for the formulation of a new law 'specific to the situation in the state'. The state government has formed a committee to look into the actual implementation of the existing law(s). But even a cursory glance at some of the early reports by various agencies gives one an idea what sort of conclusions would follow.

The 'Report on Prevention of Atrocities against Scheduled Castes' (NHRC, 2004, Delhi), which studied how the law unfolded itself, has underlined that the 'state has failed in this respect' on 'several fronts'. These are 'failure to effectively implement the laws relating to atrocities against SCs and STs', which is 'reflected both in respect of preventing violence from taking place' as well as in the 'inability to punish perpetrators of violence after the crime is committed'; 'failure to act against its own agencies involved in the commission of violence'; 'failure to strengthen the watchdog institutions' etc.

There have been innumerable reports detailing how the local police, in connivance with the perpetrators themselves, sabotages the implementation of laws basically meant to protect dalits and tribals. It is noticed that instead of filing cases under the SC-ST (Prevention of Atrocities) Act 1989, it prefers filing cases under normal provisions of the Indian Penal Code, which facilitates easy release of the accused on bail. It also facilitates the filing of 'counter cases' against the victims themselves, so that a compromise could be forced. The Third Report of the NPC (New Delhi: GOI, 1980, p.31) had rightly underlined how "[f]alse criminal cases are sometimes engineered merely for the sake of making arrests to humiliate and embarrass some specified enemies of the complainant, in league with the police for corrupt reasons."

Considering the militant character of the mass movement protesting the killings, one might easily presume that the legal wrangling in the Khairlanji massacre would not lead to a blind alley and that the perpetrators of the massacre would receive exemplary punishment. But there is no guarantee that this would be the case.

It has been the experience of activists and social workers fighting such cases that a delay in the judicial verdict is always beneficial to the perpetrators. The most important lesson is that we should be constantly on the vigil and demand that the trial be conducted by a special court and on a daily basis.

The public activism on display in the cases of Priyadarshini Mattoo, Nitish Katara and Jessica Lal has been much talked about. Can one expect a replay of the same spirit? Although, as Priti Singh put it in an op-ed piece in the *Hindustan Times* 'Priyanka's Khairlanji, I'm afraid, unlike Priyadarshini's Delhi, doesn't have an India Gate for the purpose of holding candlelight vigils.' (16th November 2006).

November 2006

Touchable Crimes

Investigations by the police or the intelligence officials even in highly contested cases manage to unabashedly work towards travesty of justice rather than what they are supposed to do. We have been witness to the nineteen year delay in the filing of the FIR in the case of the tragic massacre of Muslims at Hashimpura (1987) – thanks no doubt to the efforts of the powers that be to save the perpetrators of the heinous crime.

The recent charge sheet filed by the CBI, asked to look into the attacks and arson at a Dalit (Valmiki) *basti* in Gohana, has again highlighted this propensity of the upholders of law and order to play a partisan role in any investigation likely to be initiated. According to a newspaper report the CBI charge sheet into the 2005 Gohana riots in Haryana has '...revealed that some people in [the] Balmiki Basti had set their houses on fire themselves, allegedly for compensation." The charge sheet talks of the CBI's observations that "extensive burning was observed in 19 out of 28 houses. Of these, nine houses were inspected thoroughly and it appeared that in these houses the "simulated arsoning" was carried out, which are yet "to get compensation".

Gohana, 75 kilometres away from the national capital witnessed the burning of 50-60 houses belonging to the Valmiki community on 31 st August 2005 in broad daylight. A 1,500-2,000 strong mob comprising upper caste people, belonging mainly to the Jat community, attacked their houses in a systematic manner. The perpetrators had come armed with spears, batons, axes, petrol and kerosene. They vandalised TV sets, refrigerators and washing machines, looted the valuables and burst LPG cylinders.

I still remember our visit to Gohana (4th September 2005) as part of a fact finding team – writers, journalists, social activists – which had rushed there to get first hand details, mere five days after the incident. Haunted houses, barren faces, fear still lurking in their eyes, only some old people or relatives of the inhabitants were visible. We still have copies of photographs that we took to comprehend the magnitude of damage. None of those photographs, by no iota of imagination, convey that people residing in those houses could have themselves caused the atrocities, supposedly to get compensation (as the experienced officers of the CBI want us to believe).

The immediate reason for the anger of the Jats was the murder of a Jat youth, allegedly after a scuffle with some Valmiki youth, but the roots go deeper. The Valmikis (who have been condemned to the lowermost status in the *Varna* hierarchy) in Gohana had not only moved up a few ladders in social mobility, thanks to the efforts put in by the people coupled with the affirmative action programmes of the government, but had also begun asserting their rights. The Jats who have been dominating the polity and society in the area in innumerable ways felt threatened with the new awakening among the Valmikis. In this context the murder of the Jat youth became a rallying point for them. The compromising role of the political parties was also clearly visible. The anti-democratic, anti dalit, anti women role of the various caste panchayats has already come to the fore. In no uncertain terms they have made it clear that they are capable of taking the law into their own hands and 'teaching a lesson' to the dalits in typical medieval fashion.

It was obvious to all members of the team that the 'spontaneous expression' of anger exhibited by the upper castes against the dalits was led by an organised and experienced team of house blasters. Independent neighbours in the area, who did not want to be named, had disclosed to us how the gang of lumpens under the leadership of an advocate and son of a local MP had been the marauders. People working in a nearby hospital even told us that the marauders had brought with them mini trucks to ferry the loot from the houses. It is not beyond comprehension that the 'task' of burning and looting 50-60 houses spread over an area of three square kilometers cannot be accomplished within 15 minutes, the line that the police was initially trying to give us. Incidentally the police is on record that only 5-6 houses were burnt and the rest caught fire because of winds.

The connivance of the police and the district administration in this gory incident was also evident from the fact that they had full information of the impending attack. Contrary to taking steps to avert any untoward incident they actually asked the residents of these houses to leave the city, clearly stating that in the circumstances it would be impossible for the police to ensure their security.

When the fact finding team reached Gohana, we discovered to our dismay that attempts were on under the supervision of the sub divisional magistrate himself to 'clean' the houses, despite the fact that all the residents had still not returned nor a proper evaluation of the damages to the property been conducted. These attempts smacked of a planned cover-up of the whole incident. It was also clear that in spite of strong criticism for its inaction and connivance the administration was not ready to mend its ways. As part of the cover-up the whole basti of Valmikis, which had laboured hard and had moved up the ladder of social mobility, were being charged with being criminals. A senior police officer is on record saying that 'criminals thrive in the basti', as if this gave licence to the dominant castes 'to teach them a lesson'.

And last but not the least Gohana had elicited a media reaction said to be unique in its history. Thanks to the keen interest shown by some journalists, the burning of houses in Gohana could be witnessed by the rest of the populace on some TV channels. It would not be an understatement that but for these journalists the whole incident would have remained buried under the whimsies of the local thana itself. But what happened the next day was unpardonable. Two leading TV channels (ZEE and STAR) went in for a live telecast of a large gathering led by the dominant castes organised as a '*Sarva Jaati Panchayat*' wherein not only were the dalits further stigmatised but the administration itself was warned against taking any action against the perpetrators.

Perhaps all these details are now meaningless, as we have before us the 'official' truth scripted by the diligent officers of the CBI. Perhaps all these details would be useful for posterity, wherein some gen-next researcher might discover the metamorphosis of victims into perpetrators at the dawn of the 21 st century.

In an article written then for a magazine the undersigned had demanded that "...it would not be enough that the actual perpetrators of the attack are identified and tried according to the suitable provisions of the SC-ST Act but it is high time that immediate action is taken by the government under the Section 4 of the Scheduled Castes and Scheduled Tribes (Prevention of Atrocities) Act, 1989, against the responsible police officers and others for their willful negligence in providing protection to Dalits and their property and their complicity in the rioting incident."

Considering the fact that the premier investigating agency has held dalits as co-offenders in the burning of their own houses, it would be easy for the responsible officers to save themselves from charges of 'willful negligence'.

This is an era of 'remakes' and 'remixes'. In a way Gohana is a crude remake of the 'first' massacre of dalits in independent India (1969) at Keezhavenmani, Thanjavur. Dalits had protested there under the leadership of a radical party demanding better wages. And the dominant castes, who were big landowners, literally came to their hamlet and massacred them – mostly women and children – one by one, supposedly to teach them a lesson. In all 44 people were killed. But what was the decision of the courts? It allowed all the perpetrators of the massacre to go scot free under the specious argument that 'since all the accused belonged to upper castes, it is impossible that they would have gone walking to the hamlet'!

Perhaps it is time we listen to the voice of the legendary leader of the oppressed, Dr Ambedkar: "It is usual to hear all those who feel moved by the deplorable condition of the Untouchables unburden themselves by uttering the cry, 'We must do something for the Untouchables.' One seldom hears any of the persons interested in the problem saying, 'Let us do something to change the Touchable Hindu'."

January 2007

Thinking Kambalpalli in Times of Khairlanji

M Venkatrayappa, a dalit from Kambalapalli, Kolar district, Karnataka still remembers the last glimpses of his wife Ramakka, sons Sriramappa and Anjaneya and daughter Papammas. It has been more than six years since they died a very tragic death. All of them, with four others from their hamlet, were burnt alive by the local Reddys. The police termed it revenge killing, supposedly in retaliation against the killing of Krishnappa Reddy, a village functionary belonging to an upper caste.

The Kambalapalli massacre of March 2000 had made national headlines. The tremendous public uproar compelled the then Congress government to not only apprehend the culprits but to also shift the dalits to a new village situated around 40 kms from Kambalapalli.

Today all that is passé. During the first week of December, when the entire nation was debating the recent surge in atrocities against dalits, came the damning verdict in this particular case. All the accused were acquitted. In legalese they call it the 'case' getting 'settled' as all "witnesses turned hostile" during the court hearings.

One can imagine why all the forty witnesses, including Venkatrayappa, preferred to turn hostile rather than speak the truth for favour of justice for their near and dear ones. Although nobody is ready to share it, one can sense the fear which still pervades 'new Kambalapalli' as the new settlement is called. Gangulappa, a witness, wryly admits he changed his version in court to save his children.

This was also the time when preparations were on for the inter state council meet called by the PM to deliberate on the specific issue of dalit rage. If the killings in Khairlanji and the militant movement of dalits in its aftermath formed the backdrop of this meet, the verdict in Kambalapalli massacre also added its own melancholy tone to it.

Anyone who knows how our polity functions can well tell you that the real essence of such meets, organised primarily to exhibit to the world the concern of the powers that be towards the weaker sections, end usually with adding yet another bundle of empty promises centering around their betterment. This particular meet was no different.

At this meet the Prime Minister admitted that the continuing atrocities against weaker sections are a 'national disgrace in a civilised society'. (*The Hindu*, 10 December 2006). He also lamented the fact that 'implementation of SC and ST (Prevention of Atrocities) Act has not been effective' and 'cases continue to be registered under weaker sections of IPC'. While calling for 'comprehensive review of the existing approaches, strategies and measures' he also reiterated the 'need to show political will' and also exhorted people to be more sensitive because 'laws alone were not sufficient in dealing with social violence'. Mr Shivraj Patil, the present Home Minister, while addressing the meet also talked of tightening the police machinery as it is found to be wanting in reining in the perpetrators of atrocities on dalits.

It is worth noting that the speeches of the Prime Minister and the Home Minister did not prove to be different from similar speeches made earlier. A convention held last year under the aegis of the Social Justice Minister (Jan 2005) Meira Kumar, which was duly attended by the Home Minister, had brought home this point with emphasis. According to a newspaper report:

> Social Justice Minister Meira Kumar pointed out that the conviction rate in cases registered under the Protection of Civil Rights Act is a mere 3.75 per cent. Besides, 75 to 77 per cent cases of crimes against Dalits remain pending despite the existence of special and designated courts. Union Home Minister Shivraj Patil, who was also present at the conference, acknowledged that the system was not delivering justice and existing laws safeguarding the rights of backward classes may have to be changed or tightened. (January 12, 2005, *The Telegraph*).

Of course the verdict in the Kambalapalli case is hardly surprising. The nearly sixty year old history of independent India bears witness to the phenomenon of perpetrators of crimes against dalits being allowed to go scot free. The mechanism for denial of justice to dalits has rather been perfected down the years. Normally such cases are either not registered, and if at all they get registered, they are not filed under appropriate provisions of the law. Again, registration of cases under the proper law is no guarantee that they would be investigated by designated authority in such cases. The result is for everyone to see: acquittal on flimsy grounds.

A conclusion of a detailed and systematic study of 400 judgements passed by different district courts of Gujarat done by Vajibhai Patel, Secretary of Council for Social Justice, corroborates this. It tells us that utterly negligent police investigation at both the higher and lower levels coupled with a distinctly hostile role played by the public prosecutors is the main reason for the collapse of cases filed under the Atrocities Act. It is worth noting that he has meticulously documented the judgements delivered under this Act since April 1, 1995 in the Special Atrocity Courts set up in 16 districts of the state. The study also blasts the common perception that the inefficacy of this law is due to false complaints being lodged or compromises between the parties. In actuality it is a complicit State that has rendered the Act toothless. (*Communalism Combat* March 2005).

It is possible that all these details could be brushed aside as a story repeated ad nauseam. All the talk of atrocities on dalits could be presented as another extension of the way in which 'state in the third world' unfolds itself. But the key point worth emphasising is that caste atrocities, much like gender oppression or racial atrocities, have a specificity which transcends the binary of 'state as perpetrator' and 'people as victims'. In fact they implicate the partisan role played by the people themselves.

The 'Report on Prevention of Atrocities against SCs' prepared by NHRC (2004) presents details of the way in which the civil society presents itself. Here civil society itself becomes a distinct beneficiary of caste based order and helps perpetuate the existing unequal social reactions and frustrates attempts to democratize society because through the customary arrangements the dominant classes are assured of social control over people who can continue to abide by their commands without any protest.

Of course the uncivil nature of the civil society presents before us a unique challenge where the need then becomes to rise above a mere discourse on civil and constitutional rights to address the failure of the largest democracy of the world to go beyond mere form. We have to appreciate that it concerns the greater hiatus that exists between constitutional principles and practice and corresponding ethical ones based on a diametrically opposed ideal.

One has to concede that under the purity and pollution based paradigm which is the cornerstone of our caste system, inequality receives both legitimisation and sanctification. As inequality is accepted both in theory and practice, a legal constitution has no bearing on the ethical foundation of caste-based societies. In fact Dr Ambedkar, the legendary leader of the oppressed had this very reality in mind when he emphasised the difference between what he called 'political democracy' and 'social democracy', the difference between 'one person having one vote' and 'one person having one value'.

January 2007

Tsundur
A Milestone in the Movement For Dalit Emancipation

If we do not struggle
If we do not persist in our struggle
The enemy would finish us with his bayonets
And pointing to our bones he would tell the rest of the world
Look, these are bones of slaves!
Look, these are bones of slaves!

A Hindi couplet

D Dhanraj from Tsundur (Guntur, Andhra Pradesh) possibly does not know how the rest of the world remembers August 6th. Neither does he possibly know that there is a city called Hiroshima in far away Japan which was nearly obliterated that day. But for him too the day symbolises deaths and destruction and an endless wait for justice.

He can still recollect each and every incident of that fateful day, way back in 1991, when five people from his community were lynched before his very eyes by a mob of marauders belonging to his own village. In fact, the bloodthirsty mob had almost got to him as well, but somehow he was saved. The streets of Tsundur that day witnessed deaths of eight people, all of them dalits, when a 400 strong armed mob of Reddys – a landlord caste which has dominated the politics of A.P since independence – attacked the dalits 'to teach them a lesson'. The perpetrators of the massacre were so brutal, they cut the dead bodies into pieces, put them in gunny bags and threw them in the nearby Tungabhadra canal.

But as of now the wait for justice seems to be finally over. The recent judgement of the Special Court – which was the first of its kind formed under the provisions of the Scheduled Castes and Scheduled Tribes Act (1989) at the scene of offence- has rather vindicated their sixteen year old struggle. Twenty one of the accused have been given life imprisonment and 35 of them have been asked to serve one year rigorous imprisonment. The Court has acquitted the rest of the accused stating lack of evidence, but a coalition of dalit organisations have been pressing the government to file a petition in the higher court to challenge the acquittal.

A brief recapitulation of the events in this 'historic case' tells us that the upper caste (read Reddys') used the pretext of alleged harassment of a Reddy girl in a cinema hall by a dalit youth to attack the dalits. The planned nature of the attack was evident also from the fact that within no time a few hundred strong mob of Reddys, wielding traditional weapons (and few of them carrying modern firearms), descended on the dalit hamlet and unleashed their fury against the innocents. In fact, sensing an imminent attack, most of the men folk had already left the village. Once the marauders learnt of this they literally chased them on the road adjoining the Tungabhadra canal and lynched them one by one.

In hindsight it is clear that the preplanned attack against the dalits was another attempt by the Reddys to reassert their age-old authority, which was being challenged by the growing assertion of dalits. The changed atmosphere in the village was quite evident. Not only had many of the dalits boys and girls benefited from the affirmative action programmes in education, a few among them had even surpassed the Reddys in many respects. Many of the dalits from the village were working with Indian Railways. Overall, the situation was such that the dalits had refused to follow the medieval dictates reserved for them under the *Varna* system.

D Dhanraj was a crucial witness in the case. He did not falter for a moment despite tremendous pressure brought upon him by the powerful Reddys. One can see that Tsundur, the small village in Guntur, has created many such 'unsung heroes' – ordinary people who have faced heavy odds so that they get justice. Merukonda Subbarao, a fifty six year old daily wage-worker, who had served as the first president of the Tsundur Victims Association, was another such 'hero' who identified and named forty of the accused in the court room, from among the one hundred and eighty three people. It was clear that the whole incident was etched in his memory so strongly that he did not falter despite the judges requests to repeat the identification. And who can forget martyr Anil Kumar, a young man in his twenties, who was in the forefront of the struggle so that the perpetrators of the massacre are punished without delay. Anil was killed in a police firing during one of those struggles.

As it happens in the case of every other atrocity against the dalits, in this instance too the Reddys who have dominated the state politics since independence, tried with all their might that they may go scot free. Using their contacts in the judiciary, bureaucracy and the police administration they tried in all ways to delay the process of justice for as long as they could.

Attempts were made to buy or coerce dalits in various ways, and the state also cooperated with the Reddys. It felt that by distributing largesse to the dalits, giving jobs to a few of them, and awarding compensation to the victims' families they may dilute their yearning for justice. But dalits in Tsundur wanted nothing less than severe punishment for the perpetrators. Unitedly they raised a slogan 'Justice not Welfare'. It is worth emphasising that with their sustained resistance they were able to make Tsundur a key issue in state politics.

I.

Any independent observer of the dalit situation in the country would say that the conviction of the perpetrators at Tsundur is a significant milestone in the on going dalit emancipation movement.

The nearly sixty year old history of independent India bears witness that perpetrators of crimes against dalits in majority of the cases have been allowed to go scot free. The mechanism for denial of justice to dalits has been perfected down the years. Normally such cases are either not registered, and if at all they get registered are not filed under appropriate provisions of the law. Registration of cases under proper law is also no guarantee that they would be investigated by the designated authority in such cases. The results are for everyone to see: acquittals on flimsy grounds.

As is well known detailed and systematic study of 400 judgements passed by different district courts of Gujarat done by Vajibhai Patel, Secretary of Council for Social Justice, corroborates this. It tells us that utterly negligent police investigations at both the higher and lower levels, coupled with a distinctly hostile role played by the public prosecutors, is the main reason for the collapse of cases filed under the Atrocities Act. It is worth noting that he has meticulously documented these judgements delivered under this Act since April 1, 1995 in the Special Atrocity Courts set up in 16 districts of the state. The study also blasts the common perception that the inefficacy of this law is due to false complaints being lodged or compromises between the parties. In actuality it is a complicit State that has rendered the Act toothless.(*Communalism Combat*, March 2005).

People would recollect that in an inter state council meet called by the Prime Minister to deliberate on the specific issue of dalit rage, the Prime Minister himself had lamented that the 'implementation of SC and ST (Prevention of Atrocities) Act has not been effective' and 'cases continue to be registered under weaker sections of IPC'. (*The Hindu*, 10th December 2006).

A convention held last year under the aegis of the Social Justice Minister (January 2005), Meira Kumar, attended also by the Home Minister, had brought home this point with emphasis.

The NHRC's 'Report on Prevention of Atrocities against SCs' (2004 analyses in detail how the civil society reproduces itself. The civil society becomes a distinct beneficiary of the caste based order and helps perpetuate the existing unequal social relations and frustrates attempts to democratize society because through the existing customary arrangements the dominant classes are assured of social control over people.

2.

It would not be an exaggeration to say that the victory of the dalits in Tsundur is 'historic' in very many ways:

- It demonstrated the immense possibilities inherent in the SC and ST Prevention of Atrocities Act (1989). As rightly noted by many analysts this is the first time in the nearly twenty year old trajectory of this Act that special courts had to be set up at the scene of offence. And the dalits were saved from travelling long distances to depose in the courts and face harassment on the way at the hands of the dominant castes.

It is noteworthy that dalits in Tsundur were so united that they neither accepted any summons from the courts nor did they attend a court situated at some distance from the village. They demanded in unison that the courts should come to them and the government had to concede to their demand and set up special courts in the school premises in the village.

- They also demanded that they be provided with a Public Prosecutor and a judge who has a positive track record in dealing with cases of atrocities on dalits. After a great deal of dilly-dallying the government complied with this demand as well.

- It has been normal in all such cases that with passage of time people, including victims and their families, lose interest or tire in continuing their fight for justice. They come under pressure and are coerced into changing their statements in the courts. We have before us the recent verdict in Kambalapalli massacre of dalits in Karnataka based on a situation where the witnesses – those very people who had lost their near and dear ones – turning hostile, leading to the acquittal of the accused.

The significance of the Tsundur struggle is that those leading the campaign were successful in keeping people mobilised through these many years. Of course the help rendered by dalit and left organisations also played an important role in keeping the flame alive. Tsundur became a rallying point for different left and democratic forces in the state and it was the harbinger of a new turn in left politics, as the left also resolved to take up the issue of caste oppression.

3.

As rightly noted by an analyst the victory (albeit a partial one) at Tsundur has come as a breath of fresh air in the smouldering world of dalit oppression. And it is high time that its inspiration is spread far and wide, and a realization dawns that a united and sustained struggle can succeed.

People who have visited Tsundur would tell you that there is a 'Raktakshetram' in Tsundur – a place in the centre of the dalit basti where the massacred dalits were cremated. Till date it has remained a live reminder of the atrocity. But post-verdict one can say that it has metamorphosed into a symbol of the yearning for a life of dignity and the readiness to make sacrifices in order to make it happen.

September 2007

Dalits in 'Hindu Rashtra'

The Gujarat earthquake in the year 2001 and the consequent relief and rehabilitation programme was an eye opener to the outside world regarding the deep seated caste bias in the Gujarati community apart from the much talked about bias against the minorities. There were reports that in many places the relief and rehabilitation work bypassed the dalits and the Muslims.

The organised genocide of Muslims in the year 2002 led by the Sangh Parivar organizations, aided and abetted by the Modi government, was another occasion when the travails and tribulations of the dalits came to notice. While the cooption of a section of the dalits into the Hindutva agenda and their metamorphosis as foot-soldiers of the Hindutva brigade was duly reported, the *Varna* dominated media did not deem it necessary to emphasise some related facts. The genocide in Gujarat also involved killings of some dalits. The dalits lost 108 lives in Gujarat, 38 in the city of Ahmedabad alone. A number of these deaths occurred due to the dalits resisting Hindutva goons by siding with the hapless Muslims.

Interestingly Babasaheb Dr Bhim Rao Ambedkar had asked his followers to prevent the Hindu Raj becoming a reality at all costs.

1. Who Exhumed the Body of the Two Year Old and Why?

It was the year 2001 when Naresh Solanki's two and half year old nephew died. The aggrieved family from Hooda village, Palanpur block of Banaskantha district, went and buried him in the community burial grounds. No sooner had they reached home the news came that a member of the Patel community from the village had, literally, exhumed the body of the child with a tractor – all because the powerful Patels, who had encroached on some part of the land next to the burial ground, had felt offended with the burial.

It is more than seven years now since the incident took place and the dalits of Hooda village are still awaiting allotment of some land for burial from the collector and the village panchayat. When a community elder died last year they had no choice but to carry his body to another village, where fortunately the dalits have a separate graveyard. .

But can it be said that this problem of no land even for burials is limited to Hooda, or it is a statewide phenomenon? A report carried by *Mail Today* in the first week of February 2009 has thrown light on the issue. It tells us that dalits are not allowed to use common grounds for burial and are often forced to use a part of waste land near the villages for this purpose. Absence of any legal entitlement forces them to be pushed out of such lands by the dominant upper castes.

A survey conducted by Gujarat Rajya Grampanchayat Samajik Nyay Samiti Manch found that '[o]ut of 657 villages in Gujarat, 397 villages do not have any designated land allotted for burial for dalits. Out of the 260 villages where land has been formally allotted, 94 have seen encroachments by the dominant castes and in 26 villages it is a low lying area and therefore the ground gets waterlogged.

It would not be an exaggeration to say that when the question of burying the dead comes up dalits share a strange commonality with the Muslims. Muslims share a similar predicament when they find their graveyards getting encroached by the dominant classes. A few years ago the Gujarat High Court had to intervene and direct the State government to post police personnel as attempts were on to encroach upon the graveyard of Muslims in Patan.

2. Tell Your Caste, Lose Your House!

If the dead dalits have no dignity in 'Hindu Rashtra', one can just imagine the status of the living. One test could be house hunting for a dalit in Ahmedabad – capital of 'Hindu Rashtra' in making.

The general experience is that if a dalit approaches an upper caste builder for accommodation, he is either directly discouraged or tacitly denied it. It is immaterial whether the Dalit belongs to a sound economic background. For the builders and real estate agents, the presence of even one dalit family in a housing society becomes detrimental to sales.

Perhaps it is a marker of the deeply entrenched Varna/caste mindset, which has supposedly received a new lease of life after the 2002 carnage. One witnesses a unique trend in Ahmedabad where "only Dalit residential societies – around 300 of them" have come up in recent years. In a recent study done by him an *Indian Express* reporter emphasised that it "[is]... not a matter of choice, but of compulsion." ('A Dalit? Go find a Dalit society', DP Bhattacharya, Ahmedabad, June 17, 2007).

> Even if a Dalit can afford a flat in areas dominated by the upper castes, they are often denied by the builders or the seller," retired IAS officer PK Valera, who lives in one such Dalit society in Ramdevnagar, says. Some social scientists say the alienation started since 1982, after the anti-reservation agitation, but agree that the caste and class distinctions have become more serious in recent years. This trend can be seen not only in the walled city but also in the posh areas of west Ahmedabad like Satellite, Vastrapur, Bodakdev, Ambavadi. Socio-political scientist Achyut Yagnik says, "There are more than 300 Dalit societies in the city. In Chandkheda alone, there are 200 societies, most of which have come up after the 2002 riots when people moved out from Gomtipur, Bapunagar and Dani limda area. You will find construction contractors who only build Dalit societies.

Of course this near segregation of dalits in specific areas under the great umbrella of Hindu Unity does not stop the Sangh Parivar from using dalits for their sectarian agenda during elections and riots. Even a cursory glance at the list of the dead and wounded in the riots shows the names of only Muslims and Dalits; the other castes are nominal.

Interestingly dalits from outside the state, whose caste surnames are not identifiable, can easily get into the general housing societies.

3. Look the Other Way, While Recruiting Teachers

What is the common factor in all the non-grant receiving schools in Gujarat whose number, according the website of the Gujarat State Secondary and Higher Secondary Education Board, is around 3255. A close study of these schools may reveal many similarities but the foremost thing common between them is they routinely violate the statutory provisions of the Education Act 1972, although it is mandatory for such schools to adhere to the norms set by it. One result of this is that there are only a handful of teachers from the scheduled communities in all these schools.

Under the provisions of the Education Act 1972, it is mandatory for all the granted and non-granted schools to abide by the reservation policy while making recruitments. And the rule says that any school found to be violating these provisions is liable for having its registration cancelled. Experience shows that the rule is openly flouted by the non-granted schools. Interestingly the state government also seems to have accepted that the schools that are not given any aid cannot be compelled to follow the reservation policy.

It was only last year that the matter was publicly discussed when the *Indian Express* (Vadodara, May 26, 2008) carried a big expose about how the 'Government looks the other way as schools flout recruitment norms for teachers.' According to the Social Justice and Empowerment Department, which is supposed to supervise the implementation of the reservation policy, the simple reason for the statutory provisions of the Act being not implemented is the absence of a roster ensuring reservation.

The question naturally arises as to why the state has not deemed it necessary yet to take effective steps to stop such malpractices.

In fact, a RTI application filed by a leading social worker of Gujarat enquiring about the number of teachers who have been recruited by the non-granted schools under the reservation policy, led to this expose of details. Expressing concern over the state of affairs, the social worker demanded two things: cancelling of the registration of errant schools, and punishing the officers who were responsible for not getting the policy implemented.

4. Handling Atrocities Cases Atrociously

What is the rate of conviction in cases under the Prevention of Atrocity Act against SC/STs in Gujarat? It is mere 2.5 per cent, while the rate of acquittal is 97.5 per cent. A 23 page confidential report submitted by the state Social Justice Department to the State Chief Secretary and legal depart-

> *ments provides glaring examples of 'mishandling of cases registered under the Prevention of Atrocities Act against SC/STs.* *Indian Express*, September 15, 2006).

The report provides details of how cases are not investigated properly by the police and the hostile role played by public prosecutors during time of trials.

- The Act clearly stipulates that offences which are registered under this Act cannot be investigated by an officer below the rank of Dy Superintendent of Police but more than 4,000 such cases have been investigated by Police Inspectors or Police Sub Inspectors.

- Acquittal of the perpetrator because victim is not identified as member of SC or ST community, the simple reason being that caste certificate of the victim was not attached with the case papers.

- False claims by Public Prosecutors before the courts that the Act has been modified by the state government, although it is known that it is a central Act.

- Granting of anticipatory bails although there is no such provision in the Act. Interestingly the Parliamentary Committee on SC and ST Affairs had also expressed concern over such anticipatory bails granted 'in atrocity cases in the state of Gujarat'.

In fact a detailed and systematic study of 400 judgements done by Vajibhai Patel, Secretary of Council for Social Justice, compelled the government to take cognizance of this 23 page report. This report tells us that utterly negligent police investigation at both the higher and lower levels coupled with a distinctly hostile role played by the public prosecutors is the main reason for the collapse of cases filed under the Atrocities Act. It is worth noting that he has meticulously documented these judgements delivered under this Act since April 1, 1995 in the Special Atrocity Courts set up in 16 districts of the state. The study also blasts the common perception that the inefficacy of this law is due to false complaints being lodged or compromises between the parties. He shows that in actuality it is a complicit State that has rendered the Act toothless.

The National Crime Records Bureau had made an observation a few years ago, which went largely unnoticed. Gujarat ranks third in the country after UP and Bihar in the matter of atrocities against dalits.

(*Asian Age*, 11 April 2003). Its earlier record also revealed a similar picture. According to the Bureau's 1998 report, the total number of atrocities against dalits in the country as a whole was 25,617. Of these 8894 cases were registered in Gujarat alone. 28 cases of rapes of dalit women were recorded that year, which was seventh highest in the country. And yet the state was termed 'Vibrant Gujarat'!

The BJP government did nothing at all to check offences against the SCs and STs in the state. The special dalit courts envisaged in all districts under the SC and ST (Prevention of Atrocities) Act 1989 are still not a reality. Out of 26 districts in Gujarat, only 10 have been provided with special courts, although not even one of these 10 courts accord special status to dalit issues, according to Dalit activists. (ibid.).

5. Ambedkar's Prognosis

One can go on providing statistics on the dalit situation in the first 'Hindu Rashtra' in Secular- Democratic India. Our aim here, however, is not to present a data bank on this theme.

Our main concern is to raise two points.

- Why has the near secondary status granted to dalits not become an important issue in the anti-communal movement?

- Why does a section of the dalits still feel enamoured with Hindutva? Can it be seen as a sign of its upward mobility within the Hindu religion? Or is it a marker of the hatred they have accumulated vis-a-vis the minority communities, and they are now getting ready to play out the Hindutva agenda of their own free will?

It needs to be emphasised here that all over Gujarat one finds thousands and thousands of hoardings set up at prominent places by one or the other of the affiliates of the Sangh Parivar claiming that 'you are entering this or that locality of Hindu Rashtra', which is completely illegal and an open proclamation of 'secession' from the rest of the society.

At this juncture one thinks of Ambedkar's prognosis vis-a-vis Hindu Raj. In his book *Pakistan or Partition of India* (page 358), written before the partition of India, he clearly prophesied that if Hindu Raj became a reality it would certainly be the greatest menace to this country. Regardless of what Hindus may say, "Hinduism is a danger to Independence, Equality and Brotherhood. Thus it is an enemy of democracy. We should make all out efforts to stop Hindu Raj from becoming a reality." Is anybody listening?

March 2009

Horrors of Caste Discrimination in Ashram Schools

Higher caste teachers in India have physically and verbally abused lower caste students and India will not be able to achieve the literacy goals set for 2015. UNESCO-commissioned report on the Education For All (EFA) programme. Sarva Siksha Abhiyan (SSA) is the Indian version of EFA.

India is among 30 countries that the UNESCO feels will not make the target. Caste abuse in Indian schools: UNESCO Education for All. Report lists India among 30 countries that will miss 2015 goals. Varghese K George. Posted online: *Indian Express*, Thursday, November 10, 2005 at 0018 hours IST.

I

Few years ago a study commissioned by Ken Livingstone, the then Mayor of London had discovered how 'Black teachers face bullying and racism' in the school and had linked the plight of the black teachers to the 'continuing problem of underachievement among black pupils'. The landmark report had called for a formal investigation – akin to the Stephen Lawrence inquiry into policing – to address concerns that black teachers are isolated, maligned and robbed of proper pay and status. (Hugh Muir, Friday September 8, 2006, *The Guardian*). There were also calls for a public inquiry into racism in schools.

One is yet to come across a comprehensive study of a similar nature on how 'apartheid of different kinds' unfolds itself in schools in this part of the earth and whether teachers coming from socially oppressed communities are similarly '...isolated, maligned and robbed of proper pay and status…', or how this impacts the performance of the students coming from similar sections of society. Of course, one does get inklings of the state of affairs through related studies, reports and investigations.

As of now we have before us a number of sample studies/enquiry reports occasioned by specific complaints lodged mainly by students protesting discrimination faced inside particular institutions. It is widely known that in recent times a few premier institutions of the country made news headlines for following policies, adopting mechanisms, and continuing processes which put students coming from socially oppressed communities in disadvantageous positions, and denying them their constitutional rights.

The treatment meted out to the Scheduled Category students in the premier institutes reminds one of a three year old report of a Parliamentary Committee wherein it had expressed concern over the 'abysmally low' participation of SC and ST students, 'as compared to their percentage in total population'. It divulged that 'the enrollment of SCs in higher education has ranged between 8.6 per cent in 1990-91 to 11.3 percent in 2002-2003.' (Parliament of India, 172 nd Report on Higher Education, presented on 22 nd May 2006).

If students from socially oppressed communities going for higher education find it difficult to wage a consistent struggle against exclusions and discriminations and are condemned to face it, one can just imagine the plight of students coming from similar backgrounds who go for school education.

There is no doubt that the most vulnerable among the lot seems to be those who are admitted in the scores of 'Ashram Schools' – residential schools – where they are at the complete mercy of teachers and non-teaching staff.

Perhaps few recent news clippings from such residential schools can give us an idea of the gravity of the situation.

II

Nobody would have imagined that 66 girls studying in N Jhalarsingh Kanyashram, a government-run school for SC/ST girls in Gajapati district, (Orissa) would walk a distance of 25 kms from their hostel unannounced, to protest the behaviour of three teachers who allegedly made casteist taunts to them. Altogether there are 250 girls studying in the institution. Of them 238 live in the hostel.

It is learnt that the three would "always keep telling" them that "You all belong to lower castes." One of the girls said on condition of anonymity:

> They have inflicted unbearable torture and trauma on us. Even over a trifle thing, they make fun and remind us of our so-called low-caste background. It's very very cruel. For long, we put up with the trauma, hoping things will improve someday. But nothing of that sort happened,

Of course, it was not for the first time that SC/ST students studying in Gajapati district had undertaken such an action. Earlier, a group of students of Ekalabya Abasika Bidyalaya at Chandragiri and Laxmipur Abasika Bidyalaya near Koinpur in Gajapati district had walked out to protest against alleged mismanagement and misbehaviour of teaching staff. ('Caste taunts by teachers drive 66 SC/ST girls to run away from Orissa school', http://timesofindia.indiatimes.com/news/city/bhubaneswar/articleshow/4874588.cms, Sunil Mohan Patnaik, TNN 9 August 2009, 11:31pm IST).

Another news report which appeared in *The Statesman* which covered the incident tells us: More than 70 residential schools are run by the SC/ST Welfare Department, ITDA and the Mass Education Department in Gajapati. The students are given stipends ranging between Rs 400 and Rs 500 per month for their education and this is utilised for their food and accommodation.

It is difficult to imagine the situation in which large numbers of grown-up girls from underprivileged backgrounds, studying in various government schools, are condemned to live where they have limited protection in their own premises. Male teachers are put in charge of the girls and outsiders have free access to the girls' hostels. They stay in badly maintained accommodations and are prone to diseases due to congestion.

While the students of Gajapati could unitedly protest the humiliation heaped on them, for students of Kasturba Vanvasi Kalyan Ashram in Barwani district, (Madhya Pradesh), where around 1,071 girls are studying at present, circumstances unfolded with such rapidity that they could not get an opportunity to even say anything.

For Savita Gangaram Barela (11), Kavita Motiram (13), Rita Hawaldar (11) and Saraswati (9) the '*Khichdi*' and '*Halwa*' they consumed a day before Independence Day (14 August) – when they were getting ready to participate in the celebrations – proved fatal. They died within few hours of consuming this contaminated food in a hostel in the tribal dominated Niwali village in Madhya Pradesh.

Around 92 girls had to be admitted to different hospitals after they developed symptoms of food poisoning. ('Fourth victim dies of food poisoining in MP School', *Hindustan Times,* 19th August 2009).

If the girls from Barwani had to pay with their lives for the acts of omission and commission on the part of the management, an altogether different story unfolded in Gulabrao Ukey Adivasi Ashramshala in Wardha district, 150 km from Nagpur, which was started with the 'noble aim of providing quality education to the tribal population'. The Maharashtra government had promptly provided aid for this institution. Little could anyone have had the premonition that the Ashramshala would metamorphose into a torture chamber for the tribal children and a day would arrive when the proprietor and peon of this residential school would be sent behind bars for allegedly raping minor girl students over the past three years. It is learnt that at least five minor girls were found to be sexually exploited by the duo. (*Hindustan Times,* Aug 20, 2009).

It is 'normal' to find staff working in other similar Ashramshalas wanting in this regard on many occasions; the management also seems to condone the caste apartheid in practice before their own eyes. But the apathy on the part of the government seems to be the key factor in worsening the situation. Again, the manner in which a fifty year old school, established with the very purpose of rehabilitating children of the "denotified criminal tribes", Vikas Vidyalaya – the oldest boarding school for Dalits in Allahabad – finds itself lying in shambles just goes to vindicate this. It happens to be the only school in eastern UP where Dalit children belonging to the denotified tribes category from Azamgarh, Jaunpur, Allahabad, Pratapgarh, Mirzapur, Fatehpur, Kaushambi, Ghazipur and Sant Ravidas Nagar are admitted and can study up to class X.

One of the two hostels has not been in use for a long time, in fact after its roof had collapsed. "In the space meant for two students, eight students live in each room in the hostel," said Joshi. He added: "The school gets Rs 18 per day per child for food as opposed to Rs 40 given to other government-aided schools. Only Rs 150 per year per student is given for books and Rs 300 annually for clothes."

There are no teachers for maths and science," he said. The teachers and staff are yet to receive the benefits of the Fifth Pay Commission. ('School for Dalits running on its ruins', Vijay Pratap Singh, Posted: Aug 21, 2009 at 0246 hrs IST, *Indian Express*).

III

One can go on narrating instances of institutionalized discrimination practiced at various levels inside these schools.

Any close watcher of the situation would tell us that there is nothing 'surprising' about the situation. Some years ago hundreds of students from an Ashram School in Thane (Maharashtra) had undertaken a similar 'long march' *a la* the students of Gajapati district, to protest the inhuman treatment meted out to them inside the school where they were not even properly fed.

Only last year a few students from a government run residential school for tribal students in Jharkhand died after being fed contaminated milk.

Madhya Pradesh, which tops the list of states in 'atrocities on tribals', witnessed deaths of some students from snake bites in an Ashramshala last year. The school, constructed in a marshy area, had no provisions for protection or medication for snakebites.

Last year a two-member Bench of the Supreme Court headed by Chief Justice KG Balakrishnan and Justice Aftab Alam had issued a Notice to the central and state governments (24th October 2008) over a petition filed by a students' organisation regarding the inhuman conditions existing in 1,130 hostels meant for SC-ST students spread over 240 districts in the country. The said organisation had conducted a survey in 2006-2007 of such hostels and made it the basis of their petition. Their study had pointed out that many such hostels have been built in jungles where students have to study in candlelight and are compelled to consume impure water.

IV

The plight of the SC-ST students inside such Ashram Schools is a marker of the situation which exists at the grassroots level. One can see it as an indication of the deeper malaise in our society, one in which we are ready to protest the 'racial attacks on Indian students in Australia' but not to look inward and see for ourselves what we are doing to our own people.

It does not appear surprising, therefore, that even after 60 plus years of independence and talk of affirmative action programmes, for the majority of SC-ST boys and girls getting education still happens to be a game of hurdles today.

The recent changes in economy and polity have made the situation worse for them. Unless urgent steps are taken to ameliorate the situation there is bound to be a further shrinkage of avenues of education as well as employment within educational institutions for those belonging to the Scheduled Castes and Scheduled Tribes. First and foremost, the economic reforms of the 90s and the consequent process of privatisation and commercialisation of education and the abandonment of affirmative action in these sectors, has further marginalised these sections. Secondly, the technological changes signified by the 'information technology' revolution have given birth to a new 'digital divide' wherein the dalits and tribals are finding themselves at the bottom.

The question of apportioning blame for this state of affairs naturally arises, and it is true the State comes out in rather unflattering terms when one takes up the issue. But a point also worth emphasising is that caste discrimination, much like gender discrimination or racial discrimination, has a specificity in which the civil society is clearly implicated.

The founding fathers of the Constitution had solemnly resolved to secure to all citizens Justice: social, economic and political, Liberty of thought, expression, belief, faith and worship, and Equality of status and of opportunity, and to promote among them all Fraternity, assuring the dignity of the individual and unity among people. It also emphasised that: The State shall not discriminate against any citizen on grounds of religion, race, caste, place and birth or any form. The Directive Principles of the Constitution underlined that: The State shall promote with special care the educational and economic interest of the scheduled castes/tribes and shall protect them from social injustice and all forms of exploitation.

The plight of the SC-ST students in the Ashram schools once again proves that we are still far away from fulfilling these resolutions.

October 2009

Looking for Brahmeshwar 'The Absconder'

Myth of the Misuse of Laws meant for the Protection of Dalits and Tribals

Are the laws supposedly meant for the protection of dalits and tribals put to misuse?

While nobody can say that frivolous cases are not filed under the Act dealing with atrocities against SCs and STs, the manner in which the issue gets raised creates the impression that the only 'use' of this law is its 'misuse.' Neither the political class nor the articulate sections of our society seem ready to go in for a reality check. In fact, as a mark of respect for the 'sensitivities' of these classes towards this delicate issue, even Ms Mayawati in her earlier incarnations as Chief Minister of UP had cautioned the police about its 'misuse'. She is also reported to have issued GOs (government orders) to use this law only in cases involving rapes and murders of dalits.

The issue also came in for discussion in the Parliament recently when a member raised a query with regard to it. As reported in a section of the press, while replying to this query the Minister for Social Justice and Empowerment, Mr Napoleon, told the House that there were 6,564 false cases across India in 2008 under the Scheduled Castes and Scheduled Tribes (Prevention of Atrocities) Act, 1989, called the PoA Act. It is widely known that this Act provides for a sentence of up to five years for atrocity committed or humiliation heaped on a dalit, and provides for the setting up of special courts for trial of such cases. (*Hindustan Times*, 27th April 2010).

A break up of the figures cited by the said Minister is quite revealing. Of the numbers mentioned, 2287 of the false cases were from one state: Rajasthan. Andhra Pradesh followed with 1,577 false cases. Uttar Pradesh, the state with the largest dalit population (21 per cent of the state's 160-70 million and which stood at No. 1 as regards cases of atrocities against these sections), was third with 843 false cases. Punjab – the state with the highest proportion of Scheduled Castes at 29 per cent of the population – has had just 52 false cases registered, and Delhi is at the bottom of the list with three cases in 2008.

A quick analysis of these figures shows that around 75 per cent of the cases have been reported from three states only. What does the marginal presence or near absence of other states in this breakup tell us? Madhya Pradesh, which happens to be the state which has 'consistenly stood at No. 2 as far as atrocities against dalits are concerned', does not even find a mention in the newspaper report. Of course, this does not mean that there were no false cases from the state. The point is that there is no uniformity in the number of false cases registered, and neither are these directly proportional to the actual situation of dalits as it exists in the particular state. Gross generalisations would be too simplistic in the case.

Secondly, the nature of discussion around the alleged misuse of the Act has another negative fallout. The question of a more objective analysis of its implementation does not receive the prominence it deserves.

Take the recent case of Mirchpur (district Hissar, Haryana) where the dominant castes (namely the Jats) attacked the houses of the Valmikis in a preplanned and premeditated manner and burnt them with the district administration, especially the police personnel, turning a blind eye to this gory act (21 st April 2010). A handicapped girl, Suman, and her father Tarachand, also died in the arson. The police arrested a few of the arsonists, but neither the SHO. nor the *tehsildar* who were mute witness to this act were touched. As the issue snowballed into a major embarrassment for the Congress government at the centre with the parliament in session, only then were the infamous SHO. and the *tehsildar* put behind bars.

It is clear that despite the PoA Act making it mandatory (article 4) to take action against the government officials for dereliction of duty, it required Ms Sonia Gandhi's strong disapproval and Rahul Gandhi's trip to the village, for this step to be actually taken.

Any close watcher of the human rights situation in Haryana would vouch that this case is no exception. In fact Haryana has been witness to a number of attacks on dalits in the preceding decade, many of which reached national headlines. People can narrate incident after incident where an unholy alliance between a callous polity, an inhuman law and order machinery and a desensitized civil society made the life of dignity for the dalits a challenge in itself.

One still remembers the forcible expulsion of 250 dalits from Harsoula, District Kaithal, Haryana (February 2003). The local landowning people, mainly the jats, had objected to the dalits celebrating Ravidas Jayanti. And the ensuing fight culminated in the forcible expulsion of dalits from the village, with the police once again turning into mute spectators.

Ms Sonia Gandhi, the then leader of the Opposition, had raised the issue in the Parliament. She had lambasted the then Chautala government – a partner in the NDA then – for its failure to provide security and safety to the dalits. It has been more than six years since the Congress now wields power in the state but dalits from Harsoula are still condemned to live outside their ancestral village, somehow managing their lives in Kaithal and other places.

These days there is much talk about 'Internally Displaced Persons' the world over. One does not know whether dalits from Harsoula could be included in the list. In fact one can find many villages in Haryana similarly emptied of their dalit population under one pretext or the other by the local dominant castes. One also comes across a village named 'Devipuniya' in the state which came up when dalits from a village were similarly expelled from their village when Devi Lal had been the Chief Minister and PL Puniya, a well-known dalit leader of the area. As of now a majority of the dalits in Mirchpur, who are camping in Hissar town, are also contemplating leaving the village for good and shifting to a new location.

The National Human Rights Commission documents the state specific situation in very many ways. According to it every year at least six dalits are killed, twenty four dalit women raped and 51 houses of the dalits are set on fire in Haryana (Year 2002). Looking at the travails and tribulations faced by the dalits at various levels, most of which go unreported, it can be construed that the figures presented by NHRC are just the tip of the iceberg. This is also evident from the number of cases registered under the SC and ST (Prevention of Atrocities) Act 1989. While the number of cases registered was 32 in 1998, the figure shot up to 43 by the year 2003.

Apart from growing landlessness and continued denial of basic human rights, the most disturbing thing is that social and political visibility of dalits is minimal. It hardly seems to matter that they are around one fifth of the total population of the state (19.8%). The contrast is much sharper if one compares neighbouring UP where dalits are today the main fulcrum of the state politics.

Gohana, a town around 75 kms away from Delhi, had witnessed an organised attack on the dalit (Valmiki) basti led by the son of the local BJP MP (31 August 2005) culminating in the burning down of around 50-60 houses of the dalits. The attack was a fall out of the death of a jat youth in a scuffle with the dalit boys. The caste council (*Khap Panchayat*) of the dominant caste had played a very dubious role in the whole affair. Here also the police, present in good strength, did not act to stop the arsonists. Later it patted itself on the back as 'no lives were lost'.

Making an editorial comment on the growing dalit atrocities in the state some time ago, *The Tribune* (30th August 2007) had underlined how the state seems least bothered about the security and safety of the lives and properties of the dalits. According to it, most times that their houses come under attack, they are looted and burnt completely and the administration becomes active only when maximum damage has already been done. It also emphasised that the dalits are neither properly represented in the police and administration, nor is any special drive on to cover the backlog.

The developments in Mirchpur bear witness to the fact that despite prodding by the media there is no difference on the ground level situation. And denial of human rights to the dalits (and the tribals) is a 'national phenomenon'.

Recently the Supreme Court expressed concern that in most of the cases of violence against dalits even the necessary investigations are not completed in stipulated time. It also asked the Solicitor General, Mr Gopal Subramaniam, to give concrete suggestions to the courts so that necessary orders are passed for effective implementation of law. (*Hindustan*, 5 May 2010, 'SC-ST *mamlon kee jaanch mein deri par chinta*')

According to law, it is mandatory that such investigations are completed within a three month period in cases lodged under the SC-ST Act, 1989, by an officer not below the rank of DSP. The courts have observed that in many cases the investigations linger on for more than three years, which results in cases getting further delayed for years together. In a strong indictment of the functioning of the state machinery, on the matter of providing justice to the dalits, it said that many of the states have not even bothered to establish special courts for speedy trials of these cases. The delay in completing the necessary investigations and the absence of proper witnesses, apart from many other contingent factors, result in acquittals of the accused in 75 percent of the cases. The Supreme Court Bench concluded that delay in investigations results in denial of justice to the dalits, which in fact defeats the whole purpose of the law.

The discussion around the alleged misuse of the Act would remain incomplete without mention of the recent conviction in the case of Bathani Tola massacre. The Ara Court in Bihar recently convicted 23 people for the massacre of 21 dalits at Bathani Tola in Bhojpur in 1996.

The carnage occurred on July 11, 1996 when marauders of the Ranvir Sena (a private militia of the upper caste landlords) stormed the hamlet in Bhojpur's Sahar block and hacked to death 21 dalits. A majority of the people killed were women, teenage girls and babies less than ten months old. However, much on the lines of the April 7 verdict in the 1997 Laxmanpur-Bathe massacre case, the police pronounced Ranvir Sena supremo Brahmeshwar Singh "Mukhiya" the prime accused, an "absconder". *It is a different matter that this dangerous criminal has been in Ara jail since 2002.* It may be added here that when Nitish Kumar assumed the reins of power in 2004, one of the first things he did was to disband the Justice Amir Das Commission even as it was nearly ready with its report. This commission was appointed in the immediate aftermath of the Bathe massacre and had gone into great details about the political patronage which Ranvir Sena received from different mainstream political formations.

Expressing his clear disapproval of the way in which the Mukhiya continues to be a non-FIR accused, the Special Public Prosecutor told a reporter: "This clearly shows that both the police and the government are not interested in ensuring that justice is meted out." (*The Hindu*, 7th May 2010) The only explanation offered by the SP about this strange situation was that Brahmeshwar Singh did not stand trial as "certain court proceedings initiated against him were yet to be completed."

Anyone familiar with the pace with which courts deal with cases before them and the tremendous burden they are under would tell you that it can take decades for "certain court proceedings" to be completed, and a day could well arrive when, with all the witnesses to the case dead, Brahmeshwar Singh the mastermind of many a massacres may emerge from the jail unscathed, and would be happy to 'express full faith in the wisdom of the judiciary'.

May 2010

False Caste Certificates

Does the name of Sanjay Bhatia, ex superintendent of police, Haryana zone, sound familiar? Well, some people residing in Haryana or with some contacts in the state might have come across him during his near two-decade career as an IPS officer. Some may know his father, who also, incidentally, was a senior IAS officer. But very few would know of the great "anomaly" between father and son insofar as caste identity is concerned. Interestingly Sanjay Bhatia was registered as an "adi dharmi" (a caste falling under the scheduled category) and had duly benefited from the constitutional provisions meant for socially backward sections, whereas his parentage revealed him as belonging to the Rajput caste.

Recently the courts decided to end the anomaly once and for all. After a lengthy legal battle that continued for more than 17 years, Sanjay Bhatia has been convicted under IPC 420 for presenting a false caste certificate and has been dismissed from service. Courts have also ordered that he be sent to jail for a period of 100 days ('IPS officer convicted for fraud', *The Tribune*, July 13, 2005).

The "metamorphosis" of Sanjay Bhatia from a Rajput to an Adidharmi youth with due connivance of a section of the bureaucracy and polity may appear stranger than fiction. Those who are familiar with the purity-pollution based caste structure of Indian society – in which one is not free to choose one's caste – would be surprised if told that Bhatia is not an exception. There are thousands of people who are neither born in any of the socially oppressed castes nor have faced any caste based discrimination, but are enjoying the fruits of the "affirmative action" programmes envisaged by the makers of the Constitution.

It was only in mid-July that the chairperson of the National Commission of Scheduled Castes shared with the media a similar saga enacted by a Member of Parliament from Bijnor, UP, elected on Rashtriya Lok Dal ticket. According to him the said MP, named Munshi Pal, gave an affidavit that he did not belong to the scheduled caste when he wanted to sell his land. But at the time of elections he presented a caste certificate which showed that he belonged to the scheduled category; he contested from the reserved seat and won ('Panel to Probe MP 'Posing' as Dalit for Elections', *The Indian Express*, July 21, 2005).

It is a truism that the Sanjay Bhatias and the Munshi Pals represent just the tip of the iceberg. The gravity of the situation as it exists today can be gauged from the recent investigations done by the Central Bureau of Investigation (CBI) into the status of employees working in different ministries of the central and state governments. And the departments covered also include Delhi Development Authority (DDA), New Delhi Municipal Council (NDMC) and similar public sector undertakings (*Hindustan Times*, June 17, 2005). According to this investigation about 30 per cent of the employees in different departments of the Delhi government, who have got jobs on the basis of being belonging to scheduled tribes, have submitted false certificates for the same.

A Persistent Problem

Considering the seriousness of the problem the CBI even called a meeting of the chief vigilance officers of many central and state departments and public sector undertakings. It has also been resolved to check the credentials of the rest of the employees. CBI was rather compelled to take up this investigation since the Public Interest Litigation filed in the Delhi High Court had demanded a thorough investigation into the case. Interestingly, while the recent exposures in media have helped bring the issue into public focus it is not the case that policy-makers have been unaware of this. 'The Report of the Commissioner for Scheduled Castes and Scheduled Tribes, 1974' (New Delhi: Government of India Press, 1977) mentions the problem of false certificates although it is couched in bureaucratic language:

> ...Complaints continued to be received in this Organisation about false certificates obtained by non-scheduled caste/scheduled tribe persons to

> get the facilities admissible to members of scheduled caste/tribe communities. At times, it was observed that the authorities empowered to issue caste certificates did not satisfy themselves adequately about the genuineness of the castes to which the applicants claimed to belong. Sometimes, certificates were issued without necessary inquiries/verifications. This matter was also highlighted in the last report…The [Home] ministry has further suggested that the officials concerned may also be informed that action would be taken against them under the relevant provisions of the Indian Penal Code if any of them is found to have issued the certificates carelessly and without making proper verifications.

The very fact that the threat to use the Indian Penal Code has been mentioned implies that officials were selling certificates.

The "widespread incidence" of false certificates prompted the Commission to carry out pilot studies in several states. The third report of the National Commission for Scheduled Castes and Scheduled Tribes, (1994-95 and 1995-96, p. 192) tells us about the outcome of the process. A random check of 12 central government organisations in Tamil Nadu found 338 holders of fraudulent ST certificates. The Commission was successful in dismissing only six of them after enormous delay. In fact nearly a quarter of the individuals thwarted removal by getting stay orders from cooperative local courts.

In report after report one notices the National Commission of Scheduled Castes and Scheduled Tribes (since separated) grappling with this problem. To underline the gravity of the situation, in the Commission's 1998 report, as well as its previous one, separate chapters were devoted to the problem. It repeatedly called on the government to crack down on fraudulent certification and made detailed proposals for corrective measures, but none have been forthcoming. The fact is that few in the government really care. The Commission's 1998 report rather provided a final word:

> …certificates have been issued to ineligible persons, carelessly or deliberately... This has resulted in wrong persons availing of the benefits meant for the scheduled castes and scheduled tribes on a false pretext.
>
> …the menace of false caste certificates is on the increase...

> A considerable number of seats in the educational institutions are also secured by these wrong persons.
>
> ...there have been instances of persons being elected to elective offices on the strength of false community certificates.'

While the different dispensations at the centre as well as states have adopted a cavalier attitude about rectifying the lacunae in the affirmative action programme, we are slowly witnessing actions at the grassroots, which if properly channelised could snowball into a major agitation. A report in the *Deccan Herald*, June 20, 2002, gave details of the agitation launched by various dalit organisations in Shimoga, Karnataka. The agitators were demanding that criminal charges be filed against six personnel, who had procured false caste certificates to get jobs in a bank. The office of the State Bank of Mysore remained incommunicado for hours together due to this militant demonstration.

The UPA government has time and again declared its intentions to expand the ambit of reservation. A debate is also on regarding possibility of affirmative action in the private sector. But all such steps would be meaningless without rectifying the lacunae in the policy and showing some seriousness in the matter of false caste certificates.

It is a considered observation of activists as well as experts that since the policy of reservation is based on executive instructions, it excludes the possibility of penal provisions if officials are found to violate it. Considering the dominance of the "varna" mindset even among the bureaucracy one can envisage what ways and means could easily be devised to bypass its implementation. It is time that serious efforts are made to give the reservation system an administrative face-lift. To curb the abuse of affirmative action we also need to revise and streamline procedures. As suggested by the Commission time and again, we need a comprehensive act which would articulate the policy and which could be included in the ninth schedule of the Constitution, so that unnecessary intervention by the judiciary could also be curbed.

October 2005

Ghettos of a New Kind

Autonomy and Discrimination

What ails All India Institute of Medical Sciences (AIIMS), the premier medical institute in the country? Questions regarding its health have been in the news for sometime now. The latest concern the 'sacking' and 'reinstatement' (through judicial intervention) of its Director, Dr Venugopal, and the brouhaha that has followed.

What is most disturbing is how one of the most shocking aspects of the internal developments there has largely gone unreported in this whole fracas. The heated debate revolving around the 'autonomy' of the institution and alleged 'intrusion' into its internal affairs has papered over the quantum jump in the discrimination faced by the reserved category students there. Neither the articulate sections of our society nor the media has felt bothered over the 'medieval' treatment meted out to these hapless students by a motley combination of upper caste students and faculty members.

A shocking write-up in one of the leading dailies provides details of the deliberate herding together of the reserved category students and their 'victimisation' by a section of the faculty members.

According to the reporter 'Parts of AIIMS (All India Institute of Medical Sciences) hostels are turning into SC/ST ghettos. Reserved category students said they were being "hunted out of the remaining rooms" by upper-caste students and driven to two floors of the hostels.' (*The Telegraph*, 5th July 2006).

As things stand today, of the 250 students at the Institute, 55 belong to the SC/ST category. Of these 27 students occupy the top floors of Hostels No. 4 and 5, which have a total of 32 rooms. A cursory glance at the hostel records makes it clear that 22 out of these 27 students have moved to these floors only recently in the wake of the recent anti-reservation agitation spearheaded by the upper caste students. Graffiti engraved on one of the rooms of a SC student in the hostel makes it clear how this transfer was achieved. It warns the occupant to "get out of this (hostel) wing".

The SC/ST students also shared with the reporter how they are 'failed' in the examinations if they dare complain against the discrimination faced by them. The sub-dean of the Institute, who also belongs to the SC category, corroborated what was being shared by the students.

Incidentally, a memorandum submitted by 'Medicos Forum for Equal Opportunities' to the President of India a few days ago had expressed a similar concern about the internal situation in the premier institution. It may be remembered that this forum of doctors had supported reservation for OBCs in educational institutions and had then launched a novel campaign to further its viewpoint. The representatives of the forum apprised the President of "the open discrimination against the reserved category students and doctors being resorted to by certain members of the faculty and the administrative authorities in different medical colleges of Delhi including the All-India Institute of Medical Sciences". (*The Hindu*, 28 June 2006). A spokesperson of the forum also alleged that the incumbent Director, Dr Venugopal, and a section of the Faculty had aided and abetted the anti-reservation protest, supposedly for maintaining the "autonomy" of the Institute. He also cited instances of use of the official machinery in the day to day running of the said agitation, which according to him was an "open challenge to the constitution of India".

It is worth noting that none of the media channels which had provided the latest updates in the 'sacking' episode found it even necessary to talk to the reserved category students. Definitely such an interaction would have provided alternative viewpoints, detailing how 'autonomy' impacts upon the most marginalised sections of our society, and why there is nobody to complain against it. It would have also exposed the irresponsible behavior of the medicos who went on a lightening strike in support of the 'sacked' Director, leading to deaths of two innocent people.

It cannot be said either that incidents of such nature are an exception in educational institutions like AIIMS. Only six years ago the University College of Medical Sciences, situated in Delhi, had metamorphosed into a new theatre of conflict between the scheduled category students and the non-dalits. The dalit students studying there, in association with other like-minded groups, had launched a vigorous campaign opposing the humiliation heaped upon them by the rest of the students. It was heart rending to learn how they had been herded together on a particular floor in the hostel, and how a few tables in the mess were kept 'reserved' for them.

It is rightly said that the internal incongruities of an institution become the first casualty, if its conflict with some outside agency is presented in the simple binary of 'us' versus 'them'. Looking at the charged atmosphere in AIIMS, where a majority seems to be singing paeans to the autonomy *raga*, it appears difficult that there would be any takers for the grievances of the reserved category students.

September 2006

Viva Academic Untouchability

Reservation in Faculty Reruitment

Jantar Mantar, a unique historical place in the capital, which today serves as a 'sanctioned abode of protest' under a liberal bourgeois regime, witnessed a protest dharna in the first week of February. In terms of numbers of participants, it was indistinguishable from similar protest actions held on the same date. But the *raison detre* for this particular dharna was of considerable import in that it pertained to the entitlements of dalits, tribals or OBCs in higher education. It highlighted the surreptitious manner in which the Congress led UPA government is trying to push through a Bill which would do away with reservation in recruitment in institutions of 'national importance'.

As expected, for the media managers and for the pen pushers (or byte takers) employed by them, the whole protest action was a non event. Why have the articulate sections of our society, who claim to, and often do, stand for justice, peace and progress, joined the conspiracy of silence on this particular issue?

In this context of 'academic untouchability', which the sanction of Parliament to the introduction of such a Bill would imply, and provide further legitimacy to, the 'merit' versus 'quota' debate needs to be questioned and challenged uncompromisingly.

I.

What is common between Professor Sukhdeo Thorat, present Chairperson of the University Grants Commission; Dr Mungekar who is a member of the Planning Commission and Professor Ramdayal Munda, the ex Vice Chancellor of Ranchi University? What is well known is that they are all masters in their respective fields, but what is not appreciated is that had independent India not followed its mandatory mode of affirmative action in the form of reservation for the socially oppressed sections at various levels, it would have been very difficult for this triumvirate to prove their mettle as academics.

And if the proposed Bill 'Scheduled Castes and Scheduled Tribes (Reservation in Posts and Services) 2008 tabled and passed by the Congress led UPA government on the last day of the session of the Upper House (Rajya Sabha) becomes a reality, many talented and meritorious students coming from marginalised sections would not be able to even think of occupying important positions on the faculties of eminent educational institutions. The Bill talks of doing away with reservation in faculty recruitment for the scheduled castes, scheduled tribes and OBCs in institutions of 'national importance'.

Close watchers of the reservation debate in our country would tell you that this proposal was very much in the air and there is nothing surprising about it. In fact the Directors of the various Indian Institutes of Technology (IIT) have worked hard to ensure that the Human Resource Development Ministry drops its proposal to reserve posts for SCs, STs and OBCs in faculty recruitment. Directors of the IIMs which churn out hundreds of managers yearly for the likes of Rajus and for similar Corporate honchos had also expressed their resistance in no uncertain terms to any such proposal which would disturb the PLUs (People Like Us) in the faculty. The sole argument peddled by the Directors of these prestigious institutions revolved around the supposed negative impact on faculty quality if the reservation in faculty recruitment is not done away with. The Prime Minister on his visit to the Guwahati IIT a few months ago had dropped enough hints that the 'concern' expressed by these Directors would be given sympathetic consideration.

It is difficult to comprehend the utter silence even among the self professed champions of dalits or tribals or backwards over this disturbing development. Can it be said to be a sign of the emergent consensus among the entire spectrum of political parties who do not want to be seen singing a different tune?

As things stand today, with complete absence of any national uproar over this step, there is a strong possibility that the Bill moved by the

Department of Personnel and Training in the Rajya Sabha in December 2008 would be passed in the February session of the Lower House as well. And the long cherished demand of the "institutes of national importance" that they be exempted from reservation of posts at the faculty level would be fulfilled.

The 47 institutes that will similarly skip faculty reservation once the legislation gets Parliamentary approval include the seven older IITs, the seven IIMs, Aligarh Muslim University, Allahabad University, AIIMS. Also excluded from the faculty reservation ambit are 19 National Institutes of Technology (NITs), Jawaharlal Institute of Post Graduate Medical Education and Research in Pondicherry, Banaras Hindu University, Delhi University, Post Graduate Institute of Medical Education and Research in Chandigarh, Visva Bharati in West Bengal, Victoria Memorial, National Library, Indian Museum, all in Kolkata, and the Indian War Memorial in New Delhi.

2.

Apart from closing the doors of these 47 institutes to the historically oppressed, in one single stroke this move would also drive under the carpet many related issues centred on reservation.

Of late, the non-filling of reserved seats or the rampant use of false caste certificates by non-dalits and non-tribals to snatch posts reserved for them, have slowly emerged as key issues of the social movement. Actions at individual or collective level have not only questioned non-implementation of reservations but have also brought forth innumerable cases of phoney dalits and fake tribals enjoying the fruits of reservation at various levels.

Of course, the problem of false caste certificates, though brought into public focus by the media, is known to policy-makers as well. The practice of non-filling of posts is also a grave one. In this regard one can see a tendency towards the reserved posts for the fourth class employees getting filled with the 'eligible candidates', but as one moves up the matrix there is a noticeable reduction in the filling of seats meant for them.

For instance in Delhi University in the year 2001, out of a total strength of 6,500 teachers, one should have had a minimum 1,500 teachers belonging to this section of society. The situation on the ground was, however, entirely unsatisfactory, as merely 100 such teachers were on the rolls at the time of the survey (which later increased to 400). Delhi School of Economics, which has had luminaries like the Prime Minister himself and Prof Amartya Sen as teachers, also fared no better. It had only one dalit teacher out of the sanctioned strength of 4 (1999).

The National Commission on Scheduled Castes and Scheduled Tribes report for the year 1999-2000 provides details on the number of total posts and the numbers of people working on the reserved posts. Professors: BHU 1/360, AMU 0/233, JNU, 2/183, Delhi University 3/332, Jamia Milia 0/80, Visva Bharati 1/148, Hyderabad Central University 1/72.

Readers: BHU 1/396, AMU 0/385, JNU 3/100, Delhi Univ. 2/197, Jamia 1/128, Visva Bharati 1/70, Hyderabad Central Univ. 2/87.

Lecturers: BHU 1/329, AMU 0/521, JNU 11/70, Delhi Univ. 9/140, Jamia 1/216, Visva Bharati 16/188, Hyderabad Central Univ. 13/44.

Even a cursory glance at the figures pertaining to Central Universities (although the data is a decade old) makes it clear that, despite the fifty year old history of the UGC since its inception in 1959, more than 250 universities and the innumerable number of colleges under them, have not bothered to fill the 75,000 posts meant for the Scheduled Castes. It becomes clear that largely people belonging to the upper castes or other non-dalits have occupied these positions and have turned a blind eye to the fact that other sections remain unrepresented in the institutions of higher education.

There is a general disapproval within the *Varna* society about providing reservation to the historically oppressed sections, and sometimes the disdain becomes public as well. In formal discussions they are seen singing paens to the 'tolerance' practiced in their age-old civilisation, but in practice they are quite ruthless in sticking to the graded hierarchy as preached by Manu.

3.

Considering that most such people, the practitioners of *Varnadharma*, look towards the USA as 'model country' it would be opportune to know how the US society or even the big capitalists there have viewed the affirmative action programmes initiated in the US.

It is well-known that the sixties witnessed the launching of 'affirmative action' programmes at the national level in the US as means to providing equal opportunities to minorities, especially the blacks. The impetus towards affirmative action was twofold: to maximize the benefits of diversity at all levels in society, and to redress the disadvantages due to overt, institutional, or involuntary discrimination. Of course this was no gift by the US ruling classes to the blacks and other minorities. Rather it was the direct fallout of the civil rights movement there led by the legendary Martin Luther King.

The year 2002 witnessed the biggest challenge in recent times to this policy when two white students who failed to secure admission to the Michigan University decided to approach the Supreme Court to challenge the policy itself. Their main contention was that they did not get admission because of the 'discriminatory' policy of affirmative action and therefore the policy should be scrapped. It was an issue which literally saw a vertical division in the US society. The Supreme Court ultimately gave its consent to the continuation of this policy. Interestingly many corporate leaders ranging from the Microsoft to the smaller ones had clearly taken pro-affirmative action positions. For instance, 65 of these companies (boasting collective revenue of well over a trillion dollars) jointly filed amicus curiae (friends of the court) brief with the Supreme Court in 2003. In this brief, these corporations maintained that a racially and ethnically diverse student body is "vital" to maximizing the potential of "this country's corporate and community leaders of the next half-century."

4.

The debate around denial of entitlements to the dalits, tribals and the OBCs in higher education would be incomplete if two issues remain unaddressed.

Firstly, one needs to expose the various mythologies around merit which the *Varna* society keeps peddling to buttress its case.

Secondly, it is important to problematise the whole definition of institutions of 'national importance' and show how the hard earned monies made available by the public exchequer to these institutes (at the cost of basic educational needs of the deprived sections) end up creating doctors, engineers and other learned professionals whose majority (more than fifty percent) have no qualms in immediately moving to greener pastures – especially the USA – for good. *The Economist* (September 26, 2002) cited an Organisation for Economic Cooperation and Development (OECD) survey which found that over 80 per cent of the Indian students in the US planned to stay on after the completion of their studies. The survey also revealed that Indian students were more likely to remain in the US after higher studies than students from any other country.

Some recent studies on these institutions of 'national importance' also help create a better picture about the overall impact of such ventures.

'Media Studies Group' – a Delhi based group of media professionals and social activists – did a study of 42 batches of students who had passed out of the All India Institute of Medical Sciences (AIIMS) since its inception in 1956. In this particular study they looked at the information about the work place of these students. *The Telegraph* had carried a detailed report on their findings.

> New Delhi, Dec. 26, 2006: The All India Institute of Medical Sciences produces the country's top doctors, but more than half of them work abroad, mostly in the US.
>
> A study on the current whereabouts of most AIIMS graduates released today by the Delhi-based Media Study Group shows that the brain drain in the medical sciences may be more severe than earlier believed.
>
> Of the 2,129 students who passed out in the first 42 batches of the MBBS programme at AIIMS – from its inception in 1956 to 1997 – the researchers could trace 1,477.
>
> Of them, 780, or 52.81 per cent, are working abroad.

Interestingly a very similar picture emerges with regard to the IITs. In an informative and thought provoking article in *The Frontline*, Kanta Murali (The IIT Story: Volume 20, Issue 3, February 1–14, 2003) had analysed the IIT experience in great detail. The article starts with a piercing comment:

> Jawaharlal Nehru could not have imagined that the 'golden jubilee' of India's finest academic institution, the Indian Institute of Technology (IIT), which he was instrumental in founding, would be celebrated in the Silicon Valley.
>
> The IITs involve a considerable burden to the Indian taxpayer and this raises the important question of how the country should direct its educational investment. In a country with a woeful primary education record, government funding of the IITs is significant. In 2002-2003, the Central government's budgetary allocation to the IITs was Rs 564 crores compared with a total elementary education outlay of Rs 3,577 crores.

A few pertinent points emerge in the article:

- One glaring failure of the IIT system has been its inability to attract Scheduled Caste, Scheduled Tribe and women students in a progressive way.
- Studies suggest that close to half the seats reserved for SCs and STs remain vacant and that of those admitted a significant proportion, perhaps up to 25 per cent, is obliged to drop out
- The typical IIT student is male, hails from an urban middle class family, and does not belong to SC/ST ranks.
- The IITs have an even more dismal record in admitting women.
- It is likely that close to half the annual undergraduate output of the seven IITs, that is, anything between 1,500 and 2,000 young men and women, go abroad every year – overwhelmingly to the US. It is estimated that there are some 25,000 IIT alumni in the US.

5.

Everybody is aware that when Congress led UPA government came to power it made all sorts of pro-social justice noises to demarcate itself from the earlier dispensation. Apart from bringing forth the question of reservations in the private sector, there was also talk of making the atrocity laws more stringent and even of making reservation a statutory right.

The proposed Bill on 'Scheduled Castes and Scheduled Tribes (Reservation in Posts and Services) 2008' is being projected as elevating the provisions of reservations to a statutory right in perhaps institutions not considered important and in posts till only a certain level, and even so claims are made that it would instill a greater sense of confidence among members of the Scheduled Castes and Scheduled Tribes! As discussed earlier the Bill is based on an unreasonable presumption that members of the SCs and STs are incapable of handling higher posts. It thus bars them from making any claims for adequate representation in appointments to such posts.

One can see that the Bill lacks the constitutional spirit of providing equal opportunities to all citizens. To conclude, the Bill has the potential of undoing in one stroke what has been done so far for improving the representation of SCs and STs in services by successive governments, and is certainly a retrograde and regressive piece of legislation.

February 2009

SECTION 3

State and Human Rights

'Private' Armies & 'Public' State

It is time one looks at the 'privatisation of the internal security' with full patronage of the 'public' state, much on the lines of the privatisation being followed in the economic arena. Can it be said to be a necessary fallout of the abandonment of the so called dirigiste model or should it be considered an altogether different matter with its parameters defined by the concept and compulsions of maintaining the 'unity and integrity' of the country under a bourgeois regime?

Introduction

The national dailies are crying hoarse on Assam's slow drift towards anarchy. There are reports of a spate of 'mysterious killings' of known sympathisers and family members of militants, of ULFA militants engaged in ambushing an army squad and killing a few army people, of the BODO militants engaging in another act of arson and killings in Kokrajhar, and a small report of some obscure Bengali Tiger Force indulging in acts of vengeance over loss of their 'people'. The list continues.

The impression one gathers from the various reports is that these various insurgent/armed/terrorist groups are determined to implement their 'secessionist'/'divisive' agenda, which leaves the Indian army as the sole guaranteer of the territorial integrity of the Nation in that state.

Only very rarely does one hear about an outfit called SULFA (at least not with the same intensity or disdain). The reports filed from Guwahati and other places seem to adopt an attitude of clinical detachment about the nature of these various outfits. For the mainstream media SULFA is another militant group engaged in similar activities as the other armed groups. The question that needs to be asked is whether this is really the case. Can it be equated with, say, ULFA, or any other militant group? If so, then why? If not, then why not?

The story is the same with regard to Kashmir which has had an elected government for the past two years, meant to be controlling the situation in the state. Here also various militant/armed groups namely Hizbul Mujahideen, JKLF, Harkat Ul Ansar and countless others have been found active for almost a decade with their 'secessionist' and 'divisive' agenda. We are told that but for the army, which has established a joint command of its various wings along with the paramilitary forces and the civil administration, things would have further deteriorated. And as in Assam we also find here a few groups/outfits which are called '*sarkari* militants' in the local parlance. The likes of Ikhwahnul Musalemoon, Muslim Mujahideen and a few others, have a genesis similar with their Assamese counterparts. They have also been cobbled together out of 'renegade' militants who have surrendered to the Indian state at different times. It is also reported that these outfits aid/support the army in its fight against the 'antinational' elements in the valley.

There are also reports, yet unconfirmed, from Punjab, which tell us of some khalistani gangs propped up and used similarly by the army and the paramilitary forces during the hey days of the khalistani insurgency.

These 'renegade' militants and their actions have contributed a new dimension to the ongoing counter insurgency operations in these 'disturbed areas'. The ferocity of their actions and the blatant violation of human rights at their hands make it incumbent upon every right thinking person to understand the consequences of this phenomenon. It is time to look into the rationale provided by the powers that be for their creation. And last but not least one needs to ask with utmost urgency whether the state can be allowed to raise such apparently private criminal gangs in the name of quelling insurgency in these supposedly 'special times'.

I

What does SULFA stand for? The abbreviation stands for an organization consisting of surrendered ULFA elements. Would it not be better to rather call it *Sarkari* ULFA? This question readily comes to mind in the context of the worsening democratic rights situation in Assam and the spate of killings indulged in by this outfit. It is an altogether different matter that the Prime Minister of this country finds it politically expedient to evaluate the situation as 'slowly returning to normalcy', or 'an improvement', despite displeasure from his own party people from the state.[1]

It is worth noting that this notorious SULFA, cobbled together from the disgruntled elements of ULFA and called 'renegades' in local parlance, who surrendered to the government after the infamous Operation Bajrang and Operation Rhino in the early 90s, has recently engaged in brutal killings of the relatives and family members of the ULFA activists. From the newspaper reports of these incidents (it need not be underlined that only 'sanitised' versions of such incidents are allowed to be published in the free press of India) one can see the role of the armed forces and its men acting as cover during these 'actions' by the SULFA. The chain of events leading to the killing of the family members of ULFA activists has been widely reported.

One Tapan Dutta, a member of SULFA who had surrendered in 1991, was killed allegedly by ULFA men on the night of August 10 in Guwahati The very next morning the entire family of the publicity secretary of ULFA, Mr Mithinga Daimary (real name Deepak Das), was gunned down in Nalbari district. His mother, sister, and brother and brother's wife fell to the bullets of assailants who had barged into their house and opened fire indiscriminately. That very evening Mr Arvind Rajkhowa, brother of ULFA Chairman Dimba Rajkhowa, who was employee of the Assam State Transport Corporation, was shot dead at Dibrugarh. Brother of another ULFA leader Mr Munna Mishra, named HK Mishra, an employee of Oil India Ltd at Duliajan, was kidanapped in the morning. His dead body was recovered later in the day. In the continued killings of the kin of the ULFA top leadership Debakanta Gogoi, elder brother of Debakanta Gogoi, supreme leader of the armed wing of the ULFA was also killed at Barpathar on August 15. The local press which was quite agitated over these killings blamed the unholy nexus of SULFA and the army for these killings.

Soon after this killing spree unleashed by the SULFA as a 'retaliatory' measure against the 'terrorist actions' of ULFA, the so called Jamir Khan episode lately in the limelight, has further exposed the unholy alliance of the army with the *Sarkari* terrorist outfit SULFA.[2] The government has also been put in an embarrassing situation since it has all the time been disclaiming any connection with this outfit.

In the sensational Jamir Khan episode it was initially reported that an attack was conducted on an ULFA hideout in Jeraigaon in which four ULFA militants were killed on the spot. It was also reported that a few lakh rupees were recovered from the hideout. A few days after the killings three SULFA men, Raja Gogoi, Utpal Barua and Raju Phukan, were killed under mysterious circumstances. As usual ULFA was blamed for those murders. Then suddenly the very next day ten SULFA men in a joint statement faxed to the President, Chief of the Armed Forces, Chief Minister, as well as Chief Secretary of Assam, blamed not ULFA but some Jamir Khan, a Major in the 11th Jat regiment of the army for the murder of their men. The GOC of the Second Mountain Division, Ashok Chaki, after taking cognisance of the issue immediately suspended the Major and instituted an enquiry into the whole incident. Further investigations revealed that the three SULFA men who had participated in the initial 'action' on the ULFA hideout knew well that a few crore rupees had been recovered in the 'raid', which the Major wanted to keep for himself. The fight over the division of this 'booty' ended in the elimination of these men.

Two things are quite clear from this episode. First, this cannot be considered an isolated incident. It so happened that there was a dog fight between the actual perpetrators, which led to the matter gaining publicity. Second, this matter will, as usual, be hushed up on grounds of alleged threat to the 'unity and integrity of this country'.

What is worrisome in this whole chain of events is that under the pretext of engaging in counter insurgency operations the armed forces of this country have been given every liberty to trample on the basic democratic rights of common people, including their right to life. It appears that they have been given license to silence, maim, brutalize or kill anyone. The powers given to them under the infamous Armed Forces Special Powers Act are so sweeping that it is nearly impossible for the aggrieved party to even approach a court of law to get justice. The question confronting all democratic people's minds is: What right does the State and its armed forces have to silence, brutalize, maim or kill common people of this country under the name of protecting the geographical integrity of this country? Would one have to pay the price of one's life if it were to happen that a family member is engaged in activities inimical to the State? Arvind Rajkhowa may be a top leader of the ULFA, but the State should tackle him under the law of the land as his activities are considered improper/a 'threat' to the unity and integrity of this country. But can this be considered sufficient reason to finish his entire family, including his brother Dimba who was a state transport corporation employee?

The second and equally worrisome fact is that the State has engaged in aiding, abetting, and nurturing 'renegade militant' outfits (which have essentially been reduced to criminal activities with state patronage) whose *raison d'etre* appears to be the decimation/elimination of the anti-state militant outfits and terrorization of the wider populace to wean them away from such 'antinational' activities. The emergence/propping up of an outfit like SULFA is a case in point.

Facilitating formation of renegade militant outfits like SULFA with government patronage seems to be the 'new' game in 'counter insurgency'. What appears to be 'new' in the whole strategem of counter insurgency operations, however, is the brazenness with which the armed forces are using renegade outfits and the sanction and the encouragement these have received from the top echelons of the civilian administration. To give an example, the then governor of Jammu and Kashmir took personal credit for the policy adopted vis-a-vis the *Sarkari* militants. In an interview to the *Indian Express* (3rd Oct 1996) he narrated that there were different opinions regarding how to use the "pro-government militants" and it was he who had insisted that the most important among them, Kuka Parey's Ikwan, be kept under the control of the army.

Media has carried a great many stories on the *Sarkari* militants of Kashmir, and their role in Kashmir is quite well known.

II

Groups such as Ikwanul Muslimoon and Muslim Mujahideen, and their leaders Jamshed Shirazi alias Kukka Parey or Papa Kishtwari, were much in the news when Kashmir went for polls in the year 1996. The various Kashmiri militant groups, whether fighting for Kashmiriat or advocating full *Azadi*, or their other counterparts who were advocating integration with Pakistan, had boycotted the elections to the Lok Sabha as well as for the state assembly.

At that time one noticed the *Sarkari* militants in full form. They not only participated in the elections as candidates of their formations, but also let loose a reign of terror in those areas/localities/villages which were thought to be sympathetic to the cause of militants. They thus helped create an impression outside Kashmir that the call for boycott of elections given by the militants stood foiled since many former militants were participating in the exercise.

According to a report prepared by three civil rights organisations APCLC (Hyderabad), CPDR (Bombay), and PUDR (Delhi), 'Civil War and Uncivil Government', which deals with the issue of human rights violations under the National Conference Government

> *. .. Indeed these Sarkari militants- the Union of India's best friends in Kashmir- are a strange lot. They lead a simultaneous three in one existence. First, they are gun carrying militants who indulge in killing and blasting of their opponents and their property. Second, they are policemen who do much the same thing with the seeming authority of law. And third, they are activists and cadre of parliamentary parties such as the Jammu Kashmir Awami League, Jammu Kashmir Ikhwan, Tehreek-e-Wattan etc. but who nevertheless carry weapons in 'self defense' and do all the things they would do in their first incarnation.*

This report released in November '97 also makes the attitude of the mainstream parties to their emergence as well as their sustenance quite clear. It tells us that parties like the National Conference, Congress, and Janata Dal, who at one time or other were victims of their terror, had also raised the issue of disbanding such outfits during the elections to the Parliament or Assembly. But as with every promise made to voters these promises too were conveniently forgotten once the elections were done with. In his very first press conference after assuming office Farooq Abdullah, the new Chief Minister, admitted to the connivance of these *sarkari* militant outfits with different wings of the army and the paramilitary forces. It was a fact known to everyone in Kashmir, which the army never bothered to deny. It was told to the press that these different renegade militant outfits were working under close supervision of different wings of the armed forces; if one had the BSF as its guardian, the other was taken care by the CRPF, and the list continued. After this official acceptance one would have thought that the Chief Minister would list out the measures to disarm/disband these outfits, but on the contrary, he put forward a proposal to accommodate them in the Jammu-Kashmir Police Force at some level. Thus, if under the central rule which lasted more than six years, the idea was mooted that these criminal gangs and their members who had assisted the armed forces in the 'normalisation' of the situation in the state would be accommodated in various wings of the paramilitary forces, the government elected thereafter on the mandate of the people was also ready to accept them as guardians of law and order under its dispensation. The way was thus paved for the metamorphosis of the renegade militants into special police officers with the co-operation of the newly elected state government. One can imagine how these gangs and their members who terrorized, brutalized, maimed, raped and silenced people found to be sympathetic to the cause of the militants, who killed lawyers, human rights activists, teachers, journalists, trade union leaders and various other professionals to break the morale of the people would perform in their new *avatar*.

It becomes quite clear that the plan to freely use the surrendered militants was hatched in the highest echelons of the unified command of the army, paramilitary forces and the civilian administration as part of the counter insurgency operations.

These days not much is heard about these friends of the Union government. There could be many reasons for their lying low. First and foremost, it appears that under the new dispensation the unified command may have decided to de-emphasise them or asked them to keep a low profile. Secondly, as already mentioned, in their capacity as special police officers in the Jammu-Kashmir Police or as recruits at various levels in the paramilitary forces they are now in a position to serve the government in an official manner. Thirdly, there were also reports in the media about the offensive of the militants against these "renegades" a couple of months ago. It is just possible that with the decimation in their own ranks and the little democratic space which appears to have become available after the lapse of the central rule they may be finding it a little inconvenient to operate freely.

III

During the heyday of the militancy in Punjab, when fascist criminal gangs of the Khalistanis were engaged in killings and murder of the innocents without any mercy, there were allegations in a section of the press that the state had propped up fake Khalistani gangs to discredit the Khalistanis. It was also reported that these fake outfits did involve themselves in activities very much akin to what the Khalistanis were doing. The plight of the Punjab people, caught in the crossfire of the terrorism of the state as an antidote to the terrorism of the Khalistani brand, was unimaginable.

Last month only the Andhra press had reported on the killings of the squad members of the communist revolutionary organisations PWG or *Janashakti* of communist revolutionaries not at the hands of the police or the infamous *Greyhounds* in any encounter but at the hands of their former comrades.

Do all these examples seen together, the phenomenon called SULFA, the trigger happy *Sarkari* militants of Kashmir, or the alleged support to a few Khalistani gangs by the state, or the killings of the Communist revolutionaries in Andhra at the hands of their former comrades who had surrendered to the police, create grounds for pondering over the *modus operandi* of the State and its armed forces engaged in dealing with problems of internal security in those areas, regions, provinces where the State is engaged in direct military confrontation with groups whose *weltanschauung* differs from that of the State? What possible reasons could be attributed to this minor change in tactics? Is it the criticism leveled in the international media about the gross violation of human rights in these areas and the drubbing that representatives of the Indian government receive at the various international fora? Has this compelled the armed forces to try to maintain a human face as far as possible, and to evolve such alternate mechanisms for its 'dirty work' in insurgent situations? Should it be seen as a logical culmination of the split in the ranks of the militants of various hues, who are facing stagnation and degeneration in their ranks? What are the human rights implications of this whole exercise? Does it not throw light on the unlimited powers vested in the armed forces, which are free to operate with impunity in such areas?

One thing is certain. The same compulsions which prompted the government to go in for the formation of the Human Rights Commissions at national and state level seem to have operated in the formation of these renegade militant outfits. This may appear rather strange, but it rings true for the late 80's and early '90s phenomenon of the use of private partners in counter insurgency. In this age of the information superhighway it is incumbent upon all states that are not overtly dictatorial or autocratic or feudal and have not closed their doors to the outside world to appear as democratic as possible. The need to maintain a human face compels all such states to not appear as murderers, rapists of their own citizens, to the outside world, particularly where its armed forces are engaged in 'quelling the insurgency'. Of course it is not successful every time and on all occasions. At times it is difficult for it to rope in people from the ranks of the militants to its side and extract service from them. This can be said to be generally true in the growing stages of a movement. With the ebb in the movement or in the event of general stagnation and dissatisfaction in its cadres on grounds of its limited aims or lack of preparedness of such forces in other areas, or corruption in its ranks at any level, or the violation of democratic norms inside the organisation, the material basis for the emergence of dissidence in its own ranks gets articulated in many forms. And if this opposition or dissidence is not dealt with carefully or if there are attempts at silencing it, then it would be only a matter of time before 'dissidence' raises its head in the ugliest form.

The pro-government militant outfits serve double purpose: They can be relied on for any work which could draw flak from any section of society or media or human rights agencies. In such situations the government is also 'better placed' as it can call a barbaric act committed by such an outfit, of course with support from the army or any other wing of the forces, as an act committed by "alleged militants". Secondly, the impunity with which they are allowed to move around and the clout they enjoy acts as further incentive to dissident elements in militant movements.

In hindsight, apart from the "*people's militia*" (called "*accordists*" in common parlance after the much discussed Shillong Accord which was given shape with a section of the Naga militants, in the year 1972 to contain the Naga insurgency), which had a similar genesis to its '90s counterparts in Assam and Kashmir, and which remained effective for a very short time, rarely do we find a similar example in recent history.

IV

These developments raise serious questions on the functioning of the army and the various wings of the paramilitary forces sent in areas which are declared as disturbed. In a democratic polity it is necessary that the various arms of the State keep themselves accountable to people and always maintain transparency in their functioning. The Constitution also guarantees the right to life of citizens under article 21 and considers it of paramount importance. But in the so called "special times" all these rights of citizens in essence stand suspended in the areas so declared. The draconian *Armed Forces Special Powers Act* which is completing forty years of its infamous existence grants a soldier over the rank of a hawaldar the right to kill a person on mere suspicion, break or blast or destroy any house on mere suspicion that it harbours/harboured militants. All these actions are also very difficult to challenge in the court of law. Firstly, the central government has to give permission to inform that such and such person is being prosecuted, which is difficult to obtain. If at all the permission is given the petition can be quashed in the Supreme Court under the post-facto justification of Unity and Integrity of the Country. This Act, which was challenged in the highest court of this country by some democratic rights organisations on grounds of it being violative of the fundamental rights granted under the Constitution, including right to life and liberty, was ultimately upheld by the Supreme Court save a few cosmetic changes.

Thus the army can easily go scot-free for all the violations committed under its boot. Under the rubric of the infamous law it also becomes difficult for an ordinary citizen to even question the acts committed by the renegade militants who are acting at the behest of the army. Citizens are often caught in the unending circle of violence and counter violence, deaths and encounters. The "public" state thus holds the whole society to ransom at the expense of the apparent "private armies".

Can these things be allowed to continue in a democracy? Can we allow the State and its repressive machinery to revert to medieval times when challenge to the authority of the powers that be could result in the elimination of the entire family and kith and kin of the offender? Under what logic can the State be condoned for killing its own citizens under the pretext that their relatives or people in their neighborhood are engaged in supposedly 'anti-state activities'? At the least some transparency is in order. It should be made accountable in all such cases of omission and commission.

It is no coincidence that the constitution of a *People's Commission* at the initiative of a few eminent citizens, along with some judges, who got together to form the Committee of Concerned Citizens over Public Disappearances (CCCPD) to look into the excesses committed by the State and its armed forces during the height of the Khalistani terrorism, has raised such a controversy that the State is determined upon silencing the attempt. It reminds one of a similar controversy last year when a senior police officer, infamous for his anti-Khalistani feats, committed suicide mainly to escape the implementation of the law of the land in his case.

If this practice of using 'surrendered militants' is not checked, the day will not be far off when we would witness surrendered naxalites unleashing violence of the kind that we have never seen.

This is the 50th year of the Universal Declaration of Human Rights. The Indian State has also been a signatory to this Declaration. But this has not deterred it from engaging in 'legitimate' and 'not so legitimate' violence against its own people. It is high time that people become aware of the prevailing situation and of the midnight knocks at the doors of the Jalil Andrabis[4] before it is too late.

References

1. *The Hindu*, 30th August 1998.

2. *Jansatta*, Hindi daily, 3rd September 1998.

3. *Civil War and Uncivil Government: A Report to thePeople of India*, Nov. 1997 (APCLC, CPDR, PUDR).

4. An advocate and a famous human rights activist in Srinagar who was kidnapped and later killed by a group of army personnel with the help of the *sarkari* militants.

June 2000

Brutalising Inmates the 'Tihar Way'

We have sometimes to take tough decisions – even infringing some of our freedoms. Prime Minister Vajpayee in his inaugural address at the seventh Asia-Pacific Forum of the National Human Rights Institutions in Delhi on November 11, 2002

...[T]orture in custody flouts the basic rights of the citizens recognised by the Indian Constitution and is an affront to human dignity. Police excesses and the maltreatment of detainees/undertrial prisoners or suspects tarnishes the image of any civilised nation and encourages the men in 'khaki' to consider themselves to be above the law and sometimes even to become a law unto themselves. Unless stern measures are taken to check the malady of the very fence eating the crops, the foundations of the criminal justice delivery system would be shaken and civilisation itself would risk the consequence of heading towards total decay resulting in anarchy and authoritarianism reminiscent of barbarism. (Kashmir and India's Judiciary: AG Noorani, *Quoted in Economic and Political Weekly,* 1 December, 2001)

Jails, according to any ordinary book on jurisprudence, are supposed to be reformatory in nature. It is expected that the person apprehended for his or her act of commission and omission would come out a better citizen after his or her tenure is complete. Of course the gap between precept and practice is nowhere more evident than in jails, especially their Indian versions, which have put this wisdom on its head. Often one hears of the impunity with which notorious criminals keep 'running their empires' from the confines of the jail wall, or of 'celebrity' criminals suddenly developing chest pains and spending the entire period of their apprehension in some super speciality hospital. The nexus between the criminals, the police, and the politician, often aided by the judiciary, is quite visible. And on the other hand, ordinary prisoners being daily brutalized, with due connivance of the police and the 'senior criminals', is also not unknown. Now comes news of the police of one of the 'best' jails in this country, namely Tihar, behaving as if they were the foot soldiers of the Hindutva brigade.

The recent letter by India's leading human rights activists to the NHRC to "probe communal policies of the Tihar Authorities" ('Victims may forget torture but not verbal abuse', *The Kashmir Times*, 11 January) has once again brought into sharp focus the malady which afflicts the custodians of law. In a written complaint to the NHRC, Surendra Mohan, on behalf of All India Defense Committee for Syed Abdul Rehman Geelani, the Delhi University lecturer who was acquitted by the Delhi High Court in the Parliament attack case, has demanded to "institute a probe into the deplorable conditions inside the Tihar jail, making a pointed reference to the alleged practice of communalism inside the jail perpetrated by prejudiced jail authorities."

It is worth noting that these leading human rights activists have based their complaint on a letter written to the Defense Committee chairman, Rajni Kothari, by Syed Abdul Rehman Geelani, about the conditions in Tihar jail where he spent two years before his acquittal in November last. According to the report: "The letter has pointed reference to the torture meted out to jail inmates in the high-risk ward, where he was lodged, specially the Kashmiri inmates and the Muslims." According to the Defense Committee, "this discrimination against Muslim detainees in general and Kashmiris in particular is in violation of the basic tenets of international human rights law." It has called upon the Commission to set up a committee to visit the jail and document the problems and difficulties faced by the detenues in the 'high risk cells' and offered that it would like to be associated with the enquiry.

A cursory glance at the letter written by Mr Geelani to the Defense Committee chairman, Prof Rajni Kothari, is an eye opener for anyone concerned about Indian democracy and the future of secular values in this country. The letter says:

> Throughout my time in jail I was in an area that is called the high-risk ward in jail parlance. I do not know whether there is a provision for such a special category under the law. In my understanding it would be

highly illegal to categorise any detainee as a high risk even before he has been convicted.

> ....The detainees do not have an opportunity to go outside unless someone visits them. ...The jail authorities can and do impose all manner of illegal punishments on the detainees and prisoners lodged in the high-risk cells. I have witnessed the beating of several prisoners. The prisoners in the high-risk cells complained that the jail authorities on the smallest pretext punished them. Apart from beating, jail authorities have even tortured the detainees by pushing poles up their anus, making the men drink urine and depriving them of drinking water for several days at a time.
>
> The Kashmiri detainees are the special targets of the jail authorities. It would seem they think they can contribute to solving the conflict by subjecting the Kashmiris to indescribable brutality. Many of these men have been undertrials for many years without even a hope of getting a trial at all. Some who have been convicted have not got a fair trial and have been falsely implicated by corrupt police officers, like I was.
>
> In addition to the physical abuse is the verbal humiliation heaped on the detainees and prisoners in the high-risk cells. The majority of the men are Muslims and the jail authorities vent their prejudices and hatred without any hesitation. They also instigate the convicts to follow their example and their communalism defies description. Even if their victims forget the torture the verbal abuse cannot be wiped out of their memories....The dehumanization of the jail authorities is best seen when they do not allow the detainees to offer Namaz on the occasion of Id...

Even a layperson knows that the right to life or personal liberty, which includes right to live with human dignity, is one of our fundamental rights. It also includes an inbuilt guarantee against torture or assault by the state or its functionaries. And looking at the treatment meted out to these inmates it is worth underlining that the very apparatus which is supposed to guard the inviolable rights of citizens enshrined in the Constitution has itself become one of its biggest violators.

There is no doubt that torture of inmates on communal lines can be construed as an extension of the dehumanising behaviour of the police towards the people outside the four confines of the jail. It can rather be said that there has been a 'normalisation of brutality' or 'brutalisation of normality' which comes into full play in the interface between police and ordinary citizens. The pogrom of minorities, duly 'sponsored' by the Hindutva Brigade in Gujarat two years ago, has shown police brutality surpassing all previous limits. It was the first 'riot' in the country where the state promoted 'retribution' as a matter of *policy*. Many victims of the riot reported clearly that the police, instead of protecting them, had handed them over to the rioters. And now there is a news report of the ultimate travesty of justice – it is Gujarati Muslims who are being targeted under the extraordinarily harsh legal provisions.

Of course Gujarat was not the first instance when police forgot its 'neutrality' and joined one of the 'warring factions'. The degeneration of the police force is palpably visible at every level. It is this very force which was castigated as the "biggest organised *goonda* (goon) force" in India by Justice AN Mullah, in the mid-1950s.

In his *EPW* commentary 'Human Rights in India in the Global Context' (February 1, 2003), leading social scientist Mr Sumanta Bannerjee rightly underlined how our government's skewed policies and lack of transparency in all such cases has raised the spectre of exponential growth in cases of gross human rights violations in custody. According to him: "[B]ut along with the US, our government refuses to subscribe to this obligation. India has rejected the demand of accountability, not only by expressing its hostility to the International Criminal Court, but also by refusing to support the adoption of the 'Optional Protocol' to the UN Convention against Torture and Other Cruel, Inhuman or Degrading Treatment." This is not surprising, because the Protocol wants to "establish a system of regular visits undertaken by independent international and national bodies to places where people are deprived of their liberty, in order to prevent torture and other cruel, inhuman or degrading treatment or punishment."

The torture of the persons in 'high risk cells' is not an exception, it is a generalised phenomenon. Figures collated by the National Human Rights Commission corroborate the contention that the treatment meted out to the 'Tihar Inmates' is not an isolated case. The number of complaints with the prime human rights body has gone up from 500 in the first year to 70,000 every year in recent years. And significantly, among the complaints received by the Commission, over 40 per cent are against the police, followed by those against jails – a reflection on the state of the penal system in the country.

As regards the appeal drafted by human rights activists, one is yet to know the reaction of the NHRC. But considering the backlog of more than 40,000 pending cases awaiting disposal for several years now at the Commission, and the government's deliberate refusal to vest the Commission with adequate authority and resources – rendering it a toothless and inept institution – one cannot expect any significant move from it. If at all it takes cognisance of the appeal, it would at best be a kind of window dressing, absolving the powers that be from any involvement in this planned discrimination against the minorities.

Considering the seriousness of the matter it is clear that some positive steps are urgently needed. As things stand however, in this backdrop of increasing disregard for accountability for violations of human rights and international humanitarian laws, the task at hand may appear difficult.

It is time we make a fresh beginning in this direction. It is time that, apart from putting pressure through all possible channels and demanding greater transparency and accountability from the powers that be, we continue our efforts through all possible levels for redressal of specific grievances. It is time we also take a fresh look at the social composition of the police force and demand proper representation of different communities, sections of society in it. A glance at the recent figures available does not seem to be encouraging. According to Omar Khalidi (*Khaki and the Ethnic Violence In India*, Three Essays Collective, Delhi 2003), "For decades there was little or no recruitment of Muslims in Delhi police, so much so that they were mere 2.3 per cent of the total force in 1991 according to VN Rai" (p.78). "The National Minorities Commission gives a figure of 1446 Muslims out of a total of 51,683 in its annual report, 1995-96, New Delhi, NCM, 1996" (p.116).

Last but not least, it may be told that Mr Geelani's letter to Prof Rajni Kothari has rekindled memories of a book *My Years In An Indian Prison* written by a British national, Ms Mary Taylor. Ms Taylor, who was married to an activist of the revolutionary left movement, had to languish in Indian jails for more than five years allegedly for her 'seditious activities'. Her experiences of Indian jails had then brought into sharp focus the processes of brutalisation and dehumanisation which target especially the deprived and the marginalized, and also raised a debate on the conditions in India's jails during the late seventies and early eighties.

Let us hope that the petition by the Defense Committee for Geelani succeeds in (to quote Mr Geelani) "...focusing on the condition of detainees in the high risk cells of Tihar jail" and also some "attention on the wider problem of how communalism leads to certain dehumanisation in society and polity of the country."

May 2004

The 'Andhra Way'

On April 13 the Prime Minister is to address a meeting of states affected by Naxalite 'menace'. The media is agog with news of 'Centre Getting Tough, Action Plan to Curb Naxalism'. An inkling of how powers that be are looking at the situation can be had from a recent meeting held in Delhi.

The recent interaction between senior police officers belonging to states 'suffering from the naxalite menace' and the top echelons of the internal security establishment proved to a be a rehash of the same old mindset which pervades the custodians of law and order. Considering the quantum jump in the activities of the militant formations and the talk of 'red corridor' gaining currency, one was expecting a refreshingly novel approach, but it proved to be disappointing. To top it all, the police officials from West Bengal, Orissa, Chhatisgarh, Bihar, Jharkhand etc were advised to follow the 'Andhra Way'. *('Naxaliyon se Nipatane Mein Andhra ka Tarika Apnayen', Jansatta*, 27 March 2006).

Of course this was not the first time that there were eulogies to the Andhra model. The meeting of Home Ministers of the concerned states, held under the aegis of the present Home Minister last year, also saw projections of the southern state as model for taking steps to achieve zero tolerance of Naxalism. It is a different matter that the same Home Minister had, on the floor of the House, conceded the limits of this approach when he admitted that despite best efforts it 'was not able to bring down the level of naxalite activities as successfully as it had tackled terrorism' (*The Hindu*, 30 November 2005).

What is so significant about the steps taken by Andhra Pradesh to curb Naxalite activities?

An idea on how the state perceives the problem can be had from a protest petition duly signed by many eminent intellectuals and activists (petitononline.com) a few months ago, addressed to the President of India, which makes chilling reading. Giving details of some instances, they requested the President to intervene on the matter of the 'cruel and inhuman anti insurgency strategy being adopted by the state government.'

According to the petition, the state police department has engaged a criminal mafia gang called the 'Black Cobra'. This gang has been issuing 'death lists' in the media and brutally hacking those on the lists. And this gang has already killed two intellectuals – Mr Kanakachari, a teacher by profession, human rights activist and co-convener of Telangana Jana Sabha, and Mr M Prasad, a bank employee and district leader of Kula Nirmoolana Poraata Samithi, an organization fighting against the caste system – who were brutally hacked to death within a span of two weeks.

The petition also informs the President that when a delegation of intellectuals and journalists complained to the Lok-Ayukta (an ombudsman-like authority to enforce ethics and accountability in public office), about the state Home Minister and Director General of Police having failed to discharge their duties with respect to the 'Cobra Killings', the Cobra gang had started calling up those who were part of that delegation. This is strong proof that the police are hand-in-glove with this criminal gang. And the petition rightly points out that "rearing 'vigilante' criminal groups and using them to bump off detractors is a strategy used by cruel dictators. It is sad that such inhuman 'strategies' are being used in one of the most revered democracies in the world."

Close on the heels of these killings had also come news of the attack on the house of Prof S Seshaiah, Head of Department of Law, Sri Krishnadevaraya University in Anantpur, who happens to be general secretary of the Andhra Pradesh Civil Liberties Committee (APCLC). It has been reported that five unidentified persons attacked the house of Prof Seshaiah on 23 November at 10.30 p.m. and also tried to break open the door of the house. The next day an unknown outfit 'Rayalseema Tigers' claimed responsibility for the attack, and in a letter found outside his house demanded that Prof Seshaiah resign from the APCLC or get ready to face the consequences.

Whether it is the 'Black Cobra' or the 'Rayalseema Tigers' one is witness to a sudden emergence of many such outfits during the last few months alone, especially after the break down of talks between the Naxals and the government, now engaged in targeting people considered sympathetic to the naxalites. Their modus operandi is similar, they release a list of people affiliated to different civil and democratic rights organizations, and ask them to leave the organisation or face consequences.

It would be naive to state that all this could transpire so regularly without the government's official patronage. It cannot be denied that this killing spree by these secret groups has dampened the people's spirits, at least for now. People are asking if such things could happen to a Professor who has been a backbone of the civil liberties movement for the last twenty years and who only a year ago was one of the mediators facilitating the aborted talks between the Naxals and the Government of Andhra Pradesh, then it could happen to anyone.

The anger of the state machinery vis-a-vis the APCLC is easy to comprehend. It is an open secret that the police engage in 'encounters' with innocent persons supposedly 'to curb the menace of Naxalism'. And while the police frequently release statistics of naxalite violence, they avoid mentioning the victims of their own actions. The Andhra Pradesh Civil Liberties Committee (APCLC), the prime human rights body, has been keeping track of the police killings and two years ago it had listed more than 4,000 deaths, 2,000 in the last eight years alone.

The aborted session of the Parliament saw the tabling of a document detailing the Centre's policy on the naxalite problem (13th March) by the Home Minister. The Parliament was also informed that the said policy has been formulated keeping in mind the foremost demands of the Chief Ministers of the affected states.

Can it be then said that the powers that be have zeroed in on the Andhra model as their national roadmap to curb naxalism? Is it not time that they are told that this is another blind alley?

The well known civil rights activist KG Kannabiran, President of People's Union For Civil Liberties (PUCL) rightly pointed out to the then Andhra Chief Minister, Chandrababu Naidu: "Unless social deprivation is attended to on a war footing, the disaffection engendered by it may continue to fester fuelling never ending spirals of violence."

One does not know whether all those people singing eulogies to the Andhra model of dealing with Naxalism have ever bothered to find out for themselves how ferocious it can be on the ground. One does not know whether they comprehend that the mechanisms being put in place could also become means for instituting death squads under the canopy of democracy.

April 2006

Books as Crime

> *So you are the little woman who wrote the book that made this great (American) civil war.* Abraham Lincoln to Harriet Beecher Stowe, author of *Uncle Tom's Cabin*

Bruno Fulgini, a non descript employee at the French Parliament, would not have imagined in his wildest dreams that his tedious and boring job at the Parliament library, would lead him to a treasure hunt of another kind.

Today he finds himself metamorphosed into an author and editor, thanks to the sudden discovery of old files of the Paris police, which provided details of its surveillance work done way back in the 18th century. In a report filed by the AFP, Mr Fulgini tells us that 'Beyond criminals and political figures, there are files on writers and artists. In some cases, they go far in their indiscretions.'

An edited version of these old files, focusing on the writers of those times, has recently been published and is making waves. The said book *Writers' Police* gives details on how the greatest writers of late 18th century were kept under surveillance.

Obviously the surveillance was not dictated by the need on the part of the police to understand the lifestyles of the writers or to record how a particular author inspired new fashions or new hairstyles on the block.

In fact the Parisian police had a very specific agenda.

It was clear to those protectors of the internal security of a tottering regime that the renowned literati, viz. Victor Hugo, Balzac or Charles Dickens, may be writing fiction, but their sharp focus on the hypocrisy of aristocrats or the livelihood issues of ordinary people was adding to the growing turmoil in the country.

The Parisian police of the 18th century must have had to work hard to keep track of the daily movements of such writers. But its present day counterparts in Maharashtra have devised some 'easier' and rather 'shortcut routes' to curb the flow of ideas.

Their recent ham handed interventions at a book stall put up by well known publishers 'Daanish Books' at an ongoing book fair organized at the Deeksha Bhoomi of Dr Ambedkar in Nagpur are a case in point. A random list of books which the policemen perceived to be 'dangerous' and which they duly confiscated from the book stall makes interesting reading. According to a widely circulated email:

> The books seized by the police for containing dangerous, anti state material include books like Marathi translation of the *Thoughts of Bhagat Singh*, *Ramdeen Ka Sapna* by BD Sharma, *Jati Vyavastha- Bhartiya Kranti Ki Khasiyat* by Vaskar Nandy, *Monarchy vs Democracy* by Baburam Bhattarai, *Nepali Samargaatha: Maowadi Janyuddha ka Aankhon Dekha Vivaran* (The Hindi edition of eminent American Journalist Li Onesto's celebrated book *Dispatches from the People's War in Nepal*, Translated by Anand Swarup Varma), *Daliton par Badhati Jyadatiya aur Unka Krantikari Jawab*, *Chhapamar Yudhha* by Che Guevara and books on Marxism and Leninism and people's struggles.

Even if their fertile imagination led them to perceive that these writers scribblings may lead or add to 'social anarchy', they were quite unaware that these above mentioned books are freely available in the market and have not been banned or declared offensive by any state agency!

The Chandrapur-Nagpur police did not remain content with mere confiscation of the legally and freely available books but saw to it that the owner of the publication house, Ms Sunita, was put to three days of intense questioning by the Anti-Naxalite Special Task Force. It is clear that if friends around the world had not put in tireless efforts, and pressure had not been exerted on the Maharashtra government by the international community, Ms Sunita would be behind bars under one or other draconian provision of the 'Unlawful Activities Prevention Act'.

As the email further states, the whole incident raises pertinent questions about "… [o]ur rights vis a vis the State, as an individual citizen of a 'free country', as publishers and finally as readers?"

Of course, as an aside, one may say that while the Maharashtra Police considers selling of books a 'crime', it has no qualms in protecting perpetrators of communal violence or, for that matter, quite a few 'dirty Harrys' in its midst. This is the same Maharashtra police which preferred to look the other way when RSS-Bajrang Dal activists were killed in a bomb blast in Nanded and a well knit conspiracy by them to instigate communal riots was exposed.

Coming back to the *Writers Police*, it is clear now how all those meticulous efforts put in by the police to curtail the free flow of ideas proved futile. And how the French Revolution of those times emerged as a beacon of hope for thinking people across the world. Rather it could be said that all those efforts at surveillance became precursors to the storming of the Bastille.

If only it could be said that India is on the verge of a similar transformatory change! If only the ruling elite were losing ground!

October 2006

Irom Sharmila: 'Great Resister' of Manipur

Yes, 'n' how many times a man can turn his head,
Pretending he just doesn't see?
Bob Dylan

Irom Sharmila. (Age 34). Does that name sound familiar?

Well, like most of us this youngest daughter of Irom Nanda and Irom Sakhi Devi has many identities. For sister Vijayanti or brother Singhajit she is their dearest sister who had the 'never say die' spirit ingrained in her since childhood. For some of her dear friends she is a Yoga enthusiast who at times also dabbled in naturopathy. For litterateurs of Manipur, she is a budding poetess who has written hundreds of poems, though till date only one of her collections *Imadi Khongdai Setlaroi* has been published. And for the vast majority of Manipuris, she is not Irom Sharmila Thanu, rather she is the 'Iron Lady of Manipur' who has challenged a callous and apathetic government and its regime of draconian law with her unique struggle.

Interestingly, despite the proliferation of TV channels and a boom in the print media, not many of us from 'mainland' India would have learnt what made this young girl from a lower middle class family, who did not even manage to continue her education after Class12, such a legend in her own lifetime.

It is difficult to believe the saga of struggle of Irom Sharmila Thanu.

In fact it will be nearly six years now since she has been on her hunger strike. She has remained without solid food since then, demanding the withdrawal from Manipur, of one of the most draconian laws in the statute books, called the Armed Forces Special Powers Act (AFSPA).

At present she is lodged in AIIMS, New Delhi where she is being 'nasal fed' by a team of doctors.

Her reaching Delhi from the environs of Jawaharlal Nehru Hospital, Manipur, where she was kept in judicial custody and was nasal fed, is another saga of her glorious struggle. Taking advantage of her release after serving a 'yearlong custody' at the hospital, her supporters literally smuggled her out of Imphal to reach Delhi, to turn her "regional" campaign into a "national" one. Her first stop in Delhi was Rajghat, where she laid a wreath at Mahatma Gandhi's samadhi. Later she told a journalist "I want to tell the people of India that if Mahatma Gandhi were alive today, he would have launched a movement against the Armed Forces (Special Powers) Act. My appeal to the citizens of the country is to join the campaign against the army Act." (*The Telegraph*, October 5, 2006).

I.

Of course, the historic fast launched at Malom was no planned affair. There was a firing by security forces at Malom bus stand, which is nearly 15-16 kilometers from Imphal, on 2nd November 2000. It saw blood of ten innocents spilled on the streets. Also it was not the first event of its kind. The streets of Manipur had been witness to the killings of innocent citizens umpteen times before.

Mother Irom Sakhi Devi had no inkling of what was in store for her youngest daughter Sharmila. She merely sought her mother's blessings to work for the 'betterment of humanity'. She then straightaway went to the very spot where the bloodbath had occurred and started her fast unto death. Her demand was simple to articulate, but for the powers that be difficult to implement. She demanded repeal of the draconian law. Initially for the residents of Malom or adjoining areas it was difficult to fathom the idea of the peaceful resistance put up by this young woman. For a handful of them she was an object of ridicule. But none had imagined that she would persist in her determination in a way that would inspire support for the demand all over the state, and make it the most burning issue in Manipur. By 21st November the administration was forced to give her a 'nasal feed' in a hospital in Imphal.

The maximum sentence a Court can award for 'trying to commit suicide' is one year, and Sharmila has endured many such sentences in all these years. Every time she is released after a one year judicial detention she is immediately rearrested and put in the same ward, and the cycle continues. This year too the government officials expected the same to happen. Embarrassed police officials later admitted that they had no inkling of the plan to "smuggle out" Irom. Chief Minister Okram Ibobi Singh too was taken by surprise.

Irom Sharmila's legendary struggle for human rights has become an important symbol of the resistance of the Manipuri people against State repression. This struggle has led to 'excessive militarisation of the region' and the 'promulgations of many a black laws like AFSPA at the cost of the life and liberty of the people of this region.'

It is a sad commentary on the state of affairs that the rest of the world came to know of Sharmila's unique struggle only two and half years ago. This was in the aftermath of a militant struggle launched by Manipuri people demanding the abolition of the Armed Forces Special Powers Act, 1958, and punishment to the Assam Rifles people for killing Thangjam Manorama on 11 July 2004.

This upsurge of the Manipuri people was marked by the novel and leading role played by women in giving momentum to the movement. On 15th July 2004 around a dozen elderly and respectable Manipuri women marched to the area headquarters of the Assam Rifles, stripped naked and waved a banner which read: "Indian Army Rape Us", "Indian Army Take Our Flesh". The bold march of these taunting women had an electrifying impact and within no time the protests against the army reached new heights.

The conspiracy of silence which had surrounded Irom Sharmila's solitary struggle was not unexceptional. It is in keeping with the general silence which surrounds developments in the northeast, which for all practical purposes exists only in the 'borders of our consciousness'. A report brought out by the *National Campaign Committee Against Militarization and Repeal of AFSPA* had rightly observed a few years ago: 'Armed militancy, intercommunity killings, 'encounters' with security personnel ... conversely, pretty girls and boys dancing in traditional costume… The north east has always been a collage of the most contradictory images, that only reflect how little is known of the reality that lies behind them.'

2.

There is no doubt that if the atrocities at the hands of the security forces as are witnessed in the north east would have taken place in any region of 'mainland India' it would have caused a national uproar. But with regard to the areas which are under the Armed Forces Special Powers Act, all such acts by the security people are 'covered under the infamous Act' itself. As the provisions of the infamous Act make clear, the security forces have been given unlimited powers, and even if they commit atrocities (which are not an exception but the rule) people have no right to approach the Courts.

This 'draconian law' which has generated tremendous anger in the minds of the people, and is in many ways worse than the infamous POTA, empowers the security people in many crucial ways. It empowers the government (governor of the state, or the administrator of the union territory, or the central government) to declare any area a 'disturbed area' if it reaches a conclusion that the whole or any part of it is in such a disturbed or dangerous condition that the use of Armed Forces is necessary in reinforcing civilian authority.

Section 4 delineates the powers sanctioned to any commissioned officer, warrant officer, non-commissioned officer, in a disturbed area.

a) If in his opinion, it is necessary for maintenance of public order, to fire even to the extent of causing death, or otherwise use force against a person, who is acting in contravention of an order prohibiting the assembly of five or more persons, or the carrying of weapons or of things capable of being used as weapons.

b) If in his opinion, it is necessary to do so, then to destroy any arms dump or fortified position, any shelter from which armed attacks are made or are 'likely to be made', and any structure used as training camp for armed volunteers or as a hide out for armed gangs or absconders.

c) arrest without warrant any person who has committed a cognizable offence or against whom a reasonable suspicion exists that he has committed or is likely to commit a cognizable offence, and to use whatever force is necessary to affect the arrest.

d) to enter and search without warrant any premises to make an arrest or to recover any person wrongfully confined or to recover any arms, ammunition, explosive substance or suspected stolen property.

Section 5 makes it mandatory for the army to hand over a person arrested under the Act to the nearest police station with least possible delay.

Section 6 lays down that prosecution, suit or other legal proceedings can be instituted against a person acting under the Act only after getting previous sanction of the central government. (Ref: *The Illusion of Justice: Supreme Court Judgment on the AFSPA*, May 1998, People's Union for Democratic Rights, Delhi)

The existence of this law on the statute books has thus meant disallowing people the right of protest, the right to legal redress or right to engage in any lawful democratic activity. Ordinary persons who live a life of peace and tranquility can thus be easily framed as 'terrorists' and 'suspects' linking them to banned organizations, as often happens. Democratic rights activists who merely document excesses by the Army or demand an end to army rule have also been picked up, tortured and killed. The implementation of this law during the forty eight years of its existence has effectively meant that in our constitutional democratic set up the thirty eight million people residing in the north east have been forced to live under an undeclared emergency or de facto military rule.

Brigadier Sailo who served in the army for thirty one years, in a letter written nearly thirty years ago to Ms Indira Gandhi, the then Prime Minister of India, said: "The feelings of the entire villages and population of Mizoram are now totally alienated by the denial of all decencies of human rights, and any picture which may have been painted to you to the contrary, is totally false." (Quoted in *Where 'Peacekeepers' Have Declared War: Report on Violations of Democratic Rights by Security Forces and the Impact of the AFSPA on Civilian Life in the Seven States of North-East*, National Campaign Committee against Militarisation and Repeal of AFSPA, 2000, Delhi). It can be said without an iota of doubt that what Brigadier Sailo said about Mizoram can be applied to the whole of north east today.

3.

One cannot say with certainty what will happen next.

Hunger strike by Irom Sharmila continues undaunted by the might of the State. If earlier the venue had been the dingy rooms of the Jawaharlal Nehru Hospital in Imphal, today she lies in a similar position in a private ward in the All India Institute of Medical Sciences (AIIMS), New Delhi, where she is forcibly fed liquids through a nose-pipe. It was just last month that BBC (Tuesday, 19 September 2006, 09:46 GMT 10:46 UK) had carried a report on her marathon fast in which it had mentioned the deteriorating condition of her health: "Doctors say her fasting is now having a direct impact on her body's normal functioning – her bones have become brittle and she has developed other medical problems too."

As far as the repeal of the black law is concerned, things seem to be getting nowhere. It is being said that the Justice Jeevan Reddy Committee, appointed by the Prime Minister in 2004 in the aftermath of the militant protests in Manipur, has recommended repeal of the legislation AFPSA itself. According to reports in a section of the media, the 146 page report submitted by the Jeevan Reddy Committee says: "The Act is too sketchy, too bald and quite inadequate in several particulars." According to the report "the Act, for whatever reason, has become a symbol of oppression, an object of hate and an instrument of discrimination and high-handedness."(*The Hindu*, October 8, 2006).

According to some analysts, however, a careful reading of the report creates the impression that the Jeevan Reddy Committee merely wanted the prerogatives of the armed forces transferred wholesale onto another law, the Unlawful Activities (Prevention) Act, 1967. If this holds true we would have a situation where the dreaded black law AFPSA, which is basically applicable to North East and Jammu-Kashmir, may be scrapped forthwith while the revised ULP Act 1967, which incorporates all the necessary provisions of the AFPSA, would come into force. It would mean the whole of India may come under the ambit of a substitute of AFPSA, or in other words the whole of India would find itself under the AFPSA under another nomenclature! This cannot be tolerated at any cost.

While speaking to the BBC correspondent Irom Sharmila had declared: "My fast is on behalf of the people of Manipur. This is not a personal battle – this is symbolic. It is a symbol of truth, love and peace."

It is worth mentioning that while Sharmila is waging this unequal battle against the Indian state, many of her dear and near ones have stood solidly behind her. We are also told that not only did her brother lose a government job, because he preferred to remain by her side, but the family has also gone bankrupt since it incurred many loans during this period.

But no sacrifice can match what Irom Sakhi, Sharmila's 75 year old mother, has endured during these years. She has not met her daughter since she blessed her on the momentous day when she undertook her fast. Irom Sakhi, with tears in her eyes, told a correspondent: "It is just possible that my getting emotional on seeing her may weaken her resolve. And I do not want that my daughter lose in this battle which is for the betterment of humanity."

October 2006

Stigmatising Social Protests

What is common between Ashok of *Komu Sauhardu Vedike*, (a forum for Communal Harmony), Kadial Shamanna, a farmers' leader from Malnad region and Kalkulli Vittal Hedge who is leading an anti-displacement struggle of tribals likely to be affected by the creation of the Kudremukh National Park? Well, all these people working in different parts of Karnataka on different issues of people's concern, discovered one fine morning the similarity in which they are viewed by the powers that be. And of course, the realisation was not very pleasing.

They were appalled to find that they are part of a list released by the Karnataka police of what were called 'sympathisers of extremists'. The mischievous manner in which the list was released caused tremendous uproar in the media and civil society. The police, already under flak over its alleged involvement in fake encounters of innocents supposedly to 'control naxalite menace', was compelled to formally withdraw this list hurriedly furnishing some facile explanation for a 'mistake'.

Any sane person, however, knows that the list might have been formally withdrawn, but the government's intentions are clear. It has decided to terrorise the whole spectrum of social protests organised even within the boundaries of constitutional rights.

While Ashok, Kadial Shamanna, and Kalkulli Vittal Hedge can be cited lucky for having escaped being booked under some black law after their names were released to the public in the notorious list, Roma, Shanta and Malati were not that lucky. These women – actively involved in the concerns of the deprived sections of society in the backward district of Sonbhadra (UP) – were booked under the 'National Security Act' (NSA). Perhaps the only 'crime' committed by these dedicated women was that they were making the tribals and dalits aware of their constitutionally mandated rights. And since dalits and tribals had started claiming land which belonged to them, the land mafia in the area felt threatened and managed their arrest.

The struggle was being fought under banners depicting Dr Ambedkar, Jyotiba Phule, Savitri Bai Phule, Birsa Munda and Rani Lakshmibai and had never resorted to any violent means. In this context, where even 'such non-violent and constitutional struggle is becoming impossible in large parts of the country today' noted political scientist Aditya Nigam (www.Kafila.org) writes: "It is the state and the police that are producing Maoists by the hour. It is not without reason that former Prime Minister VP Singh had to proclaim in utter exasperation that he too wants to become a Maoist."

Any concerned observer of the interaction and interplay between various organs of the state and the people's movements or civic actions led by individuals would tell us that there is nothing unusual in the move by the Karnataka police or for that matter the UP police. Police personnel in all parts of the country are 'programmed' to follow a similar pattern. The case of Dr Binayak Sen, which has elicited international reaction, is a case in point.

It has been more than three months since Dr Binayak Sen, a pediatrician and human rights activist belonging to Chhatisgarh and the national vice president of PUCL (People's Union For Civil Liberties), has been put behind bars taking advantage of the draconian provisions of the *Chhatisgarh Public Security Act* and *Unlawful Activities Prevention Act* (a substitute for POTA which the government had to let lapse because of public pressure). As reported elsewhere, Dr Binayak Sen, who also happens to be a recipient of the prestigious Paul Harrison Award for his work in community health, was arrested basically to stifle his voice and send a clear message to the defenders of human rights in the state that they should 'remain within limits'. In fact, it was due to the consistent effort of people like him that the world came to know how the state government is creating a mercenary 'army' from among the tribals to precipitate internecine clashes. While the state government called it 'Salwa Judum' (Peace Festival), it became evident to the outside world that this strategy is responsible for precipitating violence all over the state. One can go on adding examples demonstrating the similarity in the modus operandi adopted by different state governments to condemn and stigmatise social protests.

A different dimension of the whole phenomenon is visible when one takes a look at the growing atrocities on dalits in different parts of the country. While discussing the ambit of violence against dalits and the response of the State, 'Human Rights Watch', in its path-breaking report 'Broken People: Caste Violence Against India's "Untouchables" (1999), reports :

> State agents have acted directly and forcefully against those attempting to claim their rights. Dalit activists throughout the country face charges as "terrorists", "threats to national security", and "habitual offenders". ..Dalit activists are frequently charged under the National Security Act, 1980, the Indian Explosives Act, 1884 and even the Terrorism and Anti-Disruptive Activities Act (TADA).

The criminalization of social activism in India is a pattern that has been previously documented by Human Rights Watch (pp. 153-154).

A classic case, which depicts the manner in which community leaders belonging to religious minorities are made easy scapegoats, is that of Maulana Umerji, from Godhra, Gujarat. In the year 2002, after Gujarat witnessed genocide at the hands of the Hindutva brigade, Maulana Umerji became a known face of the humanitarian work being done in Godhra. People who have visited Godhra during that tumultuous period would tell you how the Maulana tried to go that extra mile to help the victims.

It is more than four years now he has been languishing in jail, under the draconian provisions of POTA. The police claim he is among the 'masterminds' of the 'attack on Sabarmati Express' – an incident which has become doubtful and controversial because of facts to the contrary.

Post 9/11 one is witness to what can be described as 'internationalisation of this trend' with governments worldwide relying on broadly worded terrorism laws to crush social protests.

As noted by Joanne Mariner (www.counterpunch.org 17th August 2007)

> Political demonstrators in El Salvador and London have found police deploying a new weapon against them: laws designed to prevent and punish terrorism. In the town of Suchitoto, El Salvador, during a mass demonstration in early July against a water decentralization plan, fourteen protesters were arrested and charged with terrorism.
>
> Demonstrators against Global Warming at Heathrow Airport, London found themselves at their wits end when police started resorting to stop and search powers contained in a terrorism law…

She concludes with a somber warning:

> With fears of terrorism high, many governments now have tough counter terrorism laws at their disposal. But while the extraordinary powers granted to police and other state authorities under these laws are publicly defended by reference to the threat of terrorism, some of the actual conduct they apply to has little connection to the problem.
>
> Governments apparently need to be reminded: political protesters are not terrorists. Rock-throwers are not suicide attackers. People carrying placards are not people carrying bombs.

February 2007

Any Apologies For Paddars?

The name of Canadian-Syrian Mahel Arar is not unfamiliar today to the rest of the world.

The travails and tribulations of this young software engineer who became a victim of the US government's extraordinary rendition programme have been recounted umpteen times. We know how he was seized by CIA operatives during a stopover at New York in 2002 and was secretly sent to Syria. Lodged in a grave-like cell in Syria, Arar was repeatedly tortured to extract information which he did not know. Ultimately his tormentors released him after a year and half without ever being charged with a crime.

It is clear that Mahel Arar became a victim of the Islamophobia manufactured by the likes of Bush and Blair in the immediate aftermath of 9/11.

Recently Stephen Harper, Prime Minister of Canada, sought public apology for the ordeal which Maher went through and for the role played by Canadian officials in the whole affair. The Canadian government also gave him nine million dollars as compensation. Mr Harper said in full public view of the media "On behalf of the government of Canada, I wish to apologize to you, Monia Mazigh (Arar's wife) and your family for any role Canadian officials may have played in the terrible ordeal that all of you experienced in 2002 and 2003."

Mahel's saga reminds us of the recent ordeal of Tariq Ahmad Dar, a Kashmiri by birth. Tariq had carved out a niche for himself in business in Bangladesh and has also been one of the most successful models in the country. Many top corporate houses had signed him. But September 2006 changed all that.

One fine morning a team of security personnel from Bangladesh Rapid Action Force raided his house and jailed him for being a RAW agent. He was badly tortured in the jail in order to extract some confession from him. Ultimately when the security forces failed to get any evidence against him, they released him without charging him with any crime. Tariq, feeling relieved over his release, caught the next flight to Delhi to meet with his parents. But he did not know what was waiting for him. At the Delhi airport, the personnel of the Delhi police immediately arrested him for being a terrorist owing allegiance to Lashkar-e-Toiba, a dreaded terrorist organisation working across the continent.

If inside the Dhaka jail the Bangladesh Rapid Action Force had been his tormentors, in the Tihar jail he was subjected to similar harassment by Indian security agencies. Again he was released after 90 days when the police failed to gather any evidence against him and failed to present a charge sheet. Today, Tariq is a bitter man. He finds himself in a blind alley, a career ruined by false charges and a family that has undergone tremendous emotional trauma during all these months.

Is it asking too much that custodians of democracy in our country and our neighbouring country as well, come forward and apologize to this innocent young man for the wrongs done to him by our own security agencies? But such apologies from the custodians of our country are unthinkable. It is doubtful that the office of the Delhi police or the Bangladesh Rapid Action Force would have issued even a semblance of a formal apology to Tariq. And as for Tariq or his family members, it is probably beyond them to pursue the case at the judicial level, to ensure that guilty officers are punished or that the Indian government compensates him for the role played by its own people in his tragic ordeal.

Anyone familiar with the Indian situation would have noted the rampant misuse of various laws of detention and confinement. We have numerous incidences of innocent people being targeted and criminalized for no fault of theirs.

In worst cases they are also killed in fake encounters by the custodians of law and order to gain gallantry awards for themselves. It is not surprising then that Kashmir should have erupted in a show of mass anger. Many similar cases have come to limelight in the context of Kashmir. The exact quantum of such killings would never be known as the people in power go that extra mile to cover their acts of commission and omission even as human rights activists try to document each of these killings/ disappearances.

The year 2003 had seen "[o]fficial acknowledgement that many scores of people may have been killed in the custody of India's security forces." According to a report filed by Phil Reeves in Delhi (*The Independent,* 23 June 2003) 'A provincial minister told the state's legislature this weekend that there had been "144 alleged custodial killings" by security agencies and local police since 1989, when violence erupted in Indian-administered Jammu and Kashmir. Abdul Rehman Veeri also gave the number of people reported missing in the past 14 years as 3,931, a figure that will be seized on by human rights campaigners demanding an investigation into the "disappearances" in Indian-controlled Kashmir.'

Notwithstanding the recent eruptions in Kashmir, which has rather prompted the powers that be to take some corrective actions, we should not forget that within the law and order machinery the discrimination against certain communities and sections of our society has been internalised and is the norm. All of us have been witness to how the probe in the Malegaon bomb blast proceeded and the manner in which the continuous stigmatisation of the minority community was allowed to go on unabated despite clear evidence that Hindutva extremists had unleashed this reign of terror.

To be very frank, in this respect there is little to differentiate between the forces of the 'programmatic communalist' variety (like the BJP or Shiv Sena) and the 'pragmatic communalists' like the Congress.

It becomes impossible to forget Mohammad Afroz, who was arrested after 9/11 by the Mumbai police and was charged for planning a terrorist attack. It was told to the pliant media then that this 'dreaded terrorist' wanted to crash a plane piloted by him on the British House of Commons and Australia. A special team from Mumbai police specially went to these countries but could not bring back any evidence. Ultimately it found the whole charge a grand fabrication. This was during a period when Maharashtra was ruled by a "secular front" comprising the Congress and the NCP.

And what happened to the 'dreaded terrorists' arrested in connection with the four year old attack on the Raghunath temple in Jammu? The courts have finally absolved all the accused of any charges and have advised the police to properly use its minds in handling sensitive cases of such nature. These innocent people had to languish in jail for a long period for no fault of theirs.

As of now Kashmir is up in arms over the series of fake encounters staged in the central Kashmir district of Ganderbal last year. Two senior police officials, said to be at the heart of a rogue police and the army ring responsible for a series of fake encounters, have also been arrested. The cold blooded murder of Larnoo resident Abdul Rehman Paddar, a carpenter by trade, has shocked many.

It remains to be seen who will seek apologies for Paddar's near and dear ones. Who would gather the courage to stand before Paddar's widow and children with folded hands and say 'On behalf of the Government of India, I wish to apologize to you ...?

February 2007

Children's Doctor and a Mighty State

Dr Binayak Sen, a pediatrician by training and profession and a human rights activist by choice, has received a new identity, that of 'A Menace to Public Safety'. The Chattisgarh police, whose record of human rights violations is a shame, used the provisions of the draconian *Public Safety Act* and *Unlawful Activities Prevention Act* (a substitute for POTA) to detain Dr Binayak Sen in the wee hours of 14th May.

Questions naturally arise as to how a graduate from the prestigious Christian Medical College, Vellore who has been associated with several community health programmes for the last three decades, who even contributed to the state government's conceptualisation of the community health programme 'Mitanin', and who played a significant role in the evolution of 'Shaheed Hospital', a hospital started by workers for the workers under the leadership of legendary Shankar Guha Niyogi, could out of the blue metamorphose into a '*A Menace to Public Safety*' ?

One can comprehend this 'transformation' only if one takes a look at the other aspect of Dr Sen's work which he has consistently been engaged in for sometime. Close watchers of Chhatisgarh's deteriorating human rights situation would tell you that apart from his work of curing the physical health of the rural poor in general and kids in particular, he has been actively associated with bettering the social health of the downtrodden and the marginalised as a human rights activist. He is presently the General Secretary of PUCL (People's Union for Civil Liberties), Chhatisgarh region and Vice President of the organisation at the national level.

An idea of the challenging work which he, along with his comrades, are engaged in could be had from their interventions in the 'encounter killings' of twelve tribals at Santoshpur which recently made headlines in the national news (March 31, 2007). In this particular case security personnel marched into the hamlets of tribals, in the 'Naxal affected' Bastar area of Chhattisgarh, abused the villagers alleging that they were naxalite sympathizers, and took some of them away. By the evening news came that twelve such people had been killed by these security personnel after brutal torture. A few of them were simply hacked to death.

Madiyam Soni, a tribal woman from Ponjer, who lost her own son in the genocide, and who along with other villagers had to leave her village the same night, narrated her experience to a correspondent (*Indian Express*, 20th May 2007). Narrating her experience she told the reporter that the tribals are too afraid to register a complaint at the police station. She rightly asks "How can we hope to approach the police when some of their own have committed the crime?"

It needs be mentioned here that the rest of the world could get to know of the State engineered Santoshpur killings only through the painstaking work done by Dr Binayak Sen and his close comrades. Apart from the Santoshpur killings, Binayak Sen and his comrades have similarly exposed many other such incidents of human rights violation – fake killings, fake arrests. Two years ago they took initiative in the formation of an All India Committee, comprising human rights groups active in different parts of the country, to look into the brutalisation of ordinary tribals at the hands of the Police under the 'Salwa Judum' campaign.

Salwa Judum, literally translated 'Peace Festival', is a campaign organised by the police to recruit and arm tribals, put them under protected areas, and utilize them against other tribals believed to be 'under the influence of naxalites'. It is no mere coincidence that leading historian Ramchandra Guha recently filed a petition in the Supreme Court urging its intervention to stop the 'Salwa Judum' campaign.

One can easily imagine the challenges involved in exposing cases where security personnel have been given a free hand to silence the people. Incidentally, while announcing Dr Binayak Sen's arrest, a senior police officer had the audacity to threaten that two other human rights activists, namely Gautam Bandhopadhyay and Rashmi Dwivedi, would soon be similarly detained.

As rightly noted by a campaign group: "This is not merely an effort to cover up the crimes the State government has committed in the name of suppressing the Maoists. These developments are also part of a much larger agenda, driven by the Chattisgarh government's close links with large corporations and international capital and aimed at ruthlessly suppressing any resistance to the forcible seizure of people's lands and resources."

The arrest of Dr Binayak Sen under the draconian *Unlawful Activities Prevention Act* and *Chhatisgarh Public Safety Act* which can put him in jail for years together, supposedly for being connected to 'terrorist activity', reminds one of a chapter in French history which is known as the 'Dreyfus Case' .

In the early eighteen nineties a young Jewish military officer called Dreyfus was arrested, supposedly for 'treason', and was sent to St Helena. Captain Dreyfus was caught while he was playing with his young son at home. The police had made such a watertight case against the officer that it seemed everything was lost.

However, incidentally, the legendary French writer Emile Zola came to learn of this case and decided to write a series of articles in the newspapers (titled *J'accuse* meaning I accuse!) explaining the Jewish officer's innocence and describing how he was framed by the powers that be. He exposed how the people who had fabricated the case against Dreyfus 'hated Jews'. Suddenly the move to release Dreyfus gained such momentum that within a short time the government was forced to release him.

As far as Dr Binayak Sen is concerned, the 'never say die' activist community has spoken up but where are our 'Emile Zolas' who can roar *'J 'accuse*'!

June 2007

People as Trophies in Gujarat

Truth is finally out.

People who had a faint glimmer of hope regarding Kausar Bi finally know that she is no more. The Counsel for the Gujarat government admitted as much before the Supreme Court, saying she was killed, her body burnt and ashes thrown in some field. But he does not throw any light on the matter of who killed her.

It appears that the Gujarat government wants to buy time. But the CID report filed by Ms Geeta Johri is very clear on this aspect. The interim report of the IG (CID) Geeta Johri – who investigated the case as per instruction from the Supreme Court – says that Kausarbi was personally strangulated to death by DH Vanzara in the very presence of his wife and son (*Bhaskar*, 28th April 2007).

Imagine! The head of the Anti Terrorism Squad, till the other day functioning as DIG, killed an innocent woman and used his position to cover up the crime.

As things stand the story of the encounter killing of Sohrabuddin Sheikh in cold blood, followed by a similar killing of his friend Tulsiram Prajapati and later his wife Kausar Bi is getting murkier everyday. Thanks to Ruhabuddin Sheikh who persisted in his attempts to get justice and ultimately approached the Supreme Court to intervene in this matter, in which his brother was killed in a fake encounter and sister in law had gone missing, today three senior police officers – two from Gujarat and one from Rajasthan- are behind bars charged with kidnapping and murder of an innocent citizen. If the Gujarat government is compelled to follow the leads it will have to apprehend more than two dozen other police officials from both states who participated in the entire operations at some level or the other.

The manner in which the fake killing(s) have snowballed into a major embarrassment for the 'invincible looking' Modi is for everyone to see. Independent analysts have rightly pointed out that Amit Shah, a close buddy of Narendra Modi and in charge of the Home Ministry, who supposedly went all out to save the guilty officers, may also be sacrificed to save his mentor from further discomfort. And looking at the evidence which is ranged against his buddies, the day is not far off when '*Hindu Hriday Samrat*' Modi may also have to personally face the music.

II

Of course a few things are crystal clear about this killing of an innocent citizen and its packaging as the killing of a dreaded terrorist belonging to the Lashkar-e-Toiba.

Firstly, the killing of Sohrabuddin Sheikh was a joint operation of two state machineries, Gujarat and Rajasthan, both ruled by the Sangh-BJP people, executed by officers who happened to be very close to the top echelons of the people in power. It was for this reason that the Gujarat government asked Ms Geeta Johri to hand over charge to another person, just when she was to present the final report, and Gulab Chand Kataria, the home minister of Rajasthan, personally flew in in a special plane with his officers, to plead the case for Dinesh Kumar, a senior police officer with his government who is behind bars for this encounter.

Secondly, if one were to believe the journalist who played a pivotal role in exposing the killing, then the task of eliminating Sohrabuddin was undertaken at the behest of (by taking 'Supari' from) the rivals of the deceased and crores of rupees changed hands for this purpose.

Thirdly, this is not the first time the Gujarat police has organised an encounter killing and presented it as deaths of terrorists who had come to kill Modi, Togadia or any other rabble rouser from the Hindutva Brigade. One may remember the killing of Ishrat Jahan, a college girl from Bombay, along with three other persons a few years ago, and of Sami Ali Pathan, and its packaging as another 'victory' of the Gujarat police over 'terrorists'.

The Opposition has claimed that during Vanzara's tenure at the Anti Terrorism Squad 15 people were killed in 9 fake encounters. *Asian Age* (30th April 2007) tells us that the 'Rogue Gujarat Cop Killed 13'. But it would be opportune to have a look at the manner in which he went about it.

> Ahmedabad, April 29: Controversial Gujarat IPS officer and "encounter specialist" DG Vanzara, now under arrest for the death of one Sohrabuddin in November 2005, has killed at least 13 people in the past few years on the alleged grounds that they were plotting to kill Gujarat chief minister Narendra Modi and other senior BJP leaders. He has also arrested scores of "terrorists" on similar charges.
>
> To his colleagues and others he has depicted these fake encounters as "patriotic acts" which were evidence of his "deshbhakti." The alleged "terrorists" who he had caught and killed, claiming that they were members of international terrorist outfits and engaged in deadly missions to kill Mr Modi and others, were all, barring one exception, armed only with "tamanchas". These indigenously-made weapons are usually not the assassination weapon of choice employed by terrorist outfits. Mr Vanzara did this to justify the absence of injury to policemen while they were on such encounter missions.

Fourthly, it is clear that the top bosses of the state were complicit in what was being done by the ATS. Any layperson can gather that the killing spree engaged in by these rogue cops helped enhance the threat perception to '*Hindu Hriday Samrats*' inside as well as outside Gujarat and added glory to their images. This is how they ensured that not a single complaint against him reached the State Human Rights Commission. The clout which Vanzara enjoyed with his political masters can be gauged from the fact that he even managed to get his younger brother Vanraj Vanzara, who was with the state forest department, sent on deputation to the Gujarat State Human Rights Commission. It is not surprising that till date, the State Human Rights Commission has not received any complaints against Mr Vanzara.

III

It is worth noting that the BJP, which finds itself on a sticky wicket on these fake killings, has devised multiple lines of defense to avoid further embarrassment to its 'poster boy' Narendra Modi. Chances are if the interim reports of the IG (CID) become public, or the CBI or any further investigation into the case is taken up at the federal level, even for them it could become impossible to defend Modi.

They understand very well that if the investigations proceed in this fake killings case, it would be incumbent upon the agency to look at similar other recent encounters in the state, to look for the 'method in this madness'. The agencies would find it difficult to ignore all such instances where similar sounding post-facto justifications were peddled for killings and the pliant media used in their context to add to the aura of Narendra Modi and his buddies.

Another important aspect of this investigation would involve a revisit to all those cases where people were apprehended on mere suspicion of plotting to finish one or other of the Hindutva bigwigs and were put behind bars under any of several draconian laws which are there in the kitty of the government. The recent acquittal of four innocent persons who languished in jail for close to four years on similar trumped up charges is a case in point.

The BJP has decided that the concern expressed by justice loving people over the encounter killings of innocent citizens amounts to 'glorifying criminals'. They have dished out a number of charges filed against the people who were killed, which were supposedly filed in different police stations in the two states. But in their over enthusiasm they forgot the basic constitutional norms and mechanisms devised to deal with criminals in a legitimate manner. Therefore it was not surprising that on being cornered by the media, regardless of whether it believes in the rule of law or not, its spokespeople were found fumbling for words.

It has also taken a position that fake killings are a norm everywhere in today's times where the justice delivery mechanisms are already cracking under their own weight. They are thus of a considered opinion that it is not proper that Gujarat, or for that matter Rajasthan, should be singled out in this respect.

Following the old dictum that offence is the best defence, they seem to have 'discovered' that other parties are soft towards terrorism and the BJP is the only party battling terrorism. There was news in a section of the media that after lying low for some time Mr Narendra Modi is planning to go on an all out offensive on this issue. It is learnt that he has asked his colleagues to devise a plan whereby the killing of Sohrabuddin could be projected as the Saffron Party's resolute battle against terrorism. He wants to project the Congress as well as the Left as supporters of criminals/terrorists. The only flaw in this plan is the killing of Kausarbi as well as Tulsiram Prajapati, a backward caste Hindu.

IV

One hopes that further details would come out in the ensuing investigations and we would get to know the real culprits. But the moot question is: can the fake encounter killings be reduced to the depredations of few officers out to make a fast buck or gain greater proximity to political bigwigs, or must we look for the larger game plan hatched by the powers that be, which made such killings inevitable.

Perhaps one should look at the three year old plan designed by the Gujarat government, supposedly to 'counter terrorists'.

It is a bit surprising that 'revelations about the counter terrorism plan of the Gujarat police' (*The Rediff Special, Sheela Bhatt in Ahmedabad, How Gujarat Plans to Counter Terrorists, July 15, 2004*), which sent shivers down the spine of the religious minorities in the state, especially the Muslims, who were yet to recover from the tribulations and trauma of the post Godhra carnage, could not become a matter of debate among the national political leadership.

The implicit understanding (as per the Gujarat government) behind this plan was that the 'state has become a haven for terrorists' (read Islamic terrorists). In an interview to the same e-mag the additional Commissioner of Police of Ahmedabad, Mr Vanzara, had hammered this point home in no uncertain terms, stating plainly that...*After the Godhra carnage and the subsequent riots terrorists of a variety of types and shapes are aiming at Gujarat. Gujarat has become the destination for terrorists.* (*The Rediff Interview*, July 27, 2004).

As part of this plan a detailed survey was conducted of the number of mosques and madrasas, and the various Islamic organisations active in the state and their alleged linkages with other national-international organisations was also noted. As per the plan every policeperson from the constable level upwards was instructed to keep 'a close watch on the situation' at the ground level. S/He was also asked to keep tabs on meetings at masjids and the goings on in the madrasas. Activities of the Tablighi Jamaat were to be keenly watched under this plan.

It is clear to even a layperson that the neatly designed 'counter terrorism plan' of the Gujarat government stigmatised the whole minority community in no uncertain terms. As expected it did not even mention the extremist elements within the Hindu community at whose behest the post Godhra pogrom against the Muslims was undertaken. And the need to keep a close watch on the controversial activities of the plethora of organisations of the Hindutva Brigade and its leaders was thus skillfully scuttled. The action plan conveniently missed the Intelligence reports that clearly pointed towards the need to rein in the Hindutva fanatics. To quote: 'Intelligence bureau people overseeing the national scene had warned the central government to rein in elements like Praveen Togadia and Ashok Singhal if it was keen to nip the fresh sources for terrorist activities in the bud.' (*Jansatta*, Hindi Daily, 5th September, 2003, Delhi, 'Intelligence Bureau Warns the Government about Togadia and Singhal').

According to the top bosses of the Gujarat police, the plan originated after the murder of former state home minister and senior Bharatiya Janata Party leader, Haren Pandya. It is still being said that the murder of Mr Haren Pandya opened the eyes of the state government, that the state has become a breeding ground for terrorists belonging to organisations like the Pakistan-based Lashkar-e-Tayiba and Jaish-e-Mohammad. Of course it is another matter that till date Mr Vithalbhai Pandya, father of Mr Haren Pandya, has consistently maintained that his son's murder was politically motivated, and has been pointing his finger at the state leadership of the BJP for their complicity in the murder. As a mark of protest against the state government's reticence to investigate his charges, in the elections to the Parliament in 2004 he even contested as an independent candidate against Mr LK Advani.

Considering the track record of the state government in matters of governance and the manner in which its whole apparatus activated itself in a partisan manner during the 2002 pogrom, the 'counter terrorism plan' is not unexpected. It is also clear that the trauma of the minorities has not ended with the pogrom. Muslims have been subjected to all round harassment in the matter of relief distribution and in apprehending the guilty. Till date a significant section of the Muslim population in the state is facing economic boycott. The misuse of the highly draconian POTA and victimization of innocent Muslims in the aftermath of the pogrom has also been well documented. A report filed by the AFP (New Delhi, Sep 3) states that out of the 240 booked under POTA, which carries a death penalty, 239 are Muslims and one a Sikh. While Muslims have been booked for three different attacks on Hindus, including the burning of the Sabaramati Express at Godhra last year, the attack on Ahmedabad's Akshardham temple and the murder of former minister Haren Pandya, the participation of thousands of Hindus in the pogrom against Muslims did not invite POTA in even a single case.

It needs be added that this 'counter terrorism plan of the state police' has come as a sequel to the amended Gujarat Control of Organised Crime Bill (GUJCOC), which was passed by the Gujarat assembly in the beginning of June 2004. The Bill had almost all the provisions of POTA, including the authority to hold the accused in jail without trial, and provisions giving jurisdiction only to special courts to try the cases under the Act.

It would be naiveté to believe that the said action plan, so partisan in nature and communal in content, could have seen the light of day without direction from the top bosses of the Parivar.

V

Even a cursory glance at the action plan – which went largely unnoticed in the rest of the country – shows that a free hand has been given to those linked with the law and order machinery in the state to continuously harass minorities as part of their 'mission' of 'counter terrorism'. The next logical step then becomes the abduction of innocent people belonging to the minority community at regular intervals and bumping them off, supposedly to provide a post facto justification of the 'success of the action plan'.

Ishrat Jahan, Sami Ali Pathan, Sohrabuddin Sheikh and many like them – independent citizens of a secular nation – become 'trophies' displayed from time to time to convince people of the 'danger' to the nation.

The likes of Vanzara and his associates deserve the most exemplary punishment. But the real culprits in this game must not be allowed to go scott free either. People who have been peddling the agenda of hate for eighty plus years, people who have no qualms in presenting the Gujarat 2002 genocide as a 'successful experiment', people who promote such 'Dirty Harrys' to do the 'needful' must be made accountable and must be punished.

June 2007

Who Will Judge the Judges?

Rakesh Tiwari, Additional Sessions Judge in Delhi, would not have imagined that one day his name would make headlines altogether for wrong reasons. The manner in which the Delhi High Courts upbraided him for his ignorance about even elementary knowledge of the Code of Criminal Procedure (CrPC) has been widely reported. The said judge has also been asked to go on a one month study leave to upgrade his knowledge of the basics.

Close on the heels of the admonishment has come news of the caution advocated by the highest courts of the country with regard to the arbitrary issuance of non-bailable warrants. A three member jury headed by the Chief Justice himself has asked the judiciary to make a proper balancing between the right to personal liberty and the need to safeguard the interests of society in all such cases.

While both these news items have rightly made headlines, a study on the subordinate judiciary covering six states, sponsored by the UNDP, has surprisingly not received the attention it deserves. Jharkhand, one of the six states covered, has come out with its report first. Monitored by a high court judge, the aim of the study was to pinpoint the barriers, if any, in providing access to justice for the underprivileged sections of our society.

And conclusions of the study are not at all flattering for the judiciary. As reported in a section of the press it "brutally confirms the stereotypes of ignorance, indifference and inefficiency that mark the administration of justice in the lower courts."(*The Telegraph*, 27 April 2007) The study says that despite spending five hours in the Court, a subordinate judge in the district courts generally disposes just two out of the 29 cases listed for the day. Commenting on the time management of the judiciary it also alleges that the "judges actually 'loaf' around, both physically and mentally." Of course the report does not spare the police and the lawyers as well, who also contribute their share in causing inordinate delays in the disposal of cases.

Considering the arrears figures for the entire country, which has already crossed the 25 million mark, it can be expected that the conclusions of the study in the remaining states – namely Karnataka, Kerala, Maharashtra, Madhya Pradesh, Orissa and Bengal – would not be qualitatively different.

The only silver lining in an otherwise grim scenario is the growing realisation that there is a gap between precepts and practice. A former Chief Justice of the Supreme Court, Mr Bharucha, had officially lamented that at least 20 % of the judges of the higher judiciary are corrupt.

The question naturally arises as to why there have been no exposures about the malfunctioning of the higher judiciary. Noted lawyer and civil rights activist Prashant Bhushan has tried to throw some light on this matter in an article titled 'judicial Impunity' (*Outlook*, 13 September 2005). According to him:

> The primary reason for this is the lack of any practical mechanism for holding judges of the High Courts and Supreme Court responsible for misconduct. In order to keep the judiciary independent of the executive, the constitution provided impeachment as the only method for disciplining errant judges. That remedy has been shown to be completely impractical in the Ramaswami case, where the judge escaped removal by making a political alliance with the then ruling party, which abstained from voting in Parliament, even after he was found guilty of many charges of misconduct, by a committee of three judges appointed under the Judges Inquiry Act.

It is now history how evidence of misappropriation of funds in Ramaswami's case had surfaced because of an audit on purchases made by the said judge from government funds. It is obvious that without any official investigation it is nearly impossible for an ordinary citizen to get sufficient evidence of misconduct by a judge even for preparing a petition. Besides, an official investigation against a judge cannot be conducted without written permission from the Chief Justice of India. An added difficulty in initiating an impeachment process against any judge of the higher judiciary is that one requires signatures of at least one hundred members of the Lok Sabha or fifty members of the Rajya Sabha to move the motion.

To quote Prashant Bhushan once again, the higher judiciary in our country has "this triple shield of no practical remedy for removal of corrupt judges, no investigation of charges against judges, and finally, the power of contempt, have served to provide complete immunity to judges and has institutionalized judicial impunity."

The power of contempt which rests with the judges recently made headlines when the Delhi High Court sentenced four journalists of the eveninger *Mid Day* to four months imprisonment for 'lowering the prestige of the judiciary'. The Court was perturbed over a series of articles linking orders of sealing of commercial properties passed by Justice Sabharwal as Chief Justice of the Supreme Court and the benefits that his sons derived from the same through partnerships with developers engaged in building shopping malls and commercial properties. It was clear that the orders benefited his sons and their partners. Despite providing documentary evidence '[e]xposing what appeared to be a scandalous conspiracy at the Apex of the judiciary' and despite Mr Sabharwal's retirement from the post on the issue, the High Court demurred that the exposures in the media could be construed as 'Contempt of Court'. It did not deem it necessary to deliberate on the fact that by its action it is providing lifelong impunity to members of the judiciary.

In other situations, as former Chief Justice Ahmadi himself once said:

> In the context of communal riots, particularly when there is State involvement through acts of commission or omission or deliberate failure of the police to protect the targeted groups, many people ask me why the judiciary does not take *suo moto* action against those whose utterances amount to penal offences even when such utterances are bound to vitiate the peace and tranquility of the country, when otherwise in

other comparatively minor situations the Courts play a pro active role and exercise jurisdiction...Frankly, such questions leave me benumbed.

Recently under the auspices of the 'Campaign for Judicial Accountability' a seminar was organized in Delhi where all these questions were discussed and where a demand was raised for a totally independent constitutional body called the National Judicial Commission which will have the power to investigate charges against judges and take action against them.

As things stand there is nobody to judge the judges.

October 2007

Put Up a Poster, Go to Jail !

What is common between dacoity, robbery, cheating and pasting a poster on the wall? One could be chided for raising such an absurd question, for bracketing the simple act of postering with known criminal offences. But the days are not far off when the clear lines between criminality and dissent could be blurred by the mere will of the State. And this pertains to the particular manner of categorization of the act of postering in the proposed Bill moved by the Congress government in Delhi.

The recent Bill aptly titled 'Delhi Prevention of Property Defacement Act 2007' introduced in the Delhi Assembly makes depressing reading. According to its provisions a mere act of pasting posters on the walls or writing anything with chalk, paint or any other material can make one liable for a punishment of one year in jail. Additionally one can be asked to pay a fine of Rs 50,000.

The proposed Act is said to be an improvement on the existing Act in operation in the state which is considered lenient. With this Act, in legal terms, an act of putting up a poster would share a notable commonality with acts of dacoity or robbery. All such acts would be bracketed under the category of 'cognisable offence' which means one can be arrested by a police officer without the formality of a warrant from the magistrate (Court) for the simple act of postering.

Very few people are aware that the Delhi government had adopted the 'West Bengal Prevention of Defacement of Property Act 1976' supposedly to penalise people found engaging in 'defacing public property'.

And it duly arrested around 2802 people during a short span of two years (2001-2003). 1925 people were also punished for doing wall writing, pasting posters, stickers and banners. It is a different matter that this is now being considered leniency!

Considering the stringent provisions in the proposed Act, both how they bracket an act of putting posters as 'cognisable offence' and unduly empower a policeman, one can easily envisage a spurt in the number of people getting arrested or facing punishment for mere dissent. And further considering the rampant corruption in the police department, this proposed Act can only provide another handle to individual policemen to squeeze innocent people. As rightly noted in a historic judgment, in Joginder Kumar vs. State of UP, the Supreme Court (1994)4 SC 260, declared:

> The National Police Commission in its Third Report referring to the quality of arrests by the police in India mentioned the power of arrest as one of the chief sourses of corruption in the police. The Report suggested that, by and large, nearly 60% of the arrests were either unnecessary or unjustified and that such unjustified police action accounted for 43.2% of the expenditure of the jails.

Interestingly the period during which this Draft Bill was placed before the House for discussion, another decision pertained to the government's move to allow advertisements on auto-rickshaws. The goverment expects to see a quantum jump in its revenue through this. A few months ago the local Municipal Corporation also decided to allow advertisements on the radio taxis which could similarly increase its coffers by a few crore rupees.

Any layperson can see through the 'rationale' of this contrary approach of the people in power.While on the one hand the government seeks to penalise people who dissent under the specious plea of 'defacement of public property', it has no qualms/restrictions of any sort about propaganda, provided it is paid for. It is clear that only moneybags or big corporate houses would be able to avail this opportunity. In the changed ambience, where right wing outfits routinely flout the constitution in their everyday propaganda, the 'criminalization' of the democratic right of freedom of expression granted by the constitution, through this new proposed Act, would make it increasingly difficult to express one's disenchantment with the state of affairs. One cannot expect ordinary people who are living on the margins of society and who are at the receiving end of current goverment policies and social institutions to ever find themselves in a position to express their stand vis-a-vis the custodians of democracy.

One still remembers how a few years ago thousands of people working in different factories in Delhi were asked to either shift to new places of work or get ready to leave the job altogether, as the powers that be had decided to close the factories, supposedly to 'control pollution'. One also saw the well planned drive by the city authorities to demolish slums and 'decongest the cities'. A senior judge of the courts had no qualms in denying the slum dwellers any alternate accomodation, claiming that it would be 'rewarding the pick pocketeers'.

Imagine if, in a similar situation in future, people on the margins of society want to express their discontent or publicise their plight. How would they do it in the absence of even the right to put up hand made posters? They would have to be prepared for arrest and a hefty fine for what would become a daring act. Anybody can see that the situation which seems to be emerging cannot be said to be a sign of healthy democracy. And if we limit the idea of political rights to mere right to vote occasionally, then one is making a travesty of the definition.

The key thing to be noted in this debate is that under the present phase of neoliberalism – where market forces have been given free play and the State is withdrawing from key sectors of running the government- the very move to 'criminalize the right to freedom of expression' is a sign of rendering hollow the very idea of citizenship, including the denial of 'ethical and moral duties' of a citizen.

January 2008

How To Make a Terrorist of an Innocent Person and Say It Works

> Judge: The papers on my table show he is not Mukhtar. So what is his real name?
>
> Officer: He is actually Aftab Alam Ansari.
>
> Judge: That means you have arrested a wrong person. How can this horrible blunder take place?
>
> (The officer stayed silent.)
>
> Judge: If he is neither Mukhtar nor Raju, why did you not write that in the petition clearly? Have you written that? Please underline that and show it to me.
>
> (As the officer began scanning the petition, he looked puzzled.)
>
> Judge: I'm not going to accept this petition. Please go and make a fresh one.

Aftab Alam Ansari, an electrician with a power company in Kolkata, is finally free. And the ordeal that he had to go through as a 'terrorist' is finally over. Recently he met with the Chief Minister of Bengal to apprise him of the whole situation and seek help for his mother's failing health.

It is now history how he was arrested from Baranagar in Kolkata on 27th November with Bengal police's help, supposedly for 'ferrying the entire cache of explosives for the November blasts in UP'.

It is now revealed that the Special Task Force (STF) of the UP Police had been set on Aftab's trail on the basis of a vague claim by two arrested militants – Mohamad Khalid and Tariq Quazmi – that the mastermind of the court blasts in the state called himself Aftab as well as Mukhtar, Raju and Bangladeshi. The duo however, had mentioned no middle name or surname, or even had an idea of where this Aftab was.

Though Aftab is now free, Ayesha Begum, Aftab's mother, has other worries staring her in the face--whether they would ever be able to live a normal life and would ever be able to overcome the 'stigma' attached to the whole operation and Aftab's brief sojourn in Jail.

It is now clear that Aftab's arrest by the overenthusiastic UP Special Task Force was a case of mistaken identity as he, like the ringleader of the November blast, also hailed from Gorakhpur and happened to share the nickname 'Mukhtar'.

But now that Aftab, an innocent citizen of this country is free at last, can we be assured that such a tragedy is the last of its kind and will not befall on any one else in the future? And henceforth no Aftab would ever be traumatised in a similar manner? Given the track record of the Indian police and the bigotry and sectarianism of the powers that be, it seems a grand claim.

In fact on the very day the news of Aftab's freedom from jail appeared in the Press, one came across strictures passed by the Maharashtra High Court against the Maharashtra police's arbitrariness in handling the Khwaja Yunus case. Khwaja Yunus, a Gulf returned software engineer, was arrested by the police on December 27, 2002 and booked under the Prevention of Terrorism Act, in connection with the Ghatkopar blast. On January 7, 2003 Yunus was found dead amidst police claims that he had escaped after the vehicle in which he was being escorted to Aurangabad had met with an accident. Later it was revealed that Yunus was tortured to death by some police officers. After persistent protests by human rights activists on his custodial death, and the struggle for justice launched by Yunus's mother Aasiya Begum, a FIR was lodged against the guilty policemen. Of course the dilly dallying on the part of the Maharashtra government continued unabated. The High Court's query was simple: 'Why were ten top police officers initially named by the CID for their alleged involvement in the custodial death of Yunus let off?'

Again, even as Aftab is finally a free man, Mohammad Moarif Qamar and Irshad Ali, two residents of Delhi seem to be not so lucky despite languishing in jail for more than two years. Both were victims of a well-planned conspiracy hatched by the Special Cell of the Delhi Police in collaboration with the Intelligence Bureau operatives. The CBI found to its dismay that IB officials colluded with Delhi Police personnel to 'plant' RDX on these youth who were arrested as 'Al Badr' terrorists. While Qamar was abducted from his Bhajanpura residence on Dec 22, 2005 itself, Irshad Ali had gone missing from his Sultanpuri home ten days earlier. Their relatives had informed the police of their sudden disappearance. On February 9, 2006 the family members were told that both had been arrested with two kgs RDX and pistols. It was clear that they had been kept in illegal detention by the Special Cell all this while. One can imagine what would have happened to them if the High Court had not intervened in the case and directed the CBI to look into the matter. The 'terrorist' label would have stuck on them all their lives.

May it be the case of Aftab or for that matter Khwaja Yunus, or Mohammad Qamar, or Irshad Ali – it is becoming increasingly clear that framing of innocent people and branding them terrorists is the latest norm among law keepers of the country. Of course anyone familiar with the Indian situation may notice the continuity in the rampant misuse of various laws of detention and confinement. But post 9/11 a significant change has occurred. Muslims as a community are increasingly becoming the target of criminalisation and terrorization by the State machinery.

In all such cases it has also become difficult to differentiate whether the people ruled by forces of the 'programmatic communalist' variety (like the BJP or Shiv Sena) or the 'pragmatic communalists' like Congress fare better on this count.

One cannot forget Mohammad Afroz, who was arrested after 9/11 by the Mumbai police and was charged with planning a terrorist attack. It was told to the pliant media that this 'dreaded terrorist' wanted to crash a plane piloted by him on the British House of Commons and Australia. A Special Team of the Mumbai police went to these countries but could not bring back any evidence. Ultimately it accepted that the entire charge was a fabrication. All this happened when Maharashtra was ruled by a secular front comprising parties like the Congress and the NCP.

The 'dreaded terrorists' arrested in connection with the five year old attack on the Raghunath temple in Jammu also faced similar ordeals. The Courts finally absolved all the accused of any charges and advised the police to properly use its minds in handling cases of such nature. These innocent people had to languish in jail for a long period due to no fault of theirs.

It is worth noting that despite many such fiascos the powers that be have drawn no lessons, nor done anything to avoid recurrence of such incidents. On the contrary, the entire attempt is to 'individualise' all such cases and continue with the established practice of stigmatisation and brutalisation of the social and religious minorities.

Is anyone listening?

February 2008

When Lawyers Masquerade as Judges

Those who can make you believe absurdities, can make you commit atrocities. Voltaire

Ismail Jalagir, a senior counsel from Hubli (Karnataka) and Mohammad Shoaib, a senior advocate from Lucknow (UP) may not have heard of each other. But even their strongest critics would admit that they are men of some mettle. If there were awards meant for lawyers ready to go that extra mile to defend the rights of citizens these worthy men would deserve to be somewhere on the top of that list.

What they have done and achieved – without bothering about the dangers to personal security and well being – is really stupendous. They have not only defied the unethical ban imposed by fellow 'brethren' of the legal profession on taking up the defence of innocent accused Muslims, but also exposed the manner in which a particular community is being 'stigmatised and terrorised' with due connivance of the police, media and a pliant legal fraternity.

It is clearly evident that but for the efforts of Mohammad Shoaib, Aftab Alam Ansari of Kolkata, supposedly a 'Lashkar-e-Toiba' operative involved in the bomb blasts in UP courts, would have been languishing in jail, with nobody agreeing to take on his defense.

And there would have been no counsels for people like Asadullah Abubaker, Riyazuddin Nasir, Mohammad Asif and Mohammad Shakeel from Hubli and adjoining areas if Ismail Jalagir had not decided to take the plunge. In fact when Karnataka police arrested this foursome under charges of 'terrorism' there was no one to argue their case. Considering that nobody was ready to take up the cases of these people after the unanimous resolution by the Hubli Bar Association (12th February), which had resolved not to fight cases on behalf of persons charged with 'anti-national' activities, Ismail Jalagir decided to act. For this courageous act he faced the wrath of the Sangh Parivar. Miscreants tried to set fire to his office and even his junior's house was stoned. (Ref: *Justice Can't See, Won't Hear*, Suresh Bhatt, Letters, *Tehelka*, 10 May 2008). The role of the media in this matter was equally biased from day one. Despite some senior police officers' contention that there was no definite information against the accused, the local media mounted a cacophonic campaign of misinformation.

Mohammad Shoiab is handling many such cases in various courts of UP, and like Ismail Jalagir is also facing the consequences of taking a principled stand. He has come under direct physical attack on many occasions, the latest being in the Faizabad courts where he had to be literally 'cordoned' by a police team to save him from getting badly thrashed by fellow lawyers.

Neither has been cowed down by these threats and intimidatory tactics.

A disturbing aspect of the whole scenario is that neither Hubli nor Lucknow is an exception.

Today one after another Bar Associations are coming forward to pass undemocratic resolutions preventing their fraternity from taking up the defense of those accused of 'anti-national' activities. And the latest to join the bandwagon are Bar Associations in Madhya Pradesh, that have declared that they would not take up any cases where alleged operatives of a Islamic organisation were nabbed by the police. We know that the MP police arrested many people, including the ex-Chief of a particular organisation, claiming that they were associated with anti-national activities.

Let me make it very clear at this juncture that I do not hold any brief for sectarian organisations that have a very bigoted view of history – may they claim allegiance to any of the religions. But the vehemence with which these Bar Associations have come forward to declare and implement their resolve tells something about what is happening within the legal profession with regard to minority rights and how patriotism is being defined by them. And they have not limited themselves to passing resolutions, they have exhibited their 'readiness' to implement them as well. In some places they have not hesitated even in physically assaulting/intimidating anyone who opposed such a move or tried to take up cudgels on behalf of the accused charged with 'terrorism' by the police.

The cases of Khalid and Tariq, languishing in jail since the last four months supposedly (according to the police) for 'executing the serial blasts in courts of UP which left 14 people dead', presents a representative picture of the whole situation.

If one searches the records of the Jamia Tul-Salahat Madarsa in Jaunpur where Khalid taught, we learn that not only was he present in the Madarsa on the day concerned (23 November), but had also checked the copies of students on that particular day. The judge has been asked to cross-check the UP police story which says that Khalid landed in Lucknow in a bus on the morning of November 23, met other accomplices, bought new cycles, planted bombs in the Lucknow court premises and returned immediately to Jaunpur.

The recent decision of the UP government, asking a retired judge to ascertain whether both these persons arrested for the court blasts in the state are indeed terrorists or not, is an indicator of the pressure governments are facing over repeated complaints that the state police is implicating Muslims as terrorists.

STF-Special Task Force or Special Terrorist Force?

According to an investigation done by 'People's Union for Human Rights' (PUHR), parts of which have appeared in different publications (*Samayantar*, Hindi magazine, April 2008), Khalid was literally kidnapped by STF from a snacks shop on 16th evening (Mariyahu, Jaunpur), by people in civilian dress who had come in a Tata Sumo which did not carry any number plate. Hundreds of people were mute witness to the kidnapping drama. Despite best efforts by Khalid's family no case of kidnapping was registered. On 19th December the police reached Khalid's house and interrogated his family members for many hours. Khalid's uncle, Zaheer, told the PUHR team that the police took away with them the Quran and a book on Hadees, later claimed as part of 'terrorist literature' found by them.

Tariq was kidnapped by a similar team on 12th December from Rani ki Sarai, Azamgarh at 12 noon. The police registered a case of 'missing' (not 'kidnapping) on 14th December. The kidnapping case gave rise to a lot of consternation in the area with political and social organisations coming forward to protest police inaction. On 17th night around three dozen police personnel reached Tariq's house, interrogated his family members, took their signatures on blank papers and also carried with them some books in Tariq's possession (which were later declared as 'terrorist literature).

Sixteen witnesses of Tariq's kidnapping (which includes 12 Hindus and 4 Muslims) have filed an affidavit that Tariq was kidnapped before their eyes. Hundreds of residents of Mariyahu did a signature campaign and have presented a 'video recording' to the administration to show that Khalid was kidnapped before their eyes.

To go by the STF version in this case, that Khalid Mujahid and Tariq are members of Harkat-Ul-Jehad-i Islami (HUJI) and were 'involved in the serial blasts that left 14 people dead', would amount to making a mockery of justice.

Denying Legal Hearing 'Democratically'

If earlier the 'boycott' by Bar Associations, had seemed a spontaneous reaction by lawyers to imagined acts of a kind that automatically lead to revulsion in a wider populace, in hindsight they now emerge as organised efforts by vested interests owing allegiance to one set of sectarian ideologies. These forces have tried to manipulate/orchestrate people's anger over 'violent acts' in such a manner that it has created an 'us' versus 'them' like situation along religious lines culminating in the stigmatisation of a particular minority community. Much like the people in the law and order machinery, who are ready with an 'explanation' after every such act with names and addresses of the miscreants 'from across the border', a section among the lawyer community have no qualms in fixing responsibility for the violent/terrorist acts on innocent victims of police actions.

In fact the complete absence of lawyers from the courts in cases that have 'terrorist' bearings has led to the unjustifiable situation where many innocent persons are languishing in jails for no fault of theirs, and it has become impossible to get them released even on bail.

It would not be incorrect to say that Uttar Pradesh is the 'birth-place' of this phenomenon. It all started in 2005 when there was a terrorist attack on the temporary structure at the disputed site of the demolished Babri masjid. The Faizabad Bar Association took lead in the matter and unilaterally declared that lawyers would not take up the defense of the accused in this particular case. When a team of lawyers from outside the city ventured into the Faizabad courts to take up bail applications for the accused, it literally came under attack and had to leave the city under police protection. When legal proceedings in the Varanasi case began (2006) regarding the incidents of violence in the Sankatmochan temple and railway station, one was witness to a similar action by the Varanasi lawyers. November 2007 witnessed bomb blasts in the courts of Varanasi, Lucknow and Faizabad and subsequently the Bar Associations in Lucknow and Barabanki also joined in the boycott of 'terrorist' cases.

Mr KG Kannabiran, Vice President of People's Union for Civil Liberties (PUCL) and a well known human rights activist, who is also an advocate by profession, recently issued an appeal to fellow lawyers to reconsider and rescind their decision of boycott of particular cases. In his well publicised appeal he rightly said:

> The Bar Resolution stifles right of the accused to defend himself at the trial. Our right to practice this profession is part of our fundamental rights. The accused has a right under Article 21 of the Constitution. Article 22 (1) gives the right to a suspect to have a lawyer present at the time of arrest and interrogation. The lawyers' right to practice a profession or calling is directly concerned with these fundamental rights of a citizen who is an accused. Article 21 right includes the right of the accused to have lawyer for the defense. A lawyer's freedom of choice while practicing his calling has limitations. We are not here concerned with the preferences available to a lawyer for practicing his calling. We are, Respected Members, concerned here with collectively imposing a ban on lawyers making themselves available to defend a particular accused. Have the professional members such freedom to practice their calling?

> Can the members of the Bar negate the right of the accused available to him under Article 21? The position taken by the Resolution is not morally or constitutionally justified. An emotional response is not a moral response. Arguing for a fair trial cannot be equated with or confused with asking to exonerate the guilty of his crime. Emotional indignation should not degenerate into pharisaical self-righteousness. There is no dichotomy between "morality" and the Constitution if one learns to do a moral reading of the Constitution. Let us not proceed on the facile assumption that there is no affinity between law and justice and law and morality.

Over-lawyered but unrepresented!

> *When there are too many policemen, there can be no liberty.*
> *When there are too many soldiers, there can be no peace.*
> *When there are too many lawyers, there can be no justice.*
>
> Lin Yutang (1895-1976)

One does not know the context in which the Chinese-American writer, translator and editor Lin Yutang mentioned the absence of justice when one has too many lawyers. Perhaps he was making an observation on (to quote Jimmy Carter) the 'over-lawyered and under-represented' US society which has had the 'heaviest concentration of lawyers on Earth' but where 'legal skills seem to be unfairly distributed with ninety percent of the lawyers serving mere 10 per cent of the people.'

Certainly he was not contemplating the situation as it exists in many courts of India in the first decade of the 21 st century or the collective refusal by lawyers to lend their services to the accused in specific cases, thus facilitating denial of justice to them.

One can only hope that wiser sense prevails eventually. In case this does not happen it would be "...[u]pto the Bar Council of India which is a regulatory body to take serious note of the resolutions passed by the bar associations (a forum of lawyers) which amount to not merely professional misconduct but are an infringement of the constitutional and human rights of the accused."

April 2008

Writing Equals Sedition

Does critical writing on the doings of a police commissioner or his colleagues amount to sedition? Any sane person would reply in the negative. But then sanity is not the strong point of a neo-liberal and saffron condition.

The newly appointed honourable Police Commissioner of Ahmedabad has actually filed a case of 'sedition and treason' against the Ahmedabad edition of the *Times of India* for carrying a series of articles on his alleged links with a Mafia Don. According to the complaint filed by the Commissioner, the said articles 'gave the impression that state police officers were in league with criminals'. It is learnt that these reports are based on the statement given before the CBI by a henchman of the Don, in which he had claimed that the present Commissioner was once on the Don's 'payroll'. (*The Hindu*, 2nd June 2008).

The honourable Police Commissioner has every right to feel offended over such charges and if needed he can take recourse to legal action. Normally in all such circumstances cases are filed under charges of defamation. But as they say, in Gujarat they do things differently.

While the Police Commissioner's complaint vis-a-vis the newspaper has underlined the scant respect with which the fourth estate is viewed by the Super cops in a saffron regime, another incident involving a leading intellectual of our times underlines the challenges which anybody-who cares to exercise her/his right to freedom of expression has to face under such a dispensation . The case involves a lead page article ('Blame the Middle Class', 8th January 2008, *Times of India*) written by Prof.

Ashish Nandy, a well known political psychologist and sociologist of our times. According to a report which appeared in a section of the media (*Indian Express*, 31 May 08):

> The Gurajat Police has registered a criminal offence against Professor Ashish Nandy, a political psychologist and sociologist, for writing an alleged inflammatory article in the second week of January 2008 in an English daily.
>
> The case was registered on a complaint filed by advocate-activist VK Saxena, the president of the Ahmedabad-based National Council for Civil Liberties.
>
> The complaint registered under Section 153 (A) (B) of the Indian Penal Code said that the article was prejudicial to national integration and intended to cause friction and promote enmity between different communities on grounds of religion, race, language and place of birth.
>
> Nandy's article, the complaint said, was highly intemperate, vituperative and showed Gujaratis in a low light.
>
> Surprisingly, the state government gave the permission for filing the case through a notification on April 15. While granting permission for filing the criminal case against Nandy, the government notification said "there is prima facie evidence against the accused for his involvement in the commission of offences under sections of the IPC".
>
> The particular article had tried to analyse the election results of the Gujarat assembly held in December 2007, which had once again given a mandate to Mr Narendra Modi. Apart from delineating the plight of the Muslims who are condemned to a life of second class existence and the growing marginalisation of the 'secular formations/ideas' it had tried to focus its attention on the 'state's urbane middle class' which has remained 'mired in its inane versions of communalism and parochialism'.

It concluded with the observation that:

> Recovering Gujarat from its urban middle class will not be easy. The class has found in militant religious nationalism a new self-respect and a new virtual identity as a martial community, the way Bengali babus, Maharashtrian Brahmins and Kashmiri Muslims at different times have sought salvation in violence. In Gujarat this class has smelt blood, for it does not have to do the killings but can plan, finance and coordinate them with impunity. The actual killers are the lowest of the low, mostly

> tribals and dalits. The middle class controls the media and education, which have become hate factories in recent times. And they receive spirited support from most non-resident Indians who, at a safe distance from India, can afford to be more nationalist, bloodthirsty, and irresponsible.

While the state government can console itself over the fact that it has not been consulted over the case filed against the *Times of India*, it would be height of innocence to say that it has not been party to the decision which saw filing of criminal charges against Prof Nandy. And it is not very difficult to understand the growing displeasure of the Saffron lobby over Prof Nandy – who has at times been very critical of the left/secular intellectuals/formations as well. Perhaps the manner in which Prof Nandy has castigated the 'Sangh Parivar's contribution to the growth of radical Islam' in India has hit them hard.

> Events like the desecration of Wali Gujarati's grave have pushed one of India's culturally richest, most diverse, vernacular Islamic traditions to the wall. Future generations will as gratefully acknowledge the Sangh Parivar's contribution to the growth of radical Islam in India as this generation remembers with gratitude the handsome contribution of Rajiv Gandhi and his cohorts to Sikh militancy. (Quoted in *Times of India*, 8th January, 'Blame the Middle Class').

Considering the unsustainable charges against the leading newspaper and the condemnation that the state government is receiving for throttling the right to freedom of expression, one would have expected that wiser sense would prevail and the state government would actively intervene to rectify the mistake. But the way things are moving the chances seem remote.

Two years ago an editor of an eveninger from Surat was charged with 'anti-national activities', including 'instigating people against a duly elected government', and was put behind bars by the same government. As reported in a section of the media, the law and order people had felt offended when Manoj Shinde, editor of *Surat Samna*, in an editorial '...[a]ttacked several officials and BJP leaders for mishandling of the release of water from the Ukai dam resulting in the flooding of the city and causing colossal losses to the people'. (*The Hindu*, 30th August 2006, Delhi). The complaint against Shinde, on behalf of the government of Gujarat, was lodged under Section 124A (sedition: anyone who by words or expression of any kind brings or attempts to bring or provoke a feeling of hatred, contempt or disaffection towards government established by law shall be punished with life imprisonment) 292, 293, 294(b) (dealing with obscene publication), 500 (defamation), 501 (printing aggravating matter against union territory or Chief Minister) and 502 and 505(1) (circulation of false statement against the public peace) under the Indian Penal Code.

Despite the nuanced opinion of a human rights activist the government went ahead with the case. "Shinde's editorial doesn't amount to sedition as the comments were against an individual" he said. "The tendency here is that the CM considers himself to be Gujarat. It is not sedition even if he is called Hitler. It may amount to defamation but not sedition."(*Indian Express*, 31 st August 2006).

These instances raise the question of the draconian provisions in the statute books of a sovereign democratic set up, which helps the powers that be to apprehend anyone under its pretext. The leeway it gives to the ruling powers is obvious from some crucial cases of the last few years in which those apprehended as 'offenders' were in no way engaged in any activity that could be even remotely construed as connected with sedition.

Post 9/11 during the anti war protests opposing the machinations of the USA for world hegemony, a section of the participants in these protests in Delhi had tough experiences at the hands of the then BJP regime. Six students belonging to the Delhi University were charged with 'sedition' and arrested for the 'crime' of distributing anti-war leaflets and denouncing the communal-fascist war mongering stand of the Vajpayee government. It is a different matter that faced with large scale criticism in the media and civil society the government had to retrace its arbitrary move.

While Mayawati enjoyed her third stint in power in UP, with due support from of the BJP, peace activist and Magasaysay award winner Sandeep Pandey and his fellow activists also faced charges of 'sedition' and 'inciting communal violence'. A poster put up by these activists at a dharana site in Faizabad (UP) demanding a peaceful resolution of the Ayodhya issue was declared inflammatory by the government (20 March

2003). The poster in question had a quote from a poem by Laxmi Shankar Vajpayee which said "Oh God, Please don't accept the temple which is built on the foundations of the dead and has blood stained walls."

Human Rights Watch, in its report of 1999, describes the violation of dalit rights which is done with impunity. Under the heading 'Criminalisation of Social Activism' the report narrates the story of one Tirumavalavan, a dalit rights activist from Tamilnadu, and other members of his movement who were targeted by the police for organizing dalits to claim their rights. According to the testimony of Tirumavalavan he is ...[o]ften arrested under the Indian Penal Code sections 153(a) [for promoting enmity between different groups] and 120(b) [for criminal conspiracy], and also under the Sedition Act and the National Security Act.

A cursory glance at the genesis of the 'crime of sedition' would make it clear that it has its roots in an era that has nothing to do with democracy. It came to be used equally against coups and revolutions. While the British colonialists imposed it in India to rein in the natives, as an offence it originated in and had been selectively used in Britain for a long time. Prior to 1606, treason (an offence similar to sedition) was punishable under the Statute of Treasons of 1352. The offence of seditious libel was first created in 1606 by the infamous Star Chamber decision in *de Libellis Famosis*18 and continued to exist in the common law as a species of libel.

One can say that the rationale for incorporating the Sedition Act in the Indian context came in for criticism on two counts. Firstly, its clear espousal of the methods adopted by the colonial rulers to discipline 'natives', and secondly, its core concept which is clearly antithetical to the underlying premises of modern democracy. A cursory reading of passages in the 'Sedition Act', embodied under the Indian Penal Code section 124A, would make this obvious:

> Whoever by words, either spoken or written, or by signs, or by visible representation, or otherwise, brings or attempts to bring into hatred or contempt, or excites or attempts to excite disaffection towards, the Government established by law in India, shall be punished with imprisonment for life, to which fine may be added, or with imprisonment which may extend to three years, to which fine may be added...

It is symptomatic of the age we live in that in many mature democracies the law of sedition has now either formally been rescinded or is largely defunct. A considered observation of 'Global Campaign for Free Expression' is worth quoting in full:

> Pronouncements by courts and law reform commissions in a number of common law jurisdictions support the contention that the law of sedition serves no useful purpose, is anachronistic, is palpably undemocratic, and is an unconstitutional encroachment on the right to freedom of expression.

Is India, the 'largest democracy in the world', ready to pay heed to such voices? To begin with, the honourable Police Commissioner of Ahmedabad could reconsider his decision.

June 2008

Who Would Wipe Professor Radoo's Tears?

Professor Sanaullah Radoo, Principal of a Degree College in Sopore, Jammu-Kashmir still remembers the day when his youngest son Pervez had reached the airport in Srinagar to catch the next *Spice Jet* flight to Delhi.(12 September 2006). The moment the flight landed in Delhi, he had even made a call to his *Abboo* (father in colloquial terms – as he used to fondly call him) informing him that he was rushing to get the boarding pass for the connecting flight to Pune. He could not possibly have had any premonition of what was in store for him.

It is more than nineteen months now that Pervez has been in detention, and he is even now lodged in Jail No. 1, Ward No. 1, Barrack No. 2, Tihar, Delhi. And as of now all his dreams for research on the variety of rice found in Kashmir stands suspended. Young Pervez Ahmad Radoo, who had completed his post-graduation in Zoology from Modern College, Pune was hopeful of admission to PhD, for which he was going to Pune.

In fact, the moment Pervez approached the airline staff for his boarding pass at Delhi airport he realised that he had been surrounded by seven-eight people, who held him firmly and took away his luggage, and straightaway drove him to Lodhi Colony Special Cell office. In a letter (*Combat Law*, March-April 2008) he provides details of the manner in which he was 'tortured and interrogated severely' and how he was 'beaten up ruthlessly' and given 'electric shocks'.

If one were to believe the Special Cell of the Delhi Police, Pervez was arrested on October 15, 2006 from the Azadpur Mandi in the city with "three kgs. of RDX and Rs 10 lakh as hawala money along with other incriminating evidence" proving him to be a "Jaish-e-Mohammed terrorist".

Professor Sanaullah has been running from pillar to post for the last eighteen months just so that his youngest son gets a 'fair trial' and comes out of jail unscathed and is able to resume his research work. The fact is that for around a month the Professor did not even know that Pervez had not landed in Pune, rather that he was in detention. He has also presented a memorandum to the National Commission on Minorities (NCM) to impress upon them the need for intervention. Mohammad Shafi Qureshi, Chairperson of NCM, who has looked into the case and has also written to the Delhi Police, was candid enough to share his views on the subject with a reporter (*Mail Today*, Delhi, March 6, 2008 – 'NCM fights for release of J&K youth in Tihar'):

> It is hard to believe the police version when one sees the clean chits given by the police superintendent and additional district magistrate of Sopore, his native town, and from the local resident welfare association (RWA). Most importantly, the certificate given by Spicejet for the same day shows him as boarding the plane for Delhi from Srinagar and then also bound to travel further to Pune. These facts have been completely ignored by the Special Cell.

Trying to control his tears Professor Sanaullah Radoo speaks to the reporter about how the police have turned a promising young scientist into a 'bomb-man'. "He should be completing his research on a rice species in Kashmir valley, instead he is inside prison facing charges of terrorism," he says. He is categorical that the police 'are lying'. He is also not sure whether his son would receive a fair trial and whether he has been provided an able lawyer to defend his case.

Pervez's jail diary, which has appeared in a section of the media, throws further light on his plight. In his letter asking to 'Save My Career, As I Am Innocent' he poignantly asks '

> Am I not Indian, if I am Kashmiri? Why this discrimination, when tall claims are being made by the Government of India, by media, that before law all citizens are equal?

Of course the story of the metamorphosis of a student of Zoology into a 'bomb-man' is not the only one of its kind. In fact hardly a day passes that one does not hear of an illegal detention of a youth from the minority community, on some frivolous charge or the other.

Just a day before the *Mail Today* carried the above mentioned story about Pervez, it had provided details of a case involving a 'terrorist' *gutkha* manufacturer getting bail (*Mail Today*, March 5, 2008). According to the report filed by Piyush Srivastava, 'Barely six months ago, 35 year old Imran Ismail Memon was termed as a terrorist, gangster, a hawala racketeer, a smuggler and a manufacturer of adulterated Gutkha.' Imran Ismail Memon, a resident of Thane in Maharashtra was arrested by the Rae Bareli police on August 25, 2007. Police said he was part of a "terrorist module" and had started an "illegal and adulterated gutkha factory" as a cover-up to stay in the district. Lucknow bench of the Allahabad High Court granted him bail because of lack of evidence. It also added that 'the police could not even prove the power theft charge against him.'

There is the case of Aftab Alam Ansari, an employee of the Calcutta Electricity Supply Corporation who was arrested on 27th December 2007 as 'main accused behind the serial blasts in no. of courts in UP', or for that matter the case of a poor fruit vendor from Kashmir who was presented before the media as a 'prize catch' responsible for blasts on the eve of Diwali in Delhi two years ago. It is clear that with the ascendance of the Hindu right wing forces in the Indian polity, and in the atmosphere created the world over since 9/11, such targeting of innocents from the minority community has become all the more common.

All of us were witness to the travails of Aftab Alam Ansari who was tortured during the 22 days that he spent in police custody after his arrest on December 27, 2007, in order to make him confess that he was Mukhtar alias Raju, resident of Malda district in West Bengal, and had Rs 6 crores in his bank account.

The biggest irony in the whole situation is that while the terrorist acts committed by Hindutva organisations are not even reported, and in fact all attempts are made to cover them up, innocent people from the minority community are being continuously apprehended, claiming them to be associates of this or that dreaded terrorist organisation. The media, which is supposed to be a watchdog of democracy, also joins the malicious campaign, unquestioningly terming them "terrorists" rather than accused awaiting trial in court. It does not seem to be bothered that such trials by media are not only unethical but also violate the basic ethics of responsible and fair journalism.

One is saying all this not to condone terrorist acts, but rather to insist that the law of the land should be equally applicable in all such cases and it should not appear that it is favouring/targeting a particular community.

Things have reached such a pass that it would not be an exaggeration to say that the 'terrorisation' and 'stigmatisation' of the minority community is reaching menacing proportions. The pattern of mindless arrests and branding of innocent persons as terrorists and resorting to relentless torture is becoming common but also coming under increasing scrutiny. And it is quite natural that this is giving rise to perceptible anger all across the country.

Perhaps the recent decision of the UP government asking a retired judge to ascertain whether the two persons arrested for the court blasts in the state are indeed terrorists or not is an indicator of the pressure governments are facing over repeated complaints that the state police is implicating Muslims as terrorists. The case involves the arrests of Khalid Mujahid and Tariq, claiming them to be members of Harkat-Ul-Jehadi (HUJI), and their being implicated for executing the serial blasts that left 14 people dead. If one searches the records of the Jamia Tul-Salahat Madarsa in Jaunpur where Khalid taught, it becomes evident that not only was he was present on the day (23 Nov) in the Madarsa but had also checked the copies of the students. The judge has been asked to cross-check the UP police story which says that Khalid landed in Lucknow in a bus on November 23 morning, met other accomplices, bought new cycles, planted bombs in Lucknow court premises and returned immediately to Jaunpur.

One can go on narrating instances of the highhandedness of the police and the callousness of the political circles in turning a blind eye towards continuous stigmatisation of a particular community. As already mentioned this is an understanding which has received a new boost in the aftermath of 9/11 and the 'war against terror' unleashed by the US regime, to further its imperialist ambitions.

Any impartial enquiry into the state of affairs would make it clear that the need of the hour is to understand that 'terrorism' cannot be the monopoly of a particular community. It is a product of the typical circumstances which societies encounter or find themselves in and the nature of the dominant or dominated forces in operation in those societies and their larger worldview.

There is no denying also that civil society at large has accorded legitimacy to all such actions by the police. If that were not the case there would have been uproar of national proportions when it became known how 'intelligence bureau operatives colluded with Delhi police to brand two of its own informers as dreaded terrorists'. It was sheer coincidence that the matter reached the CBI, which exposed the dark machinations of the dirty tricks brigade.

A write up in the *Times of India* 'IB, cops in murky frame-up' by Sachin Parashar, New Delhi, 13 September 2007, had presented all relevant details of the case.

> New Delhi: The CBI has found that Intelligence Bureau operatives colluded with Delhi Police special cell sleuths to 'plant' RDX on two youths who were arrested as 'Al Badr terrorists', TOI has learnt. The shocking conclusion comes a month after the agency told the Delhi High Court that the special cell's probe into the murky affair "didn't inspire confidence".
>
> Top CBI sources told TOI on Wednesday that the seized RDX appeared to have been planted on the two 'terrorists' Mohd Moarif Qamar and Irshad Ali. The agency will submit its report, which indicts officers of IB and Delhi Police special cell, to the court on October 24.
>
> While similar episodes in the past have hurt the credibility of the anti-terror agencies, this one stands out because it marks a rare instance where Intelligence Bureau operatives collaborated in the plot hatched by Delhi Police's special cell against its former informers.

A few months ago one was witness to a furore over the violation of human rights and dignity of Dr Haneef in Australia. Thanks to the support provided by international media and human rights organisations and the concern expressed in the political circles here, it was not long before the Australian judiciary and executive were forced to ensure the release of Dr Haneef. We were also told then that our honourable Prime Minister Manmohan Singh felt personally disturbed about the plight of Dr Haneef and could not sleep that night.

Perhaps it is high time that the honourable Prime Minister is told that 'Dr Haneef''s is not an isolated case and Dr Haneef is not just coincidentally the name of a doctor mistakenly or wrongly apprehended in Australia – rather it is an example of a phenomenon quite rampant, and significantly, in this part of the earth as well.

And the case of Pervez Ahmad Radoo is one such important case which demands his immediate intervention. Only such a move can bring the smile back on Professor Sanaullah's face.

July-August 2008

A Two Minute Silence for Naushad Kashimji

Does a senior advocate's appearance before the Honourable Court to argue his client's case become news at the regional/state/national level? In our country of sub continental dimensions, which has thousands and thousands of courts, frequented by lakhs of advocates, this is considered to be an exception.

It only happens when the advocate (or one should say a team of advocates) is appearing for a 'celebrity swindler' a 'corporate criminal' or a ' leader who can easily double up as a criminal.'

Interestingly when the senior most lawyer of the Mangalore Bar Association, 85 year old Mr Purushottam Pujary, appeared before the District Judge, it was his own way of taking his protest to a wider level.

What was the 'special importance' of Mr Pujary's appearance before the judges? In fact, Mr Pujary was appearing for a case which was being argued by his assistant of nine years, named Naushad Kashimji, who was brutally killed by 'unknown assailants' a few days ago. A threat to his life is apprehended now that he has decided to take up the said case. Kashimji was found dead in the basement of an apartment near his house.

But who killed this promising lawyer who also acted as a human rights defender?

Mr Pujary personally went to the Pandeshwar Police station in Mangalore to lodge a complaint against the team of four police officers who had allegedly murdered this ardent legal activist and an exponent of human liberty. Mr Pujary was quoted as saying "...Not only was he my best junior and the most fearless young advocate here, he was also like a son to me." In his complaint he had accused Deputy Superintendent of Police Jayanth Shetty, District Crime Investigation Bureau Inspector Venkatesh Prasanna, Ullal Police Sub-Inspector H Shivaprakash and Circle Inspector of Panambur Valentine D'Souza of having "orchestrated the killing of his junior".

In addition to sending his complaint to the State Human Rights Commission, the Chairman of the Karnataka State Bar Council, the Chairman of the State Minorities Commission, and the Director-General and Inspector-General of Police, he had also called for a Central Bureau of Investigation (CBI) probe into the death of Kashimji.

Kashimji was defending alleged Chota Shakeel-aide Rasheed Malbari who was recently apprehended by a team led by the four police officers.

According to a report which appeared in a section of the media:

> In his complaint, Mr Poojary has alleged that a few hours before his (Kashimji) death, Kashimji was issued a "veiled threat by the four officers" at the district court complex after he finished arguing his case on behalf of Rasheed Malbari.
>
> Claiming that the slain advocate had informed him of the threat, Mr Poojary has alleged that the police officers told Kashimji, "*If you argue against granting police custody (of Rasheed Malbari), you will have no more arguments in the future.*"
>
> Attributing the alleged murder to rivalry between him and the accused police officers, Mr Poojary pointed out that Kashimji had argued several cases wherein these police officers had allegedly violated human rights or falsely implicated people in them.

It is worth noting that Mr Purushottam Pujary was not alone in raising the demand for a CBI probe into the mysterious killing of Naushad Kashimji. The Mangalore Bar Association has also voiced its concern over this brutal killing of one its finest lawyers and has demanded a CBI inquiry.

As facts tell us, the zeal with which the lawyer operated and the manner in which he was ready to go the extra mile to defend human rights, had become a 'cause of concern' for the Mangalore police. The slain lawyer had also appeared against the same police officers on behalf of Atul Rao who, he believed, was falsely implicated in the murder of Padmapriya, wife of BJP MLA Raghupati Bhat. He had also appeared for 25 persons these police officers had rounded up in connection with the murder of BJP and Bajrang Dal leader Sukananda Shetty. It is worth underlining that he was able to obtain bail for 13 of the 25 who were falsely implicated by these officers.

It is well known that whenever he heard of a case of 'custodial torture' by the police, he was ready to appear on behalf of the victims. Mr Poojary has alleged that

> ..these officers worked as "extended arms" of the Sangh Parivar and had been targeting minorities and human rights activists ever since the Janata Dal (Secular)-Bharatiya Janata Party alliance came to power in the State.

2.

Despite solid evidence which points to issues of omission and commission by the police in the mysterious killing of this advocate, the police have declared that there is no need for investigation by an outside agency. (*The Hindu*, 15 April 2009). Dakshina Kannada Superintendent of Police A.S. Rao says that investigations are progressing well and he sees no need to hand over the case to the CBI. He denied that there was any negligence on the part of the police in the investigation. Rao also said that the post-mortem of the body and the inquest had been video graphed and services of ballistic experts from Bangalore were used. The post-mortem report was awaited, he said. He said the first information report (FIR) was filed based on eyewitness accounts and there could not be a second FIR based on Mr Poojary's complaint. However, the police has included the information given by him in the scope of the investigation, he counters.

As of now, despite the solid evidence presented by Mr Poojary, the policemen themselves are investigating into allegations of involvement of top police officials in the crime.

One can imagine what would emerge out of this 'investigation'.

3.

Of course those familiar with the working of the police under the saffron dispensation should not be surprised. In its exhaustive report on 'Cultural Policing in Dakshina Karnataka' the People's Union for Civil Liberties has provided details of its working and the refusal of policemen to register cases against saffron hoodlums. It is disturbing that the communalisation and criminalisation is happening before our very eyes in Dakshina Kannada, an area otherwise regarded as very progressive in terms of socio-economic indicators. Not only is the district in the forefront in education, its progressive nature is also attested by the fact that in the 2001 census, the sex ratio recorded is 1022 females per 1000 males.

The PUCL report categorically states that "The police in Dakshina Kannada inspire little confidence. There is a widespread perception that the police are indeed part of the problem. ...With respect to cultural policing in particular, which often involves the commission of offences such as criminal intimidation, causing hurt, and outraging the modesty of a woman, the response of senior police officers has been grossly inadequate."

When confronted by the failure of the District Administration to take action against self-styled vigilante groups that have violated the criminal law with such impunity, the Inspector-General of Police (Western Range) AM Prasad said that there was no provision under the Code of Criminal Procedure (CrPC) to book cases against the vigilantes. These groups targeted people for committing "supposed moral violations" such as interacting or falling in love with people from other religious faiths or trying to proselytize someone. Of late, these groups had begun bringing their victims to the police station demanding that they be booked for their "crimes". "Everyone has the right to complain to the police when they think that someone has violated the law," Mr Prasad said (*The Hindu*, 29 November 2008).

The connivance of the police with the saffron dispensation is also evident in the report. The Superintendent of Police's statement of appreciation for the Bajrang Dal for not taking the law into their own hands but rather producing the victims before the police, also willfully ignores the fact that cultural policing by the Bajrang Dal is not an innocent act. It necessarily involves the commission of various offences possibly ranging from wrongful confinement to criminal intimidation to causing simple hurt. It is the duty of the police to inquire into and punish groups which claim to enforce morality but are actually violating the law. Surely the police should not be complicit in the violation of law to enforce morality. Such a situation is the very antithesis of a secular and democratic state committed to the rule of law.

4.

The killing of the human rights defender, allegedly by the policemen themselves, once again brings into focus the challenges faced by such people. Also, the killing of Naushad should not be seen in isolation. As we go to the Press, we learn of the Raipur satyagraha where hundreds of people are courting arrest to protest the detention of Binayak Sen, a child's doctor and a civil liberty activist. A few months ago the manner in which human rights activists were booked as 'swindlers' in UP had also reached headlines.

The real tribute to the work of people like Naushad Kasimji involves not only bringing to book the perpetrators of the crime but also carrying forward the task for which he gave his life.

June 2009

Whether Human Rights of Prisoners Stand Suspended?

> *What state of society is that which knows of no better instrument for its own defense than the hangman, and which proclaims . . . its own brutality as eternal law? . . . Is there not a necessity for deeply reflecting upon an alteration of the system that breeds these crimes, instead of glorifying the hangman who executes a lot of criminals to make room only for the supply of new ones?* Karl Marx, 1853

The letter sent by an under-trial Mukesh Kumar, at present lodged in Karnal Jail (Haryana), through his Counsel to the Chief Justice of India makes depressing reading. The letter talks about the manner in which he was brutalised by the Jail staff for disobeying their orders. It is learnt that the Jail wardens compelled him to clean the toilets calling him names and 'reminding' him of his 'caste profession'. His refusal to continue the dehumanising work led to his public thrashing and tonsuring/shaving of his head and moustache.

According to the administration, Mukesh Kumar is one of those persons arrested in different parts of Haryana from April to June 2009 as part of the state campaign 'to curb Maoist activity'.

Of course, any close observer of the human rights situation in the state would tell you that this is not the first time that jail officials in Haryana have engaged in targeting a particular section of under-trials/ detainees. Three years ago Gohana, a place around 50 kms from Delhi, had witnessed the burning of dalit houses, with police remaining mute spectators, supposedly to avenge the death of a Jat youth. A few dalit youths were arrested for the death of the Jat youth and were similarly brutalised by the jail staff.

If the matter is pending before the Court, which is already deliberating on it, then what could be the rationale for this uncalled for enthusiasm of the jail staff? It has been more than three decades since the Supreme Court verdict on such incidents. Yet the jail staff flouts it with impunity.

Responding to two separate writ petitions filed by Sunil Batra and Charles Sobharaj, two prisoners in Delhi's Tihar jail, the highest Court intervened to humanize jail conditions. As noted in a write up '*Prisoners Rights: Some Landmark Judgements*' the question before the Court was:

> Does a prison setting, ipso facto, outlaw the rule of law, lock out the judicial process from the jail gates and declare a long holiday for human rights of convicts in confinement? And if there is no total eclipse, what lucent segment is open for judicial justice? Sunil Batra, sentenced to death, had challenged his incarceration in solitary confinement, and Charles Sobhraj had challenged his confinement with bar-fetters.
>
> The Supreme Court held that there is no total deprivation of a prisoner's rights of life and liberty. The "safe keeping" in jail custody is the limited jurisdiction of the jailer. "To resort safe-keeping into a hidden opportunity to scare the ward and to traumatize him is to betray the custodian of law, safe custody does not mean deprivations, violation, banishment from the lanter barguet of prison life and inflictions of travails as if guardianship were best fulfilled by making the ward suffer near insanity.

Despite clear cut instructions from the Supreme Court, one discovers that brutalisation and dehumanisation of inmates at the hands of Jail officials is not an exception but the rule.

As recently as March 2009 the Gujarat High Court ordered the Sessions Judge to visit Sabarmati jail and to contact the detainees/prisoners lodged there. Responding to a petition filed by *Jan Sangharsh Manch* regarding the alleged atrocities committed by the jail staff on the inmates – most of whom were Muslims – it also issued notices to Inspector General of Police (Jails) and V Chandrasekhar, Jail Superintendent of Sabarmati Central Jail (*Indian Express*, 28th March 2009). Tension between the inmates and the jail staff flared on an occasion when one of the prisoners, Yunus Sareswala, was not allowed to meet his ailing mother. In the melee that ensued, twenty two prisoners were badly beaten up by the jail staff (25th March 2009).As noted in a fact finding report of human rights activists who met with prison officials as well as detainees and their relatives,

> ...[I]nmates, most of them Muslim, who were on a hunger strike, were denied medical attention after a brutal attack on them by jail staff, which left at least three of them unconscious for so long as to start rumours in the city that they had died. They were subsequently denied access to counsel, their relatives were refused permission to meet them for three days, and then the Sabarmati Police station failed to register an FIR as sought by relatives and counsel of the victims.

Questions naturally occur as to the reasons behind the current quantum jump in custodial human rights violations despite all talk of humanising jail conditions. One should see the spurt as product of faulty government policies and lack of transparency observed by the powers that be. Much on the lines of the United States of America, our government also shies away from accountability in all such matters. Figures collated at National Human Rights Commission confirm this trend. As of now complaints which have reached its offices have already surpassed the figure of 70,000. While forty percent of the complaints focus on police, violations of human rights inside the jail are a close second.

Of course, there have been instances when jail officials have been held accountable for their acts of omission and commission. In an important write up 'Walls Not A Prison Make', Editor at large of *Tehelka*, Mr Ajit Sahi, provides details of a case where "Terror accused dare to take on their brutal jailers – and win" (September 5, 2009).

The said story discusses the brutal assault in prison on Sohail and 26 other inmates on June 28, 2008 when the jail staff rained "...[b]lows, belts, bamboo sticks and stones on them, smashing their heads, breaking their bones and spilling blood." Accused of participating in the terror attack in Bombay and brought to Mumbai's Central Prison in 2006, Sohail and his fellow accused were quickly branded traitors not just by the jail staff but also by the "regular" prisoners and faced all-round hatred and contempt. To cover up their attack, jail authorities claimed that the prisoners had rioted unprovoked shouting Pakistan Zindabad, Hindustan Murdabad [Long live Pakistan, Down with India] and attacked the jail staff.

Undeterred by the ongoing brutalisation Sohail, with the help of his son Saeed, filed a case against the jail authorities despite the odds, and actually won a favourable ruling. As noted in the write up: "The order of Bombay High Court judges Bilal Nazki and AR Joshi, delivered on July 21, 2009, does not just bring justice to Sohail and the others the prison staff brutally attacked. The ruling is historic because it restores the Constitutional rights of tens of thousands of inmates who face indignities and brutalities inside Indian prisons without let or hindrance. It also prescribes criminal prosecution of the jail staff for brutalising the inmates."

According to the judges:

> … We have found [that] force was used against the under trial prisoners for no fault of theirs. Force was used excessively for extraneous reasons and [the] law was also flouted. Even as a formality, the Jail Manual was not followed. We, therefore, direct the Chief Secretary, State of Maharashtra to initiate [a] disciplinary inquiry against all the Officers involved in the incident… If need be, in addition to the departmental inquiry, criminal action be also initiated against the concerned Officers.

The said judgment unequivocally lays down that the jail authorities have no authority over an inmate's life:

> Once a charge sheet has been filed, nobody has authority over the custody of an under-trial except the Court... It has to be remembered that the convicts or the under-trials are human beings and they have to be treated like human beings. The jail authorities who have custody over them have [a] special responsibility to protect their rights and in fact they are their custodian, reformer and counsellor.
>
> They cannot assume the role by which they turn into [a] villain. They in fact should command respect from the prisoners and that respect should come as a result of their conduct with prisoners. This is no longer in debate in this country whether or not the prisoners have fundamental rights available to them as this has been decided in [a] number of cases by the Supreme Court.

It need be noted that the judges also slammed the Jail Superintendent at the Central Prison, Swati Sathe, a female officer who is infamous for her brutalities among inmates. As of now a departmental inquiry has been instituted against Sathe and there are hopes of her criminal prosecution once the departmental inquiry is completed.

September 2009

Social Profiling, Indian Style

The Muslim is not wanted in the armed forces because he is always suspect – whether we want to admit it or not, most Indians consider Muslims a fifth column for Pakistan. [*Vengeance! India after the assassination of Indira Gandhi* (New Delhi, Norton, 1985), pp. 1995-96] George Fernandes

Amnesty International defines racial profiling as the targeting of individuals and groups by law enforcement officials, even partially, on the basis of race, ethnicity, national origin, or religion, except when there is trustworthy information, relevant to the locality and time frame, that links persons belonging to one of the afore mentioned groups to an identified criminal incident or scheme.

I

Is racial/social profiling practiced in India?

If one were to pose the question before the powers that be we would obviously encounter a strict 'no'. Tons of statistics would be put before us to 'prove' that our sixty plus years experience of democracy is living proof that such things do not happen here. Interestingly, barring exceptions, the articulate sections of our society would also be found singing paeans to this 'largest democracy' in the world and would rather shy away from accepting the simple fact that the 'largeness' of this democracy has not prevented it from practicing all kinds of 'apartheid' against its own people.

It is a different matter that some occasions do arise when neither representatives of the government nor spokespersons of civil society are able to deny the prevalence of such discrimination.

A few weeks ago newspapers were agog with the case of Maulvi Noor Ul Huda, who runs a Madrasa in Faizabad, who was forcibly alighted from an international flight and put in detention by the Delhi police because a lady co-passenger complained of his 'suspicious behaviour.' It was told that his talk on his mobile informing his relatives about the expected take off of the plane ("*jahaz udane wala hai*") aroused suspicion in the minds of his co-passenger. We were also told that it required the Home Minister's intervention to free him from detention without any false charges slapped against him. In fact, a few enthusiasts in the police department were keen he be booked under some pretext or the other to save face. It is equally disturbing that the lady co-passenger who had lodged the false complaint against him and made him as well as his family members suffer many agonising moments, was allowed to go scot free.

Can one say that this case was an exception (as a section of the media wants us to believe) or is it a reflection of the ongoing institutional discrimination against religious minorities, especially Muslims, which has societal sanction and legitimacy as well?

II.

Close on the heels of this news came an important announcement from one of the premier agencies of the government which was an indirect acceptance of the fact that religious minorities as well as other deprived sections of our society have faced unfair treatment in terrorism related incidents at the hands of the investigating agencies.

Reports which have appeared in a section of the media (viz. *Jagran Rashtriya*, 3rd June 2010, '*Alpasankhyakon se poochtach mein satark rahegi NIA*') tell us that the said directive issued by its Director General Mr SC Sinha – which discusses the planning and the priorities of the agency – asks the investigating officers to be 'extra careful and sensitive towards the emotions of the minority communities as well as other oppressed and deprived sections of our society' and 'respect the rights of the accused during investigationss'. Also that the agency is committed to complete the investigations in any particular case within a year, and if for any reason it is not completed, the investigating officer would have to seek permission directly from the Director General.

For any close watcher of the 'terrorism related investigations' the context of the said directive was very clear. This was the same period during which the investigations into the Ajmer bomb blast had unearthed the connections of the Rashtriya Swayamsevak Sangh (RSS). The exposures in this case had revealed that it was members of the RSS who had executed this plan, and one key member of this terrorist module had been working as a whole timer/*pracharak* for the entire state of Jharkhand. It had also come to light that a team of Rajasthan police personnel had in fact revealed these links way back in 2008, but the then dispensation in power in the state, namely the BJP, had not exhibited any keenness to follow the case.

The manner in which biases and prejudices entertained by the police and the officials of the investigating agencies affect the outcome of the probe were thus on full display in this case which had seen the deaths of two innocents. As of now the Rajasthan Police is said to be trying to unearth the linkages of these Hindutva terror modules to the blast which was earlier blamed on fanatic Muslims despite clear evidence of involvement of Hindutva organisations. It is also learnt that Central Bureau of Investigation (CBI) will soon take into custody two people who had been arrested by the Rajasthan Police in connection with the Ajmer blast, to probe their role in the Mecca Masjid blast in Hyderabad as well following evidence of links between the two incidents.

One can look at the history of any terrorism related incident in recent times and the manner in which investigation proceeded and one would discern a pattern in the responses of the law and order machinery. Barring exceptions, one would find that the responses have not been balanced and have contributed significantly to stigmatising the minority community.

III.

Of course, it is not only during such investigations but generally too that those in power as well as the investigative agencies have systematically targeted the minority community. A few months ago the news magazine *Outlook* made the revelation that Muslim-dominated areas of two important Indian cities were targeted for telephone tapping at the behest of then National Security Adviser MK Narayanan ('Phone tapping: Why target us, ask Muslims', April 25, 2010 19:45 IST, Mohammed Siddique in Hyderabad,(rediff.com). This was under the Congress led UPA regime, in utter disregard of the fact that telephone tapping is a serious violation of the right to privacy guaranteed by the Constitution. According to a news item which appeared in a section of the media:

> Muslims in Hyderabad have expressed their unhappiness over reports that they were target of a sophisticated telephone tapping operation by Intelligence Bureau.
>
> Reacting sharply to the revelations made by news magazine *Outlook* that Muslim-dominated areas of Hyderabad and Lucknow [Images] were targeted for telephone tapping at the behest of then National Security Advisor MK Narayanan, community leaders said that this was yet another proof of how Muslims were being eyed with suspicions by those in power as well as the agencies.
>
> All India Muslim Personal Law Board secretary Abdul Raheem Qureshi has urged the Centre and the state to immediately put an end to the abominable practices of targeting of Muslims for telephone tapping and other espionage operations in the name of fight against terrorism.

IV.

One can go on enumerating instances when minorities have received a rough deal at the hands of the powers that be, and how the articulate sections of society have not bothered that a more inclusive, non-discriminatory atmosphere be maintained.

An outcome of this situation is very much visible on the educational front as well. A recent report by the National Sample Survey Organisation (NSSO), a central government body, tends to confirm this. Its surveys show that Muslims, India's largest religious minority, is the most backward community in terms of educational attainment. According to it the ratio of the Muslims in higher education is lower than that of even Scheduled Tribes (STs), who are considered to be the most backward.

A letter circulated by Mr Faisal Khan, an activist of the National Alliance of People's Movements, provides vivid details of the unfolding situation.

> ..[A]ttached to the Union Ministry of Statistics and Programme Implementation, NSSO, in its report titled 'Education in India, 2007-08: Participation and Expenditure', says that of every 100 Muslims in the education system, just 10 are enrolled in high school and above. Similar ratio for STs is 11, Scheduled Castes (SCs) 12 and Other Backward Classes (OBCs) 14.
>
> The report also says that higher education among urban Muslims is lower than their counterparts in rural areas. This despite the fact that urban areas have better educational facilities. According to the NSSO report published on May 19, just seven out of 100 urban Muslims in the education system were enrolled in high school or above as compared to 12 in rural areas.
>
> This is because poor Muslims in urban areas do not have easy access to education as they have in rural areas. The landless poor "labourers, rickshaw pullers etc" are hardly able to make both their ends meet, leave alone education for their children.
>
> The report is based on the household survey on participation and expenditure in education conducted in its 64th round. The field work of the nationwide survey was carried out during July 2007 to June 2008. The survey covered a random sample of 4,45,960 persons, from 63,318 rural households and 37,263 urban households spread over 7953 villages and 4682 urban blocks, covering the entire geographical area of the country.

V.

To come back to the issue of racial/social profiling, another simple query concerns the effectiveness/ineffectiveness of social profiling as a crime prevention strategy. In the absence of available data the task would seem difficult but one can perhaps look at figures collated by the US and Britain to know its impact.

Studies by Amnetsy International USA tell us that a staggering number of people in the United States are subjected to racial profiling. Approximately 32 million people, a number approximately equivalent to the population of Canada, report they have already been victims of racial profiling. Victims of racial profiling include Native Americans, Asian Americans, Hispanic Americans, African Americans, Arab Americans,

Iranian Americans, American Muslims, many immigrants and visitors, and under certain circumstances, white Americans.

Interestingly racial profiling is not officially admitted in the UK but statistics do show otherwise. According to section 44 of the Terrorism Act 2000, police officers are permitted to stop and search individuals with justifiable cause. The statistics provided by the Ministry of Justice tell us that some police people do seem to be using racial profiling. Asian people were over five times more likely to be stopped and searched than white people. Black people were seven times more likely to be stopped and searched than white people. Only 0.6% of the searches ended in arrests for terrorism offences.

Human rights organizations, such as Liberty, active in the UK have stated that racial profiling is not as effective as rational police methods. The manner in which racial profiling undermines law enforcement efforts is evident from the classic Oklahoma City bombing case in the US. Facts tell us that the white male assailant, Timothy McVeigh, was able to flee while officers reportedly operated on the theory that "Arab terrorists" had committed the act.

June 2010

And Quiet Flows the Yamuna

A Court Order and its Aftermath

Introduction

It was the end of the year 1996 when a joint initiative took shape in Delhi in the shadow of a controversial Supreme Court Order, to protect the rights of workers. The Order pertained to the alleged violation of the Master Plan by 168 industries and the Court had ordered their closure/relocation. The controversial Order affected around 50,000 workers.

This is just to 'recapture' the story of that joint effort, the only one of its kind in the recent history of Delhi, when the Joint Action Group, comprising various types of mass organisations, christened itself as the 'Delhi Janwadi Adhikar Manch' and mediated its path through the complex and complicated maze of environment and labour interface. It was a journey to understand the intricacies of the 'red' versus 'green' debate; it was also a coming to grips with the dynamics of judicial activism and comprehending how vested interests can make any sensible action in an iniquitous society turn into its opposite.

This is just to share with a wider audience the experiences we gathered, the difficulties we faced and the questions we encountered in the whole journey.

The Day After

In mid-1996 the highest Court of the country delivered the 'historic judgement' citing need for 'environment protection at any cost' and decided to close down 168 industries operating in the confirming/non-confirming areas of Delhi. The judgement was delivered by the Bench of Kuldeep Singh and Saghir Ahmad and was in response to a petition filed by MC Mehta, a 'green' lawyer, in 1985, about the pollution of the Yamuna. According to the Honourable Court, since the said industries were violating the provisions of the Master Plan of Delhi they had to be either closed or relocated. In the initial judgement given on July 8 the Court had set the compensation to the workmen who were to be affected by the Order as equivalent to one year of their wages. After the intervention of the aggrieved parties the compensation was raised to six years of the wages in case of closure of the industries.

The Court also decided on the matter of the real estate involved in this *l'affaire* closure/relocation in a detailed manner. In cases where a relatively smaller piece of land was involved it gave the owner of the industry complete right to develop the land, and where a relatively larger piece of land was involved it stipulated that a portion of the land be handed over to the Delhi Development Authority or any such concerned authority.

With regard to the violations of the Master Plan and the role/complicity of the bureaucracy and the industrialists in causing the environment to deteriorate to such a miserable condition, the Honourable Court merely passed strictures. The crimes and the connivance of the bureaucracy in turning a blind eye to the progressive deterioration of the environment was left to be investigated by an officer of the level of Secretary rank in the Delhi Government. (It would be not only interesting but revealing as well to know the findings and the consequent action taken by that Secretary.) Neither the industrialists/mill owners who through their unscrupulous ways had bypassed the provision of the Master Plan or had deliberately played with the environment received any penalties for their 'crimes' nor did the courts find it fit to invoke the provisions of the famous Environment Protection Act (1986) in this 'historic judgement'. It is known that the Environment Protection Act (1986), which was passed in the aftermath of the Union Carbide disaster in Bhopal, had even stipulated penal provisions for those industrial units considered involved in causing irreparable damage to the environment.

For the workers the Order came as a bolt from the blue. Even as the judgement was about to be delivered they were made to believe that all talk of closure/relocation was a mere hoax. They became fully aware of their situation only when ultimately under the clear instructions from the Supreme Court the industries were forced to close shop. Also, by denying intervention on behalf of the workers' representatives when the case was subjudice, the SC itself violated the principle of natural justice.

It has been more than three years since the judgement was implemented. As ordered by the Court the said industries were either shut down or a decision on their relocation was conveyed to the workmen by the night of December 31, 1996. Out of the 168 industries one industry, Sahni Rubber Industries, gave an affidavit to the SC to exempt it from implementing the shut down order since it was not producing any hazardous or polluting substance. The Court, after verifying the facts, allowed it to continue its operations.

Till date, apart from a small section of workers belonging to a public undertaking, the majority of workers have not received any compensation and a number of cases are pending in the Court over the definition of the term 'workmen' by the Court in its judgement.

As things stand today, the industries have been closed, the major industrialists have been allowed to mint millions of rupees by selling the land situated in prime localities, the bureaucracy has been allowed to go scot-free and the whole burden of providing 'lung spaces' to the city has been borne by the workers, numbering more than 50,000. And to make matters worse a new Order has come from the Honourable Court as part of its drive for an environment-friendly Delhi which has the potential of putting the right of around one million more workers to live a life of dignity in jeopardy.

It is worth noting in this connection that the Supreme Court, taking notice of a newspaper article in July 1994 about the polluted Yamuna, had directed the government to build CETPs (Central Effluent Treatment Plants) in twenty eight industrial areas of Delhi in February 1996. The whole issue of setting up of the CETPs culminated in a game of 'shirking of responsibilities' between the government, the industries and the Pollution Control Board. Finally, on January 24, a two-judge Bench of Kirpal and Rajendra Babu forbade the discharge of untreated effluents from any factory in Delhi and Haryana into the Yamuna, immediately affecting the running of around 1000 industries.

And the SC, 'learning' from the earlier experience of providing 'continuity of employment' (at least in the judgement) to the workmen, has not bothered to even mention what needs to be done about them. The fate of the workers is left to the mercy of the factory owners, the bureaucrats and the politicians, with the judiciary washing its hands off any meddling in their fate.

As has been widely reported, many workers have died pending payment of compensation by the management of the industries; quite a few have committed suicides. The self-immolation of Sarvesh Chand, a worker of the SB Mills, before Parliament on May Day is a case in point. The death of Bharat, who died in Baddi last year braving the cold wave while participating in an indefinite dharna outside the proposed factory gate, did not get much publicity.

For the ordinary worker, the Order has come as a 'double punishment'. While working inside the factory he/she was compelled to work in unhealthy and hazardous circumstances and the closure/relocation of the factory has deprived him/her of dues. For the mill owners and the industrialists the Order has come as a double reward: they could rake in millions when their units were running; and now with the units legally closed they could sell the land and even get monetary support for shifting the units.

How the Other Half Lives

As is widely known, all the industries employ workers in various categories ranging from permanent, temporary, *badli* and contract. It is estimated that around 50 to 60 per cent workers in any unit come under the 'non-permanent' category. And with the intensification of the trend of informalisation and casualisation of labour, there has been a significant shift away from employing permanent workers. And since these 'other' workers are not enrolled on the live registers of the company/industry, their 'continuity of employment', as guaranteed in the SC order, becomes a casualty presuming that the Company shifts its base to a new location. An added factor, which acts as further hindrance to their 'continuity of employment', presents itself in the form of the policies adopted by various state governments for the industrial development of their state. The case of Himachal Pradesh is worth mentioning in this regard; any new industry being opened there has to provide employment to a fixed percentage of the local populace.

No sane person would dispute the need for sustainable development as defined by the famous Brundland Report of 1987 wherein it underlined the importance of 'development which meets the needs of the present without compromising the ability of the future generations to meet their own needs'. It is not for nothing that people of all types the world over have become more conscious about safeguarding the environment and there is even talk of environmental rights of people apart from social, cultural and economic rights.

But sometimes the way the question of environment is posited smacks of utter disregard for the rights of those sections of people who are ultimately compelled to face a 'double burden' for cleaning the environment. Looking at the particular case under discussion, one notices that quite a few eco-activists even proclaimed: how does the livelihood of a few thousand workers matter when the right to life of more than ten million people is at stake? Granted that the right to life of more than ten million people is more precious as compared to the fate of a few thousand workers; but how does that give licence to the powers-that-be to play havoc with their hard-earned rights?

It has been widely reported that as far as air pollution is concerned, more than 64 per cent of it is caused by vehicular emissions. In its first publication, *The Order that Felled a City*, the Manch had provided details of the state of pollution in the cities, especially the metropolises. An NGO, the Centre for Science and Environment (CSE), in its publication, *Slow Murder*, has also given horrific details of the state of pollution in the metropolises. As far as Delhi is concerned, the total number of cars/vehicles running in Delhi is more than the total number of cars and other vehicles running in the other three metropolitan cities, namely, Bombay, Calcutta and Chennai. One also notices that disregarding the caution voiced by environmentalists about the "more polluting" nature of diesel, permission continues to be being granted for passenger cars running on diesel.

The power plants (three in number operating in Delhi) come next as far as degradation and deterioration of the environment are concerned. A few years ago details of the malfunctioning of the electrostatic precipitators installed in these power plants were published in one of the issues of *New Scientist.* The matter was shelved and only cosmetic steps were taken to ameliorate it.

A related question was also raised: how is the Supreme Court going to ensure that the said factories would not begin polluting the atmosphere at their new places? It is also clear that the present laws provide little or practically no scope for the people (especially the workers) to take action against the polluting employers. It is also essentially they who bear the impact of the poison and hazardous material created by the working of the factories. If concrete steps are not taken to reduce/stop pollution at the shop floor the Order essentially gets reduced to the not-in-my-backyard attitude of the Supreme Court.

It was rightly pointed out that the highest Court after taking on an interventionist stance should have dealt with the question in a holistic manner.

Justice is Not Even Blind

> *The punishment prescribed for violations of the law are not exactly designed to ensure compliance. The "polluter pays" principle has undergone metamorphosis in India and become a "pay and pollute" principle, because paying or avoiding penalties are less expensive than installing treatment plants.* [('Enforcing Environmental Laws' by Rahmatullah Khan, quoted in *Environmental Challenges* (ed. Varshney and Sardesai)]

The juggernaut of the Supreme Court still rumbles on. Even while the debate over the harmonious relationship between the three pillars of democracy – namely, legislature, executive and the judiciary – continues, the interventionist role adopted by the judiciary vis-à-vis the other two 'pillars of democracy' is still unfolding before our eyes. It is not surprising that the inefficient, corrupt and lethargic executive and a compromising legislature has helped the judiciary don an 'activist' garb in the outgoing decade.

While nobody can doubt the concern of the judiciary towards matters directly affecting society and polity, it does not augur well for a true democracy that one of its 'pillars' oversteps its limits and 'infringes' on the 'space' of the other. Certainly quite a few of its interventions have had a positive impact on society, but does not the whole process create a 'superior' image of the judiciary which, while 'dispensing justice', has also been at the same time disempowering the wider populace?

The progressive deterioration of the environment and the growing consciousness of the people, especially the middle classes, about ecological issues has led us to a situation where one finds many a petition being filed before the various courts. It is also evident that the courts have become the sole arbiters in many a technical issue. A perusal of many of its Orders would in fact make us aware that often the courts are dishing out 'technical' solutions rather than setting policy guidelines. In future a neutral observer might well be amazed at how in the nineties the courts were giving such Orders as that the streets be cleaned regularly and how hospitals should treat their wastes.

And how does one expect the judiciary to remain aloof from the goings-on in society, sort of a lotus in muddy waters? Not long ago even the Chief Justice of this country felt compelled to make an exposure in the Court on how he was being pressurized while handling the sensitive *hawala* case.

AG Noorani, an authority on constitutional law, rightly puts it: "No Apex Court works in an ivory tower."

The manner in which the Supreme Court, or for that matter any other court, deals with a particular case reflects the prevailing climate of opinion. If in the eighties the Court felt itself restrained to intervene in cases which were apparently beyond its purview, the same Court within a decade had earmarked Fridays to hear cases centring on environmental issues.

In this era of LPG (Liberalisation, Privatisation and Globalisation) and triumphalism of the market, one is not very surprised to see the judiciary becoming more and more insensitive to the rights of the marginalised and the unprivileged, whether it is the workers in a polluting industry or squatters in one of those sprawling slums. If the Jagmohans were determined to remove the plague called unauthorised colonies in the seventies during the Emergency, their judicial *avatars* at the beginning of the new millennium have been insensitive enough to compare them with 'pickpockets'. The Order of the SC explicitly stating that in the event of failure to install effective effluent treatment plants the industries should simply be closed is a reflection of this insensitivity. The said Order does not even mention 'workmen' or what is to be done with him/her – a concern that had found some reference in the 1996 Order.

The Silver Lining

> Marx's partner, Frederich Engels, crossing a Lancashire river, spoke of "the most disgusting blackish green pools from the depths of which bubbles of miasmatic gas constantly arise and give forth a stench unendurable even while on the bridge 40 to 50 feet above the surface." *Ecology for Beginners*

While the preparations for a seminar on these issues were on there was an interesting piece of news from the southern corner of the country. The news dealt with the goings on at the Mavoor Factory (run by the Birlas) which has been in the news. As is widely known, a citizens' movement has been going on in that area for the last three decades centring on the pollution of the Challiyar river caused by the said factory. It is worth noting that the citizens' movement has involved people from different vocations and occupations and it has been demanding that the factory control its pollution. They have also been pressurising the government to ensure that the Birlas comply with the pollution regulations. Fearing retrenchment, the trade unions have been objectively on the opposite side of the citizens' council.

Recently the management has applied for closure of the industry giving rise to apprehensions that it wants to wash its hands off the workers' dues and the penalties for polluting the environment. Many are of the opinion that this is another ploy of the management to hoodwink the people who are being exposed to untold miseries both inside and outside the factory. This new move by the management has given rise to a new bond of solidarity among the trade unions and the citizens' council who were hitherto in an adversial relationship vis-à-vis each other. It is a good sign that these 'contending' camps are realizing that real danger to the rights to life and livelihood of both, the wider populace and the workers, lies in the logic of capital itself which is ready to plunder, loot the natural resources and exploit labour.

The experience of campaigns like the 'Delhi Janwadi Adhikar Manch' also brings home the point that a sustained effort of some magnitude can facilitate the process of bringing together 'contending camps' in a dialogue that can create a positive consensus around particular cases.

Summing up, what can one say on the role of the Manch in this closure/relocation saga? Apparently it failed on all major counts. The special leave petition supposed to be filed could not actually be filed, nor was a petition given to the parliamentary committee to look into the judicial intransigence. The Manch could not halt relocation/closure, or gather resources to support thousands of workers of the SB Mills who went to the site of relocation braving cold winds to get their meagre compensation.

The eleven-year old Court battle was already over and the courts had already given their final orders. In fact the memorable joint initiative to halt the process took shape effectively only in the shadow of the SC order. But it was clear from day one that the Manch was trying to retrieve a battle which was already lost. The formation and continuation of the Manch was an event in itself as intellectuals and ordinary workers, party people and concerned individuals associated with different types of activities came together and worked together in a completely democratic manner. The initiative of the Manch was exemplary in another sense, that it awakened from deep slumber the major trade unions, who were finding themselves clueless as to how to act/intervene in this issue.

The Road Ahead

From the experience of the DJAM, or for that matter the Citizens' Council at Mavoor, and the various local resistance movements all over the country to one or other such devastating project, one fact is becoming increasingly evident – that during the last decade or two new types of movements/campaigns mobilising different strata of society on issues of local and general concern are acquiring some prominence.

In today's times when the traditional organisations of the workers are locked in many a defensive battle, and the custodians of capital are happy thrusting market-friendly legislations on people to cut their hard-won rights, and when the major political formations have reached a consensus over the direction of the economy, the role and scope of the activities of these forums/campaigns/movements, even if they are of a transitional nature, becomes quite crucial for supporting the struggles of the marginalised and the unprivileged.

As things stand today, the trade unions, the torchbearers of the working class, also need a lot of introspection on the state of affairs in which they currently find themselves. Why is it that during the last five decades they could not lodge any significant struggle on the working conditions on the shop floor, in addition to the usual monetary struggles centring on wage increase and bonus? Why is it that they failed to link in their struggles the issues of lowering of working hours and better wages with those of increased productivity and better technology in such a way that more jobs are created and better working conditions are attained? Why is it that they could not join the vast majority of workers in the unorganised sectors? Why is it that the issue of occupational hazards could not become an important issue in their schema of things? Have orders such as this, which effectively make the workers serve a 'double punishment', not made them painfully aware of the things which lie ahead?

A related question which arises in the whole debate is: how does one look at the whole issue of "development" as it is understood today?

Certainly a crucial aspect of all such attempts should be to rearticulate our agenda in a way that we are clearly able to expose monopoly capital's constant search for new profits as the major source of environmental crisis which seems to threaten humanity, and are also able to decide our stand vis-à-vis all those social movements which have taken up with vigour many such issues that have so far remained neglected in the overall schema of 'traditional Left politics'. Certainly those who still swear by *The Communist Manifesto* or cherish the dreams of the Paris Communards will have to engage in a lot of introspection over the fact that despite our claims of a scientific understanding of nature and society we have remained neglectful of an entire range of these new phenomena. Was this the result of our mechanical understanding or was there something amiss in the revolutionary project itself as claimed by many a radical intellectual?

Has the time come for a "historical compromise" linking the labour movement with the social movements, as claimed by Rudolf Bahro in one of his earlier writings? That as "people are fighting the system in many different ways and because resistance is cutting across class and party lines a grand coalition of anti-capitalist forces is needed to unite them"? Should it be the case that the Left in its mass activities and engagements joins with the new social movements? There are growing indications that the Left would need to take up the challenge and move in this direction. The clever and flexible *modus operandi* of a more evolved capitalism often succeeds in pitting the interests of the citizenry against those of the organised labour which is under renewed attack from Capital. On the other hand a large majority of the same citizenry is forced to eke out a living under the severely exploitative conditions in the unorganised sector. The Left needs to make a double move out of its traditional base in the organised sector. It must join with the issues and struggles of the unorganised sector. At the same time it would have to actively take up the issues and interests of the citizenry. To take the issue of environment as an example, it is a mistake to consider it an issue of the elite. It is a bigger mistake to leave such an important issue to the initiative and leadership of the elite. Of course, there are complex and thorny issues on the way as has been underlined in the experience of the DJAM. In the final analysis the complexity arises because the issue rubs against systemic issues. Capitalism as a system comes under a new and more serious question-mark. The complexity arises also because an alternative system which has a realistic chance in the near future, to replace capitalism and to address such issues as sustainable development and better living conditions for all, is not considered to have been worked out, at least in the common perception.

This should not discourage us from pressing on. After an honest, hard day's struggle, if we win a small bit for the people even as we lose quite a bit in the face of entrenched capitalism, it is a big gain. For after an honest, hard year's or decade's struggle in this mode we should be able to make substantive contributions towards putting capitalism in the dock. That will have a different kind of Court then and it will for sure give a different kind of verdict.

December 2000

Sex Choice as Advertisement, Rape as Infotainment!

It was early eighties when amniocentesis arrived on the Indian scene. Primarily devised for detection of genetic diseases in the foetus and to assist in delivery they soon became widespread in determining the sex of the foetus. "Better Rs 500 now than Rs 5 lakhs later." One could see billboards advertising these 'tests' aggressively. Expectant parents were invited to resort to these 'tests' and eliminate an 'unwanted foetus' (another acronym for doing away with female foetuses). Clearly the argument that prevailed was that hefty amounts as dowry (for the girl) could be saved if one could get an idea of the sex of one's child at such low cost, and act upon it.

Two decades later, with the figures of the 2001 census staring us in our face (which further confirmed the skewed gender ratio), one expected that the corporate world which cannot stop patting itself for its show of 'social responsibility' would exercise more sensitivity on this issue. But from the recent case against a telecom firm (Reliance Infocomm) under the Pre Natal Diagnostic Techniques (Prohibition of Sex Selection) Act it becomes clear that for bigwigs in the corporate world all talk of gender sensitivity is only for public consumption. The company in question, Reliance Infocomm, has been charged for 'displaying an advertisement on its website pertaining to sex determination of the foetus.' The ad gave Chinese tips for predicting the gender of the child. It also talked about "techniques ensuring and increasing probability that an embryo will be of a particular sex." (*Hindustan Times*, Feb. 1, 2005)

Of course Reliance Infocom, which has also been under scanner for minting money by converting international calls into local calls, cannot be singled out for sanitising violence against women to enhance its business prospects.

The great villain of yesteryears, Pran, had not expected that a senior and well known television programmer would ask him the kind of discomfiting questions that he did. In a programme in Hindi, modeled on the famous 'Hard Talk', (*Seedhi Baat, Aaj Tak,* 5 Sep 2004, Prabhu Chawla interviewing Pran) Prabhu Chawla, all of a sudden broached the topic of the 'rapes committed by the villain' in many of the scenes he had enacted in films. Despite the visible discomfiture on Pran's face he unashamedly asked him: "Looking at the galaxy of 'sexy heroines' in the industry today whom would you 'prefer' in the upcoming film if given a chance?" Taken aback, the 'great villain' who had carved out a niche for himself in the industry then with his acting, somehow wriggled himself out of this humiliating situation. Of course the compere continued along similar lines, all the time with his impish smile.

It is really disturbing that this trivialisation of rape in the full glare of cameras largely went unreported. Barring a single commentator in Hindi, none from the fraternity of media watchers even deemed it necessary to comment on how the most obnoxious and inhuman violence against women had been trivialized and joked about. (Anil Chamadia, *Kathadesh,* Hindi Magazine, Oct 2004). It is no less a surprise that one did not hear a single voice of protest even from the vibrant women's movement or from the battery of gender activists who have at times single handedly taken up cases of gender oppression and helped get justice.

Such incidents signifying the denigration and objectification of women by the media cannot be considered an exception. They can even be said to be part of media strategy. In her well researched piece 'Media Culpability in the Continuum of Violence against Women', Lucinda Marshall (feminist artist, writer and activist, founder of the Feminist Peace Network, feministpeacenetwork.org/) critically examines the issue (30 September, 2004 Countercurrents.org) "...[M]ost disturbing is the disproportionate coverage of sensationalized violence. Invariably, rape stories get far more coverage than domestic violence stories. In all likelihood, this is because rape stories usually focus on one individual woman. If she is attractive, and particularly if she is white, she is a very marketable victim."

While Ms Marshall's study may have been based on how media in the west presents women, it cannot be said that her observations are irrelevant for Indian conditions. Even a random look at the programmes or ads on the media circuit here makes it clear that things are unfolding here in a similar manner.

In this connection the ad series launched by a leading auto major in India last year for their new car model was representative of this trend (Economictimes.com, Monday, November 24, 2003 05:01:16 pm). "The controversial ad showed a young beautiful blonde being stalked by a tiger through the city at night. The girl passes through the various areas of the city. ...Whenever she is on the road, it is the new look car that follows her. The moment she is on stairs or over bridge, the car is transformed into a tiger. The TVC ends with the girl finally giving up the chase with a deep male voiceover 'Surrender, to the new...' The advertisement fashioned on the "predator concept" was chosen to attract young consumers below the age of 35, and it was deliberately selected to "build excitement around the brand in a completely different manner".

Only a persistent protest by a small but determined group of gender activists and intellectuals compelled the company to withdraw this ad which '... had converted rape into a commodity'.

In the petition which this group sent to the big bosses of the company and concerned organisations it was clearly stated that the said ad 'completely ignored the campaign against carjacking and rape'. It also overlooked the fact that cars in general had become a weapon for men, who abduct and rape women. It has been repeatedly argued that the projection of cars as predators, women as sexual objects and travel as a hunt constitutes rape culture.'

As Jennifer L Pozner (former director of the FAIR Women's Desk) makes clear, controversy rather than facts sells in a 'media climate that considers news a "product" and readers and viewers "consumers".' As an example, female genital mutilation affects millions of women worldwide, yet you rarely hear about this. According to Ms Pozner the 'economic benefits' of 'rape – the most titillating crime' are immense. According to her 'The sexual brutalization of women is a highly marketable business, bringing in some $10 billion in profits in the US every year. As lucrative as the portrayal of rape is in the adult entertainment industry, it stands to reason that it is also a profitable story for the news media as well.'

UNIFEM (United Nations Development Fund for Women) published a report in Nov 2003 according to which one out of three women is likely to be sexually assaulted during their lifetime. We know that in many cases the perpetrators of such crimes have stated in an unambiguous manner that the 'media' has played a role in it.

Considering the gravity of the situation it is high time people become aware of the role media can play in ameliorating the condition. Coming back to the successful intervention of the small group in compelling the company to withdraw the ad, there is a need to 'empower the viewer' and make her/him 'media literate'. With the growing importance of media in politics as well as public life the importance of such 'watchdogs' is being felt more urgently.

February 2005

Can India Emulate the 'Other Bombay'?

The sublime and the ridiculous are often so nearly related, that it is difficult to class them separately. One step above the sublime makes the ridiculous, and one step above the ridiculous makes the sublime again. Thomas Paine, *The Age of Reason*

The most detestable wickedness, the most horrid cruelties, and the greatest miseries that have afflicted the human race have had their origin in this thing called revelation, or revealed religion. ibid

The demolitions in Bombay which have led to the displacement of lakhs of people and the continuing hostile attitude of the state government towards those displaced has caused some uproar all over the country. One can say that the callous attitude displayed by the administration towards the slum dwellers was a marker of the neo-liberal changes in the economy which have accelerated the process of the cities metamorphosing into showcases for investors rather than congenial living spaces for citizens. And it is rightly said that this 'Bombay plan' (of a very different kind) would be replicated in many parts of the country if there is no united resistance to the machinations of the ruling classes and the building mafias.

The only silver lining in this attempt to transform Bombay into a new Shanghai at tremendous human costs is the role of the media and civil society organisations who have kept the issue alive compelling even the party in power to stop the onward march of the bulldozers.

While media's role as a watchdog was commendable in this case, it is puzzling to note that the demolitions of a different kind which visited the same city at the end of the year 2003 did not receive the attention they deserved. The local media gave them some coverage but the national media by passed them despite their tremendous import for the nation. And it related to the knocking down of more than a thousand roadside illegal shrines belonging to various faiths by the Brihanmumbai Municipal Corporation (BMC) as part of a judicial directive. Interestingly the Bombay High Court had intervened in the matter of these illegal constructions on roads in response to a public interest litigation filed by a social crusader, Mr Bhagwan Raiyani, who had moved the Court in 2002 after calculating the number of illegal shrines in Mumbai which were an obstruction to the public in various ways. One year later, the High Court ordered that all illegal shrines-temples, mosques or churches – should be demolished.

As expected the attempts by the BMC to comply with the High Court order, which was also asked to submit an action taken report by 12 Nov 2003, were resisted by a motley combination of political formations and religious groups who gave different pleas. The custodians and/or owners of such religious shrines too tried to raise lot of hue and cry over this drive, but ultimately everyone had to comply with the orders.

Of course it cannot be said with guarantee that for now the phenomenon of illegal religious shrines has been completely done away with in Mumbai. Considering the strength of sectarian forces of different hues in the city it would be unbelievable. But a major achievement of the whole drive has been that a step forward in this direction has ultimately been taken in a city which was the scene of inter-communal killings merely 12 years ago during which such structures had played an important role.

Any sane person can understand that it is no easy task. It requires suitable mechanisms in place so that the concerned authorities are held responsible for the proliferation of such shrines. It is also important that ordinary people realise that they must abstain from providing any legitimacy to such 'illegal shrines' by their active participation. Every person needs to learn that s/he may have her/his religious beliefs and has a right to practice it, but this does not mean one becomes a mute participant in the breaking of laws in the name of her/his spiritual quest.

When the financial capital of the country was cleansed of some of its illegal religious shrines nobody could have imagined that a city in Tamilnadu, which has a special place in ancient Tamil literature, would carry the baton forward. All those people who face nightmares daily on the streets simply because of the public display of religiosity around illegal structures would be delighted to know that the people of Madurai, the city of historic temples, have co-operated wonderfully in the cleansing of their beautiful city.

News has come in that the municipal corporation of the city took the unprecedented step of demolition of more than 250 temples, two churches and a dargah which had been built on unauthorised land and were causing a great deal of inconvenience to the wider populace. It need be added that these demolitions were part of a wider drive undertaken by the corporation to demolish six hundred other illegal structures which had sprang up in the city.

This is, of course, not to say that the people who matter in the functioning of the city had overnight metamorphosed into overenthusiastic atheists or nastiks. Here too they had been compelled by a judgement of the High Court (3rd February 2005) which directed the concerned authorities to remove all such impediments on the road which were disturbing the smooth flow of traffic.

Certainly also it did not prove to be a cakewalk for the administrators to implement this decision. A few fanatics even raised the issue of the 'injustice' being done to Hindus for targeting only temples. There were also attempts to mobilise devotees in different places, particularly sit-ins inside the temples, where the police was challenged that it could not touch them.

But the people in charge of the drive took care to defuse the situation. The most significant aspect of this chain of events was that they convinced the general public that the move was not meant to 'insult' any particular community. By citing examples of churches as well as dargahs which were to be targeted in the drive they were able to communicate their point forcefully. They had even formed secret teams to talk to the key persons in this illegal encroachment of government land.

Today if you visit Madurai, you will discover a different city. No doubt there are some disgruntled elements who had been minting lakhs of rupees every year through this purely 'temporal exercise', but most people understand the actions of demolition.

One may have different opinions on the matter but it needs emphasis that the experiments undertaken by the municipal corporation in Madurai or by the BMC in Bombay have national ramifications. All of us are witness to the phenomenon of such illegal shrines coming up all over our city spaces. Within a span of a mere five years during my stay in northwest Delhi one can see how more than two dozen temples or religious structures have come up with the civic authorities turning a blind eye. The modus operandi followed in the 'emergence' of such 'ancient' shrines which slowly eat into vital spaces on the streets or government land is widely known and does not need repetition. The transformation of the spot decorated with a simple photograph or a vermillion coloured stone into a full fledged shrine does not take much time if the people of the area are also made participants in this process. Considering the money these shrines start generating, the number of people for whom these places give 'employment', and the 'ancillary industry' of flowers and other necessary things which go along with these shrines, the involvement of organised groups in running of these places is obvious.

One does not know of any nationwide survey undertaken by any researcher which can divulge the actual status of the 'illegal shrines' in the country. But even a cursory glance at our surroundings would make it clear that the total number must be running into a few hundred thousands all over the country. One can also imagine the amounts of money that such exercises of a 'temporal' nature are generating and the role such places can play in vitiating the harmony in our society comprising of people from different communities and different faiths. All of us have been witness to the organisation of *maha artis* all over Mumbai in the roadside temples way back in 1993 and the consequent mayhem perpetrated by fanatic elements, the scars of which are still visible on the social fabric of the city.

Is it not time that all of us – with differing religious identities or those like me who have opted to be atheists – who yearn for a more civilized and a more just society see to it that public thoroughfares are not transformed into places of religious congregations that can turn aggressive given opportunity? Is it not our duty to see that serpentine queues on special occasions at such shrines do not choke the cities more than they already are? Is it not time that all of us strive hard to ensure that democracy –which implies participation of everyone in the running of society – does not get substituted by majoritarianism?

It would be opportune to listen to Bhagwan Raiyani, the social crusader who also happens to be atheist, who had filed the historic petition in the Bombay High Court which led to the unprecedented order. In an interview to rediff.com (11 Nov 2003) this builder by profession explained the purpose behind the petition in simple words "...Suppose, I am a Hindu and construct an illegal temple then this will affect other passers-by from different religions. The same is true with other co-religionists; if they construct an illegal mosque or church it creates problems for people from other religions. Another point is that they create unhygienic conditions around that area. They go on to build communication centres or sometimes people play cards near those places. So to clean all these things from society, I took this step. This is to help the society. .."

Simple words, so difficult to achieve!

May 2005

'Sacred' Pollution

This is the time when sounds of *Ganpati Bappa Morya or Ganesh Maharaj ki Jai* are reverberating in large parts of India. Time when lakhs of idols of Ganesh, the elephant headed God of the Hindus, are installed at different places and the festival is celebrated with lot of fanfare and religious fervour. But people are now becoming aware of the irreparable damage to the environment caused by the immersion of Ganesh idols in public ponds and there are attempts by enlightened citizenry to take some corrective action.

It was the beginning of the month of August when Hyderabad witnessed a heated debate over immersion of Ganesh idols in Hussain Sagar. The city happens to be second only to Mumbai in organising the festival on a massive scale during which more than 15,000 huge idols are normally installed at various places. In fact the debate was precipitated by a decision of the High Court which had asked different departments to make alternate arrangements for idol immersion. The High Court was responding to a petition which had provided details about the pollution caused by this yearly ritual. The Advocate General of the state had also made a presentation before the courts which elaborated on how idol immersion adds to the level of water pollution (*Hindi Milap*, 5th August 2006, Hyderabad).

Taking umbrage at this order a section of the citizenry, with significant participation of Hindutva brigade leaders, flatly denied that idols cause any pollution and asked the state government to intervene to protect the 'religious rights of Hindus'. As of now the immersion of idols in the Hussain Sagar will be taking place under strict monitoring by state authorities as the Andhra Pradesh High Court has issued orders to minimise pollution.

One does not know whether the state leaders of the Hindutva brigade – namely BJP or VHP – who had raised a hue and cry over this issue, had any knowledge of how their counterparts in Gujarat were contemplating the control of pollution similarly caused. While the High Court in AP had asked merely for alternate arrangements for idol immersion, the guidelines issued by the Gujarat state government had stated that the idols be made of clay and no synthetic colours be used to make them. These guidelines were necessitated taking into consideration that thousands of Ganesha idols are immersed in Kankaria Lake in Ahmedabad, Sursagar Lake in Baroda and in the Sabarmati river. According to a news item 'Gujarat's bid for Clean Ganesh' which appeared on BBC news:

> The new guidelines, originally prepared by India's Central Pollution Control Board and reproduced by its Gujarat state counterpart, have been sent to district officials for implementation. From now on Ganesha idols should be made of clay and not of plaster of Paris – a fine white chemical powder which solidifies when mixed with water. Environmentalists say plaster of Paris takes longer to dissolve; it also reduces the oxygen level in the water resulting in the death of a large number of fish. Clay, on the other hand, dissolves quickly and does not harm aquatic life. The pollution control board has also appealed to the organisers of the festival to commission smaller idols which dissolve more easily in water. (www.bbc.co.uk: Monday, 21 August 2006, 14:53 GMT 15:53 UK)

The raging debate over idol immersion reminded one of a tragic scene on the Juhu beach, Bombay, last year. The sudden appearance of thousands of dead fishes – small as well as big – had made policy makers as well as citizenry sit up and wonder what precipitated this phenomenon. When asked to divulge the possible reasons the officials of the fisheries department had made a few general comments focussing on increased pollution of water leading to such deaths. But nobody was ready to say clearly that the immediate reason for the increase in level of pollution had something to do with the immersion of thousands of idols in the months of September and October. One electronic channel (NDTV) followed up the particular story and investigated into the quality of sea water at various places. It found to its dismay that the sea water has turned poisonous at different places because of dissolved mercury and other heavy metals.

One can understand why two years ago the Chennai High Court had imposed a temporary ban on immersion of idols of Ganesh. The Court had upheld a petition which said the idols are made of chemicals which pollute the sea and other water sources. (www.bbc.co.uk, Wednesday, 8 September, 2004, 18:30 GMT 19:30 UK).The Court had also issued notices to the state government and the Pollution Control Board to explain their stand on this issue.

A study of the pollution levels of Yamuna river in September done by the 'Central Pollution Control Board' (*Indian Express*, 13 September 2005) had similarly underlined how immersion increases the quantity of metals and decreases dissolved oxygen in the river and thus leads to choking of the river. It was observed that while mercury concentration in the river is nil in normal periods, it increases dramatically in the festive season after the idol immersion. Disposal of flowers, plastics, ashes in the river also adds to the pollution levels. The CPCB tells us that Delhi witnesses around 1700 immersions every year. Considering the enormous popularity of Ganesh festival in many parts of India one can imagine the enormity of the pollution caused by this yearly ritual.

Certainly the immersion of idols is not the only example which demonstrates how rituals of a section of people can become a nuisance of sorts for the wider populace or for that matter the ecosystem itself. Whether it be mass deaths of fishes or the inconvenience caused to the broader public because of holding of religious processions every other day, or for that matter the holding of *namaaz* prayers on the street itself to accommodate a large gathering, or the sprouting of 'ancient' temples on busy thoroughfares and in colonies, one can say that manifestations of faiths of sections of people are not as neutral as they are sometimes presented. While the onset of communal riots on some minor pretext could be said to be the extreme manifestation of this phenomenon, the non riot time situation which otherwise exists is not a guarantee that things are as they should be at the societal level.

It is clear that the makers of the Constitution, who had rightly added freedom of faith including its propagation as one of the cardinal principles of the democratic experiment, could not have envisaged this state of affairs. Considering the state of affairs now and the possibility of mischievous elements benefiting from it, is it not high time that saner elements in society came together to ensure that a faith practiced by a section of society should not become an alibi for harming the larger life world around us?

September 2006

God and Faith in the Life of Indians

What is common between golfer Jyoti Randhawa and actress Khushboo? In fact, considering their distinct fields, it would certainly be difficult to discern any thread of commonality. But if one came across the latest survey published in a leading newspaper one would already have got an answer. According to this survey, both do not believe in 'any higher power'. For Jyoti 'the only power I believe in is willpower- the power within you', for Khushboo 'my power is within me. I live for people whom I love and who love me'.

Interestingly people like Jyoti or Khushboo cannot be considered lone rangers in this society which is becoming rather more religious with time. (A trend which is definitely at variance with what is happening in the West) Sixty six respondents out of a group of thousand plus clearly stated that they are non-believers.

Of course, the commonality shared by these two stalwarts of their own fields regarding their understanding of a 'higher power', is not the only interesting fact which emerges from the survey done by the *Times of India* people with TNS, a leading market research agency to know 'how Indians view God and their faith'. ('10 city TOI-TNS poll', *TOI*, 26th November 2006)

To be very frank, the recent survey done across ten cities – Delhi, Mumbai, Kolkata, Chennai, Bangalore, Hyderabad, Ahmedabad, Patna, Lucknow and Nagpur – with 1,007 respondents, which was restricted to people falling in socio-economic categories A, B and C, present a mixed set of conclusions.

According to the survey three fourths of Indians are strong believers; 72 per cent of those in their twenties strongly believe in god; mere 11 per cent of respondents saw god as explicitly male; number of people who said they are more religious today than they used to be was considerably larger than those who felt they had become less religious; God is perceived as a source of energy and not someone to be feared; people are not convinced that God is a micromanager, around 46 % said s/he was an observer, not a controller. Despite the fact that 87 % of the respondents in the survey were Hindus, only one third of them said that they sensed the presence of God in *murtis* (idols).

The survey also brought to the fore the unwritten divide existing between the south and the north. While according to the survey 92 % of the respondents in the north had expressed their belief in God, the figure slipped to 86% in South. The skepticism of the south is also evident in things like belief in spiritual gurus or on questions less directly connected to religiosity. As the paper puts it "Whether it is belief in miracles, astrology or communicating with the dead, Chennai and Bangalore are consistently the least given to such ideas". As far as the non-believers were concerned, their attitude towards life was 'whatever has to be done, we have to do it ourselves'.

The observations tend to emphasise the growing religiosity of the Indian people, especially its younger lot, and thus could boost the ratings of social/political formations whose *weltanshauung* itself revolves around 'god'. They also demonstrate the growing 'market of spirituality' in our country where we find ourselves amidst Jet set gurus or channels beaming out sermons by these self-proclaimed representatives of god.

One is witness that neither social life nor polity has remained aloof from how people viewed religion. Psephologists keep relating the voting behaviour of a people to their religious affiliations. A presumption is also at work here that one's other worldly view has a great deal of bearing on one's this worldly views.

Interestingly, however, despite a growing interest in becoming more religious or exhibiting one's religiosity to the hilt, people are smart enough to differentiate between the spiritual and temporal.

When the respondents were specifically asked whether they think religion is a private or a social affair, a majority of them (43 %) were of the opinion that it should be a private affair and only 29% were of the opinion that it should be a social affair. Of course 28 percent of the respondents underlined that it should be both. Despite the ongoing propaganda by the Hindutva brigade organizations regarding religious conversion, 67 percent of the respondents clearly opined that people should be allowed to convert. As an aside it may be emphasised here that the Constitution gives right to faith and its propagation, and if properly fought by a team of legal luminaries in the highest courts of the country, all those laws which have been put in place by different states (mainly the Hindutva ruled. Of course they are not the only guilty ones. We are told that MP and Orissa have drafted laws to ban 'religious conversions long before the Hindutva attained legitimacy in the eyes of the people) could prove *ultra vires.*

The respondents were very clear about the alleged correspondence between 'being religious' and 'being moral'. Everybody is aware that a social common sense has emerged down the years (thanks to the manner in which religion plays a normative role in modern societies and the concerted campaign undertaken by institutions/individuals who think that it is their duty to communicate to the wider people the 'ultimate truth') which establishes a direct relationship between religiosity and morality. The connection between belief and goodness of an individual was also posed before the participants and the overwhelming opinion was that it has nothing to do with one's non/beliefs.Sixty five per cent of the respondents were of the opinion that 'it is not necessary to be believer to be a good person.'

It cannot be denied that all such surveys have their own limitations. At times they suffer from the initial premise provided by the respective organisation, or there are constraints in reaching any fruitful conclusion if the sample size chosen is not representative. And looking at the fact that the above mentioned survey focussed itself on socio-economic categories A,B and C and left the categories D, E out of its ambit, one can always say that the conclusions are skewed in favour of the middle or upper middle class.

Does the present survey carry any import for all such people who are worried about intrusion of matters of faith in the running of the state and society?

First of all the survey does provide resource(s) of hope for all those people/formations who yearn for secularism to prevail in this country. It is true that the idea of secularism and its practice has received a lot of battering during last sixty years of independence. One need not mention the genocide of Muslims *a la* the Modi brigade in Gujarat or the carnage against Sikhs with due connivance of the 'secular' Congress regime at the Centre or the killings of lakhs of innocents of different communities at the altar of vested interests camouflaged under a religious garb.

But despite the high voltage propaganda by the by religio-centric people, if more than 6 per cent of people have no qualms in emphasising their (non) belief or if a major chunk of the target population still considers religion to be a private matter or have no qualms if people convert according to their own will, then it should be considered as a silver lining. It gives an impression that notwithstanding the majoritarian assault, by and large people still cherish pluralism. Political Hinduism or political Islam may create conditions conducive for harbouring illusions about 'others' but people seem to be still keen that the state should remain above any particular faith or creed.

Perhaps this explains the silence maintained by the wider populace when the Shankaracharya and his junior were put behind bars for being 'party to the planned killing of one Shankar Raman – an employee of their Ashram itself. It also explains the absence of any big uproar in a city like Mumbai or for that matter Madurai when illegal religious structures – may it be temples, mazaars or churches – in their hundreds were pulled down by the municipal authorities sometime back. It also explains why it took around 60 years of consistent work for the Hindutva formation to attain some sort of legitimacy in the eyes of the people.

This 'silver lining' to an otherwise sense of gloom brings forth the task of defense and rejuvenation of secularism high on our agenda, a task which has been largely neglected even by forces/individuals whose credentials vis-a-vis secularism can never be questioned. One thinks that the gigantic task of promotion and strengthening of secularism has been left to the state to deal with, which has culminated in grievous consequences for the fabric of our society which retains its composite heritage despite heavy odds.

While there seems to be a fresh need to revisit the whole idea of secularism as it is understood and practiced in our country, there is also an urgent need to take into consideration the efforts we – as individuals/ formations/ parties – need to put in. Is it not high time that one moves forward from the 'Sarva Dharam Samabhav' position to a position of what an intellectual calls 'militant or uncompromising secularism' where we employ all the resources at our disposal to hold high the banner of secularism.

And looking at the fact that the purity and pollution based regime of caste as well as gender oppression practiced by the majority community derives sanction and legitimacy from religion, is it not necessary to integrate 'anti-caste struggle' and struggle against gender oppression in our fight for secularism?

December, 2006

Bailing Out Dow Chemicals

> *The lessons of Bhopal do not lie in our past but in our future. By refusing to meet the people of Bhopal who have suffered for decades after the Union Carbide/Dow Chemicals gas leak Prime Minister Manmohan Singh, who is at the forefront of the Corporatization of India's Economic Policies, is sending out a clear message to the Corporate World: In India you are free to poison, rob and kill our people. The Government will protect you. You will never be brought to book.* Arundhati Roy, 'Bhopali Children Beaten Up by Cops – Prime Minister Sir, What are you doing?'

> *Has India's main opposition party, the BJP, which is yearning to return to power at the centre, accepted a donation of $ 2,500 from a controversial company – Dow Chemicals? The information revealed by the Election Commission of India, in response to a freedom of information request on the funding of political parties and donations received by them between 2005 and 2007, makes the situation clear. It is a different matter that the BJP spokesperson has yet to acknowledge it formally.* 'BJP in row over party donations', Panini Anand, BBC Hindi Service, page last updated at 16:49 GMT, Wednesday 11 June 2008 17:49 UK).

Why is Dow Chemicals, the US multinational company so notorious in India? And why are people uniting in different forums to protest its entry in the Indian market? The hostile reaction that the name evokes was evident when Dow Chemicals attempted to construct a Rs 300 crore R&D facility in Chakan, Pune. The villagers dug up the approach roads to the construction site and forced the Government to rethink its permission for Dow's proposal. (January 2008). Dow's attempts to forge alliances with the Indian Institutes of Technology have also run into rough weather. Citing Dow's mishandling of the Bhopal legacy issues as reason, students and teachers of six prestigious engineering institutes across the country have joined hands to bar the company from any truck with the IITs.

It is well known how Dow Chemicals had purchased the 'Killer' Union Carbide company in 2001 and was now reneging on commitments to the gas victims and their families. Dow claims that its 100 percent subsidiary, Union Carbide, is a separate legal entity with its own system of liability management, and that Dow has inherited only assets and not Carbide's liabilities. In 2005 Dow began intense lobbying for legal immunity against Carbide's liabilities prompted by a May 2005 application by the Ministry of Chemicals in a case relating to toxic waste clean-up in the Madhya Pradesh High Court. The application sought Rs 100 crores ($25 million) from Dow towards clean-up costs.

It is now more than 23 years (2-3 December 1984) since the fatal leak of tonnes of methyl isocyanate from the pesticide plant in Bhopal owned by Union Carbide – now a subsidiary of Dow Chemicals – had resulted in the world's worst environmental disaster. According to concerned citizens engaged in bringing succour to the victims of the deadly poisonous gas, more than 23,000 people have died painful deaths in the last 23 years and today there are more than one lakh survivors who continue to suffer from chronic illnesses.

It is a tragedy of epochal proportions that despite 23 years of the disaster, more than 25,000 people still living next to the abandoned factory are condemned to drink the same contaminated water polluted by thousands of tonnes of toxic wastes from the factory. Health activists have noted rise of cancers in the exposed populations and horrific birth defects among thousands of children born to gas exposed parents.

While Union Carbide has managed to abscond from the criminal case relating to the deaths and injuries caused by the disaster, its present owner, Dow Chemicals, has neither produced its subsidiary Union Carbide in the court in Bhopal, nor has it paid for the clean up of the abandoned factory which still stores thousands of tonnes of toxic wastes.

It is widely known that but for the connivance of the ruling parties in India – whether the Congress or the BJP or their different allies- it would have been impossible for Union Carbide/Dow Chemicals to escape the liabilities of the corporate crime. A joint appeal issued by the Bhopal survivors (namely, *Bhopal Gas Peedit Mahila Stationery Karmachari Sangh, Bhopal Gas Peedit Mahila Purush Sangharsh Morcha and Bhopal Group for Information and Action*) on the eve of the historic *padyatra* from Bhopal rightly claims that 'There is abundant documentary evidence that indicts the Indian government as an accomplice in the corporate crime in Bhopal... The collusion between the American multinationals and the Indian government is the main reason why the Bhopal victims have been denied justice in the last 23 years.'(www.bhopal.net)

It is worth noting that senior leaders of the BJP have been accusing the Congress party for its lack of seriousness in taking action against those responsible for the gas leak. Yet they have had no qualms in taking donations from the very same company which has shown scant regard for the welfare of the people affected by the gas leak.

The Congress Party which has held the state and the central governments during this interregnum for a considerable period of time has not covered itself with glory either with its inaction and apathy towards the victims. The latest in the series of its complicity is the role of the Commerce and Industries Minister, Kamal Nath, who is being charged with helping Dow Chemicals and Union Carbide escape their liabilities in Bhopal. In a press conference (3 June 2008) the activists associated with the organisations of Bhopal survivors have said that "...[M]inister approved the sale of Union Carbide's Unipol technology to Reliance Industries in 2006 knowing fully well that it was approving the sale of intellectual property of an absconding criminal. They pointed out that in March 1992 the Bhopal District Court directed the government to confiscate all property belonging to Union Carbide in India." (www.bhopal.net).

It is no less shocking that the government has so far ignored the Supreme Court's recognition of Bhopal victims' right to proper health care as a constitutional right. Neither has it followed the Supreme Court's directions that the Indian government must pay for the medical insurance of at least 1 lakh children born to exposed parents. Nor has it followed the directions of the criminal court to the CBI to bring the absconding Union Carbide to book.

As of now Bhopal survivors have undertaken a fast unto death in Delhi to press for their demand for a special commission on Bhopal and criminal action against Dow Chemicals/Union Carbide. But nobody seems to be listening.

On 9 June, 2008 14 Bhopali children, along with 22 adults, were arrested for staging a peaceful protest outside the Prime Minister's office in South Block. Arresting the women and children is not the worst of it. Beginning 7 p.m., plainclothes policemen and some uniformed police belonging to the Parliament Street Police Station began roughing up the Bhopalis. 19 year old Imran was belted so fiercely by the policemen that he hurt his eye. 11-year old Yasmin Khan, 6-year old Nagma and 27-year old Meera More were slapped and punched by male police, even while senior women gas victims were dragged against their will into police lock up.

One can gauge how much pressure is being exerted by the corporate lobby, if despite the Prime Minister's Office underlining the 'legal liability' for Dow Chemicals things are yet not moving forward. An internal document dated 7.2.2008 from the PMO, which says that "Irrespective of the manner in which [Union Carbide Corporation] has merged or has been acquired by Dow Chemicals, if there is any legal liability, it would have to be borne by Dow Chemicals," attributes this opinion to the Ministry of Law. This document contradicts Dow's stated position to its shareholders, and clearly outlines the risks faced by Dow Chemicals' investments in India. The document was unearthed on 8 May, 2008, through Right to Information from the Prime Minister's Office by organizations of survivors of the 1984 Union Carbide disaster in Bhopal.

A case involving bribes paid by Dow officials to Indian Agriculture Ministry staff to register three toxic pesticides is also under investigation. Last year Dow Chemicals was charged with violations under the Foreign Corrupt Practices Act (FCPA) by the US Securities and Exchange Commission (SEC). As per the Indian Penal Code "bribe" is a criminal offence punishable by up to one year of rigorous imprisonment. As part of its investigation into this crime the Central Bureau of Investigation has recently sent a Letter Rogatory seeking judicial assistance from the US Justice Department.

Eleven year old Yasmin, who was born to gas exposed parents, is a living example of the continuing tragedy in Bhopal. She suffers from hormonal disorders and skin and gastrointestinal problems. This little girl participated in the *Padyatra* from Bhopal to Delhi yearning for the day when she might get clean water in her colony Shiv Nagar, which is an area contaminated by ground water behind the Union Carbide factory.

She is still waiting for a call from the Prime Minister's office to agree to meet the kids from Bhopal who have walked all the way to Delhi. Perhaps she does not know that the big iron gates at the Prime Minister's Office can genuflect before corporate criminals but can never let people like Yasmin get in.

June 2008

Beyond Ableism

Union Finance Minister P Chidambaram revealed a part of his mind at a national conference organised by the FICCI recently. Addressing the meet on 'Engaging Industry in Employment of Persons with Disabilities' he appealed to the captains of industry to 'show their humanitarian side' and 'employ the physically challenged people'.

The question naturally arises as to what prompted him to issue such an unusual appeal in that gathering. Perhaps the immediate provocation was the news that even six months after the commencement of the current financial year the budget allocations and incentives for the differently abled persons remained completely unutilised. To be frank, not a single application to avail this scheme had reached the Finance Minister's office.

What was so special about this scheme?

The government had earmarked Rs 1,800 crores in the budget, which included social security cover as well, for those employers who were ready to give employment to the specially abled people. It had envisaged that it would be able to give regular employment to 1,00,000 physically challenged people by encouraging industrialists through incentives.

Surprisingly instead of raising a question about the lacunae in the recruitment policies of the corporate sector, the finance minister himself appeared to be defensive on this issue and was ready to call it a 'failure of the government'. According to him "A large number of people have told me, including PM Sinha who heads Bata, that he had no idea of such a scheme until a week ago."

Even if one were to give benefit of doubt to individual entrepreneurs or industrialists on their 'ignorance' of this part of the budget pronouncements, it appears rather incredible that the corporate sector as a whole which has a battery of highly paid financial advisers -who analyse the budget in great detail – failed to note this important part which involved enough subsidies and grants.

Or was it a case of selective amnesia?

A close look at the employment situation of the specially abled persons in the corporate sector can throw light on the subject. According to a World Bank report on *'People with Disabilities: From Commitments to Outcomes'* which was released sometime ago, a mere 0.3 per cent of the large private firms' workforce comes from the disabled category. And for all their talk of equal opportunities the MNCs seem to be the worst, as a mere 0.05 percent workforce in them is from this category.

Contrary to all pronouncements for their betterment, in a decade when we had a 'landmark legislation' to promote the rights of the disabled, one witnessed five per cent drop in their employment rates. The fall in the employment rate of working age disabled people from 42.7 per cent in 1991 to 37.6 percent in 2002, was almost universal across the country.

But can the corporate sector be singled out for its policies of exclusion vis-a-vis the specially abled persons? In fact the callousness of the state governments also is visible at various levels. The year 2006 saw approval of National Policy on Persons with Disabilities by the Government of India. But till date only two states – Chhatisgarh and Karnataka – have drafts on policies for the disabled ready.

As per the report, people with disabilities are among the most excluded in the country. Multiple deprivations faced by the disabled range from lack of educational opportunities to lower consumption levels and assets. It is found that children with disabilities are around 4 to 5 times less likely to be in school than SC and ST children.

While the said report was being discussed in forums committed to the specially enabled, one came across an order by the Delhi High Court wherein it directed the Centre and Delhi government to advise all its agencies to compulsorily make all public spaces – including railway station, airports and heritage sites, disabled friendly. The Court's intervention came only after disability rights activists approached them under the Persons with Disabilities (Equal Opportunities, Protection of Rights and Full Participation) Act, 1995.

However, would it be right to put the entire blame on the state and its various organs or for that matter the corporate sector for the plight of the disabled? There is also the silence of the articulate sections of our society towards them. Rather one needs to understand that social stigma and social attitudes in general play an important role in limiting opportunities for the disabled in different walks of life.

It was late 70s when Frank Bowe, a disability rights activist from the US had written a monograph *Handicapping America* (1978) in which he tried to explain how the key issue in any debate around disability is the societal response to it. For Bowe, the main point was not the status of physical or mental impairment of a particular person, but the way society develops strategies to cope with it.

In fact the nature of societal response is a marker of the subtle manner in which the mainstream society practices what can be called *ableism*. It is argued that *ableism* is like *racism* and *sexism*, a derogatory reaction of mainstream society to the physical or intellectual capacities of the disabled in combination with the behaviour of the disabled person. An *ableist* society treats non-disabled people as the standard of 'normal living'. In an *inclusive* society, on the other hand, all products and services are fully accessible and usable for as many people as possible. An *ableist* society tends towards isolation, whereas an *inclusive* society tends towards *integration* or inclusion.

The enormity of the challenge which faces humanity vis-à-vis the question of disability can be gauged from the fact that around ten per cent of the world population suffers from disability of some sorts. The World Health Organisation (WHO), for example, estimates that there are as many as 600 million persons with disabilities. The United Nations estimate is 650 million. There is also widespread agreement among experts in the field that disability is more common in developing than in developed nations.

Interestingly till the early 80s, the dominant trend in the disability discourse was the adoption of 'social welfare measures' and it was yet to be recognized as a 'human rights issue'. But things have started moving since then and the resolve of the international community to fight the scourge of disability became clear when the United Nations decided to celebrate 1981 as the Year of the Disabled. The UN Decade of Disabled Persons (1983-1993) featured a World Programme of Action Concerning Disabled Persons. In between, much was accomplished. For example, in 1984, UNESCO accepted sign language for use in education of deaf children and youth.

A positive aspect of the otherwise grim scenario is that the year 2006 saw the adoption of the 'International Convention of the Protection and Promotion of the Rights and Dignity of Persons with Disabilities', and the key 'thinking behind the Convention was that welfare and charity should be replaced by new rights and freedoms.' It also recognized that 'a change of attitude is vital if disabled people are to achieve equal status – countries that ratify it will be obliged to combat negative stereotypes and prejudices and to promote an awareness of people's abilities and contribution to society.' For countries like India, which has been a signatory to the Convention, an important provision is the Article that obliges governments to expand the reach of inclusive education- the education of disabled children together with the non-disabled ones. The basic idea is to do away with 'special schools' specifically run for them.

There are many prisms through which one can look at societies to understand the level of human freedom available. It is for us to decide when we would cross the *ableism* mark.

December 2008

Company Secretary to Replace Inspector

Another Move to Appease India Inc and Let Down the Workers

While the Manmohan Singh government's Left-free second innings is expected to usher in changes to India's archaic labour laws, the labour ministry is working on a quick-fix solution to help drop the country's notorious 'inspector raj' tag.

If all goes to plan, India Inc would no longer have to deal with labour inspectors turning up at their premises to check compliance with 43 central and myriad state labour legislations. Instead, firms can submit a certificate from a company secretary that validates their compliance with the numerous employment laws. Vikas Dhoot in *The Indian Express,* Posted: Wednesday, August 5, 2009 at 0137 hrs IST, Updated: Wednesday, August 5, 2009 at 0137 hrs IST.

Prime Minister Manmohan Singh led government's 'left-free second innings' seems to be taking the battle against 'archaic labour laws' full steam ahead. The outgoing Union Labour Secretary, Ms Sudha Pillai, recently shared with the media the proposed contents of the draft being prepared in the Labour Ministry for this purpose.

The proposal, which would be shortly submitted in the form of a Cabinet Note, seeks to 'permit company secretaries to file compliance reports for labour laws, just like they give compliance reports for other laws.' As of now the role of the company secretary is limited to certifying the said firm's compliance with various statutes, which includes the Companies Act, 1956 and also the listing of agreements with stock exchanges. The issue of compliance with labour laws is handled by the labour inspectors.

According to the government this new regime, freeing companies from the drudgery of visits by the labour inspectors, would boost India's global perception. Ms Sudha Pillai, who has since demitted the post of Union Labour Secretary and has joined Planning Commission, explained the 'rationale' behind this move. "At most international fora, the pathetic compliance levels of Indian labour laws, especially in small and medium enterprises and the services sector [have come up]...our labour laws were made purely for industry, but services now contribute over 55% of GDP and operate under a vague Shops & Establishments Act. Many countries are using labour issues..."

As can be expected the proposed change is a win-win for industry, employers and regulators who had been clamoring hard to do away with 'labour market rigidities'. A key point which usually finds mention and supposedly provides legitimacy to these changes veers around a simple argument. It is said that with such institutional rigidities which result in high levels of labour costs it becomes difficult for the developing economies to compete in the world market which includes new production sites having weak labour institutions and hence, lower labour costs. Ranging from the IMF to the World Bank to the OECD, everybody seems to be pushing for what is known as labour market flexibility. It is a different matter that employers in countries like India "..[e]njoy the freedom to employ and exploit more than ninety percent of the workforce without taking account of any norm of civil society or rule of law. And, contrary to the European case, productivity of labour and profitability of capital increased manifold over the last two decades." ('Employment and Labour Market: The Myth of "Rigidity"' – Satyaki Roy, *Alternative Economic Survey*, India 2007-2008, Daanish Books, Delhi).

Interestingly, despite more than a month since the business dailies covered this press conference, there is no reaction from the unions, organisations engaged in uniting labour at various levels. Should it be seen as indicative of how the 'inspector raj' normally unfolds itself before the labour – which seems to cover rather than expose violations of labour friendly laws at the shop floor level – or is it just that under reporting has meant that the concerned people/formations have not noted it?

I.

For close observers of the labour scene in India, there is nothing surprising about this 'radical' sounding proposal. In fact, the issue of de-institutionalising and dismantling labour has been high on the agenda of the proponents of neo-liberal changes in the Indian economy for a long time. And the proposal to do away with 'inspector raj' – which is constituted to verify compliance with labour laws – is only an aspect of this agenda.

Of late, one has been witness to the determined assault on labour laws in India through judicial caveats or legislative measures. A decade ago the then NDA government led by Mr Vajpayee had formed the 'Second National Labour Commission' (Oct 1999) to suggest rationalisation of existing laws relating to labour in the organised sector and also suggest 'umbrella' legislation for ensuring a minimum level of protection to workers in the unorganised sector. And without waiting for this Commission to submit its report important changes were announced in the Industrial Disputes Act and Contract Labour System (Abolition and Regulation) Act.

The growing clamor to end the 'Inspector Raj' raises a few disturbing questions. Why is it that the 'Inspector Raj' becomes a dirty word in case of labour *laws* alone, and why do the rulers gloss over the fact that the practice of 'Inspector Raj', as it is termed, plays havoc with the lives of the ordinary wo/men? Again, there has been no attempt at curtailment of the powers of the Inspector Raj of the Indian police which was castigated as the 'biggest organised *goonda* force' in the country in a famous judgment by Justice AN Mullah decades ago.

Corruption is rampant in the labour department and it is always a difficult task to locate genuine personnel in the department who are above it. Labour inspectors or their seniors who act as the interface of the department and the public seem to be afflicted with this 'disease' more. Certainly that does not seem to be the reason why the government is keen to end this 'regime'. Had that been the case, the powers that be would have been forced to take the unusual step of 'shutting down' all the government departments as none seems to be free from this malaise! Transparency International, the global corruption tracking watch dog, recently downgraded India's ranking from 72 to 85 in the list of world's corruption-plagued countries.

Why is it that the government plans to substitute the labour inspector by the company secretary?

A point worth noting is that despite corruption at various levels in the labour department, the whole formal arrangement in which the labour inspectors are authorised to verify compliance with labour laws in different units does help the workers (albeit in a very limited way) to get some relief, and ensures that the employers cannot wish away the labour laws completely. Apart from this there are occasions of judicial intervention leading to workers getting some relief or ensuring that the labour personnel deal with a case properly. One can get some idea of the significance of even this limited impact of the 'notorious inspector raj' on the issues of conflict between workers and industrial units/owners/contractors from the number of cases filed by these personnel in different courts of the country and the amount of fine they have been able to recover from employers as penalty. This amount runs into crores, which could definitely be enhanced if we were to have a stringent application of the laws and were able to overcome many of its loopholes, instead of suggesting that they be done away with. Another significant aspect of the intervention by the labour inspectors can be noted from the judgements by different courts in all those matters where the labour inspectors have filed criminal cases against employers. A cursory glance at such judgments tells us that in more than 95 per cent of such cases the judgments have been in favour of the government, i.e., in favour of the labour inspectors, and the employers are forced to admit mistakes.

It is clear that for the owners of factories/industrial units/contractors/other employers the 'notoriety' of the 'inspector raj' arises from the 'nuisance' they seem to create at various levels. One can easily notice the glee with which they welcomed the proposed move to substitute the labour inspector by the company secretary.

2.

Who is a company secretary? First and foremost s/he is an employee of the industrial unit/service centre. Can we expect an employee of a company to go against the interests of the owner, or take steps which could hamper its immediate/long term interests?

To be fair to them they are not even trained for this work. A cursory glance at the syllabus formulated by the Indian Company Secretaries' Institute (ICSI) for training company secretaries brings out the correct picture. During the three year degree course the students have to cover subjects worth 1,800 marks, out of which only 40 marks are meant for labour laws. In fact, they are taught only a limited number of labour laws.

The move to substitute labour inspectors by company secretaries has many other drawbacks. The system of having a company secretary exists only in the organised sector, in which merely 7 per cent of the working population finds employment. The remaining 93 per cent of the working people are engaged in the unorganised sector. It is clear that the government wants to leave the broad masses of the working people at the mercy of the owners/employers/contractors by dismantling all such structures/arrangements which can provide relief to them in their unequal battle against Capital.

Proponents of wide ranging changes in labour laws – obviously to serve the interests of Capital better – also package their move in the binary of 'old' versus 'new'. They talk in terms of doing away with 'archaic labour laws'. By such logic we would have to rid ourselves of many other laws which are not only older but also better known. For example, the Indian Penal Code – 1860, Transfer of Property Act – 1882, Trust Act – 1882, Telegraph Act – 1885, Registration Act – 1908, Negotiable Instrument Act – 1881, Land Acquisition Act – 1894 and so on. One can go on listing similar laws still in operation and older than the so called 'archaic' labour laws. As a matter of fact these labour laws are quite 'young' in comparison with many other laws/acts/ codes etc.

An appraisal of labour laws in the country shows that they came up in the post second world war period which witnessed the emergence of a socialist bloc and militant working class movements in many other countries. The rulers of newly independent India too felt the pressure and many leaders were fired with the utopian sounding imagination of building an inclusive, equitable society. The State thus willingly entered into a historic pact with labour, which was reflected in the different labour laws in India meant to regulate the labour market, protect employment and ensure social security of workers. It was also seen then as a State's entering into a historic pact with labour. One can also see the impact of the International Labour Organisation (ILO) in their formulation, which had come into existence then as part of the building and strengthening of United Nations Organisation (UNO).

In its hurry to placate India Inc. and help boost the 'Global Perception' of India, the government seems to have suffered a selective amnesia regarding its commitments on labour and labour laws in the international fora. It would be opportune to look at Convention -81, related to labour inspection. It needs to be underlined that the Indian government has not only accepted this Convention but is also a signatory to it. The task of labour inspectors facilitates the implementation of the recommendations of the International Labour Organisation. In the ILO Conference held in 2006, in the discussions on a report on labour inspection, it was duly emphasised that labour inspectorates should be fully independent of local authorities, and labour inspectors should be such public servants who have permanent tenures and are free from any external pressures.

It was also underlined that to ensure proper implementation of labour laws it is incumbent that inspections take placc at regular intervals and labour inspectors are allowed free access to different establishments and production units. Para 17 also seeks to ensure immediate legal action in case of violations of labour laws.

The report also mentions that in its 60 plus years history the ILO has always recognised the importance of labour inspection. And noting the recent changes in world economy – namely segmentation of labour markets, quantum jump in the number of migrant labourers, privatisation, growing sense of job insecurity and increasing pressure in the workplace – it says that it is all the more necessary that labour receives extra protection.

It further adds that the mere fact of more and more countries implementing Convention 81 is a marker that labour inspection has played an important role in the security of workers and implementation of labour laws. It concludes with the observation that a strong and effective labour inspectorate not only provides better protection to labour but also guarantees productivity of labour which is good for all.

Is anybody in the labour department listening?

September, 2009

Index